LABOR IN HARD TIMES

Labor in Hard Times examines how organized labor in Turkey and the United Kingdom turned to international human rights law in response to domestic repression and neoliberal restructuring. Drawing on extensive fieldwork and a unique database of labor rights cases, the book traces how workers used litigation at the European Court of Human Rights not just to win legal victories, but to build political pressure, assert legitimacy, and reclaim space for collective action. Focusing on public sector unionists in Turkey and blacklisted construction workers in the UK, it offers a rare view of how grassroots activists and lawyers mobilized international law as a tactical resource: Workers engaged rights discourse strategically to pursue concrete goals, while remaining rooted in class-based solidarity. With vivid case studies, this book speaks to readers interested in international courts, human rights, and the evolving strategies of labor movements in an era of democratic backsliding and global inequality.

FİLİZ KAHRAMAN is Assistant Professor of Political Science at the University of Toronto. Her research on law and politics has been supported by the National Science Foundation, awarded the ISA's Best Dissertation in Human Rights prize, and received an article award from the Law and Society Association.

CAMBRIDGE STUDIES IN LAW AND SOCIETY

Founded in 1997, Cambridge Studies in Law and Society is a hub for leading scholarship in socio-legal studies. Located at the intersection of law, the humanities, and the social sciences, it publishes empirically innovative and theoretically sophisticated work on law's manifestations in everyday life: from discourses to practices, and from institutions to cultures. The series editors have longstanding expertise in the interdisciplinary study of law, and welcome contributions that place legal phenomena in national, comparative, or international perspective. Series authors come from a range of disciplines, including anthropology, history, law, literature, political science, and sociology.

Series Editors

Mark Fathi Massoud, University of California, Santa Cruz

Jens Meierhenrich, London School of Economics and Political Science

Past Editors

Chris Arup, Martin Chanock, Sally Engle Merry,
Pat O'Malley, Susan Silbey, Rachel E. Stern

A list of books in the series can be found at the back of this book.

LABOR IN HARD TIMES
Workers' Legal Mobilization at the European Court of Human Rights

Filiz Kahraman
University of Toronto

Shaftesbury Road, Cambridge CB2 8EA, United Kingdom

One Liberty Plaza, 20th Floor, New York, NY 10006, USA

477 Williamstown Road, Port Melbourne, VIC 3207, Australia

314–321, 3rd Floor, Plot 3, Splendor Forum, Jasola District Centre, New Delhi – 110025, India

103 Penang Road, #05–06/07, Visioncrest Commercial, Singapore 238467

Cambridge University Press is part of Cambridge University Press & Assessment, a department of the University of Cambridge.

We share the University's mission to contribute to society through the pursuit of education, learning and research at the highest international levels of excellence.

www.cambridge.org
Information on this title: www.cambridge.org/9781009732369
DOI: 10.1017/9781009732321

© Filiz Kahraman 2026

This publication is in copyright. Subject to statutory exception and to the provisions of relevant collective licensing agreements, no reproduction of any part may take place without the written permission of Cambridge University Press & Assessment.

When citing this work, please include a reference to the DOI 10.1017/9781009732321

First published 2026
Cover image: Kibele Yarman

A catalogue record for this publication is available from the British Library

Library of Congress Cataloging-in-Publication Data
Names: Kahraman, Filiz author
Title: Labor in hard times : workers' legal mobilization at the European Court of Human Rights / Filiz Kahraman, University of Toronto.
Description: Cambridge, United Kingdom ; New York, NY : Cambridge University Press, 2026. | Series: CSLS Cambridge studies in law and society | Includes bibliographical references and index.
Identifiers: LCCN 2025048505 (print) | LCCN 2025048506 (ebook) | ISBN 9781009732369 hardback | ISBN 9781009732376 paperback | ISBN 9781009732321 epub
Subjects: LCSH: European Court of Human Rights | Labor laws and legislation–Turkey | Labor laws and legislation–Great Britain | Employee rights–Turkey | Employee rights–Great Britain | Labor laws and legislation, International
Classification: LCC K1705 .K325 2026 (print) | LCC K1705 (ebook)
LC record available at https://lccn.loc.gov/2025048505
LC ebook record available at https://lccn.loc.gov/2025048506

ISBN 978-1-009-73236-9 Hardback
ISBN 978-1-009-73237-6 Paperback

Cambridge University Press & Assessment has no responsibility for the persistence or accuracy of URLs for external or third-party internet websites referred to in this publication and does not guarantee that any content on such websites is, or will remain, accurate or appropriate.

For EU product safety concerns, contact us at Calle de José Abascal, 56, 1°, 28003 Madrid, Spain, or email eugpsr@cambridge.org

CONTENTS

List of Figures	*page* vii
List of Tables	viii
Acknowledgments	ix
Table of Cases	xiv
List of Abbreviations	xviii

1	Introduction	1
2	Theorizing Legal Mobilization at the International Level: Lawyers, Movements, and Courts	21

PART I WHY DID WORKERS TURN TO THE EUROPEAN COURT OF HUMAN RIGHTS?

3	Domestic Drivers of Human Rights Litigation: Unraveling Trade Union Power Under Two Variants of Neoliberalism	55
4	A New Avenue for Workers at the International Level: The European Court of Human Rights	74
5	Lawyers as Strategists: Between the Local and the International	105

PART II WHAT IS THE IMPACT OF LITIGATION AT THE EUROPEAN COURT OF HUMAN RIGHTS?

6	Direct Remedies: Limits of Compliance with European Court of Human Rights Rulings	139
7	On-Stage and Off-Stage Mobilization: Blacklisted Workers in the United Kingdom	175
8	Mobilizing to Unionize: Public Sector Workers in Turkey	201

CONTENTS

9   Litigating in Hard Times: Fragile Gains, Enduring
    Struggles   230

Appendix I   Strasbourg Labor Cases Database (StrasLab)   240
Appendix II   Qualitative Data   243
References   251
Index   292

FIGURES

3.1	Trade union density in eight European countries	page 61
3.2	Collective bargaining coverage in eight European countries	62
4.1	Annual number of labor cases at the ECtHR	79
4.2	Convention articles and protocols invoked and violated in labor cases	84
4.3	Types of labor claims and the most important cases	85
8.1	Key moments in Turkish public sector unionization and international legal mobilization	204
8.2	References to human rights law and discourse in *abece*	207
8.3	Membership levels in public sector unions	223

TABLES

3.1 Trade union rights cases before the ECtHR 1960–2021   57
4.1 Notable ECtHR rulings on trade union rights across three phases   95
6.1 Execution of ECtHR's trade union rights cases from Turkey and the UK 1960–2021   146

ACKNOWLEDGMENTS

This book started its journey as a dissertation. But the ideas and the frustrations that motivated it, along with the encouragements and inspirations that sustained it, go back beyond my graduate school years. So, there is more than a decade's worth of people across three continents to whom I am grateful.

First, I would like to acknowledge the courageous struggles led by KESK (Confederation of Public Employees Trade Unions) and the Blacklist Support Group, whose stories gave life to this book. I am grateful to the activists and lawyers, named and unnamed, who generously shared their time and insights with me. I would especially like to thank a few individuals who facilitated my fieldwork by helping me access critical documents or reach new contacts: Gökhan Candoğan, Başak Çalı, İsmail Çınar, Görkem Doğan, Mert Ertan, Sakine Esen Yılmaz, Mesut Gülmez, Sevgi Karaduman, İrfan Kaygısız, Sinan Ok, Necdet Okcan, Yusuf Şenol, and Öztürk Türkdoğan in Turkey; and Kate Ewing, Keith Ewing, Michael Ford, John Hendy, Declan Owens, Victoria Philipps, and Dave Smith in the UK. Discussions on workplace homicides at the İşçi Sağlığı ve İş Güvenliği Meclisi (Health and Safety Watch/Turkey), where I volunteered for several years, profoundly shaped my thinking about labor rights and legal accountability. I especially thank Murat Çakır and Aslı Odman from this network for their support and their inspiring work.

My interest in collective action, human rights, and organized labor took root during my undergraduate years at Boğaziçi University, in the classrooms, student protests, and the many hours of conversations I had with friends. Lisya Yafet, my dearest friend since those formative years, was by my side at every step. During fieldwork in London years later, she hosted me, grounded me, and reminded me – "like a repotted plant" – to give myself time to recuperate between travels. Mehmet Kentel was my favorite intellectual antagonist in those years; the friendship we carried from Istanbul to Seattle has only deepened. I thank Ayşen Candaş for lighting the way toward a contemplative life, introducing me to the giants and puzzles of political theory, and encouraging me to find my own voice.

Many of my professors who opened up a new intellectual and moral universe for me have since been forced into exile. Those who remain, at Boğaziçi and elsewhere, continue to mount an admirable defense against government-appointed rectors and escalating repression in academia and beyond. I especially want to honor Barış için Akademisyenler (Academics for Peace), many of whom disproportionately bore the consequences of a petition we signed, but their defiance in the aftermath gave me hope during dark times.

I cannot imagine a more supportive environment to complete a dissertation than the one I found at the University of Washington (UW). I owe the greatest debt to my co-supervisors, Michael McCann and Joel Migdal, for their intellectual influence and unwavering support. Sociolegal readers will recognize that this book builds on Michael's approach to legal mobilization, which opened the door for me to explore its international dimensions. During my time at UW and after, he offered a hand whenever the ground beneath my feet began to crack and reminded me that professionalization, if left unchecked, can consume the social justice commitments that first brought me to this work. Joel has been a towering figure of moral and intellectual integrity, and I strive to carry those values into my own teaching, writing, and research. I also benefited from the mentorship and insights of many faculty members, especially James Caporaso, Rachel Cichowski, Reşat Kasaba, Selim Kuru, George Lovell, and Jamie Mayerfeld.

Outside the department, three communities sustained both my growth as an interdisciplinary scholar and my commitment to praxis at UW: the Comparative Law and Society Studies (CLASS), the Harry Bridges Center for Labor Studies, and the Turkish Circle. During my final year, the Bridges Center – led by Michael and run by Andrew Hedden – gave me a room of my own where I completed the dissertation. Many participants in workshops hosted by these three networks helped shape the initial ideas in this book. I especially thank Hind Ahmed Zaki, Emily Christensen, Elizabeth Chrun, Sarah Drier, Yoav Duman, Amanda Fulmer, Sema Kentel, Tania Melo, Onur Mete, Chelsea Moore, Özge Sade, Zeynep Seviner, and Ayşe Toksöz for making Seattle a home away from home. My closest companions, Zeynep Kaşlı and Esra Bakkalbaşıoğlu, were there for me through the emotional, intellectual, and political ups and downs of these years.

Milli Lake was my unofficial mentor, role model, and a friend who never forgot to toast the small victories.

Georgetown University was the first institution where I began transforming my dissertation into a book during my postdoctoral fellowship at the Mortara Center. Among the regular participants in research seminars at Mortara, I thank Nik Kalayanpur, Abe Newman, and Erik Voeten for their thoughtful engagement with my research and support. Over the years, I have developed the ideas in this book through exchanges with many scholars whose work inspired me, whether they remember them or not. I am grateful to Celeste Arrington, Mark Berlin, Zoltán Búzás, Lynette Chua, Lisa Conant, Chuck Epp, Lucrecia García Iommi, Heidi Haddad, Larry Helfer, Courtney Hillebrecht, Alex Huneeus, Susan Kang, Dilek Kurban, Mikael Madsen, Virginia Mantouvalou, Kelly Morrison, César Rodríguez Garavito, Wayne Sandholtz, Lisa Sundstrom, Whitney Taylor, Freek Van Der Vet, and Andrea Vilán. Sid Tarrow's work shaped my thinking long before I met him, and I am so thankful for his generous feedback on the entire manuscript.

After years in Istanbul, Seattle, London, Baltimore, and Washington DC, I felt unmoored when I first arrived in Toronto. But the friends, colleagues, and communities across the three campuses of the University of Toronto gave me a new intellectual home and taught me that a city of immigrants is perhaps the best place for me to settle. I owe much gratitude to Geoff Dancy, Randall Hansen, Tom Pavone, and Ed Schatz, as well as Dan Kelemen and Lisa Vanhala – who made the trip to Toronto – for attending a book workshop supported by the political science departments at the University of Toronto and the University of Toronto Scarborough (UTSC), and the Munk School's Centre for European and Eurasian Studies (CEES). Watching six experts discuss my book for an entire day was an intellectual feast; their incisive feedback helped make this a far better book. I also thank Janine Clark, Catherine Evans, Connor Ewing, Diana Fu, Ran Hirschl, Egor Lazarev, Sida Liu, Andrew McDougall, Alex Reisenbichler, and Lucan Way for their invaluable feedback on my work, tips on the publishing process, as well as for their cherished friendships. I'm grateful to Chris Cochrane and Peggy Kohn for facilitating the institutional support that made this book possible.

I wrote most of this book in the company – and sometimes in the solidarity – of an amazing group of women at the University of Toronto: Liz Acorn, Hülya Arık, Martha Balaguera, Nicole

Bernhardt, Janine Clark, Nadège Compaoré, Fidan Elçioğlu, María Méndez Gutiérrez, Julie Moreau, Nidhi Subramanyam, Lauren Richter, Rania Salem, and Lana Salman. The many hours we spent writing, debriefing, laughing, celebrating, and conspiring reminded me that no part of this journey had to be taken alone. I do not believe that I could have completed the book without Martha, whose companionship brought clarity to tangled ideas, warmth to difficult days, and a daily dose of insight, humor, and care that carried me through. With Çağrı Yoltar and Ömer Özcan, I found both intellectual kinship and a chosen family; our conversations about the personal and the political made everything feel a little more possible. Randall has been an unfailing source of wit and wisdom on all things academic and a friend always great at listening, provoking, and entertaining.

The initial research for the dissertation was funded by the National Science Foundation's Law and Social Sciences Program along with the Chester A. Fritz and Boeing Fellowship, the David Olson Research Fellowship, the European Union Center of Excellence, and the Harry Bridges Center at UW. Support for the book came from CEES, UTSC Department of Political Science, UTSC Office of the Vice-Principal Research and Innovation, and a Social Sciences and Humanities Research Council of Canada (SSHRC) Partnership Development Grant. I would also like to thank the brilliant graduate and undergraduate research assistants who helped build the Strasbourg Labor Cases Database (StrasLab) and assisted with research for this book. At UW, I thank Dashni Amin, Katherine Beyer, Travis Bjork, John Flanagan, Carlee Goble, Christine Hanzawa, Mark Lee, Jisoo Lee, Kasumi Maeda, Kyle Martin, Hannah Schwendeman, Skye Terebey, Lindsey Trimmer, and Aya Yousuf. At the University of Toronto and UTSC, I thank Zubeir Ahmed, Salar Asadolahi, Esma Boztaş, Gözde Böcü, Reyanna Bridge, Dalraj Gill, Christos Kakaletris, Selin Kepenek, Momina Malik, Mher Mamajanyan, Hadi Qarizada, James Vlahos, and Lina Zuluaga.

I thank Matt Gallaway, my editor at Cambridge University Press, for his guidance and thoughtful engagement throughout the publication process, and the series editors of *Cambridge Studies in Law and Society* – Mark Massoud, Jens Meirhenrich, and Rachel Stern – for welcoming this book into a series that I've long admired. I also want to acknowledge the two anonymous reviewers for their thoughtful comments, which helped sharpen the book's core arguments. Portions of Chapter 7 draw on ideas first developed in my 2018 *Law & Social Inquiry* article, and some of the empirical material in that chapter also appears in my 2026 *Perspectives on Politics* article. Parts of Chapters 2 and 5 build on arguments originally developed in my 2023 *Law & Society Review* article. I'm grateful to Kibele Yarman for designing a book cover that captures so much of what the book is about.

Finally, I thank my family, near and far. My parents have been my most enthusiastic supporters; above all, I thank them for teaching me how to dream without losing sight of the joy in what is already mine. My sister has lifted me up when I needed it most and has been a model of strength and brilliance that I have always looked up to. Our extended families, spread around the US and Turkey, shared their cheer, love, and care as Zach and I moved from one place to the next.

River Kahraman was worth every bit of the delay her arrival brought to this book. Her cuddles and warmth are the best reasons for late starts and frequent pauses. And Zach Richer has been with me through every storm and every celebration as my lover, carer, editor, and as a challenger with one of the sharpest minds I know. I'm so grateful to have him by my side; I never take that for granted.

TABLE OF CASES

CJEU

International Transport Workers' Federation and Finnish Seamen's Union v. Viking Line ABP and OÜ Viking Line Eesti (Viking) (2007), 119, 123
Laval un Partneri Ltd v. Svenska Byggnadsarbetareförbundet and Others (Laval) (2007), 119, 123

ECTHR

AB Kurt Kellermann v. Sweden (2007), 86
Airey v. Ireland (1979), 81
Aizpurua Ortiz and Others v. Spain (2014), 87
Akarsubaşi v. Turkey (2015), 157
Akdivar and Others v. Turkey (1996), 160
Akkoç v. Turkey (2000), 132
Almaz and Others v. Turkey (2024), 102
ASLEF v. The United Kingdom (2007), 97, 113, 122, 151–153
Atalay v. Turkey (2024)
Bariş and Others v. Turkey (2021), 102, 124
Beck, Copp and Bazeley v. the United Kingdom (2002), 89
Brincat and Others v. Malta (2014), 92
Brough v. the United Kingdom (2016), 2, 123, 177, 181, 188
Bucur and Toma v. Romania (2011), 88
C. N. and V. v. France (2012), 90
C. N. v. the United Kingdom (2012), 90
Case of United Communist Party of Turkey and Others v. Turkey (1998), 216
Chowdury and Others v. Greece (2017), 90
Copland v. the United Kingdom (2007), 93
Council of Civil Service Unions et al. v. The United Kingdom (1987), 65, 94, 115
Dahlab v. Switzerland (2001), 91
Danilenkov and Others v. Russia (2009), 99
Dedecan and Ok v. Turkey (2015), 160–161
Demir and Baykara v. Turkey (2008), 3–5, 74–75, 98, 120, 127–128, 130, 163–164, 180, 208, 212, 215, 17
Dev Maden-Sen v. Turkey (1999), 124

TABLE OF CASES

Dikici v. Turkey (2009), 93
Dikici v. Turkey (2013), 92
Dilek and Others v. Turkey (2007), 129, 98, 167–168
Dudgeon v. the United Kingdom (1981), 114
Ebrahimian v. France (2015), 91
Eğitim ve Bilim Emekçileri Sendikası v. Turkey (2012), 134, 159
Eğitim ve Bilim Emekçileri Sendikası v. Turkey, 101
Eker v. Turkey (1998), 91
Emel Boyraz v. Turkey (2014), 89
Enerji Yapi-Yol Sen v. Turkey (2009), 74–75, 98, 129–130, 166–167
Erenler and Others v. Turkey (2023), 161
Ertaş Aydın and Others v. Turkey (2005), 160
Eweida and others v. the United Kingdom (2013), 91
Ezelin v. France (1991), 56
Fábián v. Hungary (2017), 88
Fatma Akaltun Fırat v. Turkey (2013), 169
Garcia Mateos v. Spain (2013), 88
Guja v. Moldova (2008), 88
Gül and Others v. Turkey (2010), 169
Güneri and Others v. Turkey (2005), 160
Gustafsson v. Sweden (1996), 96
H. M. v. Turkey (2006), 169
Halford v. the United Kingdom (1997), 93
Harman and Hewitt v. the United Kingdom (1992), 123
Heinisch v. Germany (2011), 88
Hirst v. the United Kingdom (2005), 142
Hirst v. the United Kingdom (2006), 186
Hulea v. Romania (2012), 87
Humpert and Others v. Germany (2023), 102–103
I. B. v. Greece (2013), 89
Junta Rectora Del Ertzainen Nazional Elkartasuna (ER.N.E.) v. Spain (2015), 98
Karaçay v. Turkey (2007), 99, 129, 167–168, 210
Karademirci and Others v. Turkey (2005), 169
Kavala v. Turkey (2020), 235
Kavala v. Turkey (2022), 142
Kawogo v. the United Kingdom (2013), 90
Kaya and Seyhan v. Turkey (2009), 168
Kaya v. Turkey (2024), 102
Kjartan Ásmundsson v. Iceland (2004), 87
Konstantin Markin v. Russia (2012), 87
Köpke v. Germany (2010), 93
Koufaki and ADEDY v. Greece (2013), 87

TABLE OF CASES

L. C. B. v. the UK (1998), 92
L. E. v. Greece (2016), 91
L. R. v. the United Kingdom (2011), 90
Lautsi and Others v. Italy (2011), 91
López Ribalda and Others v. Spain (2019), 93
Lustig-Prean and Beckett v. the United Kingdom (1999), 89
M. A. and 39 Others v. the United Kingdom (1987), 65
Massa v. Italy (1993), 86
Matelly v. France (2014), 98
Meier v. Switzerland (2016), 91
Melike v. Turkey (2021), 89
Metin Turan v. Turkey (2006), 160
Müslüm Çiftçi v. Turkey (2010), 160–161
N. K. M. v. Hungary (2013), 87
The National Association of Teachers in Further and Higher Education v. the United Kingdom (1998), 67
National Union of Belgian Police v. Belgium (1975), 94
National Union of Rail, Maritime and Transport Workers v. The United Kingdom (2014), 64
Nerva and Others v. the United Kingdom (2002), 87
Norman v. the United Kingdom (2021), 88
Obst v. Germany (2010), 91
Öneryildiz v. Turkey (2004), 92
Palomo Sánchez and Others v. Spain (2011), 101
Paulet v. the United Kingdom (2014), 87
Pay v. the United Kingdom (2008), 89
Pellegrin v. France (1999), 86
Perkins and R. v. the United Kingdom (2002), 89
Petrovic v. Austria (1998), 87
POA and Others v. The United Kingdom (2011), 154
R. A. and W. M. v. the United Kingdom (1987), 65
Rantsev v. Cyprus and Russia (2010), 90
Redfearn v. the United Kingdom (2012), 89
RMT v. The United Kingdom (2014), 101–102, 122–123, 154, 155–156, 182
Rommelfanger v. Germany (1989), 91
S. L. v. Sweden (1971), 56
S. M. v. Croatia (2020), 91
Sabeh El Leil v. France (2011), 86
Saime Özcan v. Turkey (2009), 99
Schmidt and Dahlström v. Sweden (1976), 94
Schuth v. Germany (2010), 91
Selahattin Demirtaş v. Turkey No. 2 (2020), 142, 235
Sidabras and Džiautas v. Lithuania (2004), 89

Siebanhaar v. Germany (2011), 91
Siliadin v. France (2005), 90
Smith and Grady v. the United Kingdom (1999), 89
Smith v. the United Kingdom (2017), 2, 177, 196, 198
Sørensen and Rasmussen v. Denmark (2006), 99
Sosyal-İş Union and Kodaş v. Turkey (1995), 69
Stummer v. Austria (2011), 88, 91
Süheyla Aydın v. Turkey (2005), 132
Süleyman Çelebi and Others v. Turkey (2016), 171
Swedish Engine Drivers' Union v. Sweden (1976), 94
Tek Gıda İş Sendikası v. Turkey (2017), 158
Tüm Bel Sen v. Turkey (2014), 164
Tüm Emekliler Sendikası v. Turkey (2017), 124
Tüm Haber Sen and Çinar v. Turkey (2006), 97, 126, 158, 201, 204, 208, 212
Tyrer v. the United Kingdom (1978), 81
Ülger v. Turkey (2007), 86
Urcan and Others v. Turkey (2008), 167–168
V. C. L. and A. N. v. the United Kingdom (2021), 91
Van Der Mussele v. Belgium (1983), 91
Vilho Eskelinen and Others v. Finland (2007), 86
Vilnes and Others v. Norway (2013), 92
Wilson, National Union of Journalists and Others v. The United Kingdom (2002), 6, 17, 56, 75, 102, 106, 116, 118, 120, 122–123, 149–150, 153, 155
X v. Federal Republic of Germany (1974), 91
Young, James and Webster v. The United Kingdom (1981), 67, 94, 115, 153
Zengin v. Turkey, 132–133

UNITED KINGDOM

Metrobus Ltd v. Unite the Union (2009), 154
Milford Haven Port Authority v. Unite (2010), 155
R (UNISON) v. Lord Chancellor (2017), 109
RMT v. Serco Ltd and ASLEF v. London and Birmingham Railway Ltd (2011), 154–155
Secretary of State for Business and Trade v. Mercer (2024), 155
Serco Ltd v. RMT (2011), 154
Smith v. Carillion (JM) Ltd (2015), 188

ABBREVIATIONS

AKP	Adalet ve Kalkınma Partisi (Justice and Development Party)
ANAP	Anavatan Partisi (Motherland Party)
ASLEF	Associated Society of Locomotive Engineers and Firemen
BES	Büro Emekçileri Sendikası (Office Workers Union)
BNP	British National Party
BSG	Blacklist Support Group
CA	Consulting Association
CCSU	Council of Civil Service Unions
CEACR	Committee of Experts on the Application of Conventions and Recommendations
CESCR	Committee on Economic, Social and Cultural Rights
CFA	Committee on Freedom of Association
CHP	Cumhuriyet Halk Partisi (Republican People's Party)
CJEU	Court of Justice of the European Union
CM	Committee of Ministers (of the CoE)
CoE	Council of Europe
COPS	Campaign Opposing Police Surveillance
DİSK	Devrimci İşçi Sendikaları Konfederasyonu (Confederation of Revolutionary Trade Unions of Turkey)
DYP	Doğru Yol Partisi (True Path Party)
ECHR or the Convention	European Convention on Human Rights
ECJ	European Court of Justice
ECSR	European Committee on Social Rights
ECtHR or the Court	European Court of Human Rights
EEC	European Economic Community
Eğit-Der	Eğitimciler Derneği (Educators' Association)
Eğit-Sen	Eğitimciler Sendikası (Education Workers' Union)

LIST OF ABBREVIATIONS

Eğitim-İş	Eğitim İşkolu Kamu Görevlileri Sendikası (Education Sector Public Employees' Union)
Eğitim-Sen	Eğitim ve Bilim Emekçileri Sendikası (Education and Science Workers' Union)
EIN	European Implementation Network
ERA	Employment Relations Act
ESC	European Social Charter
ETUC	European Trade Union Confederation
EU	European Union
FBU	Fire Brigades Union
GCHQ	Government Communications Headquarters
HDP	Halkların Demokratik Partisi (People's Democratic Party)
HRA	Human Rights Act
ICC	International Criminal Court
ICESCR	International Covenant on Economic, Social and Cultural Rights
ICO	Information Commissioner's Office
IER	Institute of Employment Rights
ILO	International Labor Organization
ITUC	International Trade Union Confederation
JCHR	Joint Committee on Human Rights
KCK	Koma Civakên Kurdistanê (Kurdistan Communities Union)
KÇSP	Kamu Çalışanları Sendikaları Platformu (Public Employee Unions' Platform)
KESK	Kamu Emekçileri Sendikaları Konfederasyonu (Confederation of Public Employees Trade Unions)
Memur-Sen	Memur Sendikaları Konfederasyonu (Confederation of Civil Servants' Unions)
MP	Member of Parliament
NCCL	National Council for Civil Liberties (Liberty)
NGO	nongovernmental organization
NUJ	National Union of Journalists
OECD	Organisation for Economic Co-operation and Development
OPEC	Organization of the Petroleum Exporting Countries
PACE	Parliamentary Assembly of the Council of Europe
PKK	Partiya Karkerên Kurdistanê (Kurdistan Workers' Party)

LIST OF ABBREVIATIONS

POA	Prison Officers' Association
PWAB	Public Workers Arbitration Board (Kamu Görevlileri Hakem Kurulu)
RMT	National Union of Rail, Maritime and Transport Workers
SDS	special demonstration squad (of the Metropolitan Police, UK)
SEE	state economic enterprises
SES	Sağlık Emekçileri Sendikası (Healthcare Workers' Union)
SHP	Sosyaldemokrat Halkçı Parti (Social-Democrat People's Party)
SNP	Scottish National Party
StrasLab	Strasbourg Labor Cases Database
TİP	Türkiye İşçi Partisi (Workers' Party of Turkey)
TUC	Trades Union Congress
TULRCA	Trade Union and Labour Relations
Tüm Bel Sen	Tüm Belediye ve Yerel Yönetim Hizmetleri Emekçileri Sendikası (Union of All Municipality and Local Administration Services Employees)
Türk-İş	Türkiye İşçi Sendikaları Konfederasyonu (Confederation of Turkish Trade Unions)
UCATT	Union of Construction, Allied Trades and Technicians
UCU	University and College Union
UN	United Nations
YSP	Yeşil Sol Parti (Green Left Party)

CHAPTER 1

INTRODUCTION

Dave Smith was a construction worker in the United Kingdom who devoted years of his life to developing his skills in the construction industry. Despite his experience, in the late 1990s Smith suddenly began to see his applications for new contracts rejected. Unable to find a project that would take him on, he was forced to give up his career completely by 2001. Smith had always heard rumors among fellow construction workers about an employer-run list of workers active in the trade unions, but nobody he knew had concrete evidence of it. It wasn't until an official investigation was commissioned in 2009 that the rumors were confirmed: Several firms across the industry had colluded in compiling a massive roster of names – a blacklist – of the union workers deemed likeliest to push for better and safer working conditions. A raid of the Consulting Association by the UK's national data protection authority, the Information Commissioner's Office (ICO), revealed that forty-four companies – including several major multinational corporations – had conspired in the blacklisting of more than 3,200 people.

A blacklist this extensive required collaboration among several actors. Construction firms collected information on workers without their knowledge or consent and reported it to the Consulting Association, which was founded and funded by construction firms to run organizational operations by systematically compiling, analyzing, and selling data about workers. Firms could then purchase these data, including names of workers deemed "troublemakers, criminal elements or other undesirable people," for use in their hiring and firing decisions (Department for

Business, Innovation and Skills 2009: 9). Investigations into blacklisting later showed that undercover police officers regularly provided information to the Consulting Association regarding the political activities of workers. The institutional effort was complex and layered, but the effects were simple: Employees who had raised their voices on health and safety issues in the workplace and/or were active in the trade union movement lost their jobs and essentially became unemployable. Smith's own file reached thirty-six pages, documenting such offenses as filming unsafe working conditions and sharing the footage with the press (*Smith v. the United Kingdom* 2017, para. 7).

As a result, thousands of workers like Dave Smith went unemployed for years or were forced to look for jobs as unskilled workers, unable to seek employment in the industry to which they had devoted years of work. Workers seeking state remedy were further frustrated by the weakness of domestic laws on blacklisting. In the aftermath of the raid, only the Consulting Association head, Ian Kerr, was officially prosecuted for breaching the workers' privacy. Kerr's penalty was a £5,000 fine, which was swiftly paid off by one of the blacklisting firms in exchange for his agreement to take the blame and keep the blacklisting companies' names out of the court hearings.[1]

Several aspects of this story stand out. These include the extent and nature of blacklisting in a country that has long expressed a commitment to democratic values and the protection of individual rights, the discovery of police complicity in the crime, the inability to prosecute the blacklisters under British law, and the devastation of the targeted workers' careers and livelihoods. But it was not just the scale or the severity of these crimes that is noteworthy, it is also the response of those it victimized. After losing their cases in domestic courts, Smith and one other worker, guided by their lawyers, decided to pursue remedies at the international level and applied to the European Court of Human Rights (ECtHR, or the Court) (*Smith v. the United Kingdom* 2017; *Brough v. the United Kingdom* 2016).

The blacklisted workers' cases were part of a rapidly developing case law on trade union rights at the post-2000 ECtHR. In response to a new deluge of cases across the continent, the ECtHR set precedents that for the first time recognized basic trade union rights – including the

---

[1] Daniel Boffey, "Construction Bosses 'Tried to Hide Evidence of Their Blacklist,'" *The Guardian*, May 14, 2016, www.theguardian.com/business/2016/may/14/blacklist-construction-workers-mcalpine.

rights to organize, bargain collectively, and strike – as fundamental human rights. This emerging case law culminated in *Demir and Baykara v. Turkey* (2008), which concerned a labor dispute caused by the failure of a municipal council to fulfill its obligations under its collective bargaining agreement with the public sector workers' union. The claim emerged in 1993 when the Turkish public sector workers were striving to unionize for the first time since the violent 1980 coup crushed all trade union activism in the country. The Turkish courts dismissed the case, ruling that, according to Turkish laws, public servants were not even permitted to form a union, let alone engage in collective bargaining. In a landmark judgment, the ECtHR reversed its earlier jurisprudence and recognized collective bargaining as "an essential element" of the right to association (Article 11).

The development of this trade union rights case law, which has garnered little attention from social scientists, is surprising for at least two reasons. First, an overwhelming majority of ECtHR cases come from Turkey, followed by cases from the UK. These two countries are an unlikely couple to be leading the labor case law: One is a repeat offender before the ECtHR with the highest number of violation rulings on all issues, the other is a liberal democracy and a drafter of the European Convention on Human Rights (the European Convention or the Convention). The high number of cases, some of which set important precedents, coming from these two countries compels us to look beyond regime type and economic development to understand the conditions that drive workers to look for remedies at the international level.

Second, labor and human rights are strange bedfellows. For decades, most workers avoided litigation as a strategy that took too long and tended to individualize and depoliticize the collective nature of workers' claims. Instead, they preferred to resolve their issues as an extension of their collective identity, through rank-and-file mobilization. Litigation at an international court was barely a consideration for organized labor. And for good reason: As a court established to protect civil and political rights with no clear mandate on labor rights, the ECtHR dismissed the few labor rights claims brought before it during the first four decades of its existence. What, then, explains organized labor's sudden embrace of international litigation? Does the developing labor case law at the ECtHR signal a new era for labor activism?

The first part of this book traces the struggles of British and Turkish unionists and lawyers as well as the changing political power and jurisprudence of the ECtHR to show how the Court has become a new terrain for labor activists to seek remedies for the violation of workers' rights. Despite major differences between these countries, common features motivated organized labor in both countries to turn to litigation at the ECtHR. Although not without reservations, labor activists in both countries have seized on the ascendence of human rights at a time when neoliberal policies have curbed the power of organized labor since 1980. Labor lawyers played key roles in this process by drawing workers' attention to the emerging legal opportunities at the international level and leading strategic litigation efforts.

The second part of the book turns to pressing questions concerning the impact of these legal mobilization efforts. Do these landmark rulings on trade union rights merely serve as "window dressing" (Keith 2002), or do they actually improve the lives of workers on the ground? To what extent do states implement rulings issued by a distant international court? Are workers wasting valuable resources and energy on litigation efforts when they could be pursuing more effective tactics, like rank-and-file mobilization? Can human rights law and institutions become counter-forces against the declining power of organized labor?

At first glance, there is hardly any reason to be hopeful about the prospects of human rights litigation for workers. The ECtHR took eleven years to decide on the *Demir and Baykara* case, and when the period required for exhausting the domestic remedies, is included, the workers had to wait for fifteen years for legal proceedings to be completed. By the time the ECtHR delivered its judgment, the government had already granted public sector workers the right to unionize and the right to engage in collective bargaining. On the surface, these legal reforms cannot be attributed to the landmark ruling of the ECtHR. The blacklisted workers in the UK had even less obvious reason to cheer the ECtHR, as the Court eventually dismissed both of their cases. All told, the ECtHR appears to offer little more than a "hollow hope" (Rosenberg 2008; see also Gearty 2010).

A closer inspection of the dynamics on the ground, however, reveals a different picture. A year after the ICO findings, Smith read a report on blacklisting written by a prominent labor scholar and lawyer, Keith Ewing (2009a). In the report, Ewing drew attention to the weakness of domestic laws and pointed to how the UK was violating its obligations under the European Convention and ECtHR case law. After reading the report, Smith had a "eureka!" moment: The best way to draw public attention to their plight would be by framing the issue as a human rights scandal.[2] Smith joined forces with other blacklisted workers to establish a grassroots organization called the Blacklist Support Group (BSG) committed to claiming workers' rights as human rights. Smith was a labor organizer not a lawyer: The series of campaigns launched by this new group fought for their rights in multiple venues, from rallies in front of the parliament building with other human rights activists to inventive protests outside the headquarters of blacklisting firms. As a result, the BSG was able to leverage policy changes, initiate a public inquiry into police surveillance, and win a multimillion-dollar civil settlement from the blacklisting companies. Most of these developments occurred *before* the ECtHR even issued its final rulings. Indeed, the ECtHR dismissed the cases due in part to the remedies workers had already received from a domestic court. In Turkey, too, the availability of an international enforcer sparked mobilization by providing public sector workers safeguards against state repression in a post-coup environment and legitimacy to their claims to unionize. Workers initiated a massive mobilization campaign through which they pressured the government to undertake legal reforms recognizing some basic trade union rights *before* the landmark ruling of *Demir and Baykara*.

These cases draw our attention to an often neglected factor in studies assessing the impact of human rights courts: the power of grassroots mobilization. The direct remedies provided by international courts often come too late to offer much relief to the applicants named in the suit. And international courts lack strong enforcement mechanisms to persuade states to undertake structural changes that would prevent future violations. Yet the transformative impact of international courts can be activated indirectly. Litigation at the international level can serve as a catalyst for grassroots mobilization, generating momentum for change. When activists build a movement in conjunction with litigation efforts, they secure tangible gains even before the court issues its final judgment.

At the same time, labor's engagement with the ECtHR demonstrates a new approach to human rights: the *strategic* mobilization of human rights. Workers do not target courts out of a love of litigation or an ideological commitment to universal rights. They invoke international law *because it helps them advance concrete goals*. The availability of an international enforcer gives legal backing to activists' demands,

---

[2] Interview with Dave Smith, October 2014.

facilitates recruitment and coalition-building, and provides a resonant frame for gaining visibility in political environments hostile to labor. However, despite adopting human rights language in their public campaigns or recruitment efforts, workers are skeptical of using human rights frameworks. In planning meetings, social media groups, and social hours, they still form their collective identity and solidarity ties around class-based themes rather than human rights.

I draw these conclusions based on two types of original data. First, I constructed the Strasbourg Labor Cases Database (StrasLab), which compiles sixty years of ECtHR case law on labor rights ($n = 1{,}161$). This is the first cross-national, longitudinal database to systematically identify and categorize the ECtHR's rulings on labor issues. Second, in order to examine why workers turn to international litigation and how ECtHR rulings affect them on the ground, I conducted fieldwork in Turkey and the UK and collected in-depth data on two labor movements. These sources combined provide a comprehensive account of the causes and consequences of workers' legal mobilization at an international court.

1.1 A NEW ERA OF ACTIVISM FOR LABOR: CLAIMING LABOR RIGHTS AS HUMAN RIGHTS

When two Turkish union leaders, Kemal Demir and Vicdan Baykara, complained to the ECtHR about the blanket ban against public sector workers' right to engage in collective bargaining in 1993, they did not have high hopes of winning their case. The only article with explicit reference to trade union rights is Article 11 on the freedom of assembly and association. But at the time, the ECtHR did not have a single violation judgment on cases brought by trade unionists.[3]

The ECtHR's reluctance to recognize trade union rights in its early years was not surprising. Established in the aftermath of World War II, the Council of Europe (CoE) followed the dominant human rights framework at the time, privileging civil and political rights such as freedom of expression or prohibition of torture, while delegating the

---

[3] Article 11 states that "Everyone has the right to freedom of peaceful assembly and to freedom of association with others, including the right to form and to join trade unions for the protection of his interests." The first time the ECtHR issued a pro-union judgment under Article 11 was in *Wilson, National Union of Journalists and Others v. The United Kingdom* (2002).

protection of socioeconomic rights to the European Committee on Social Rights (ECSR) with a much weaker monitoring system.[4] The few cases workers filed during the ECtHR's first four decades were all dismissed.[5] Labor activists, in turn, spent this period prioritizing rank-and-file mobilization to address their grievances. Seeking recourse at an international institution was not an option they considered.

The conditions that led a skeptical group of activists to turn to an international court for relief constitute the first theme of this book. I suggest three factors to explain this tactical shift to international litigation in the post-1990 period. First, *political opportunities for organized labor started to close off* with the ascendance of neoliberal policies. As governments implemented policies that structurally disempowered – or, in more authoritarian contexts, violently repressed – trade unions, labor activists' ability to advance their grievances through democratic or judicial channels at the domestic level became severely restricted. In response to their waning strength, organized labor adopted various revitalization strategies, such as restructuring organizations, building coalitions with other grassroots activists, partnering with employers or governments, and establishing transnational links with unions abroad (Baccaro, Hamann, and Turner 2003; Frege and Kelly 2004; Ibsen and Tapia 2017; Seidman 2007). One of the understudied responses of unions in countries where organized labor experienced a sharp decline was seeking legal remedies at an international court. Domestic repression – whether through policy or by force – constitutes a major "push factor" that brought unionists' claims to the Court.

During the same period, *international courts rose to prominence* by weighing in on an increasingly broad range of important policy issues. The rapid expansion of the labor case law at the ECtHR can be viewed as part of this broader trend of "judicialization" or the "rights revolutions" unfolding at international courts (Alter 2014; Hirschl 2008; Kelemen 2011; Stone Sweet and Shapiro 2002). Over the past thirty years, the ECtHR's case law has exploded in both volume and significance as the Court has increasingly addressed contentious issues such as women's right to wear a headscarf, the treatment of terrorism suspects, and prisoners' right to vote. During this period, the ECtHR became "the supreme European Court" shaping policy outcomes across the

---

[4] The United Nations (UN) similarly had a divided approach to human rights under the twin covenants (Alston and Goodman 2013).

[5] Chapter 4 provides a detailed discussion of these trade union rights cases.

continent (Madsen 2016). Most studies on human rights, including those on the ECtHR, focus on how historically marginalized groups have turned to these institutions, with particular attention to civil and political rights. Despite the increasing number of studies on legal mobilization at the ECtHR (Anagnostou 2013; Cichowski 2016; Hodson 2014; Kurban 2020; Sundstrom, Sperling, and Sayoglu 2019; Van der Vet 2012), we lack a study that examines the social and political causes of the unexpected growth of the Court's trade union rights case law.[6] The emergence of the ECtHR as an influential actor in policymaking at the international level constitutes a "pull factor" that made the Court newly attractive to labor activists and their lawyers.

In response to the early trade union rights cases brought before it, the ECtHR was initially more deferential to member states, leaving the settlement of these contentious issues to national courts. But after gaining confidence and experience on a wide range of issues throughout the 1990s, the Court became more receptive to new rights claims. The violations faced by trade union members resonated easily with the ECtHR as breaches of freedom of association (Article 11). The workers' need to find remedies beyond domestic channels coincided with a period of expanding ECtHR jurisprudence and growing responsiveness to new rights claims. Consequently, the push from repressive domestic regimes in the post-1980 period, coupled with the pull of a stronger international human rights court, created appropriate conditions for workers to seek remedies at the international level.

International courts, however, are not in the usual toolkit of activists operating at the domestic level. For organized labor – a group accustomed to resolving labor disputes through traditional bargaining and collective action tactics – resort to long-term litigation at an international court constitutes a highly unexpected course of action. An explanation based solely on structural changes leaves unanswered the question of how workers became aware of remedies at the international level. Furthermore, the ECtHR, as an institution designed as a civil and political rights court without any favorable rulings on labor rights at the time, was not an obvious choice for labor activists. Workers had other venues to consider, many of which could be

---

[6] Legal scholars provide comprehensive analyses of the labor jurisprudence at the ECtHR (see, for example, Dorssemont, Lörcher, and Schömann 2013; Sychenko 2017), but there have not been any studies on labor activists' legal mobilization at the ECtHR.

expected to have more applicable law, if not ideological sympathy, for their claims. The International Labor Organization (ILO) and the Court of Justice of the European Union (CJEU), for example, both have provisions that explicitly protect trade union rights. The ILO, in particular, has a clear institutional commitment to advancing unions' concerns. However, my comparative case studies and case law analyses show that workers rarely chose these other institutions to seek remedy. A second related question, then, is the workers' choice of target institution for legal mobilization: Why did labor activists choose the ECtHR over other international institutions?

I show that a small group of lawyers facilitated workers' legal mobilization by probing different international legal institutions to identify the right venue for unions, directing labor activists' attention to international courts, and leading strategic litigation efforts. In so doing, this research contributes to studies that emphasize the agency of lawyers in leading legal mobilization. New rights claims, buttressed by strong legal argumentation and compelling evidence prepared by expert lawyers, not only expand international courts' jurisprudence into new issue areas but also steer the direction of this expansion by shaping court dockets (Caserta and Madsen 2024; Cichowski 2007; Duffy 2018; Haddad 2018; Hodson 2014; Kurban 2020; Pavone 2022; Sundstrom 2014; Van der Vet 2018). The majority of the existing literature on international legal mobilization, however, explains why and how lawyers engage in litigation at a single international court. Despite a growing literature on regime complexity and forum shopping by private actors at the international level (Busch 2007; Gomez-Mera and Molinari 2014; Hafner-Burton, Victor, and Lupu 2012), we know little about how lawyers navigate a landscape of multiple international institutions to identify the best venue for advancing their claims. Findings in this book advance the study of legal mobilization by demonstrating how lawyers operate in a field of international legal pluralism. This process of strategic litigation at the international level is based on lawyers' legal expertise on the institutional features of these bodies, as well as their evaluations informed by prior litigation experience.

1.2 BEYOND COMPLIANCE: THE MOBILIZING POWER OF HUMAN RIGHTS LITIGATION

The first part of the book shows how organized labor in Europe identified a new way to combat precarious work conditions and restrictions on unionization. But is litigation at the ECtHR an effective strategy? What tangible impact do international rulings have for aggrieved workers on the ground?

1.2.1 Conventional Wisdom on the Impact of Human Rights Regimes

There is hardly a consensus among scholars on the impact of international human rights institutions. Established as "the crown jewel of the Council of Europe" in the aftermath of World War II in order to promote democracy and human rights in Europe (Madsen 2007: 148), the ECtHR is often regarded as a highly effective human rights court (Alter, Helfer, and Madsen 2016; Hillebrecht 2014; Stone Sweet and Keller 2008). In 2020, the CoE proclaimed the ECtHR a leading force "in maintaining and fostering democratic stability across the Continent" and highlighted its "extraordinary contribution ... to the protection and promotion of human rights and the rule of law in Europe."[7] Studies on compliance with ECtHR rulings confirm the CoE's proclamation, demonstrating that Court rulings shape state behavior and facilitate policy changes across Europe (Helfer and Voeten 2014; Stiansen 2019). Many scholars argue that increased litigation at international human rights courts over the past few decades – in Europe and beyond – has helped protect the rights of marginalized groups against state oppression, bring human rights violators before justice, and facilitate democratization in transitioning regimes (Alter 2014; Brysk 2000; Cichowski 2016; Duffy 2018; Engstrom 2019; Simmons 2009).

Pessimists – also referred to as realists – argue, on the other hand, that human rights commitments of states are "empty promises" and that states avoid making structural changes that would produce substantive impact at the domestic level (Hafner-Burton and Tsutsui 2005; see also Hathaway 2002; Vreeland 2008). Posner (2014) declares that the human rights project failed spectacularly: International institutions, including the ECtHR, are too feeble and lack the resources necessary to compel states into compliance. Case studies on the ECtHR raise similar concerns in less alarmist language: Member states often find ways to superficially comply with the letter of the law while evading structural reforms that would provide meaningful protections (Anagnostou 2013; Búzás 2021; Kurban 2020; Von Staden 2018).

---

[7] CM 130th Session, November 2020 decision, https://rm.coe.int/0900001680a03d50.

Many labor scholars are also skeptical about the promises of human rights, albeit for different reasons. Some point out that human rights law undermines the collective nature of labor claims by encouraging workers to seek remedies for their individual problems on their own rather than engaging in rank-and-file mobilization (Savage and Smith 2017). Others lament the concurrent development of neoliberalism and human rights, pointing out the lack of remedies the latter provides for rising global inequality. After all, human rights gained prominence in the late 1970s, precisely when welfare states started to retreat from their redistributive role and corporations' increased demand for flexible labor left workers in a vulnerable position.[8] In this telling, human rights at best shadowed neoliberalism as a "powerless companion," providing few tools to combat these restrictive policies (Moyn 2018: 180). At worst, human rights served to legitimize structural injustices by becoming an "ideological alibi" of market fundamentalism (Hopgood 2015: 2).[9] While human rights became the dominant framework for advancing social justice claims globally, these scholars argued, its narrow focus on establishing a minimum floor of human protection depoliticized and curbed the ambitions of most other social movements, including labor movements (Baxi 2008; Rajagopal 2003). Consequently, there is nothing to celebrate about the human rights revolution from the perspective of labor (Gill 1995).

1.2.2 A Grassroots Theory of International Legal Mobilization

The pessimists are to a degree right. Reforms taken by states in compliance with court rulings often fail to fulfill the expectations of trade unionists. In most cases, states undertake the minimum requirements to appease Court officials and manage to close the supervision of the case without taking robust measures that would prevent future violations. Moreover, due to the excessive length of legal proceedings at international courts and the supervision process, these changes in state behavior often come too late – a decade or two after the initial violation occurred – to provide any actual remedies to the applicants.

But they are also wrong, because they fail to look beyond the direct remedies to understand the real impact of international courts.

---

[8] Flexible labor refers to temporary or subcontracted work with no benefits or welfare safety nets (Felstead and Jewson 1999).
[9] For similar arguments in this critical vein, see Brown (2004), Marks (2011), and Whyte (2019).

Litigation at an international court can instigate grassroots mobilization on the ground. The possibility to litigate at an international court can give activists new resources and motivation to launch their movement when domestic institutions are unresponsive to their demands. It can also recruit new members to the movement by providing safeguards against state repression. The case studies in this book show that, rather than waiting for a final ruling from the ECtHR, activists simultaneously engage in multiple forms of activism, including street protests, marches, lobbying, social media activism, as well as new domestic litigation campaigns with references to human rights law. Human rights litigation provides activists a whole new set of opportunities and resources to advance their agenda, such as a globally resonant discourse to frame their grievances, new tools for tactical innovation, support from sympathetic political or judicial elites, legal backing and legitimacy to their claims to recruit new members, and alliances with other human rights groups to expand their movement. Consequently, rather than having a depoliticizing effect on workers, as some critics have cautioned, human rights law can arm activists with new resources to build and amplify grassroots mobilization.

At the same time, I find that workers do not completely buy into the promise of law and instead engage in *strategic mobilization of human rights*. Aware of many of the limitations of human rights institutions, they use human rights as a means to an end. They incorporate human rights language in their mobilization efforts in order to achieve specific goals, such as gaining the sympathy of an audience or, in repressive environments, mitigating the fears of government retaliation among new recruits. But they define themselves primarily as workers and labor activists, rather than as human rights activists. Labor's commitment to human rights is purely pragmatic; activists are ready to break their ties with human rights when they no longer serve a purpose.

The findings from Part II of the book advance scholarly debates on the impact of human rights courts, legal mobilization, and labor politics in several important ways. First, this book builds on efforts to understand the importance of domestic politics in giving effect to human rights law and institutions (Alter 2014; Dai 2007; Dancy and Michel 2016; González-Ocantos 2016; Haglund 2020; Hillebrecht 2014; Sikkink 2011; Simmons 2009). A growing body of research confirms realists' claim that international mechanisms (i.e. international institutions, other countries, and transnational activist networks) fail to provide sufficient incentives for states to take action (Dai 2007;

Hillebrecht 2014; Simmons 2009; Von Staden 2018). While these external pressure mechanisms provide political or legal opportunities to strengthen human rights practices, the main engine of improvement is effort from pro-compliance domestic actors, such as judges, executives, legislators, or civil society actors. These groups may be committed to implementing a state's international human rights obligations for either normative or strategic reasons. Politicians, for instance, may promote compliance because of ideological commitments to liberal values or their socialization within an international organization where compliance is the norm (Finnemore 1996; Goodman and Jinks 2008). Alternatively, government leaders may expect to receive political gains for their state, such as joining the EU, as a result of implementing human rights law (Holzhacker 2013). For their part, judges may start referencing international human rights laws as a result of their participation in transnational judicial dialogue (Koh 2005; Slaughter 2003) or being prompted by human rights activists and lawyers (González-Ocantos 2016; Pavone 2022). Domestic non-governmental organizations (NGOs) can initiate naming and shaming campaigns at the domestic level to hold states accountable to their international obligations.[10] Most of the existing research, however, demonstrates how elite actors or NGOs induce compliance through institutional means. We know little about how social movements use disruptive or non-institutional means to instigate change. *Labor in Hard Times* demonstrates how litigation at an international court can empower groups directly affected by government policies to become agents of change. Hence, in explaining the divergent impact of human rights courts, I shift attention away from international factors and elite actors to the determinants of grassroots mobilization at the domestic level.

Second, research on international human rights courts generally operationalizes impact as compliance with court rulings. Studies on the ECtHR, for instance, often measure the impact of the Court by analyzing whether member states pay the damages awarded to

---

[10] The most famous example of NGOs initiating naming and shaming campaigns, of course, is Keck and Sikkink's (1998) boomerang model, where activists form transnational ties with international NGOs. (See also Risse, Ropp, and Sikkink 1999.) Other scholars point out that local NGOs can launch such campaigns at the domestic level (Engstrom 2019; Simmons 2009; Sundstrom 2012). Overall, NGO campaigns include publishing reports, organizing collective petitions, or lobbying activities, rather than demonstrations or other disruptive tactics. See the discussion in Chapter 6.

individual applicants or undertake relevant legislative changes in order to comply with the judgments of the Court (Grewal and Voeten 2015; Hawkins and Jacoby 2010; Hillebrecht 2014; Stiansen 2019). The CoE's official website facilitates such research by providing a detailed online database on the execution of ECtHR judgments. Such data have some merits. Direct remedies resulting from court rulings demonstrate some of the general patterns of compliance. And they are limited. Case studies that look at the actual implementation of reforms undertaken by states show that states often find ways to evade undertaking steps that would result in systemic changes (Anagnostou 2013; Búzás 2021; Kurban 2020; Von Staden 2018). Compliance with the Court's ruling may fall well short of activists' intentions or ambitions.

Yet evaluating compliance based on data provided by the courts or states can provide a limited and misleading picture because it obscures the social and political changes that occur in the shadows of official law.[11] I join sociolegal scholars' call to look beyond the legal documents and courtrooms to analyze the "radiating effects" of law, including how litigation efforts can change norms, discourses, social relations, and modes of contestation (Galanter 1983; see also Cover 1983; Epp 2009; McCann 1994; Moustafa 2018; Taylor 2023). To this end, *Labor in Hard Times* builds on legal mobilization theory, which draws insights from social movements theory and constructivism, to examine the relationship between law and social change. Comparative studies, including those based in the US, demonstrate that litigation in domestic courts can be constitutive of mobilization (Albiston 2011; Arrington 2016; Hunt 1990; McCann 1994; NeJaime 2010; Scheingold 1974). Participation in collective litigation efforts fosters legal consciousness by shaping actors' aspirations, norms, and perceptions of their own grievances, all of which are essential factors in building a movement. At the same time, litigation efforts can create more tangible benefits, such as attracting new financial resources for their cause or providing legal backing to activists' claims in their lobbying efforts. Litigation, even if unsuccessful, can thus act as a force-multiplier in raising expectations, attracting new supporters, and increasing the bargaining power of activists.

Most studies that examine international legal mobilization, however, examine the role of legal advocacy groups or lawyers in leading

---

[11] Merry (2016) refers to this case in measuring impact of human rights as compliance with a set of rules as the "seductions of quantification."

litigation efforts or in leveraging policy changes through institutional channels, such as lobbying efforts or follow-up litigation (Alter and Vargas 2000; Caserta and Madsen 2024; Cichowski 2007, 2016; Duffy 2018; Hodson 2014; Kelemen 2011; Pavone 2022; Sundstrom 2012; Vanhala 2010, 2018). As discussed earlier, lawyers play pivotal roles in facilitating labor's strategic litigation at the ECtHR. But lawyers are not the protagonists in actualizing international court rulings, and nor is the ECtHR. Rather, labor activists that build movements and engage in multiple forms of mobilization to advance their claims are the main agents in this struggle. This book, therefore, advances the legal mobilization theory by demonstrating the mechanisms through which international litigation can be constitutive of grassroots mobilization on the ground.

Distinct from others' findings on legal mobilization, workers' legal mobilization at the international level shows that human rights litigation does not necessarily shape the cultural drivers of social movements such as collective identity formations and inter-personal relationships. Classic legal mobilization theory shows that consistent engagement with legal institutions shapes the social construction of rights-based collective identity and solidarity ties among activists (Arrington 2019; McCann 1994). In some cases, these processes can occur naturally as a consequence of participating in collective litigation efforts or socializing in an environment where rights discourse is the dominant framework for talking about social justice issues. Activists can develop a sense of camaraderie based on shared grievances articulated through rights talk. In others, victims can be coached to articulate their grievances as human rights abuses and to adopt a rights-bearing individual identity. Drawing on a multi-sited ethnographic work, Merry and her collaborators argue that knowledge about international human rights law is communicated, or "vernacularized," to local people through transnationally connected "intermediaries" – activists or legal professionals who are "fluent" in human rights language (Levitt and Merry 2009; Merry 2006; Merry and Stern 2005). The adoption of human rights language and identity is encouraged and desired in order to help people view themselves as rights-bearing individuals rather than helpless victims (Chua 2020; see also Tsutsui 2018). My findings on labor activists differ from these accounts as labor activists' ideological convictions and collective identity are already shaped by class-based themes, and human rights do not replace these strong commitments. Activists use human rights law and language in order to advance specific goals. This instrumental approach allows activists to pursue more radical agendas and not be absorbed into conventional politics as cautioned by critical labor scholars (Gearty 2010; Rajagopal 2003; Savage and Smith 2017).

1.3 RESEARCH DESIGN AND CASE SELECTION

This research generates and analyzes two types of data. First, in order to examine workers' legal mobilization at the international level, I created a comprehensive database of labor-related cases at the ECtHR, covering the period from its inception in 1960 until 2017 ($n = 1,161$). StrasLab traces the evolution of the Court's labor jurisprudence, documenting trends in case volume, the countries most frequently involved, and the most salient issues in both quality and quantity. It also identifies the outcome of the cases and novel rights claims rejected by the Court. This analysis provides an overview of the Court's changing approach to labor rights, capturing the broader "rights revolution" that has unfolded since its inception. Appendix I provides detailed information on the database and the coding process.

Second, I draw on qualitative data based on comparative case studies of legal mobilization of trade unions in Turkey and the UK, the two countries that have brought the highest number and the most important cases before the ECtHR. Comparing these two countries, which differ in key respects, such as levels of economic development, regime type, and overall compliance rates with ECtHR rulings, gives me analytical leverage to identify the shared mechanisms that drove organized labor in both contexts to pursue litigation at the ECtHR.[12] In each case, unions faced the erosion of labor protections under post-1980 neoliberal reforms – implemented through legal restructuring in the UK and through more repressive means in Turkey – found strategic value in the ECtHR's growing receptiveness to labor claims, and were supported by committed lawyers who recognized the Court as a viable venue for contestation.[13] The UK became the site of the first successful challenge

---

[12] See Tarrow (2010) for a discussion of how paired comparison can be used to identify common mechanisms that drive seemingly different cases to similar outcomes (see especially pp. 244–45).

[13] While the ECtHR created similar incentive structures in both countries, the differing severity of domestic violations prompted Turkish and British lawyers to adopt divergent litigation strategies. I explain these differences in more detail in Chapter 5.

that elevated trade union rights within the Court's jurisprudence. Starting with *Wilson, National Union of Journalists and Others v. The United Kingdom* in 2002, the ECtHR began to recognize trade union rights as a core component of human rights law. Similarly, Turkish trade unions set numerous precedents, including the landmark *Demir and Baykara* (2008).

In the second part of the book, I present two cases of grassroots trade union activism to analyze the broader impact of ECtHR litigation: public sector workers' mobilization efforts that culminated in the formation of Kamu Emekçileri Sendikaları Konfederasyonu (KESK, Confederation of Public Employees Trade Unions) in Turkey and the BSG in the UK. I gathered rich data from participant observation, interviews, archival materials, media coverage, social media, parliamentary records, and reports published by NGOs and international organizations. The case studies underpin a bottom-up approach to examining workers' perspective on human rights litigation and the actual impact of ECtHR rulings on the ground. I provide detailed explanations on all qualitative data sources and research methods in Appendix II.

Analyzing these two movements enables me to theorize distinct pathways through which human rights litigation can catalyze grassroots mobilization under varying conditions. In Turkey, following a crushing military coup, public sector workers sought legal backing to demand their right to unionize for the first time. Human rights litigation provided safeguards against government repression to recruit new members and increased the likelihood of achieving their goals. In the UK, the blacklisting scandal, exacerbated by police collusion and union inaction, prompted blacklisted workers to seek new avenues for organizing and demanding justice. The ECtHR became a potential venue to address grievances in a national context where domestic protections were weak. Distinct from Turkish public sector workers, the BSG activists launched their movement in the late 2000s when the ECtHR had already issued several precedents on trade union rights, and human rights had become a dominant framework for advancing social justice claims. The BSG, therefore, launched a public campaign claiming their rights as human rights.

Although StrasLab includes a broad range of labor cases, the fieldwork data focus on trade union rights issues in part because it is the area of labor rights to which the ECtHR has been most attentive. At the same time, trade unions assume an enabling role for all other labor rights protection, allowing workers to collectively demand fair wages, social

17

security, health and safety at work, and other labor rights (Rosenfeld 2014). For this reason, in both Turkey and the UK, as well as in other parts of the world, disempowering unions has been an integral part of neoliberal policies (Daniels and McIlroy 2009; Harvey 2005). Through litigation at international human rights courts, unions have sought to reclaim public legitimacy, strengthen their bargaining power with governments, and enhance their capacity to recruit members.

1.4 ROADMAP

The next chapter establishes the theoretical framework of the book. I first discuss the conditions that drive activists to litigation at an international court, including the decline of domestic opportunities, the rise of new legal opportunities at the international level, as well as the agency of lawyers in driving activists' attention to these new legal remedies and identifying the target organization within a field of international legal pluralism. Next, I turn to the question of impact of human rights courts on the ground. I shift attention away from direct compliance with court rulings to the indirect effects of international courts on mobilization at the grassroots level. I offer a theoretical model that demonstrates how litigation at an international court can spark and expand social mobilization.

Part I of the book addresses the question of why and how workers have begun to turn to the ECtHR. Each of the three chapters examines the changes that occurred at the domestic, international, and grassroots levels, respectively. Chapter 3 explores the domestic origins of unions' turn to international law. I start with a brief analysis of StrasLab to identify the countries most frequently targeted in applications and those involved in the Court's most significant trade union rights rulings. I then provide a historical institutional analysis of how shifting political opportunity structures under two post-1980 variants of neoliberalism rolled out in Turkey and the UK created conditions that pushed workers to seek remedies elsewhere. The chapter ends with a brief analysis of the rising legal opportunities at the international level.

Chapter 4 presents StrasLab, which should appeal to legal professionals and scholars interested in finding out how the ECtHR overturned its previous case law to incorporate a wide range of labor rights into its jurisprudence. In addition to the labor case law analysis, the chapter identifies three eras in the ECtHR's approach to trade union rights: an initial phase of conservatism, when labor claims were dismissed; a golden period of expansive responsiveness; and a later phase of retrenchment, marked by political backlash and judicial caution.

Chapter 5 places lawyers center stage as agents who precipitated a scale shift in trade union strategy. The analysis complements the findings in Chapter 4 by pointing out how the labor jurisprudence developed through an iterative process between the top-down initiative of a new responsive court and the bottom-up legal mobilization led by lawyers. It shows how a group of committed lawyers in both Turkey and the UK identified the ECtHR as their target institution due to its judicial responsiveness and authority, and how they adapted their litigation strategies in response to differing levels of domestic violations. The chapter also highlights the lawyers' ideological commitments and their role as allies of organized labor.

Part II assesses the direct and indirect effects of legal mobilization at an international court. Chapter 6 evaluates the direct impact of ECtHR rulings on trade union rights through an analysis of ECtHR data on the execution of judgments, along with reports published by trade unions, pro-labor organizations, and labor scholars. This analysis will appeal to labor lawyers and activists interested in the compliance measures undertaken by Turkey and the UK in response to the ECtHR's trade union rights rulings. I show that, despite formal closure of most cases under supervision, the actual implementation of these rulings often falls short of reflecting the spirit of the ECtHR judgments. By foregrounding the limitations of a narrow compliance lens, the chapter sets the stage for those that follow, which trace how labor movements engage international human rights law as part of wider campaigns for political transformation.

Chapters 7 and 8 build on this argument by moving beyond a compliance-centered approach to examining the indirect effects of litigation on social movements. Chapter 7 illustrates these broader effects through an analysis of BSG's legal mobilization at the ECtHR, highlighting the on-stage and off-stage dynamics of strategic mobilization. On-stage, activists use human rights as a framing device in order to gain national attention and change the negative perceptions of trade unionists in the public opinion. Off-stage, when they are away from the spotlight, they rarely discuss or identify with human rights. Chapter 8 turns to the case study of Turkish public sector workers' struggle for recognition of fundamental trade union rights. The chapter brings into focus the role human rights law played in the 1990s by providing legal protections against state repression and legitimizing unionists' claims. However, the analysis of the post-2000 period draws out the limitations of legal victories in the absence of sustained grassroots mobilization. Without strong organizing on the ground, litigation alone proved insufficient to drive meaningful change, highlighting the need for legal strategies to be reinforced by collective action.

The concluding chapter returns to the question of whether litigation is a recourse or curse for labor activists in light of the findings in this book. It considers the future of strategic mobilization of human rights law in an era of backlash against international courts, the continued decline of trade unions, and the rise of authoritarianism. Litigation at an international court is no panacea for the structural problems confronting organized labor today. Yet the case studies in this book show that it can help rebuild labor's mobilization capacity, allowing activists to win concrete gains in the short term and to press for broader reforms through other venues and strategies in the future.

CHAPTER 2

THEORIZING LEGAL MOBILIZATION AT THE INTERNATIONAL LEVEL
Lawyers, Movements, and Courts

The end of the Cold War ushered in a new phase in the evolution of international human rights courts, marked by their growing prominence and increasingly assertive jurisprudence (Alter 2014; Alter, Hafner-Burton, and Helfer 2019). Yet despite the growing volume and significance of international rulings over the ensuing decades, their relationship with social movements has received little attention from social scientists. Most studies have focused on the role of legal professionals, state officials, or NGOs in giving effect to human rights rulings at the domestic level. This chapter changes the focus by analyzing international courts from the perspective of grassroots activists.

I develop a theoretical framework for understanding both why activists turn to international courts and how such courts influence mobilization on the ground. I argue that structural conditions – namely, the closing of political opportunities domestically and the growing availability of legal avenues internationally – set the stage for international litigation. Yet these conditions alone are insufficient to account for activists' pursuit of international litigation. Lawyers, as guides directing activists' attention to international remedies and as tacticians identifying the target venue among multiple institutions, are the central figures of Section 2.1.

In Section 2.2, I move from the question of why activists litigate internationally to what effects such litigation can generate. While many realists and critical scholars see international courts as largely symbolic, allowing states to appear responsive to human rights norms while avoiding substantive change, I focus instead on their indirect effects. Legal mobilization, I argue, can catalyze grassroots organizing well before any ruling is issued. It is activists – rather than judges or states – who are the central actors, repurposing international legal tools for movement building and political leverage. In doing so, I theorize the shadow effects of international courts on social movements.

2.1 WHY DO ACTIVISTS TURN TO INTERNATIONAL LITIGATION?

The increased salience of international courts notwithstanding, international litigation is often a last resort for activists (Alter and Vargas 2000; Conant et al. 2017; Hilson 2002). Activists have good reasons for favoring other strategies, such as lobbying or disruptive/contentious action, over litigation at an international court. First, international litigation can take a very long time as activists typically have to exhaust domestic remedies before a case can proceed, and final rulings can take years, if not decades. Second, international courts tend to wield less authority in the eyes of states than their domestic counterparts. Most governments "pick and choose the measures with which they will comply" according to political exigencies or resource constraints (Hillebrecht 2014: 64; Staton and Moore 2011). Third, international legal mechanisms are not in the usual "toolkit" of most grassroots actors (Swidler 1986). Knowledge about legal remedies offered by an international court requires legal expertise that is not always readily available to activist groups. Finally, some activist groups avoid litigation for ideological reasons, on the grounds that courts reinforce existing hierarchies and are unlikely to deliver transformative change (McCann and Lovell 2020). Radical groups, in particular, tend to favor contentious action over pursuing institutional channels (Hilson 2002; Vanhala 2018). Given these challenges, when can we expect activists to seek remedies at an international court?

A second, related question pertains to the target institution. The proliferation of legal avenues in the international arena – a phenomenon sometimes referred to as "international legal pluralism" (Burke-White 2004) – presents activists with a range of options. How do they choose where to submit their legal claims among the available international venues? Do they pursue multiple venues simultaneously or focus on one preferred institution? Do they select courts based on favorable precedent, institutional reach, or enforcement capacity?

2.1 WHY DO ACTIVISTS TURN TO INTERNATIONAL LITIGATION?

Where can they look for information to make the right decision? Most scholarship picks up the story after these decisions have been made, focusing on legal mobilization at a single international court (Anagnostou 2014; Cichowski 2007, 2016; Conant et al. 2017; Engstrom 2019; Guillaume 2015; Kahraman 2018; Kurban 2020; Pavone 2022; Sundstrom, Sperling, and Sayoglu 2020; Van der Vet 2018; but see Caserta and Madsen 2024). This approach fails to account for a critical first step: how activists navigate the institutional complexity and overlapping jurisdictions of the international legal field (Kahraman 2023).

Where scholars have examined regime complexity and forum shopping, they have tended to focus on trade disputes involving states and corporations, contexts in which litigants often possess bargaining power and where compliance rates are relatively high (Busch 2007; Gomez-Mera and Molinari 2014; Hafner-Burton, Victor, and Lupu 2012). By contrast, human rights activists rarely wield comparable leverage in the international arena and often struggle to ensure that rulings are enforced. As a result, we know little about whether and how activists choose among international legal institutions to advance social justice claims (but see Helfer 1999).

I argue that labor activists' turn to international litigation is motivated by two structural conditions: (1) the erosion of political opportunities at the domestic level and (2) the concurrent rise of judicial bodies at the international level. But these conditions alone do not account for the decision to litigate at the international level. Lawyers are the driving force behind this transition. They draw activists' attention to international legal remedies, identify the target institution, and lead strategic litigation efforts. Absent the guidance of a committed group of lawyers, most activists would not consider international litigation a viable option.

I also develop a theoretical framework for understanding how lawyers navigate the field of international legal pluralism to identify their target organization. Lawyers first probe multiple options to determine where to direct their litigation efforts. Conventional indicators, such as de jure rights protections or favorable case law, are not always the decisive factors guiding their choice of venue. Instead, I find that activists target courts with strong *judicial authority* and a high degree of *judicial responsiveness*, even when these institutions lack robust rights protections on paper. Through strategic litigation, they seek to transform such courts into effective venues for advancing labor rights.

Trade union rights offer a theoretically rich arena to investigate how activists engage in legal mobilization within a field of international legal pluralism, as multiple adjudicative bodies, both at the regional level in Europe and internationally, have jurisdiction over this issue. Moreover, since most trade unions in Europe have historically preferred rank-and-file mobilization over litigation, this shift in tactics provides an opportunity to examine why and how activists turn to international courts. The theoretical insights derived from the path that led organized labor to Strasbourg, however, have implications that extend beyond both trade unions and specific geographic regions.

2.1.1 Declining Political Opportunities at the Domestic Level

Scholars of human rights have traditionally focused on regime type to explain why activists mobilize around international human rights institutions. According to this perspective, transitioning democracies – rather than stable liberal democracies or autocracies – provide the most fertile ground for international mobilization (Risse and Sikkink 1999; Simmons 2009). But to understand when and why activists turn to international litigation, we need a different framework that captures the political openings and constraints activists face across different domestic contexts.

According to regime type theories, international treaties are unlikely to mobilize citizens in liberal democracies, where a system of protection for rights and liberties already exists. Conversely, autocracies have little regard for international human rights treaties, while posing greater risks of repression for activists.[1] Transitioning democracies, these scholars argue, offer both the opportunity and the motive: political leaders are more likely to seek international legitimacy (Risse and Sikkink 1999) and their economic or political dependence on stable democracies makes them more vulnerable to external pressure on human rights issues (Greenhill, Mosley, and Prakash 2009; Hafner-Burton 2009). Some scholars have even suggested that liberal democracies can assume the role of "global good Samaritans" (Brysk 2009) or exercise "stewardship" (Hafner-Burton 2013) in promoting human rights abroad, especially in transitional contexts.

While this perspective offers some general patterns for understanding when activists turn to international human rights institutions, it does

---

[1] But see Hendrix and Wong (2013) for an argument that autocracies can be more sensitive to international naming and shaming.

not capture the full range of variation. Different groups' access to domestic institutions can vary widely even within the same regime. Many liberal democracies have historically employed illiberal means – including violence and covert repression – to control marginalized populations, particularly along lines of race, class, gender, and sexual orientation (Davenport 2007; McCann and Kahraman 2021; Meierhenrich 2008), and these "illiberal practices" and "authoritarian enclaves" persist within ostensibly liberal systems (Chua 2019; Glasius 2018). Closer attention to labor rights, in particular, reveals that liberal democracies often fail to meet even basic human rights norms, much less serve as "stewards" for norm-violating states (McCann 2020). There is now a fairly well-developed literature documenting that states from all around the world deviate from and contribute to developing human rights frameworks (Rajagopal 2003; Somers and Roberts 2008; Waltz 2001).

The concept of political opportunities offers a more nuanced framework to analyze the conditions that drive activists to seek remedies at the international level. Political opportunities refer to the extent to which an activist group can access state institutions and the responsiveness of the institutions to activists' demands (McAdam 1999; Tarrow 2022). Social movement scholars have identified four key dimensions of political opportunities: the openness of the political regime, the presence of elite or civil society allies, fragmentations among political elites, and the likelihood of state repression (McAdam 1996; see also Smith, Chatfield, and Pagnucco 1997; Tarrow 2022). Researchers further distinguish between stable patterns of political opportunity *structures* and political opportunities (Kriesi et al. 1995). The former aligns more closely with regime type distinctions made by human rights scholars, referring to broader features like open political systems that provide regular channels for institutional participation. The latter allows for more nuanced analyses across different regimes by examining various state practices, such as repression, judicial tactics, and policies, that govern different groups in society.

Political opportunities can wax and wane over time. Major political events, changes in power configurations among the elites, or evolving judicial landscapes can all alter the receptiveness of a regime to certain rights claims. For example, the decline of the cotton economy in the American South created openings for civil rights activists to challenge segregationist policies (McAdam 1999). Yet activists' efforts to appeal to international institutions were stymied by Cold War dynamics, and they ultimately pursued domestic channels to push their agenda (Anderson 2003; Somers and Roberts 2008). Similarly, changes in party alignments, the political salience of an issue, or new judicial appointments can alter the opportunities available to social movements (Pedriana 2006).

The kinds of political opportunities available to a group shape the strategy they will pursue to advance their goals (Hilson 2002). Movements with legislative allies may pursue lobbying; those facing a receptive judiciary may favor domestic litigation. A key precondition for turning to international courts, however, is the closure of domestic political opportunities; in other words, state institutions, including the judiciary, must be unresponsive to activists' demands.[2] In the face of closed political opportunities at home, activists increasingly look outward, turning to international legal institutions as new arenas for contestation.

2.1.2 Rising Legal Opportunities at the International Level

Just as repressive domestic conditions can push activists to look for remedies elsewhere, rising legal opportunities can pull activists toward international litigation.[3] To theorize the features of international courts that encourage legal mobilization, scholars have examined legal opportunity structures (Alter and Vargas 2000; Conant 2006; Hilson 2002).[4] While the term generally refers to static features that shape actors' decision-making processes, such as judicial access, legal fees, and existing laws and regulations, I draw here on sociolegal scholarship to generate expectations on both the structural and contingent factors that can make an international court attractive for activists. I then show how lawyers assess these factors and identify the institution with the highest *judicial authority* and *responsiveness* as their target organization.

---

[2] Findings from litigants at the CJEU mostly confirm this assumption that applicants turn to international law when domestic remedies are unavailable (Alter and Vargas 2000; Hilson 2002; Passalacqua 2021), but Hofmann and Naurin (2021) argue that groups that have access to policymakers can still use litigation in conjunction.

[3] For an argument on how push factors, rooted in neoliberal retrenchment and the erosion of traditional channels of interest representation, and pull dynamics, created by the expansion of rights frameworks and new institutional venues can motivate citizens to pursue their claims in judicial and administrative arenas at the domestic level, see Gallagher, Kruks-Wisner, and Taylor (2024).

[4] See Andersen (2006), Pedriana (2006), and Tam (2012) for theorization of legal opportunities at the domestic level.

2.1 WHY DO ACTIVISTS TURN TO INTERNATIONAL LITIGATION?

First, rules regarding standing constrain who has *access to international judicial institutions*. Some organizations only accept petitions from designated civil society organizations or member states, while others permit individual petitions. Jurisdiction also varies: Some international institutions have mandatory jurisdiction over all member states, while others allow individual or collective petitions only from states that have ratified specific provisions. Although international courts typically do not impose legal fees, the requirement to exhaust domestic remedies can generate substantial costs that deter litigation for activists with limited resources.

Second, the presence of favorable case law can make a court more attractive for activists. *De jure rights protection* refers to the body of formal legal rights guaranteed in treaties and the precedents established by courts that can be drawn upon by judges in their decision-making process. They therefore shape the kinds of legal remedies available for activists who bring their grievances before courts (Cebulak, Morvillo, and Salomon 2024; Conant 2006; Hilson 2002). As Helfer (1999) notes, such protections can influence not only the choice of tribunal but also whether litigants pursue simultaneous or successive petitions, depending on where favorable precedent is most likely to be found. Institutions differ in the strength of their de jure protections depending on treaty ratifications and reservations made by member states. All else being equal, institutions that prohibit reservations and possess an established body of favorable case law should be more appealing to activists.

Third, *judicial responsiveness* to new claims can encourage legal mobilization. As recognized by many scholars, human rights are malleable and contested; judicial interpretations of human rights can evolve alongside social norms (Ayoub 2016; Finnemore and Sikkink 1998; Merry 2006; Wiener 2007). The ECtHR, for example, treats the Convention as a "living instrument" and incorporates "European consensus" when revisiting previous rulings or setting new precedents (Dzehtsiarou 2015). Studies show that judges respond both to external political pressures – such as deferrals or threats of override from executives or legislatures – and to their own normative commitments or strategic considerations (Carrubba, Gabel, and Hankla 2008; Graber 1993; Hilbink 2009; Hirschl 2004; Larsson et al. 2017; Moravcsik 2000; Pevehouse 2005; Stiansen and Voeten 2020; Weiler 1994). Whether driven by internal beliefs or external signals, international courts experience periods of activism and restraint. During periods of judicial activism, courts are more likely to be responsive to new rights claims, which encourage legal mobilization.

Fourth, the *judicial authority* of a court can shape activists' strategies. While favorable rulings may go unenforced, courts with strong judicial authority are more likely to be taken seriously by member states (Alter, Helfer, and Madsen 2016; Madsen, Cebulak, and Wiebusch 2018). Judicial authority is strengthened when states take "meaningful steps" to comply with rulings, even if full compliance with international human rights courts remains rare, since these institutions do not have the same means as their domestic counterparts to guarantee enforcement (Alter, Helfer, and Madsen 2016; Hawkins and Jacoby 2010; Staton and Moore 2011). Oversight mechanisms and peer pressure among member states can further expand the judicial authority of an institution (Alter, Helfer, and Madsen 2016; Çalı and Koch 2014). However, compliance often varies across member states, depending on political will, state capacity, and the political salience of specific issues (Alter, Helfer, and Madsen 2016; Anagnostou 2013; Helfer and Voeten 2014; Hillebrecht 2014). States are more likely to resist compliance when rulings concern contentious issues, though their overall willingness also varies with electoral realignments. Lawyers' assessments of a court's judicial authority are thus informed by both temporal shifts and the specific political context of the activist group.

Relatedly, lawyers may also consider what Alter, Helfer, and Madsen (2016) term *extensive authority* – the extent to which an international court's rulings are recognized by and influence broader audiences, including other international or domestic court judges, government officials, activists, and scholars. Institutions with extensive authority can shape international norms even when compliance with individual rulings is low. Quasi-judicial institutions such as the ILO or other UN agencies may wield greater extensive authority than some regional courts, especially since they are widely recognized as norm-setters (Anner and Caraway 2010; Weisband 2006). References to such decisions by domestic courts, other international institutions, and human rights groups can bolster an institution's extensive authority. Therefore, recognition of new rights claims by quasi-judicial institutions with high extensive authority can be particularly appealing for activists seeking to reframe public narratives or build momentum for later legal change, rather than to secure immediate enforcement.

Finally, it is important to distinguish between judicial authority, measured based on actual practices of courts, and judicial legitimacy, measured based on actors' normative perceptions of an institution's rightful authority (Alter, Helfer, and Madsen 2016; Peters and Schaffer 2013). Although normative considerations about legitimacy can guide activists' behavior when organizing public campaigns (see discussion in Section 2.2), lawyers leading strategic litigation efforts are typically motivated more by pragmatic assessments of judicial authority than by considerations of legitimacy.

2.1.3 Agents of International Litigation: Lawyers

When domestic institutions are hostile to activists' claims and new opportunities are arising at the international level, seeking remedies at an international court might seem like a natural result. From today's perspective, when the ECtHR's case law has reached over a million, taking a case to an international court is not a far-fetched idea for most European citizens. But in the early 1990s, when international courts were only beginning to gain reputations as actors that can potentially influence political outcomes, international litigation was hardly an obvious route for activists. Workers themselves are unlikely to pave the way to the international legal arena. Without legal guidance, activists are often ill-informed about these institutions and are unlikely to consider litigation at an international court as a viable option to address their grievances.[5]

The first key function lawyers perform in facilitating legal mobilization is drawing activists' attention to the remedies available at the international level. Lawyers act as "intermediaries" or "interpretive mediators" between the local and the global by communicating information about international human rights law to activists (Merry 2006; Pavone 2022). Their legal expertise on international law, coupled with their close ties with activists, situate lawyers in a distinct position to bridge the gap between the local and the international. Lawyers convey this information to activists through reports, workshops, and ongoing collaboration with activist organizations.

Deciding which court to select as a target among the multitude of international institutions is far more challenging for activists. The second key function lawyers perform in initiating legal mobilization is

---

[5] Recent studies show that there is widespread misinformation, some of which is deliberate in order to fuel backlash against international courts in the media and speeches given by politicians (Jay 2022; Voeten 2013).

identifying the target institution toward which mobilization efforts should be directed.

2.1.4 Identifying the Target Institution

Legal and political opportunities are not fixed structures that have uniform effects on actors' decision-making processes (Andersen 2006; McCann 1994; Pavone 2022; Vanhala 2018). The perception of opportunities can shape actors' behavior in different ways. Lawyers, in particular, can assume the role of "strategy entrepreneurs" by "introducing new tactics into an organization's repertoire" (Vanhala 2018: 398), devising litigation strategies aligned with the movement's goals (Epp 1998; Hilbink 2006; McCann 1994), and shaping activists' legal consciousness (Chua 2020; McCann 1994). However, most of the studies on international legal mobilization focus on the role of lawyers and activists in devising a litigation strategy at a single international court (Anagnostou 2014; Cichowski 2007, 2016; Haddad 2018; Hodson 2014; Kurban 2020; Pavone 2022; Sundstrom 2014; Van der Vet 2018; but see Caserta and Madsen 2024). We know little about how activists navigate a plurality of legal institutions at the international level.

In practice, the development of an international litigation strategy is far from linear. I argue that a group of committed lawyers guide activists to craft strategies suited for the goals activists wish to pursue. In strategic litigation, where lawyers pursue long-term goals, the choice of target institution is motivated primarily by influencing *structural reforms* and international *norm-setting*.[6] Seeking remedy for individual applicants is not a priority in strategic litigation, but if activists fail to instigate reforms to prevent further violations, repeat litigation may become necessary to secure incremental victories.

The complexity of the international legal system requires lawyers to engage in an initial probing phase, filing applications across multiple institutions. I suggest that the institution ultimately targeted for sustained litigation is likely to be the one demonstrating the highest *judicial authority* and *judicial responsiveness*. This process of probing and selecting an institution draws not only on lawyers' formal legal expertise but also on their accumulated experience with how different

---

[6] Lawyers' aim to keep their eyes on long-term goals is consistent with other studies on litigation at a single international court (Anagnostou 2014; Pavone 2022; Sundstrom 2014; Van der Vet 2012).

institutions operate in practice. The type of judicial authority an institution wields is critical. Lawyers prefer institutions with high compliance rates to leverage structural reforms at the domestic level. However, they also take cases to international institutions with low rates of compliance if these institutions have extensive judicial authority – the ability to shape international norms and influence broader audiences. This approach signals an understanding that recognizing new rights claims can produce long-term gains, as these norms may later be incorporated by other international courts with high compliance rates or by domestic legal systems.

A major challenge in selecting a target institution is assessing judicial responsiveness in the absence of relevant precedents. Lawyers initially submit claims to multiple venues in order to probe for signals of receptiveness. Once an institution responds favorably, they are likely to concentrate their litigation efforts on this institution. In contrast to the emphasis that legal opportunity structure scholars place on de jure rights protections, I argue that formal legal rights are largely meaningless unless activated by responsive judges and probing lawyers. This iterative process creates a signaling game between courts and lawyers: The more receptive judges are to lawyers' claims, the more cases lawyers bring before them. Over time, strategic litigation efforts can transform courts initially weak on certain rights protections into more powerful defenders in those areas.

This process, however, amounts to more than simple forum shopping. Legal remedies are not static structures, as much of the regime complexity and legal opportunity structure literatures tend to assume (Alter and Vargas 2000; Busch 2007; Gomez-Mera and Molinari 2014; Hilson 2002). As the empirical analyses in Chapters 4 and 5 will show, lawyers' ability to transform the ECtHR – from a civil and political rights court into one increasingly protective of labor rights – demonstrates that legal and political opportunity structures are malleable and can be reshaped through bottom-up mobilization. Building on sociolegal research (Andersen 2006; González-Ocantos 2016; Taylor 2023; Vanhala 2010), I show that international courts' jurisprudence on a new issue area is constructed through an iterative process between activists' strategic litigation efforts and judicial responsiveness.

At the same time, this mutually constitutive relationship between bottom-up legal mobilization and judicial responsiveness is not an endless virtuous cycle. External factors, such as threats from member states, executive signals, or popular backlash against international courts, can disrupt judicial activism and trigger periods of judicial restraint. Domestic responses can also inform litigation strategies. If a state persistently commits repeat violations, lawyers may reorient their strategy away from norm-building litigation to repeat violation cases aimed at securing remedies for individual applicants. Thus, both international and domestic political dynamics critically mediate the trajectory of international legal mobilization.

***

Overall, the closure of domestic political opportunities pushes activists to seek remedies elsewhere, while the emergence of new international openings pulls them toward transnational litigation. Yet this shift does not occur automatically. Lawyers play a central role in mediating between activists and legal institutions by identifying promising venues and adapting litigation strategies to movement goals and changing political conditions. Through their probing and iterative litigation efforts, lawyers not only navigate but also reshape the international legal field, expanding the possibilities for future mobilization.

2.2 IMPACT OF INTERNATIONAL COURTS: MOBILIZING IN THE SHADOW OF HUMAN RIGHTS LAW

Section 2.1 addressed the question of why and how activists engage in legal mobilization at the international level. A more critical question, however, is whether the favorable rulings activists obtain translate into meaningful change on the ground. In this section, I review the existing scholarship on the impact of international court rulings and offer a theoretical model that shifts the focus from formal compliance to the indirect effects of litigation. More specifically, I argue that international legal action can catalyze social movements and help activists advance their goals.

2.2.1 Compliance with International Court Rulings

Scholars are divided on whether international human rights law delivers "empty promises" (Hafner-Burton and Tsutsui 2005) or produces tangible effects on state behavior. The realists point out that international human rights regimes neither provide adequate incentives for compliance nor possess a strong coercive mechanism to

2.2 IMPACT OF INTERNATIONAL COURTS

prevent further abuses (Posner 2014; Vreeland 2008).[7] Seen from this perspective, litigation at an international court is a poor use of activists' limited resources. Instead, mechanisms such as preferential trade agreements or conditional economic aid are more likely to supply the hard power needed to persuade states to improve their human rights record, including, in some cases, implementation of better labor standards (Hafner-Burton 2009; Greenhill, Mosley, and Prakash 2009; Postnikov and Bastiaens 2014).

Constructivists are more optimistic about the impact of human rights regimes, emphasizing the power of norms, transnational civil society actors, and socialization processes in shaping state behavior (Chayes and Chayes 1998; Checkel 2005; Finnemore and Sikkink 1998; Meyer et al. 1997; Koh 2005; Risse, Ropp, and Sikkink 1999; Wotipka and Tsutsui 2008). On this account, states are not necessarily bad-faith actors seeking to avoid compliance (Goodman and Jinks 2008). Rather, they can be socialized into compliance through reputational incentives, normative pressures, and institutional learning. International courts, in particular, function not only as enforcement mechanisms but also as sites of socialization, encouraging states to participate in a cooperative international order and deepen their engagement with human rights norms (Helfer 2008).

A third line of scholarship points out that the preoccupation with international forces in human rights scholarship is misguided and that we should instead focus on domestic politics in order to understand the impact of international human rights regimes. Simmons (2009) finds that ratified international human rights treaties have a positive effect on state behavior and that domestic politics principally determines variation in countries' compliance records. The presence of domestic compliance partners, such as active civil society organizations, receptive judges, or reform-minded politicians, can significantly improve the likelihood of implementation (Alter 2014; Dai 2007; Haglund 2020; Hillebrecht 2014; Simmons 2009).[8] These studies draw attention to

---

[7] For a similar argument on the ineffectiveness of international human rights treaties, see Hafner-Burton and Tsutsui (2005, 2007); Hathaway (2002); Keith (2002); and Neumeyer (2005).

[8] Similarly, studies examining the causes behind the rise of domestic prosecutions of human rights crimes, particularly in Latin America, emphasize the importance of judges, victims, human rights NGOs, and lawyers operating at the domestic level (Dancy and Michel 2015; González Ocantos 2016; Sikkink 2011).

the fact that states are not monolithic entities with a single, unified approach to human rights law. Different branches or actors within the state may pursue pro-compliance agendas and work to implement rulings, while others resist or publicly denounce them.

Sweeping realist claims that human rights regimes amount to "cheap talk" carry less weight within the context of the ECtHR, since it is consistently singled out for its high compliance rates and consistent policy impact across Europe (Alter, Helfer, and Madsen 2016; Helfer and Voeten 2014; Hillebrecht 2014; Stiansen and Voeten 2020; Stone Sweet and Keller 2008). Unlike many other human rights regimes, the ECtHR enjoys a generous budget provided by its member states and the authority to issue legally binding judgments, as well as broad accessibility for individuals and civil society organizations. Nonetheless, these institutional advantages do not eliminate compliance challenges. Studies that examine the actual implementation of ECtHR rulings – beyond the Court's own supervision data – show that states often find ways to evade undertaking reforms that reflect the essence of norms stipulated in ECtHR rulings (Anagnostou 2013; Búzás 2021; Kurban 2020; Von Staden 2018). Even liberal democracies undertake minimal measures that fulfill the technical criteria of the supervisory bodies of the ECtHR, while avoiding structural reforms that would prevent future violation cases.

2.2.2 Impact Beyond Compliance: A Grassroots Theory of International Legal Mobilization

Skeptics are largely correct that international human rights regimes, even the most generously supported ones like the ECtHR, lack effective mechanisms to ensure full compliance. Measures undertaken by states in response to court rulings often fall short of fulfilling the expectations of victims and human rights advocates. Yet solely focusing on state compliance provides an incomplete picture of the impact of international human rights courts. To understand the broader impact of international courts, we need to look at changes that start to occur before a violation judgment is issued. The very availability of international human rights courts can alter state–society relations. I argue that improvements in states' human rights records can be achieved through a mechanism that is largely understudied: grassroots mobilization. Litigation at an international court can catalyze social movements at the domestic level, enabling activists to advance their goals even before a final judgment is handed down.

This argument draws from and extends the efforts to understand how compliance with human rights law can be activated through domestic mechanisms. I concur with the contention that the realists have overly focused on the international level and neglected the domestic channels through which international human rights law can gain traction (Simmons 2009). However, most research on domestic human rights politics emphasizes the role of elite actors – politicians, judges, lawyers, and institutionalized civil society organizations – in pressuring the state toward compliance (Alter 2014; Dai 2007; Haglund 2020; Hillebrecht 2014; Simmons 2009). I contribute to this literature by demonstrating how international human rights courts can mobilize social movement actors to push for reform.

In order to analyze these "radiating effects" of human rights courts, I build on sociolegal studies which urge us to look beyond compliance to assess judicial impact (Galanter 1983; see also McCann 1994; Moustafa 2018). These studies show that the power of courts does not merely reside in their ability to induce compliance, but in their ability to spark political action and confer legitimacy on social justice claims (Epp 2009; Galanter 1983; Rodríguez-Garavito and Rodríguez-Franco 2015; Scheingold 1974; Taylor 2023). In particular, legal mobilization scholars have demonstrated how litigation in domestic courts can catalyze and strengthen social movements (Arrington 2019; Hunt 1990; McCann 1994; NeJaime 2010). Yet research exploring how these broader dynamics between litigation and social change play out at the international level has been scarce.

The Power of Social Movements
By social movements, I refer to groups that engage in sustained, organized collective action aimed at instigating social and political change. Distinct from NGOs or other interest groups, social movements use non-institutional channels and engage in contentious action – such as demonstrations, protests, boycotts, and strikes – rather than routine interactions with state institutions (Snow, Soule, and Kriesi 2008; Tarrow 2022).[9] They also mobilize broad-based constituencies, rather than depending on experts and technocrats. But why should we care whether international litigation can spark social movements?

---

[9] This does not mean that social movements only use non-institutional mechanisms; instead, they often employ a wide range of actions, including petitioning and lobbying, in their "repertoire" (Armstrong and Bernstein 2008; Tarrow 2022: 88).

One reason is that a large body of research links an active civil society with greater respect for human rights in a country. Even realists acknowledge that NGO presence is a key mechanism: "[T]he positive institutional effects of the international human rights regime on local practices ... operate not through the treaty system, but through nongovernmental actors" (Hafner-Burton and Tsutsui 2005: 1380; see also Neumayer 2005). Case studies from around the world similarly show that transnational naming and shaming campaigns have played a central role in holding the authoritarian regimes of Latin America responsible for forced disappearances and torture (Duffy 2018; Engstrom and Low 2019; Keck and Sikkink 1998), changing employment practices in sweatshops in Mexico, India, and Guatemala (Rodríguez-Garavito 2005; Seidman 2008), and ending apartheid in South Africa (Thörn 2006).

While these studies provide valuable insights, the actors driving the change are typically internationally connected and well-funded NGOs, rather than grassroots social movement activists (Wong 2012: 2; but see Smith, Chatfield, and Pagnucco 1997). In Keck and Sikkink's (1998) famous boomerang model, global campaigns led by NGOs like Amnesty International are vital in pressuring Western states to act against authoritarian regimes (see also Risse and Sikkink 1999). Studies of international courts similarly emphasize the role of legal advocacy groups, many of which are based in or funded by actors in the Global North (Cichowski 2006, 2016; Duffy 2018; Engstrom 2019; Haddad 2018; Holzhacker 2013; Jacquot and Vitale 2014, Sundstrom 2014; Van der Vet 2012). One notable exception that aims to take a bottom-up approach is Simmons's book, *Mobilizing for Human Rights* (2009), where she theorizes the mechanisms through which ratified human rights treaties can catalyze grassroots mobilization. Yet, despite the theoretical insights on the conditions under which international law can motivate domestic actors to engage in mobilization, the case studies primarily draw on secondary literature on NGO campaigns that utilize institutional mechanisms, rather than on movements that engage in contentious action.

A focus on social movements allows for an examination of the agency of grassroots actors in determining the goals they want to pursue and the means they take up to achieve them. Rather than seeking support from transnational actors, social movements take direct action, using non-institutional and disruptive tactics such as demonstrations and protests, not typically used by NGOs, alongside other forms of political pressure. The preponderance of evidence from social movements literature shows that the involvement of institutionalized actors can stifle activists' use of novel, contentious, and disruptive tactics, which are linked to social movement success (Koopmans 1993; Kriesi et al. 1995; Staggenborg 1988; Wang and Soule 2016). Studying social movements enables us to explore the conditions under which victims themselves become the protagonists of their struggles.

Relatedly, unlike NGOs, social movements are not bound by the limited set of issues that resonate with donors or transnational audiences. Campaigns that attract international attention often focus on dramatic crises, which may marginalize locally relevant but less visible concerns, or fail to reflect the perspectives and sensitivities of local activists (Bob 2002; Chouliaraki 2013; Kent, Skoutaris, and Trinidad 2019; Waites 2019). Trade union rights issues, for example, rarely gain much traction in international campaigns unless extreme working conditions are involved (Rodríguez-Garavito 2005; Seidman 2008). Social movements can center issues that matter to local communities, regardless of their appeal to the international community.

Finally, the emergence or strengthening of labor movements can produce long-lasting results. Increased mobilization capacity can make labor movements formidable challengers against the power of states and businesses. With the ability to disrupt production through rank-and-file mobilization, a unified voice of labor in collective struggles has the potential to alter employment relations not only within individual workplaces but across the national economy. Beyond their importance in advancing the collective interests of workers, labor movements have historically played pivotal roles in promoting democratic change, including the formation of social democratic parties (Przeworski and Sprague 1986) and the downfall of authoritarian regimes (Collier and Collier 2002; Rueschemeyer, Stephens, and Stephens 1992).[10] Even in more stable regimes, strong labor movements often build durable alliances with labor-friendly political parties to influence policy outcomes. Therefore, the revitalization of labor movements can shift the balance of power in lasting ways.

That said, critical scholars are hardly sanguine about the catalytic potential of human rights law on social movements. Resort to human rights is viewed as a precursor to being absorbed in conventional

---

[10] More recent research shows that sustained mass mobilization is a predictor of democratic regime durability (Kadivar 2018).

politics and giving up revolutionary ideas (Corntassel 2007; Moyn 2018). As Savage (2009: 9) observes, relying on human rights "foster[s] a sense of individualism in workers rather than the sense of collective worker power required to transform society."[11] Skepticism expressed by these scholars about using human rights frameworks to address entrenched hierarchies of power is valid, yet we lack an empirical study that investigates whether and how litigation at an international court shapes dynamics of mobilization on the ground.

Legal Mobilization Theory: From Domestic to International Level
Much of the early theoretical insights on legal mobilization theory emerged from studies on the American legal profession, particularly the civil rights movement's efforts to utilize the US Supreme Court for reform. Against the critics who argued that court rulings amounted to little more than a "hollow hope" (Rosenberg 2008; see also Gearty 2010; Tushnet 2000), sociolegal scholars pointed to the indirect effects of litigation: legitimizing the claims of civil rights activists, emboldening broader participation in the movement, building political coalitions, and placing racial segregation at the forefront of the liberal political agenda (Eskridge 1991; Polletta 2000; Scheingold 1974; Schuck 1993). McCann's analysis of the pay equity movement combined social movements theory with a constructivist understanding of law to demonstrate the mechanisms through which litigation efforts can catalyze grassroots mobilization (McCann 1994). He contends that, "although judicial victories often do not translate automatically into desired social change, they can help to redefine the terms of both immediate and long-term struggles among social groups" (McCann 1994: 285). Legal mobilization, then, involves not just efforts to change legislation but broader projects of social transformation, including reframing public discourse, altering perceptions, and building solidarity networks. Comparative studies extending this work show that domestic litigation can foster coalitions among activist groups (Arrington 2016), equip movements with discursive tools (Chua 2020), and create new spaces for deliberative democracy with participation from civil society (Rodríguez-Garavito and Rodríguez-Franco 2015).[12]

---

[11] See also Glendon (1991) for the argument that rights discourse encourages individuals to prioritize self-interest over the common good.

[12] For a recent overview of the law and social movements literature, see Taylor and Tarrow (2024).

Despite these insights, research exploring how the dynamics between law and social change play out at the international level has been scarce.[13] Can international human rights litigation also spark grassroots mobilization? Can movement actors leverage international legal proceedings to push states beyond symbolic or evasive compliance? How can grassroots activists translate the promises of a distant international court into concrete outcomes at home?

I argue that litigation at an international court can indeed *catalyze* and *expand* social mobilization. First, the prospect of a favorable judgment and the enforcement powers of an international court can provide activists safeguards and credibility, encouraging them to initiate mobilization. Unlike legal mobilization at the domestic level, where movements often emerge in response to precedent-setting rulings, activists at the international level tend to mobilize around the threat of litigation or pending cases already underway. In many instances, they achieve key goals through domestic mobilization efforts before a final ruling is even issued.

Second, pending cases can help sustain and expand mobilization efforts by introducing new discursive frames, encouraging tactical innovation, building alliances with other activist groups, and opening institutional channels within the domestic system for activists to advance their agenda. In this way, international litigation can facilitate political change – including changes in the practices of the government, legislature, and the judiciary – through changing the landscape of mobilization and reshaping activists' expectations, narratives, and strategies.

Another key distinction from domestic legal mobilization is that international litigation does not typically shape the cultural foundations of social movements. Instead, I find that activists engage in *strategic mobilization of human rights*. While human rights language may inform the public face of the social movement, it does not necessarily shape activists' ideological commitments, self-understanding, or internal solidarity. The appeal to human rights is often instrumental: a means of gaining traction, legitimacy, and institutional access, rather than a foundational source of activist identity.

---

[13] But see Simmons (2009) for theoretical insights on these dynamics at the international level.

Movement Building Before the Ruling
In classic legal mobilization theory, landmark court rulings often serve as impetus for grassroots mobilization. For example, the pay equity movement in the US gained national traction after a key Supreme Court decision in the 1980s, following years of groundwork by activist lawyers through experimental litigation in the 1970s (McCann 1994). Schmidt (2018) shows that pivotal rulings like *Brown v. Board of Education* indirectly fueled the sit-in protests during the civil rights era by inspiring hope among activists and intensifying frustration with the gap between constitutional principle and the persistence of segregation in everyday life (see also Coleman, Nee, and Rubinowitz 2007). In Colombia, the Constitutional Court's recognition of internally displaced persons' rights produced indirect effects, such as issue resonance and the reframing of public discourse surrounding their plight (Rodríguez Garavito and Rodríguez-Franco 2015). While legal mobilization scholars acknowledge that court victories alone do not bring about political change, there is near consensus that recognition of a new rights claim in a landmark ruling can become an inflection point by reshaping activists' perception of legal and political opportunities.[14] Precedents not only raise public awareness but also help foster rights consciousness among potential recruits and unlock political and financial resources.

The threat of litigation, especially when backed by an existing favorable precedent, can also shape social and political behavior. Drawing on five case studies, Duffy (2018) urges us to move beyond the celebratory focus on "the champagne moment" of a favorable ruling and instead consider how strategic litigation operates before and after the judgment. She shows that legal processes can produce important forms of impact – mobilizing civil society organizations, attracting allies, and influencing public discourse – even in the absence of legal victory. As McCann notes, the possibility of legal intervention, "either implicitly or explicitly threatened, ... tends to shape social interaction and bargaining relations far more than actual direct official interventions" (McCann 2006: 22; see also Galanter 1983; Pavone and Stiansen 2022). Rights struggles may advance more effectively and at lower cost "when conducted in the shadow of favorable legal norms and threats of judicial intervention" (McCann

---

[14] See NeJaime (2010) on how a negative ruling could also spur mobilization.

2006: 30). Legal precedents thus provide a framework of "legalized accountability" through which activists can hold states to established standards (Epp 2009).

In strategic mobilization of human rights, activists begin organizing in the shadow of an international court before they receive a favorable ruling. These movements typically do not emerge from scratch but are reactivations of groups with a shared history of collective action that had gone dormant due to government repression or previous failures. For such groups, the utility of an international court is not in its ability to foster a rights-based consciousness among group members, but its promise of curbing state power. This potential, the possibility of legal protection or vindication, can help activists re-emerge and revive their movement.

But the challenge of legal mobilization at the international level is that the legal proceedings take too long. Courts like the ECtHR often take a decade or more to deliver a final ruling, and most require that domestic legal avenues be exhausted first, adding years to the process. For activists confronting urgent and ongoing violations, these timelines provide little recourse. By the time a ruling is issued, momentum may have waned, public attention may have shifted, and the structural conditions driving the violations may become even more entrenched. Therefore, for international legal mobilization to be successful, activists must mobilize domestically while litigation is still pending, relying on the prospect of international legal support as a source of leverage.

I argue that the mere availability of an international court can facilitate mobilization in two ways. First, it can raise activists' *perceived likelihood of achieving their substantive goals*. People are more likely to engage in collective action when they believe that change is possible. In hostile domestic environments, where national courts or legislatures are unresponsive, the possibility of a favorable ruling at the international level may be the only viable legal path forward. This prospect can boost morale, strengthen activists' belief in the validity of their claims, and inspire renewed organizing. Scholars have suggested that treaty ratification can change activists' perception of political opportunity by increasing the perceived "likelihood of success" (Simmons 2009; see also Dai 2007; Goodman and Jinks 2008; Tarrow 2001: 16; Tsutsui, Whitlinger, and Lim 2012). Yet despite human rights researchers' optimistic approach, empirical examples of treaties galvanizing mass movements are scarce, partly because treaty-monitoring bodies often lack binding authority and rely heavily on state self-reporting.[15] Conversely, international human rights courts like the ECtHR issue binding judgments and accept individual petitions, offering a more credible form of external enforcement. As Alter observes, "the external, independent, and legal nature of international courts is their chief attraction [and] their main source of power" (Alter 2014: 54). The authority of such courts can shape domestic actors' behavior: Anticipating litigation, executives or domestic court judges may interpret ratified treaties more expansively to avoid violations, to recognize new rights claims, broadening the legal space available for activists.

Second, international courts can *provide safeguards against government repression*, encouraging activists to launch their movement. In repressive political environments where retaliation by the government against peaceful protestors is a common occurrence, the lack of legal redress for arbitrary arrests or police violence can create a chilling effect (Jeffries 2002; McAdam 1996; Muller and Weede 1990; Tilly 1995).[16] Existing research presents mixed findings on the impact of ratified international treaties on government repression. Some studies find that treaty commitments lead to little or no change, and may even exacerbate repressive practices (Hafner-Burton and Tsutsui 2007; Hathaway 2002; Hill 2010; Vreeland 2008). Others argue that treaties reduce repression by increasing the likelihood of mobilization and altering states' risk calculations (Ritter and Conrad 2016; Simmons 2009). Once again, international courts offer stronger accountability mechanisms against repression than treaty-monitoring bodies.[17] Their potential to publicly condemn state violence or issue binding rulings can embolden activists to overcome their fears and take greater risks. For instance, some may participate in banned demonstrations or form "illegal" associations, trusting that international courts offer recourse. These procedural resources can lower the perceived costs of activism and encourage activists to join the movement.

---

[15] But see Tsutsui (2018) for an example of how international treaties can spark mobilization by constituting new "movement actorhood."

[16] But in some contexts, indiscriminate state violence can incite moral outrage and trigger a backlash (Blaydes 2020; O'Brien and Deng 2015; Wood 2003).

[17] The ICC also reduces the risk of violent repression in member states (Dancy 2017; Hillebrecht 2016; Jo and Simmons 2016). But the ICC's jurisdiction is mass atrocities, and individuals do not have access to it; therefore, it is less likely to affect activists' decision to engage in mobilization.

2.2 IMPACT OF INTERNATIONAL COURTS

Strategic Mobilization of Human Rights in Contentious Politics
For social movement activists, the power of an international court to induce compliance matters only insofar as it provides opportunities and resources for activists. In particular, litigation at an international court allows activists to expand their mobilization across multiple fronts before any ruling is issued. These expansions can take four forms: (1) *developing new discursive frames*; (2) *facilitating tactical innovation*; (3) *opening institutional opportunities at the domestic level*; and (4) *building new alliances*. By simultaneously engaging in various forms of activism, movements can increase political pressure and build momentum for reform while litigation is still pending.

First, international courts can provide *new discursive frames* that resonate with wider audiences. Social movement scholars have long emphasized the importance of framing – strategically aligning the movement's messages with broadly accepted values to increase persuasive power (Benford and Snow 2000; Goodman and Jinks 2013). Discursive tools used by activists are often shaped by structural or cultural factors that are beyond the control of the framers (Polletta 1999: 63; Steinberg 1999). For example, the US labor movement's focus on individual rights, as opposed to the French movement's emphasis on collective associations, emerged from the distinct cultural and political contexts in which they developed (Tarrow 1996: 50). Similarly, court-generated norms can influence narrative tools available to activists. Such rulings have helped activists counter stigma on marriage equality in the US (NeJaime 2010) and change media narratives on internally displaced people in Colombia (Rodríguez-Garavito and Rodríguez-Franco 2015).[18] While in some cases frames can grow organically out of these contingent factors, activists can also take a calculated approach to framing, selecting language that maximizes the appeal among their target audiences. For example, both proponents and opponents of reproductive rights use rights-affirming language – "pro-choice" and "pro-life" – in order to frame their positions in positive terms (Djupe et al. 2014; Williams 2019).

Strategic mobilization of human rights involves activists deliberately invoking human rights law and language to broaden support internally and externally. Internally, activists may reference international human rights to help alleviate fears among potential recruits and inspire

---

[18] See also Andersen (2006) and McCann (1994).

confidence in the movement's goals. Externally, they can use human rights discourse to craft resonant public narratives that appeal to broader audiences and elevate the legitimacy of their claims. Since the ascendance of human rights in the 1970s, human rights have functioned as a "master frame," a broadly resonant, flexible idiom that different movements can adapt to their causes (Dancy and Fariss 2018; Johnson 2006; Snow and Benford 1992; Tsutsui and Smith 2018).[19] The indeterminacy of human rights language – what McCann (2014) calls its "unbearable lightness" – makes it a particularly useful tool for groups seeking to challenge stigmatizing narratives and associate themselves with internationally respected norms (Ayoub 2016; Finnemore and Sikkink 1998; Merry 2006; Wiener 2007). This strategy is especially important for movements aiming to dismantle negative images commonly associated with their group (e.g., unions labeled as corrupt or activists branded as terrorists).

Second, international litigation can *facilitate tactical innovation*. Inventive and disruptive actions can attract media attention and disrupt routine state responses (Almeida and Stearns 1998; McAdam 1983). Yet tactical innovation is difficult to sustain – it is more common in the early stages of mobilization and in coalitions comprised of diverse constituencies (McAdam 1983; McCammon 2012; Wang and Soule 2016). International legal processes can similarly expand the tactical repertoire of activists by organizing symbolic arrests or mock trials. For groups operating in repressive environments, the legal backing of an international court can encourage protests, defiance of restrictive laws, or the reopening of closed venues. By leveraging international legal norms, activists may pursue actions that are unlawful domestically but consistent with international human rights standards.

Third, the threat of litigation and the presence of pending cases at an international court *open new institutional pathways for domestic advocacy*. A state's membership in an international court usually implies that there are some "compliance partners" (or allies within the state institutions), such as officials or sympathetic judges that are interested in ensuring the government's adherence to international human rights laws and rulings (Alter 2014; Hillebrecht 2014). Even ratified international treaties without a third-party enforcer could create unexpected

---

[19] Tracking references to human rights language throughout the twentieth century, Moyn (2018) claims that "human rights became our highest moral language" after the end of the Cold War.

allies within the state or present an opportunity for activists to exploit divisions among the elites (Goodman and Jinks 2008; Simmons 2009; Tsutsui, Whitlinger, and Lim 2012). While some supporters may be solely interested in the substantive goals embedded in a particular treaty, others may be motivated by a normative principle of compliance with international human rights obligations (Alter 2014). Activists can lobby these allies to frame parliamentary debates in the preferred terms used by the activists or, when conditions permit, to propose policy reforms to advance activists' agenda. Pending cases can also force state officials to take pre-emptive action in order to avoid receiving a violation judgment that will force their hand (Pavone and Stiansen 2022). Moreover, judicial decisions against one country can also reverberate in others, where receptive domestic institutions may adopt similar reforms (Helfer and Voeten 2014). These kinds of pressures create opportunities for grassroots activists to push for policy changes before the international court issues a violation ruling against the state.

Domestic court judges can also prove to be important allies for activists. For example, International Criminal Court (ICC) investigations have prompted domestic prosecutions of state officials for human rights violations (Dancy and Montal 2017). Activists can more forcefully demand domestic courts to take states' obligations under international law into account when they have the option to appeal to an international court. Lawyers, once again, play a crucial role by reminding judges of the applicability of ratified treaties or the relevant precedents set by the international court. They can develop a legal strategy by targeting the domestic courts that are more likely to be receptive to human rights claims (Alter 1998; Pavone 2022). High-profile cases or class-action suits can attract media attention, increase public awareness, and help recruit new members. However, in countries where respect for the rule of law is weak, enforcement of international human rights law by domestic courts may provide limited gains for activists.

Finally, litigation at an international court can *foster new alliances with other grassroots activist groups*. Building coalitions help movements recruit new members, diversify tactics, and, overall, extend their longevity (Diani 2013). While most mobilization efforts remain parochial, the formation of inter-group alliances can lead to a "scale shift," or "a change in the number and level of coordinated contentious actions leading to broader contention involving a wider range of actors"

(McAdam, Tarrow, and Tilly 2001: 331).[20] The broader goals and worldviews represented by a growing number of activists increase the reach of the grievances of the activists. Establishing such links can be challenging for activists as it requires finding frames that unite diverse grievances and viewpoints without compromising the group's internal coherence or collective identity. Human rights, as a master frame with flexible and inclusive language, can help bridge these divides, allowing varied groups to advance distinct claims under a shared umbrella. As Tarrow notes, "[i]nternational institutions serve as a kind of 'coral reef,' helping to form horizontal connections among activists with similar claims across boundaries" (Tarrow 2001: 15). These connections enable activists to coordinate demonstrations, adopt shared slogans, and lobby for reforms using a common rights-based vocabulary. The availability of an international human rights court also creates opportunities for activists and their lawyers to exchange strategies and build networks through legal workshops and collaborative training.

In sum, international courts do more than adjudicate violations; they help catalyze new modes of organizing, reshape activist strategies, and open up new political possibilities. These indirect effects are central to understanding the impact of international courts in domestic politics.

Enabling Conditions for Strategic Mobilization
While international litigation can catalyze and expand movements, these effects are not inevitable. The indirect impacts of international courts depend on a set of enabling conditions that shape whether, when, and how litigation catalyzes domestic mobilization. The following factors are especially important: the court's judicial authority and perceived legitimacy, its judicial responsiveness, and the form of state repression.

For an international court to have such a catalytic effect on mobilization, it must wield sufficient judicial authority within that country and be seen as a credible venue where activists have a real chance of winning. Otherwise, litigation provides little strategic advantage to activists or reassurance to new recruits. That said, political backlash can diminish this credibility. Backlash refers to systemic efforts to undermine the authority and legitimacy of a court, ranging from budget cuts and procedural obstruction to formal withdrawal (Hillebrecht 2021; Voeten

---

[20] See Arrington (2019) for how litigation in domestic courts can foster transnational ties among activists and lead to a scale shift.

2022). Even in such hostile environments, activists may still mobilize around human rights by publicizing the incongruence between the government's international obligations and its actual behavior, as leveraging such dissonance is a common feature of contentious action (O'Brien 1996; Simmons 2009). Moreover, backlash by political elites does not always express public opinion. Indeed, determining public attitudes toward international courts is not a straightforward task, since public opinion data on international courts are limited and most people are unfamiliar with international courts (Dinas and Gonzalez-Ocantos 2021).[21] Activists can capitalize on this ambiguity among the population to shape public narratives and demand stronger rights protections.

Second, judicial responsiveness matters. Courts that demonstrate a willingness to engage with new rights claims, issue bold rulings, or challenge state behavior – even in other member states – can provide extra fuel for mobilization efforts. But even in the absence of favorable rulings, the prospect of a legal victory – as long as the court has demonstrated responsiveness and is setting new precedents in other areas – can provide a strong enough foundation for activists to launch their movements.

Finally, the nature of state repression shapes whether and how activists mobilize. Repression is not uniform; its type and intensity depend on state capacity and how threatening the government perceives a movement to be (Davenport 2007; Earl and Braithwaite 2022; Earl and Soule 2010). Covert repression – such as surveillance, infiltration, or cooptation – tends to be more effective than overt repression – such as physical violence or arrests – in quelling collective action as it weakens a movement's cohesion from within (Davenport 2014). Moreover, covert tactics are more difficult to document and therefore harder to litigate at international courts. As a result, international human rights courts may be ill-equipped to address these subtler, yet highly effective, forms of repression.

Group Identity and Legal Consciousness in Strategic Mobilization of Human Rights

One distinctive feature of strategic mobilization of human rights, compared to legal mobilization at the domestic level, is the absence of any significant effect on activists' identity formation and legal

---

[21] Even courts that receive regular media attention often remain poorly understood by the general public, including confusion about their parent organizations and core functions (Voeten 2013).

consciousness. According to legal mobilization scholars, mobilizing the law can serve an educative purpose by changing the way people perceive and articulate their grievances (Engel and Munger 2003; Zemans 1983). A shared sense of experiences, interests, and grievances formed around legal frames can, in turn, shape group identity (Albiston 2005; McCann 1994; Pedriana 2006). The formation of such social constructs are core elements that facilitate and sustain collective mobilization (Armstrong and Bernstein 2008; Polletta and Jasper 2001). But because international law exists on a more distant and abstract terrain than domestic law, it does not shape everyday social interactions or inform people's legal consciousness in the same way.

Some scholars argue that the constitutive power of human rights law can still be activated via mediators. As part of their effort to communicate or "vernacularize" international law to local people, human rights activists and legal professionals can try to instill legal consciousness among the locals by encouraging them to see their grievances through a human rights lens. These efforts are often led by transnationally connected NGOs or advocacy organizations that run workshops and training sessions to educate local actors. Merry and her collaborators (Merry and Stern 2005; Merry et al. 2010) document cases from New York to Hong Kong where such groups helped participants reframe experiences – such as domestic violence – as human rights violations. Other scholars find that these types of efforts can catalyze movements by fostering collective identity around human rights and facilitating member recruitment (Chua 2020; Tsutsui 2018). Yet, as Merry and Stern (2005) note, activists often adapt and repurpose the meaning of human rights depending on context, and not all participants fully internalize them (see also Merry 2006: 44).

Distinct from these studies, *strategic mobilization of human rights* points to a more instrumental approach to human rights. Decades of social movement scholarship show that decisions to participate in contentious action are not purely based on cost–benefit calculations; people need to be moved by normative commitments (Armstrong and Bernstein 2008; Polletta and Jasper 2001; Wood 2003). Yet the moral outrage that motivates labor activists does not come from a realization that their human rights are being violated. Instead, their motivation comes from a recognition of the stark power imbalance between individual workers and employers, and they see unionization as their only viable means to demand better working conditions or fair wages. Their sense of solidarity and collective identity are rooted in class-based struggle, not in a shared understanding of themselves as rights-bearing individuals. In that sense, activists use human rights language as a tactical weapon to advance their cause or as a shield against state repression, not as an inspiration for contentious action.

The empirical studies examined in this book demonstrate two forms of strategic mobilization of human rights. In the first, activists widely incorporate human rights language in their campaigns to broaden public support for their cause. They appeal to the cultural legitimacy of human rights not to persuade their own members, but to gain public sympathy and political traction. They also undertake targeted campaigns in order to draw attention to the fact that the abuses they suffer violate the state's legal obligations under international law. Hence, the vernacularization efforts target external audiences rather than the group's own members (Kahraman 2018). Activists want to persuade the general public that trade union rights are human rights; workers themselves do not require additional convincing about the urgency of their claims.

The second model works in more repressive contexts where activists strategically use human rights to provide a legal foundation for organizing and to mitigate potential recruits' fears of retaliation by the government. Here, vernacularization targets in-group members, but activists or lawyers do not try to persuade members of the moral legitimacy or the inherent worth of their claims. Instead, activists emphasize the legality and official endorsement of their demands, aiming to convince potential supporters that participation is both lawful and aligned with the state's professed values. In both cases, human rights frames have little to no effect on activists' belief in the legitimacy of their claims or on the formation of their collective identity. These cultural drivers of mobilization are forged around preexisting ideological commitments and shared normative convictions within the group, rather than in their engagement with international human rights. Strategic human rights mobilization, then, is more likely among groups that already possess a strong sense of solidarity and identity prior to their adoption of human rights language.

Why would activists take a utilitarian approach toward human rights rather than fully endorsing them? There are sound reasons for activists to be skeptical or ambivalent toward human rights. For most groups, having to appeal to a distant international court can seem arduous, costly, and slow. This is especially true for labor activists who have historically used rank-and-file mobilization to address their grievances, international courts are distant and elitist institutions that individualize and depoliticize workers' demands. A substantial body of scholarship argues that litigation is a defeated strategy that ultimately serves to replace collective bargaining mechanisms with individual rights claiming, weakening the foundation for collective labor action (Marks 2011; McCartin 2005; Savage and Smith 2017). Similar arguments have been advanced by critical legal scholars who warned against pursuing social change through litigation (Gearty 2010; Rosenberg 2008; Tushnet 2000).

Still, even the most repressive systems are never entirely closed, and tools of domination can sometimes be repurposed for resistance (Mitchell 1991; Scott 2000). Turning to human rights frameworks does not mean that workers are deceived by the promise of law (Lovell 2012), or that they naively embrace the "myth of rights" (Scheingold 1974). Sociolegal scholars have shown that activists may engage with litigation strategically, fully aware of the risks of cooptation and disempowerment (Dukes and Kirk 2024; Kahraman 2018; Madlingozi 2013; McCann 1994; McCann and Lovell 2020; Mehta 2024; O'Sullivan et al. 2015). Some of these scholars also argue that sustained legal engagement may, over time, cultivate rights-consciousness and rights-based identity (Chua 2020; McCann 1994; Scheingold 1974). Strategic human rights mobilization builds on this insight while emphasizing that activists can employ legal tactics and rights-based rhetoric without endorsing human rights as a cause around which to build a movement and solidarity ties. They remain cautious about what human rights law can deliver, and their belief in the legitimacy of their cause continues to be shaped by preexisting normative convictions. This tentative engagement suggests that activists' relationship with human rights is conditional and may be abandoned if it no longer serves their political goals.

2.3 CONCLUSION

This chapter has theorized both the conditions under which activists turn to international courts and the impact of international litigation on mobilization. Structural conditions – namely the decline of political opportunities at the domestic level and the rise of legal opportunities at the international level – lay the groundwork for activists to engage in international litigation. Yet such a turn is hardly inevitable; without the guidance of lawyers, activists are unlikely to perceive these new opportunities as such or act on them. Lawyers bridge the international and the local by communicating these new possible remedies to grassroots activists. After probing several venues, they identify the international court with the highest judicial authority and judicial responsiveness to direct litigation efforts, and coordinate strategic litigation efforts.

Section 2.2 shifted focus to the impact of international courts on domestic politics. I argued that solely analyzing states' compliance record with international court rulings provides an inadequate picture of the impact of international human rights courts. In order to fully comprehend how international courts matter, we need to analyze their indirect effects and turn our attention to the developments that occur before the court issues its final ruling. By centering the catalytic rather than just the compliance effects of international litigation, the chapter extends legal mobilization theory into the international domain. I outlined the mechanisms through which human rights law can be constitutive of grassroots mobilization by safeguarding activists' ability to join collective action and by fostering hope that their goals are attainable. Litigation at an international court can also expand and sustain movements by creating new institutional opportunities, attracting allies, and broadening the tactical and discursive repertoires available to movements. International human rights courts may lack strong enforcement powers, but they can still empower activists to engage in diverse forms of action that put direct pressure on governments. At the same time, I theorized strategic mobilization of human rights as a distinct mode of legal mobilization that is pragmatic and rooted in preexisting collective identities, rather than shaped by an internalized rights-based legal consciousness.

The next chapter takes up the first core question: What drives workers to seek recourse through international litigation? It traces how two variants of neoliberalism in Turkey and the UK created the conditions for organized labor to look beyond their national borders for legal remedies.

PART I

WHY DID WORKERS TURN TO THE EUROPEAN COURT OF HUMAN RIGHTS?

CHAPTER 3

DOMESTIC DRIVERS OF HUMAN RIGHTS LITIGATION

Unraveling Trade Union Power Under Two Variants of Neoliberalism

Why have the most important trade union rights cases before the ECtHR emerged from Turkey and the UK – two countries with sharply divergent regime types and human rights records? The UK is an established liberal democracy that played a leading role in drafting the European Convention and has a long history of upholding human rights. Turkey, on the other hand, has a spottier democratic record marked by several military coups over the past half century. Despite being one of the founding members of the ECtHR in the 1950s, Turkey did not accept the jurisdiction of the Court until 1990. Placing this puzzle at its center, this chapter examines the domestic drivers of workers' turn to international litigation.

It argues that anti-union policies adopted by both countries in the post-1980 era drove workers to seek remedies outside of the domestic system. In the UK, neoliberal policies structurally disempowered trade unions, whereas in Turkey, their implementation was accompanied by overt state violence that undercut the power of organized labor for years to come. While the difference between the two variants of neoliberalism is noteworthy, both ultimately eroded labor's mobilization capacity.

In the 1990s, new opportunities started to emerge at the international level as both countries took steps toward Europeanization and made new legal commitments. The analysis suggests the need to move beyond regime type as the primary explanatory framework and instead focus on changing domestic political opportunities to understand the conditions that prompt activists to pursue international legal remedies.

3.1 TRADE UNION RIGHTS LITIGATION BEFORE THE ECTHR

Starting in the 1990s, the number of labor rights cases brought before the ECtHR rose precipitously. The Court's rulings on trade union rights have been the most striking, as it overturned its previous case law to recognize some basic trade union rights, such as the right to collective bargaining and the right to strike, as human rights (Chapter 4). Table 3.1 shows the breakdown of ECtHR trade union rights case law by country from 1960 to 2021.[1] Rulings include all judgments and decisions on trade union rights where Article 11 was invoked.[2] Many East European countries joined the CoE during the 1990s, and in 1998 the Court's jurisdiction became compulsory for all member states.

Therefore, the analysis in the table focuses on cases issued after 1998. In order to offset the effect of repeat cases, the table illustrates the *most important* cases, which include those that the ECtHR identified as key cases and high-importance cases.[3] The Court issued its most influential rulings on trade union rights by folding trade union rights under Article 11, which protects freedom of association. The ECtHR issued its first case where it found a violation of trade union rights in 2002 (*Wilson, National Union of Journalists and Others v. The United Kingdom* 2002).[4] The table also shows the number of cases where the ECtHR found a violation of Article 11 by country.

---

[1] See Appendix I for a methodological note on StrasLab.

[2] All decisions were declared inadmissible or were struck out, except for one decision where the case was declared admissible without a follow-up judgment on the merits (*S. L. v. Sweden* 1971). There are twenty-eight cases brought by individuals or employers complaining about the rights and protections provided to trade unions; these are not included in the analysis here. The vast majority of these cases concern the closed-shop agreements in the UK, Sweden, and Denmark. For a discussion on such cases, see Chapter 4.

[3] The Court assigns an importance level to its own case law based on the significance of a judgment or decision in developing the existing jurisprudence. Key cases are those that have set precedents since the inception of the new Court in 1998. High-importance cases make a significant contribution to the development of the case law. Medium-importance cases go beyond merely applying existing case law, while not making a significant contribution. Low-importance cases simply apply the existing case law.

[4] Prior to *Wilson*, the Court found a violation of Article 11 in a case where the applicant, who was a trade union leader, joined a protest for the Guadeloupe independence movement (*Ezelin v. France* 1991). Although the applicant joined the protest as a trade union leader supporting the movement, the issue at stake was not about the right of unions to take collective action.

TABLE 3.1 Trade union rights cases before the ECtHR 1960–2021

	Post-1998	Most important (post-1998)	A-11 (post-1998)	Total (1960–2021)
Turkey	94	7	38	97
UK	10	4	2	16
Romania	8	2	0	8
Russia	5	2	3	5
Ukraine	5	1	1	5
France	4	0	2	6
Greece	4	0	0	7
Spain	3	2	0	8
Hungary	3	0	1	3
Sweden	1	0	0	5
Germany	0	0	0	4
Other	16	1	1	21
Total	153	19	48	185

Source: StrasLab.

Rulings from Turkey and the UK rank highest in terms of the frequency and importance of the cases activists brought before the Court. Turkey, accounting for more than half of all trade union rights cases, stands out in terms of sheer volume. Of the 153 trade union rights cases brought before the ECtHR since 1998, 94 originated from Turkey, followed by 10 from the UK. France – a country that shares much in common with the UK – produced only four, none of which qualify as most important. This pattern holds in the post-1960 period as well, with Turkey and the UK continuing to lead. At the same time, nearly half of the cases from the UK have set precedents compared to just 8 percent of cases from Turkey, indicating a lot of repeat cases brough by Turkish workers before the Court.[5]

The only countries approaching the UK and Turkey are the recently transitioned East European democracies and Russia.[6] Romania follows the UK with eight cases, though the Court has not found any Article 11 violations in these cases. Ukrainian workers have brought

---

[5] Chapter 5 discusses the different litigation strategies adopted by British and Turkish lawyers.
[6] Russia's membership of the Council of Europe was terminated in 2022 due to its invasion of Ukraine.

five cases, one of which was a high-importance case where the Court found an Article 11 violation. Russian workers have also brought five cases, with the Court finding Article 11 violations in three of them. Chapter 4 demonstrates that the ECtHR has primarily built its trade union rights jurisprudence with precedent-setting cases from Turkey and the UK. In short, cases from these two countries form the core of the ECtHR's case law in this area.

The Court's frequent findings of labor rights violations in cases from Eastern European countries may not be surprising, given that this is a common occurrence not just in labor rights cases but also in other issue areas. Turkey has the highest number of judgments delivered against it, comprising 16 percent of all violation judgments of the ECtHR, followed by Russia (13%), Italy (10%), Romania (7%), and Ukraine (7%) (ECtHR 2022).[7] The UK comprises only 2 percent of these judgments. Yet these similar outcomes emerge from sharply different contexts. The UK is an established democracy with a long-standing commitment to the rule of law and human rights. Turkey's democratic record is inconsistent, interrupted by intermittent military coups and periods of populist authoritarian leadership. The puzzling coupling of Turkey and the UK raises a critical question: Why do so many – and such significant – labor rights cases come from these two countries?

3.2 DOMESTIC ORIGINS OF UNIONS' TURN TO INTERNATIONAL LAW

The answer partly depends on the political opportunities they have; that is, the extent to which activists can access state institutions and the responsiveness of those institutions to activists' demands. The availability of political opportunities encourages activists to take collective action by providing some access to formal state institutions, whether through the courts or political allies. Conversely, when these opportunities are closed off, activists will be unable to push their agenda through domestic channels and will likely face repression when they engage in collective action. Despite the differences in regime type, both countries fundamentally redesigned industrial relations under neoliberal policies, which left little room for labor activists to

---

[7] Italy's slow legal system is driving the overwhelming majority of these judgments as citizens flooded the Court with Article 6 cases due to not being able to receive a ruling within a reasonable time in domestic courts.

advance their grievances through democratic channels in the post-1980 period.

In some respects, labor activists' turn to international litigation due to a decline in political opportunities resonates with findings from other human rights and labor studies. Studies on human rights show that repression at the domestic level motivates activists to seek alliances or remedies at the international level (Risse and Sikkink 1999; Simmons 2009). Though most of these studies associate repression with authoritarian or newly transitioning regimes, the focus on political opportunities here allows us to see how labor activists in a liberal democracy can similarly experience despair in seeking remedies at the domestic level. This is not to say that regime type does not matter. The mountain of repetitive cases from Turkey dwarfs the number of cases from the UK because the labor conditions Turkish workers face are much harsher and the violations are more frequent than those in the UK. Nevertheless, the UK's position as the country with the second highest and most important cases tells us that regime type by itself does not explain the conditions under which activists turn to international law.

Though we lack a systematic study on when labor unions turn to international organizations, existing studies suggest that countries where neoliberalism had a more drastic impact as well as those with regional free market zones, such as North America and the European Union (EU), are more likely to engage in transnational activism and coalition building with other social movements (Frege and Kelly 2004; Gentile and Tarrow 2009). Findings here show that in countries where unions' ability to influence domestic policy has been curtailed, or where restrictions on trade union rights have been imposed, unions are more likely to resort to litigation before international courts. In both Turkey and the UK, labor activists turned to international litigation when political and legal opportunities were unfavorable for advancing their claims at the domestic level.

3.3 LABOR RIGHTS UNDER TWO VARIANTS OF NEOLIBERALISM

Organized labor has been in decline in many parts of the world since the late 1970s. The neoliberal turn is often contrasted with the demand-side economics of the Fordist era and is characterized by a range of economic policies that aim to liberalize trade and foreign capital entry, privatize state enterprises, dismantle social welfare provisions, regressively cut taxes, remove capital controls, weaken trade unions, and deregulate financial institutions (Harvey 2005). The most significant feature of neoliberalism distinguishing it from classical liberalism is the involvement, rather than the retreat, of the state in the economy – that is, intervention on behalf of capital through bailouts, tax cuts, subsidies, or policies that favor investors and employers. The legitimacy of the state is tied to its efficiency in *governance* – not only in the sphere of production, but also in non-economic spheres through promoting individual self-sufficiency, entrepreneurship, and adaptation to unpredictable market conditions (Brown 2006; Keil 2009; Ong 2006). For the purposes of the analysis of political opportunity structures in this chapter, the most important aspect of neoliberalism is the sustained assault on collective labor rights.

The rise of neoliberal policies can be traced back to the stressors that the Organization of the Petroleum Exporting Countries (OPEC) crisis created in the global economy, including the departure of manufacturing jobs in search of cheap labor in other parts of the world and a growing reliance on subcontracting and flexible labor (Hansen 2023). With a few exceptions, unions in most advanced economies failed to rise to the challenge of organizing workers in these new sectors (Disney, Gosling, and Machin 1995; Hansen 2023; Hardy, Eldring, and Schulten 2012). At the same time, these developments incentivized governments to lower labor standards, offering fewer regulations and low wages in order to attract global companies. While this "race to the bottom" manifested itself as sweatshop labor and inhuman work conditions in the Global South, governments in most advanced industrialized countries responded by crushing trade unions (Hansen 2023).[8] Baccaro and Howell (2017) provide a path-breaking analysis of neoliberal convergence by drawing on a statistical analysis of macroeconomic indicators in 15 advanced industrialized countries, 12 of which are Western European countries. In a challenge to the "varieties of capitalism" literature, which emphasizes sustained divergence between economies, they find a "common neoliberal trajectory" characterized by weakening trade unions, declining industrial conflicts,

---

[8] See Fourcade-Gourinchas and Babb (2002) and Wallerstein, Golden, and Lange (1997) for earlier studies of how implementation of neoliberalism takes different forms, albeit in the same direction.

Trade union density

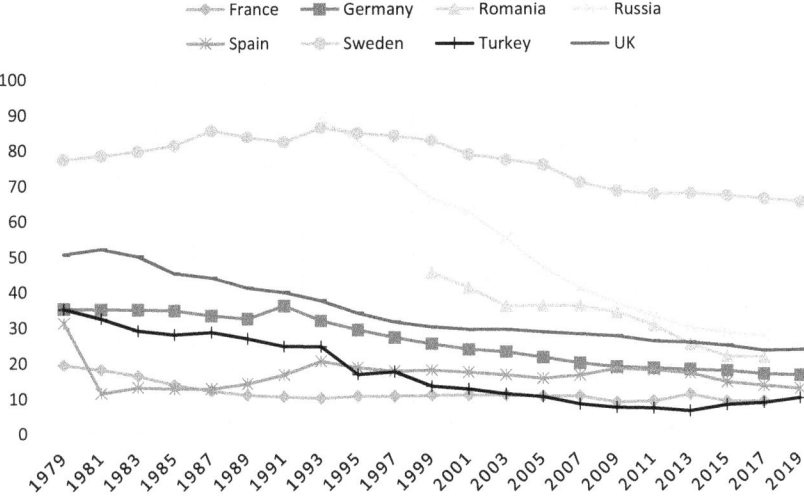

Figure 3.1 Trade union density in eight European countries
Source: OECD-AIAS-ICTWSS 2021 (variable UD_hist) and ILOSTAT 2020

and decentralized collective bargaining.[9] While these findings are common in both liberal market economies and coordinated market economies, the UK stands out in their analysis as a country where "industrial relations underwent decollectivization on a massive scale in a relatively short period of time ... through the direct erosion and ultimately the dismantling of existing institutions" (Baccaro and Howell 2017: 83). According to the International Trade Union Confederation (ITUC), the UK has the worst conditions for trade union activism in Western Europe, with a ranking of 3 out of 5, and Turkey is among the world's ten worst countries.[10]

Figures 3.1 and 3.2 illustrate the decline of collective bargaining coverage and trade union density in eight European countries, encompassing a range of geographical regions and levels of economic

---

[9] For a prominent defense of the resilience of domestic institutions despite economic liberalization see the varieties of capitalism literature (Hall and Soskice 2001).
[10] The ITUC's Global Rights Index ranks countries based on an analysis with indicators derived from ILO conventions and examines violations of workers' rights in law and practice (ITUC 2014 and 2022).

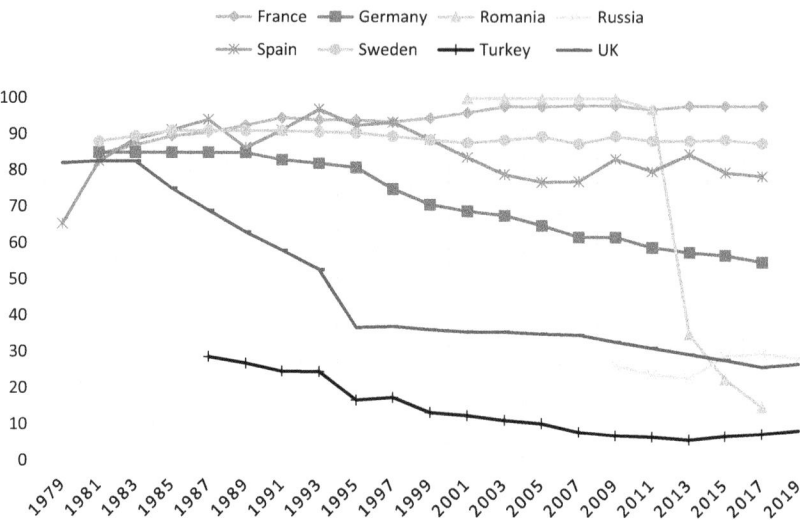

Figure 3.2 Collective bargaining coverage in eight European countries
Source: OECD-AIAS-ICTWSS 2021 (variable AdjCov_hist) and ILOSTAT 2020.

development.[11] These countries are notable in Table 3.1 for their high number of trade union rights cases and the violation judgments issued against them. The figures show that even in Germany, once regarded as an alternative success model to extreme forms of neoliberalism, collective bargaining coverage declined and trade unions lost power.[12] In France and Spain, while the collective bargaining coverage remained relatively stable, the role of trade unions in the process has been progressively weakened.[13] The UK exhibits the sharpest decline (67%) in collective bargaining coverage – second only to Romania – bringing the 2019 rate to 27 percent. The unionization rate similarly decreased by 54 percent, reflecting a steep decline consistent with other liberal democracies.

---

[11] Trade union density refers to the ratio of trade union members among wage and salary earners. Collective bargaining coverage refers to the share of workers covered by valid collective agreements in the workforce.
[12] See also Baccaro and Howell (2017), Hassel (1999), and Kinderman (2005).
[13] See also Baccaro and Howell (2017) and Howell (2009).

The situation of unions in East European countries is often worse than the unionization rates suggest. While post-Soviet states have given up on "overt authoritarian corporatism," in Russia, state-sponsored or elite-controlled unions still control many sectors of the economy (Cook 2010; Robertson 2007).[14] Romania is in a relatively better situation among post-Soviet states, as the legacy union was displaced after transition to democracy. However, in 2011, the government unilaterally scrapped the collective bargaining scheme in the country and introduced a new system with significant restrictions, resulting in the sharp decline shown in Figure 3.2 (Trif 2013). In Turkey, a state-sponsored union came to dominate the public sector in the post-2000 period (see Chapter 8). But a major transformation across the labor force was propelled in the post-1980 period with the introduction of neoliberal policies. The figures demonstrate a steady decline of union power since 1980 and Turkey ranks lowest on both indicators.[15] Trade union density fell from 35 percent in 1979 to only 10 percent today, while collective bargaining coverage dropped to a meager 8.5 percent, placing Turkey second to last among all Organisation for Economic Co-operation and Development (OECD) countries, after Estonia.

The grievances of Turkish and British workers before the ECtHR do not only result from the dire situation workers are in today, but also the relative deprivation they experienced compared to the pre-1980 period when organized labor was a major political actor shaping policy decisions in both countries. Focusing on Turkey and the UK enables an analysis of how neoliberal policies, implemented within different regime types, undermined the power of organized labor – albeit to varying degrees. In both cases, neoliberalism ultimately drove workers to seek remedies at the international level. In Turkey, the defining feature of neoliberalism was the violent form it took following a military coup in 1980. As a result, trade unions lost their organizing power as their relations with political parties were severed. In the UK, there was no such overt state violence against unions. Neoliberal policies nonetheless structurally disempowered trade unions, curtailing their influence and capacity for collective action.

---

[14] I discuss how a state-sponsored union took over the public sector in Turkey in Chapter 8.

[15] The trade union density is similarly low in France. In 2017, the rate was 9 percent in France and 8.6 percent in Turkey. The 2019 rate for France is not available.

3.4 UNITED KINGDOM

3.4.1 Institutional Disempowerment of Organized Labor

Former Prime Minister Margaret Thatcher's rise to power in 1979 marked the beginning of a new era for the UK.[16] The Conservative government did everything in its power to curb union strength and to impose measures restricting collective action, defending its anti-union policies and austerity measures by famously proclaiming that "there is no alternative." As noted above, trade union density has halved since 1979 and collective bargaining coverage has shrunk even more drastically. Within the first two decades after the introduction of neoliberal policies, the number of work stoppages fell by 90 percent (Colling 2006: 142).

The Conservatives rolled out a series of policies aimed at sapping union power: banning closed shop agreements – arrangements between the employer and unions stipulating that all workers at a workplace would be represented by a single trade union – restricting the right to take industrial action, and prohibiting certain groups, such as teachers, from engaging in collective action altogether. They introduced complex ballot mandates, including an open ballot requirement for collective action that compromised union democracy, adding red tape and confusion to even routine union proceedings.[17] Tory leadership also tipped the balance of the public body responsible for preventing and resolving industrial disputes – the Advisory, Conciliation, and Arbitration Service – in favor of employers by removing its statutory duty to promote collective bargaining. The Thatcher government went as far as breaking its own collective agreements with workers in the public sector, perhaps the most blatant example of the Tory approach to trade union rights. The government cast union power as "the enemy within" crippling economic growth, at the same time as it failed to provide any protection for individual workers against corporate power.

In 1984, the government banned all workers of the Government Communications Headquarters (GCHQ) from joining trade unions.

---

[16] The literature on neoliberalism in the UK is extensive. For an overview, see Harvey (2005), King and Wood (1999), Smith (2009), and Wedderburn (1991).

[17] This requirement was later unsuccessfully challenged in a case brought before the ECtHR (*National Union of Rail, Maritime and Transport Workers v. The UK* 2014). See Chapter 5.

The workers, who had been unionized for almost four decades, were offered a sum of money in exchange for giving up their union membership at the Council of Civil Service Unions (CCSU); those who refused were dismissed. The ban triggered widespread protests across the country and public sector workers in other industries engaged in work stoppages in solidarity with GCHQ workers.[18] The union and the workers later brought the case before the ECtHR to no avail (*Council of Civil Service Unions et al. v. The United Kingdom* 1987; *M. A. and 39 Others v. the United Kingdom* 1987; *R. A. and W. M. v. the United Kingdom* 1987). This ban was one of the first major victories of the Thatcher government against organized labor. But its most defining victory was the defeat of the striking mine workers in 1985. Thatcher's resolve in breaking the solidarity of thousands of workers after a yearlong strike had symbolic importance, since the National Union of Mineworkers was considered among the strongest unions at the time, and the government policies that led to the strike were emblematic of the transformation of the UK labor market under neoliberal policies (Towers 1989; Winterton and Winterton 1989).

In addition to institutionally disempowering organized labor, the government demonstrated a lack of regard for the UK's obligations under international law. During this period, the UK denounced thirteen ILO Conventions, violated several of its obligations under the European Social Charter (ESC), and failed to sign the new protocols of the ESC regarding workers' rights (Kang 2012). The refusal of the UK – a founding member of the CoE, with a leading role in drafting the European Convention – to comply with important international agreements was yet another hallmark of the Thatcher government.

The unions' prospects improved only marginally under "New" Labour. Prime Minister Tony Blair promoted "flexibility" and "security" to work, while continuing the conservative erosion of unions and decollectivizing industrial relations.[19] The Labour Party continued the Conservative rhetoric of portraying unions as a regressive force for economic development from which individual workers needed protection, casting

---

[18] Jon Nordheimer, "Strikes Disrupt Public Services in Britain," *The New York Times*, February 29, 1984, www.nytimes.com/1984/02/29/world/strikes-disrupt-public-services-in-britain.html.

[19] In order to differentiate the anti-union policies of New Labour from the Thatcherite period, some scholars have defined it as "social neoliberalism" (Crouch 1997: 358) or a "social-democratic variant of neoliberalism" (Hall 2005).

collective bargaining as coercive over workers. To reassure business interests, Blair publicly declared, "We will not be held ransom by unions. We will stand up to strikes," and pledged "there will be no return to the trade union laws of the 1970s" (Kang 2012: 136). Despite pressure from the unions, Blair refused to reverse many of the restrictions on trade union activities introduced by the Conservatives, such as the ban on closed shops, prohibitions on secondary action (or solidarity strikes), and the onerous requirements imposed on unions for taking industrial action (Daniels and McIlroy 2009; Smith 2009). The government also failed to introduce stronger protections against the blacklisting of unionized workers, despite being urged by the unions and the ILO (Chapter 7). Without union power, the limited provisions aimed at providing "security" to workers fell short of fulfilling Labour's promises.

Under Blair, the Labour government strangled the labor movement which had given birth to the party. The government actively tried "to marginalize union influence both inside the party and over government" (Hamann and Kelly 2004: 110; see also Daniels and McIlroy 2009). Consequently, organized labor's relations with the party significantly weakened: Unions reduced their funds to the party and the party reduced the unions' share of votes at Labour Party conferences (Daniels and McIlroy 2009; Schulman 2019). As union contributions to the party budget fell from 54 percent in 1995 to 30 percent in 1999, Labour more than compensated with increased funding from wealthy business owners (Schulman 2019: 119). In 2004, the Fire Brigades Union (FBU) and the National Union of Rail, Maritime and Transport Workers (RMT) severed all ties with the party to protest at Blair's policies, particularly privatizations and restrictions on strike action.[20]

3.4.2 Steps toward Europeanization: The ECtHR Emerges as a New Legal Opportunity

Amidst this restrictive domestic environment for labor, a new avenue emerged to combat anti-union policies as a result of New Labour's commitment to international instruments and its efforts to mend relations with Europe. Tony Blair's election success could in part be

---

[20] "Rail Union Breaks with Labour," *BBC News*, February 7, 2004, http://news.bbc.co.uk/2/hi/uk_news/scotland/3467637.stm.

attributed to his promises to restore the UK's image in Europe as a country committed to basic rights. In addition to the promise to introduce the Human Rights Act (HRA) to strengthen the protection of international human rights domestically, the Labour Party pledged to "make the protection and promotion of human rights a central part of our foreign policy" in its election manifesto (Labour Party 1997, quoted in Kang 2012). Unlike the previous government's isolationist policies, the UK made strides in strengthening ties with the EU, empowered international treaties at the domestic level, and once again assumed a leading position in human rights in Europe.

Under the HRA, judges are to interpret UK legislation in a way that gives effect to the Convention rights. While the ECtHR rulings were already legally binding in the UK, the HRA put in stronger measures to ensure domestic institutions complied with the European Convention. In cases where the judges find UK laws incompatible with the Convention or ECtHR rulings, they can issue a "declaration of incompatibility," effectively placing the burden on parliament to change the relevant legislation accordingly. In that sense, the HRA integrated the Convention into British law. In 1998, the Blair government showed no concerns about passing the HRA and giving effect to the Convention articles and protocols at the domestic level. At the time, the Convention and the ECtHR protected primarily civil and political rights, which were deemed harmless by New Labour from an economic standpoint. In *Young, James and Webster v. The United Kingdom* (1981), the Court had upheld the government's ban on closed shop agreements. More recently in *The National Association of Teachers in Further and Higher Education v. the United Kingdom* (1998), the Court had rejected the trade unions' complaints regarding the allegedly unfair restrictions on the right to strike. Thus, the Labour government did not anticipate that, by giving teeth to the ECtHR rulings at the domestic level, it would open the door for an international body to weigh in on some of the major industrial disputes, such as anti-union discrimination, the right of unions to choose their members, blacklisting, and ballot requirements for collective action (see Chapter 4).

3.5 TURKEY

3.5.1 The Violent Destruction of Organized Labor

Turkey's transition from an inward-looking economy to a market-oriented one took place in an undemocratic and violent political environment. This pattern was typical: In countries where the labor movement was strong and democratic institutions were weak, states often resorted to violence to enforce neoliberal economic policies.[21]

Turkey's history of democratic transition is fraught with military coups and constitutional overhauls.[22] The 1961 Constitution, drafted after a military coup, granted broad associational rights that laid the groundwork for the golden age of organized labor as well as the rise of militant left-wing movements (Belge 2006). As one observer noted, "the 1961 Constitution had permitted Turkish society to be politicized; the [post-coup] 1982 version attempted to reverse the process" (Ahmad 1985: 2013). Devrimci İşçi Sendikaları Konfederasyonu (DİSK, Confederation of Revolutionary Trade Unions of Turkey) and its political correspondent Türkiye İşçi Partisi (TİP, Workers' Party of Turkey), the first avowedly socialist party, were home to many radical left-wing activists and politicians. TİP had surprising success in the 1965 elections by winning 3.3 percent of the votes and sending fifteen members to the parliament. The establishment of DİSK, splitting from the then-leading trade union Türkiye İşçi Sendikaları Konfederasyonu (Türk-İş, Confederation of Turkish Trade Unions), was a major blow to the corporatist union structure that dominated organized labor until then.[23] Leftist politics of the era was based strictly on achieving social justice through class politics. Human rights and democratization without class struggle were unthinkable for activists at the time.[24] With few notable dissenters, activist groups rallied around the common cause of socialist revolution. Labor led the left.

In 1980, the military seized power, accusing the government of failing to manage the deeply polarized political demands from society.

---

[21] Turkey's neoliberal restructuring closely parallels that of Latin American countries (Dogan 2010; Öniş 2006; Taylor 2006)

[22] For an analysis of military tutelage in Turkey and its similarities and differences from the bureaucratic-authoritarianism in Latin America (O'Donnell 1973), see Cizre-Sakallıoğlu (1992), Özbudun (1996), and Tachau and Heper (1983).

[23] See Cizre-Sakallıoğlu (1992) for a discussion on the corporate ties between Türk-İş and the governing Democrat Party at the time. In particular, the agreement between the two institutions rested on an understanding that the union would not engage in politics. This decoupling of union strategy and politics was the main source of the rift between DİSK and Türk-İş.

[24] Socialist movements around the world peaked globally around the 1970s (Moyn 2018).

The coup facilitated the implementation of neoliberal policies by crushing and silencing all dissent. Many labor unions were shut down and their leaders and activists imprisoned. DİSK suffered the worst of all unions at the time, with its assets confiscated and fifty-two of its leaders tried on charges carrying the death penalty. Banned for over a decade, it was only allowed to reopen in 1992. The new power structure severed the political ties between organized labor and the state. The 1982 Constitution and subsequent employment legislation severely restricted trade union rights. As Figure 3.1 shows, unionization has steadily declined since 1980. Strikes were permitted only when they did not violate the procrustean definition of "national security." Collective bargaining was granted only to unions that unionized at least 10 percent of the relevant sector in addition to at least 50 percent of workers in an enterprise. This restriction, which was later unsuccessfully challenged by DİSK before the ECtHR (*Sosyal-İş Union and Kodaş v. Turkey* 1995), emerged as a major impediment for unions in the following decades. As a result, about one-third of unionized workers do not have the right to sign a collective bargaining agreement, and the overall coverage rate plummeted to a mere 8.5 percent by 2019 (Figure 3.2).[25] The new regulation also excluded smaller, independent, and radical unions from representing workers. The Turkish economy took a sharp neoliberal turn through the privatization of state-run industries and the liberalization of trade and foreign investment. Throughout the 1990s, structural adjustment programs, familiar to many other developing countries at the time, encouraged public expenditure cuts, wage depreciation, and an economic transformation that resulted in a volatile economy dependent on capital influx and short-term investments (Boratav and Yeldan 2006; Öniş 2006).

Until the Adalet ve Kalkınma Partisi (AKP, Justice and Development Party) took an authoritarian turn in the post-2010 period, Turkey's integration into the global economy was hailed as a success story, and its democratic reforms were recognized by the EU with candidacy status in 2005. Turkey now ranks as the twelfth largest economy in the world (adjusted by purchasing power parity) and maintained high growth rates throughout the 2000s (IMF 2024).[26]

---

[25] The 10 percent threshold was finally lowered to 1 percent for all unions in 2015, but by this point the unions had already lost most of their organizing power.

[26] For example, even after the 2008 global financial crisis, its growth rate rebounded to 8.2 in 2010 (CIA 2012).

However, alongside the ongoing economic crisis and soaring inflation, this growth came at the expense of deteriorating labor conditions and rising inequality. The ITUC ranks Turkey as one of world's ten worst countries for labor conditions and trade union rights (ITUC 2014 and 2022). Among the OECD countries, working hours are highest in Turkey.[27] It also has the highest rate of fatal occupational injuries among European countries (ILO 2020).[28] Each year, more than 1,500 workers die due to unregulated, insecure working conditions (Health and Safety Watch/Turkey 2024).[29]

The rapid expansion of subcontracting and the informal economy is degrading working conditions faster and further. Eighty-five percent of total employment is provided by small enterprises, where most labor violations occur (Adaman, Buğra, and İnsel 2009) and unionization rates remain below 10 percent.[30] According to the Turkish Statistical Institute (TurkStat), about 35 percent of workers in Turkey were in the informal sector between 2011 and 2015, but the actual numbers are likely to be much higher.[31] People working under precarious conditions do not have access to labor unions or any other rights, most are not covered by social security, and are paid well below the minimum wage. Adaman, Buğra, and İnsel (2009: 179) describes the Turkish labor market as "a shrinking island of privileged union members in a vast sea of underprivileged workers." Consequently, these employment problems have brought with them new forms of poverty and social exclusion, particularly in urban areas (Adaman, Buğra, and İnsel 2009; Buğra 2007; Keyder 2005).

---

[27] Turkey shares this position with Colombia, with average weekly working hours of 46–51 hours between 2010 and 2020 (OECD 2023).
[28] From 2010 through 2020, Turkey had the highest rates per 100,000 workers.
[29] The actual numbers are likely higher due to underreporting and difficulties in collecting data, especially on deaths resulting from occupational diseases.
[30] The number of unionized workers is hard to determine, as the Ministry of Labor and Social Security tends to exaggerate the numbers. One challenge in calculating these rates, of course, is the informal sector, where the unregistered and non-unionized work of millions goes unreported. The same is true for estimations on collective bargaining coverage. For instance, the Ministry reported Turkey's 2016 unionization rate at 11.5 percent, but DİSK-AR (2017) estimated it at no more than 10 percent, while the OECD placed it at 8.2 percent (OECD-AIAS-ICTWSS 2021)..
[31] TurkStat's estimate is based on a household survey that identifies informality as being not registered with any social security system. But Acar and Tansel (2016) estimate the actual number to be at 65 percent, based on job attributes, social security registration, scale of enterprises, and employment type.

As unions weakened, most also lost their internal democratic governance and accountability to their traditional base. Many became susceptible to cooptation by the state and employers, as workers increasingly lost trust in union leadership. As a result, unions ceased to be key actors in the governance of employment relations in the post-1980 era.

3.5.2 Steps toward Europeanization: The ECtHR Emerges as a New Legal Opportunity

By the late 1980s, Turkey began taking concrete steps toward Europeanization, and its rapprochement with Europe became institutionalized. Turkey applied to become a member of the European Economic Community (EEC), the predecessor of the EU, in 1987. The EU accession process had a significant impact on Turkey's democratization and prompted its commitment to numerous international human rights obligations. Turkey accepted the right of individual petition (Article 25) to the European Convention in 1987 and the jurisdiction of the ECtHR in 1990. In 1989, Turkey ratified the ESC, albeit with major reservations, including the right to organize (Article 5) and the right to collective bargaining (Article 6). In 1993, ILO Convention 87 on the freedom of association and the right to organize was ratified, adding to its earlier ratification of Convention 98 on the right to organize and collective bargaining in 1952. Turkey's efforts finally came to fruition in the 1999 Helsinki Summit where it was recognized as a candidate for full EU membership, with formal negotiations to begin in 2005. As in the UK, these new international commitments led to unintended consequences for the Turkish state and opened up a new avenue for Turkish workers to claim trade union rights.

The gradual relaxation of trade union restrictions, coupled with Turkey's new international obligations, set the ground for an unlikely group of workers to mobilize and demand trade union rights – white-collar public sector workers. Although public sector unions often make up the largest share of unionized workers globally, white-collar public employees – or civil servants – have historically faced greater restrictions in exercising trade union rights, often justified by their supposed political neutrality or the need to ensure uninterrupted public services (Bach and Bordogna 2016). In more centralized or authoritarian contexts, civil servants have been viewed primarily as extensions of the state apparatus, bound by loyalty to the state, rather than as workers entitled to collective labor rights (Bishara 2018). In line with this latter logic, *memurs* (civil servants) in Turkey were long excluded from basic trade union protections. Prior to the 1980s, public sector workers had organized under *derneks* (associations) that provided them some support and a solidarity network, though they had never formed unions.[32] The 1982 Constitution was the most restrictive constitution in terms of the rights and liberties it set out not just for trade unions but for civil society activism at large. Nonetheless, it provided two openings. First, the Constitution gave direct effect to ratified treaties in domestic laws, empowering the domestic application of already binding Convention rights and ECtHR rulings. Second, it did not include a ban on public sector workers' right to unionize, which was likely an oversight by the junta leaders who regarded public sector workers' unions as such a far-fetched idea that they saw no need to prohibit it. These two openings created opportunities for public sector workers to decisively demand the right to organize for the first time.

3.6 CONCLUSION

This chapter examined the changing political opportunity structures under two variants of neoliberalism in Turkey and the UK. In both countries, restrictive trade union rights regimes left workers with few domestic avenues to address their grievances, driving them to seek remedies at the ECtHR. As a result, workers from these two countries have brought both the highest number and the most important trade union rights cases before the Court.

Despite their distinct political histories, Turkey and the UK share a common trajectory in the erosion of organized labor under neoliberalism. Turkey has some of the worst labor conditions in Europe, and labor activism has been severely restricted since the 1980s. The military coup marked a turning point, ushering in a period of violent repression in which trade unionists were imprisoned, exiled, and even killed, and trade unions were banned for nearly a decade. Trade unions have not been able to organize a strong movement since this harsh crackdown,

---

[32] There was a brief five-year period within the liberal era following the 1961 Constitution when public sector workers were granted the right to unionize. Yet the structure of these unions was not too different from that of associations, since public sector workers did not have the right to engage in collective bargaining or to strike (Gülmez 2002).

nor have they been able to adapt to the needs of workers in a changing economic landscape.

The UK, despite its history of commitment to democratic values, assumed a leading position in the world in implementing neoliberal policies that systematically undermined organized labor. Here, neoliberalism took the form of institutional disempowerment, with successive governments introducing policies that dismantled trade union power over time. Even though British workers have never faced the level of violence experienced by their Turkish counterparts, organized labor in each country experienced stark relative deprivation – losing power, abandoning socialist ideals, and struggling to maintain relevance in the post-Cold War era. These repressive conditions at the domestic level pushed workers to seek alternative strategies to voice their demands.

At the same time, both governments made new commitments to international law. When the Turkish and British governments made these commitments, the ECtHR had yet to establish clear protections for trade union rights. By the late 1990s, however, the Court took a sharp turn, expanding its interpretation of labor rights and imposing new obligations on domestic governments. How did this transformation come about? What role did cases from Turkey and the UK play in building the Court's case law on trade union rights? The next chapter addresses these questions by tracing the Court's development of labor jurisprudence within a broader political and historical context.

CHAPTER 4

A NEW AVENUE FOR WORKERS AT THE INTERNATIONAL LEVEL
The European Court of Human Rights

> [T]he Court considers that its case-law to the effect that the right to bargain collectively and to enter into collective agreements does not constitute an inherent element of Article 11 ... should be reconsidered, so as to take account of the perceptible evolution in such matters, in both international law and domestic legal systems. While ... the Court should not depart, without good reason, from precedents established in previous cases, a failure by the Court to maintain a dynamic and evolutive approach would risk rendering it a bar to reform or improvement.
>
> Demir and Baykara v. Turkey (2008)

In 2009, the ECtHR issued one of its landmark rulings on trade union rights in *Enerji Yapı-Yol Sen v. Turkey*, concerning a government circular that barred public sector workers from participating in a planned one-day national strike organized by the public sector union confederation KESK. This blanket ban was announced just five days before the scheduled action in April 1996, leaving no time for the union to legally challenge it. Despite the prohibition, members of Enerji Yapı-Yol Sen – a KESK-affiliated union – joined the strike and were subsequently subjected to disciplinary sanctions. The case carried particular significance for unions at the time since the strike action aimed to secure the right for public sector workers to engage in collective bargaining. Appeals against these sanctions were dismissed by Turkish courts, which upheld the circular and emphasized public servants' obligation to adhere to existing legislative provisions regarding union activity.

The ECtHR's ruling – which found that the prohibition effectively deprived all public servants of their right to strike and thus amounted to a violation of Article 11 (freedom of association) – came a year after its most momentous judgment, *Demir Baykara v. Turkey* (2008), which had established collective bargaining as "an essential element" of the right to unionize. Together, these cases represented the apex of the ECtHR's golden period for trade unions, extending freedom of association (Article 11) to include key trade union rights, like the rights to strike and bargain collectively, that are not explicitly protected in the Convention.

The ECtHR, however, had not always been so responsive to workers' claims. As illustrated by the quote above, these rulings mark a sharp departure from the Court's previous case law. During the four decades ensuing its establishment in 1959, the ECtHR largely avoided labor disputes, deferring these contentious issues to national courts.

Part of this shift can be attributed to the nature of the new cases that started to appear in its docket in the 1990s. None of the earlier cases matched the urgency of those filed by the Turkish public sector workers who faced blanket bans on union activity or British workers challenging the government's overt support for employers' attempts to undermine the existence of unions (*Wilson v. UK* 2002). As shown in the previous chapter, these cases emerged in the wake of post-1980 neoliberal reforms that left workers with little recourse in domestic institutions, pushing them to seek international legal remedies.

The other part of the puzzle behind the ECtHR's new approach to labor cases lies in changes occurring at the international level. At around the same time, the ECtHR rose to prominence with new judicial powers and a growing willingness to expand its jurisprudence into new domains. This chapter takes a top-down perspective and tells the story of this labor case law from the perspective of the ECtHR. Situating the growth of labor case law within a historical and political context, the analysis here shows that the workers' international legal mobilization coincided with the ECtHR's institutional evolution. Moving away from its conservative origins, the ECtHR became more assertive and, by the end of the 1990s, started intervening in contentious policy areas across Europe. The sheer volume and the pressing nature of claims brought by workers presented an opportunity for the Court to expand its case law into new issue areas.

In order to document the scope of this shift, I present findings from the Strasbourg Labor Cases Database (StrasLab) in this chapter. The analysis shows that the growth of trade union rights cases was part of a trend, and that the ECtHR applied this new pro-worker approach to a wide range of cases, including workers' health and safety, surveillance in the workplace, undocumented migrant workers' rights, and unfair dismissals. In response to these new types of claims, the Court interpreted the Convention articles expansively, establishing new rights in the workplace. The most innovative cases came in the area of trade union rights.

The chapter also shows that the ECtHR's judicial responsiveness to trade union rights evolved across three distinct periods. In the *Initial Phase*, the Court remained faithful to its conservative origins and dismissed the few labor cases brought before it. This was followed by the *Expansion Phase*, a golden era in which the ECtHR's responsiveness to labor rights peaked. In the most recent *Retrenchment Phase*, the Court has faced intensifying political pressure and has become reluctant to recognize new trade union rights as human rights, though it has not overturned its case law on established rights.

4.1 INSTITUTIONAL DESIGN AND THE AUTHORITY OF THE EUROPEAN COURT OF HUMAN RIGHTS

The ECtHR is the most active human rights court in the world. Since its establishment in 1959, the Court has issued over a million cases (ECtHR 2022). One key reason behind this massive case load is the direct access it grants to individuals, corporations, societal associations – including NGOs and trade unions – and member states that are victims of human rights abuses. There are no legal fees for bringing a case to the Court, but applicants must first exhaust all domestic remedies before applying to the ECtHR. Individuals, regardless of being a national of a member state, can directly take their cases to the ECtHR, provided that they are complaining of a violation committed by a member state. Trade unions' ability to bring cases before the Court as applicants has undoubtedly played an important role in the development of the labor case law. Additionally, societal groups and member states can make third-party interventions – a system similar to amicus curiae briefs in the US – to advocate on behalf of the applicant or the member state. These third-party submissions have supported many trade union rights cases, as discussed in the previous chapter.

Much of the ECtHR's strength comes from its institutional structure and resources. The ECtHR's budget has grown steadily since its inception, with regular contributions from member states, which allows the Court to continue its operations much more smoothly than its counterparts in other regions. For example, the ECtHR's 2015 budget was six times bigger than the budget allocated for the African Court on Human and Peoples' Rights and eleven times bigger than the budget of the Inter-American Court of Human Rights.[1] While this privileged position has allowed the ECtHR to process more cases, the immense backlog remains a major challenge for the Court. As of January 2025, there were 60,200 applications pending before the Court (ECtHR 2025). Though this is a large number, it represents a significant improvement, considering that the number of pending cases has almost halved within the past decade. As the next section will show, the Court has gone through a series of reforms to be able to manage its case law more effectively.

The ECtHR was established by the thirteen founding member states of the CoE as the judicial body that protects the rights set out in the European Convention. Today, the CoE, based in Strasbourg, France, has forty-six member states, including many countries not in the European Union, encompassing some 675 million inhabitants. The number of judges serving at the ECtHR (46) is equal to the number of member states. Judges are appointed for a non-renewable nine-year term by the Parliamentary Assembly of the Council of Europe (PACE) among the three candidates proposed by each state. All rulings are reached by a majority vote in a transparent manner whereby judges may issue separate dissenting or concurring opinions. These opinions provide a window into the judges' interpretive process.

Once a case reaches the ECtHR, the Court first issues a *decision* on admissibility. Every year, the Court receives thousands of applications, a vast majority of which are ineligible. In 2022, the Court decided on almost 40,000 cases, 89 percent of which were declared inadmissible or struck out (ECtHR 2023).[2] After an application is deemed admissible,

---

[1] The ECtHR's budget in 2015 was €85,109,200 (excluding the funds allocated for the execution of judgments and enhancing the effectiveness of the ECtHR), which constituted 21 percent of the Council of Europe's total budget. The Organization of American States allocated $8,088,900 for the Inter-American Court and the Commission, constituting almost 10 percent of its total budget. And the African Union allocated $9,857,665 to the African Court and the Commission, which constituted about 4 percent of its total budget.

[2] This percentage also includes cases that were administratively disposed of before allocation to a judicial formation.

negotiations may ensue for a *friendly settlement* between the applicant and the government. If a friendly settlement is not reached, the Court then examines the merits of the case and issues a *judgment* on whether there has been a violation of the Convention or not. Judgments are generally issued by a committee of three judges or a chamber of seven judges. In exceptional circumstances, cases may be referred or appealed to the Grand Chamber, composed of seventeen judges, to reach a final judgment.

4.2 ECTHR'S LABOR CASE LAW IN POLITICAL CONTEXT

My analysis of the labor cases brought before the Court since its inception shows that it was not just the unionists that turned to the ECtHR; workers that experienced all sorts of rights violations – from unfair dismissals to safety in the workplace, from discrimination in hiring practices to workplace surveillance claims – urged the Court to consider their grievances as human rights violations. Since the 1990s, the number of labor cases has risen steeply, turning the ECtHR into a site of contestation for workers' rights (Figure 4.1).

That courts are political institutions is hardly a revelation for political scientists (Hirschl 2008; McCann 2020; Shapiro 1986). Scholars point out a number of factors that can explain the judicialization of politics, including increased demand for courts following economic liberalization or democratization (Alter 2014; Kelemen 2011; Keohane, Moravcsik, and Slaughter 2000; Stone Sweet 2000); changes in world historical events (Alter 2014); bottom-up mobilization, with lawyers or NGOs leading the way with new rights-claims (Cichowski 2007; Epp 1998; Pavone 2022; Tate and Vallinder 1995; Vanhala 2010); elite-level interactions, such as legislative or executive deferrals (Carruba, Gabel, and Hankla 2008; Gallagher 2017; Ginsburg 2006; Larsson et al. 2017); and judges' preferences based on normative commitments or their pursuit of institutional power (Graber 1993; Hilbink 2009; Hirschl 2004; Moravcsik 2000; Pevehouse 2005; Weiler 1994).

The making of the ECtHR into a labor court was in part driven by mobilization from below. Innovative and committed lawyers brought well-argued cases regarding blatant rights violations workers experienced after the neoliberal transformation in their countries, as

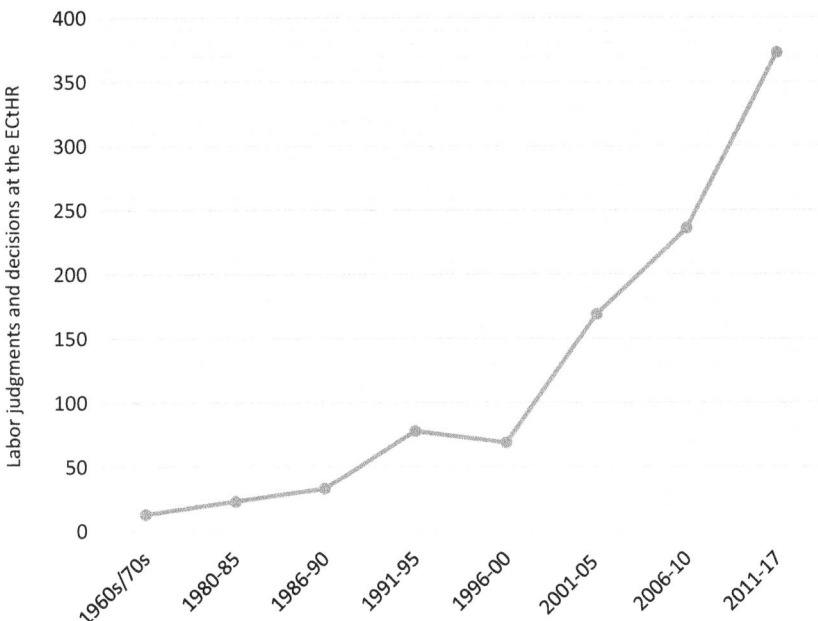

Figure 4.1 Annual number of labor cases at the ECtHR
Labor judgments and decisions before the ECtHR, 1960–2017 (N = 992)
Source: StrasLab.

will be discussed in the next chapter. But it is not just the sheer number of these cases that is noteworthy. The Court's finding of at least one violation in its judgments on labor cases rose from 36 percent in the pre-1990 period to 85 percent in the post-1990s. In response to the cases brought before it from workers across Europe, the ECtHR started to interpret the Convention to include some basic labor rights and became judicially more responsive to labor claims. Tracing the political context within which the Court was established and developed over time highlights the significance of political and institutional forces that shaped the ECtHR's judicial responsiveness to labor rights.

4.2.1 The Conservative Origins of the ECtHR
Established in the aftermath of World War II, the CoE followed the dominant human rights framework at the time and established the

ECtHR primarily as a civil and political rights court.[3] The protection of socioeconomic rights, along with labor rights, was delegated to the ECSR under a much weaker monitoring system. Unlike the ECtHR, the ECSR accepts collective petitions from certain governmental and non-governmental bodies, and only fifteen out of forty-six CoE members (not including Turkey or the UK) have accepted the collective complaint mechanism. Many member states have either not ratified or expressed reservations on many articles of the ESC, which the ECSR oversees. As a result, core labor rights are protected under a charter that allows states to selectively opt out of compliance.

The conservative origins of the ECtHR are rooted in the ideological commitments of its inventors. Duranti's historical research on the creation of the Court shows that these inventors, including prominent British Conservatives, intended to design a supranational court that upheld values of classical liberalism not only to contain communism and fascism in Europe, as is commonly argued (Bates 2010; Moravcsik 2000), but also to constrain the ability of national governments to pass left-wing economic policies favored by social democrats in Europe (Duranti 2017). As a result, while the Convention includes strong protections for property rights, core labor rights – along with other socioeconomic rights – are largely excluded, except for a vague reference to the right to unionize under Article 11. Indeed, earlier legal studies indicated that the ECtHR's interpretation of Article 11 in response to the few labor rights cases brought before it was "formalistic" (Wedderburn 1991: 144) and that the Court was more interested in "defense of individual autonomy than collective solidarity" (Novitz 2003: 238). It is also important to note, however, that during these early years, most CoE member states had relatively strong welfare regimes and trade unions. The Court had not yet been presented with the kinds of cases where trade unions faced existential threats, as they did in the post-1980 period.

4.2.2 From Marginal Player to Judicial Powerhouse: The ECtHR's Rise to Authority

The workers' search for an alternative venue to claim their rights coincided with the ECtHR's rise to prominence in European

---

[3] The UN, similarly, established two separate covenants for civil and political rights on the one hand and socioeconomic rights on the other, and put in place a weaker oversight mechanism for the latter. Nevertheless, the ILO was already in existence to protect workers' rights when the UN human rights system was being set up in the postwar period.

politics.[4] The first signals of the ECtHR's willingness to diverge from the intentions of the drafters of the Convention and expand its jurisprudence can be traced back to the 1970s when a new cohort of young and progressive judges assumed their positions (Madsen 2007: 152–153). In *Tyrer v. the United Kingdom* (1978: para. 31) the Court established its doctrine of the Convention being "a living instrument" that "must be interpreted in the light of present-day conditions." The following year, the ECtHR moved toward adopting a more holistic approach to human rights by rejecting a strict separation between civil and political rights versus socioeconomic rights (*Airey v. Ireland* 1979). However, the Court had yet to issue rulings that provided any protections for labor rights during this period.

Throughout the 1980s, the Court continued to expand its thematic reach, and human rights started to influence national politics. Human rights centers and legal advocacy organizations started to proliferate across Europe and national judges increasingly incorporated the ECtHR's rulings into their jurisprudence. Though the ECtHR had not yet secured a prominent place in public discourse in this period, "the Europeanized concept of human rights effectively entered the mainstream of the legal field" (Madsen 2007: 154).[5]

The most dramatic shift occurred in the 1990s, as the ECtHR's case law expanded both in scale and scope. The number of cases before the ECtHR surged from 596 in 1985 to 8,400 in 1999 and 41,700 in 2020.[6] This increase partly reflects the growing awareness and willingness among European citizens and lawyers to appeal to the ECtHR as a legitimate institution. The Court released landmark rulings on issues considered to be "mega-politics" (Hirschl 2008), including the treatment of terrorism suspects, women's right to wear a headscarf, and the rights of migrants. At the same time, the post-Soviet period saw the doubling of the ECtHR's member states, with most Central and Eastern European countries joining the CoE system. In particular, Russia and

---

[4] I emphasize the concurrent development of these two processes because there is no evidence to suggest a causal relationship between the ECtHR's rising political influence and the spread of neoliberal policies in Europe. For an argument on how the rise of human rights strengthened or legitimized neoliberal policies, see Brown (2004), Marks (2011), and Whyte (2019).

[5] The rise of the ECtHR and human rights more generally aligns with parallel trends around the world (Alter 2014; Moyn 2012).

[6] The numbers represent the applications that were received by the Registry and allocated to a judicial formation each year (ECtHR 2002, 2007, 2021).

Turkey's membership posed new challenges for the Court; it was presented with new forms of human rights abuses, including state violence during civil wars, as well as a mountain of repetitive cases stemming from compliance issues.[7] Despite the challenges, the growing importance and volume of its rulings elevated the Court to a key player in European politics, widely regarded as having a positive impact on democratization in these countries (Brems 2011; Sweeney 2013).[8] This was also a period of eastward EU expansion, and the prospect of joining the EU provided an additional incentive for these countries to strengthen human rights protections because the EU made direct references to ECtHR rulings when evaluating candidate countries' human rights record (Holzhacker 2013; Kochenov 2008; Schimmelfennig and Sedelmeier 2005).

To consolidate its position after these developments, the Court underwent a major institutional reform in 1998 (Protocol 11). Under the old system, the ECtHR operated under a two-tier framework: Applications were first filtered by the Commission, which then referred the admissible cases to the Court or the CM to determine the merits of the cases. With the adoption of Protocol No. 11, the Commission was abolished, and the adjudicative powers of the CM were consolidated under the body of a single court. Most notably, the right of individual petition and the jurisdiction of the Court became mandatory for all member states. Prior to 1998, member states could formally opt out of the ECtHR's jurisdiction, even after ratifying the Convention. Thus, when workers turned to the ECtHR in the 1990s, the Court had already cemented its position as the "supreme European Court" with binding jurisdiction on all member states (Madsen 2007: 154). The ECtHR was ripe for legal mobilization.

4.3 BROADENING THE SCOPE: LABOR RIGHTS IN ECTHR CASE LAW

The only articles in the Convention that explicitly protect workers' rights are the prohibition of slavery and forced labor (Article 4) and

---

[7] Turkey had been a CoE member since 1950, but it accepted the Court's jurisdiction in 1990.

[8] www.routledge.com/The-European-Court-of-Human-Rights-in-the-Post-Cold-War-Era-Universality-in-Transition/Sweeney/p/book/9780415544337; https://doi.org/10.1093/ijtj/ijr010.

the freedom of assembly and association (Article 11).⁹ Yet, within the first four decades of its existence, the Court did not find any violation of workers' rights under these articles.¹⁰ By the late 1990s, however, the Court started not only to issue violation rulings under these two articles, but also to include a wide range of labor rights under other provisions of the Convention. This turn became particularly pronounced in the 2000s, when the Court delivered judgments with far-reaching implications for workers. The growing number and variety of cases pointed to a significant transformation taking place at the ECtHR: Workers across Europe were turning to international human rights mechanisms to seek remedies for myriad labor rights violations.

The analysis below provides an overview of the trajectory and breadth of this case law, illustrating how a court originally designed to safeguard civil and political rights became a labor court. To demonstrate both the ECtHR's new approach toward labor rights as well as its limitations, I highlight some of the key cases in each category – though the discussion is far from exhaustive.¹¹ Trade union rights under Article 11 arguably constitute the area where the Court has issued its most influential and controversial rulings. The ECtHR's attention to trade union rights is particularly significant because labor activists and scholars consider trade union protections as foundational for securing other labor rights (Flanagan 2006; Rodríguez-Garavito 2005; Rosenfeld 2014). Strong trade unions are viewed as critical safeguards for fair wages, social security, health and safety at work, and other labor rights. Unions demand these rights collectively, amplifying the bargaining power of otherwise isolated workers. The overview is followed by a section that zooms in on trade union rights.

---

[9] Article 11 states that "Everyone has the right to freedom of peaceful assembly and to freedom of association with others, including the right to form and to join trade unions for the protection of his interests."

[10] The only exception is that the ECtHR found Article 11 violation in cases brought by workers complaining about closed shop agreements, which is a system that strengthened the power of trade unions, as discussed below.

[11] StrasLab includes cases from 1960 to 2017, but the discussion includes some of the more recent examples from the Court's case law. See ECtHR Factsheets on Work-Related Rights (2003), Forced Labor (2012), Surveillance at Workplace (2017) and Trade Union Rights (2014) for more examples of landmark cases in each category. See also Dorssemont, Lörcher, and Schömann (2013) and Sychenko (2017) for a jurisprudential analysis of the Court's evolving labor case law.

A NEW AVENUE FOR WORKERS AT THE INTERNATIONAL LEVEL

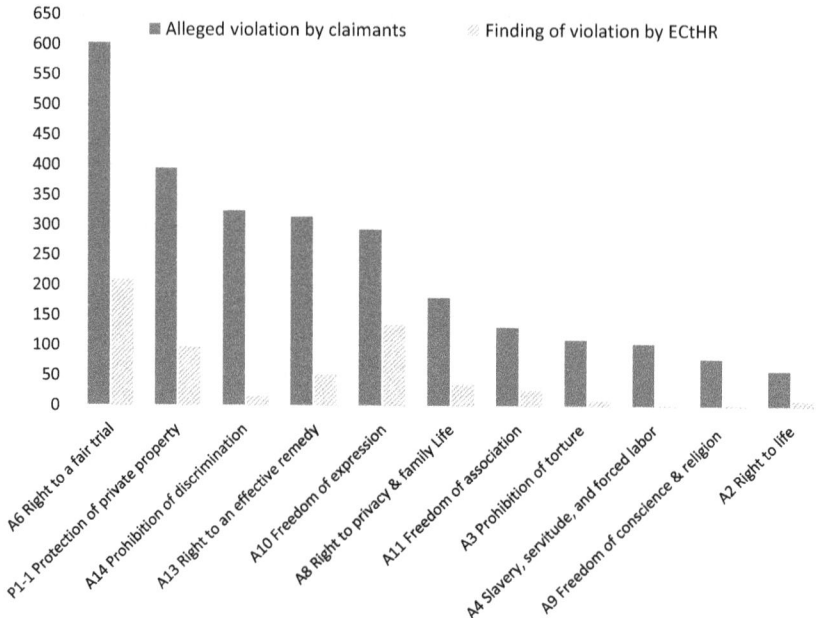

Figure 4.2 Convention articles and protocols invoked and violated in labor cases
Labor judgments and decisions before the ECtHR, 1960–2017 (N = 992)
Source: StrasLab.

4.3.1 Overview of the Diversity of Labor Cases

Figure 4.2 depicts the breakdown of the Convention articles and protocols that were invoked by claimants in decisions and judgments (alleged violations) alongside the ECtHR's findings of violation in judgments. Since most labor rights are not explicitly protected under the Convention, I have categorized labor rights claims under different thematic groups. Figure 4.3 visualizes these different types of labor claims, including judgments and decisions. The categories in the figures are not mutually exclusive since applicants often complain of multiple types of labor rights violations within a single case. The "most important cases" are those that the Court identified as precedent-setting or significantly shaping the ECtHR's case law.[12]

---

[12] As explained in Chapter 3, the Court assigns importance level to its own case law based on the significance of a case in developing the existing case law: *case reports* are precedents since the inception of the new Court in 1998, *high-importance* cases

84

4.3 BROADENING THE SCOPE

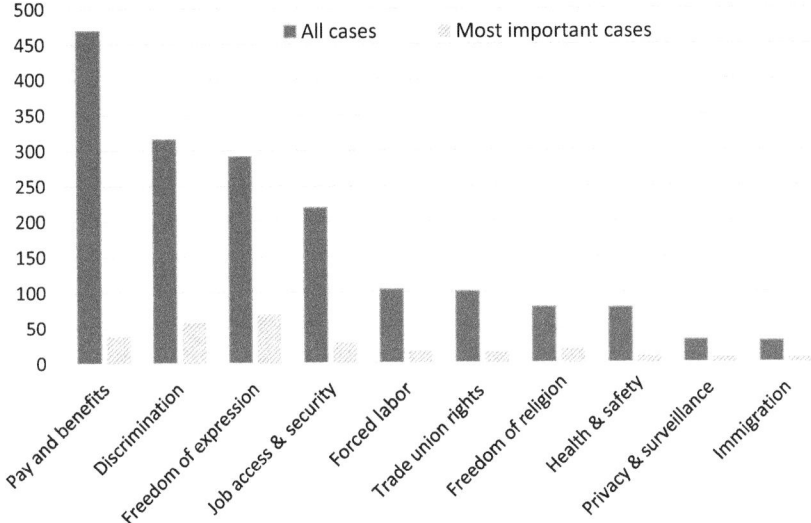

Figure 4.3 Types of labor claims and the most important cases
Labor judgments and decisions before the ECtHR, 1960–2017 (N = 992)
Source: StrasLab.

A separate focus on these cases allows us to see where the Court's labor case law expanded with new rights claims, whereas "all cases" include many repetitive cases.

The highest number of cases is in the wages and benefits category, though this is not the area where the ECtHR's rulings have been the most transformative. Notably, the proportion of the most important cases in this area is the lowest (8 percent), compared to cases concerning freedom of religion or freedom of expression, where approximately a quarter qualify as most important cases. Trade union rights cases – alongside other Article 11 claims – do not represent the highest number of claims overall, nor do they constitute a large percentage of the most important cases. However, qualitative analysis shows that the

make a significant contribution to the development of the case law, *medium-importance* cases go beyond merely applying existing case law, while not making a significant contribution, *low-importance* cases simply apply the existing case law. The category of "most important cases" includes case reports and high-importance cases. While these data illustrate general trends, my qualitative analysis of labor case law across categories is not limited to the Court-ascribed precedent-setting designations.

Court's changing approach to trade union rights claims has been the most salient, as I shall discuss below.

Access to a fair trial (Article 6) is the most frequently invoked article in labor cases, and the Court is most likely to find violation of this provision (Figure 4.2), a pattern that aligns with the ECtHR's overall case law.[13] Since repetitive cases often result from systemic problems, the Court's violation findings in such cases tend to be high.[14] The same goes for property rights cases (Protocol 1 of Article 1, P1-1); both the alleged violations and the finding of violations are elevated due to repetitive cases. Only 11 percent of cases where the claimant alleges a violation of Article 6 are classified among the Court's most important case law. The percentage of most important cases among property rights cases is even lower at 8 percent. The low proportion of most important cases among fair trial and property rights claims confirms that most of these cases are repetitive cases.

Nonetheless, the Court's expansive interpretation of Article 6 in labor cases strengthened protections provided for workers.[15] In its earlier case law, the Court contended that "disputes relating to the recruitment, careers and termination of service of civil servants are as a general rule outside the scope of Article 6" (*Massa v. Italy* 1993: para. 26). However, the ECtHR later overturned this principle, effectively allowing public sector workers to seek procedural justice in cases regarding dismissals or promotions (*Vilho Eskelinen and Others v. Finland* 2007; see also *Pellegrin v. France* 1999; *Sabeh El Leil v. France* 2011). The Court further expanded its case law by finding an Article 6 violation in a case where a worker's access to justice was obstructed due to financial difficulties (*Ülger v. Turkey* 2007) and by holding that the impartiality of domestic labor courts is not necessarily compromised because representatives from workers' and employers' associations serve on a judicial board (*AB Kurt Kellermann v. Sweden* 2004).

---

[13] Nearly 40 percent of the ECtHR's violation judgments from 1959 to 2017 concerned an Article 6 violation (ECtHR 2018). Among the Court's violation judgments in labor cases during the same period, 49 percent concerned Article 6 violations.

[14] The structural problems in the justice system of a few countries – mainly Italy, Turkey, Russia, and Ukraine – dominate these cases (ECtHR 2018).

[15] Cases where the applicant invoked only Article 6 or 13 are not included in the database. Although the dispute concerned workers' rights in the domestic courts, the application before the ECtHR raised only procedural complaints rather than substantive labor rights issues. See Drooghenbroeck (2014) for an extensive analysis of the Court's labor rights jurisprudence under Article 6.

4.3 BROADENING THE SCOPE

The highest number of labor disputes concern issues related to workers' *pay and benefits*, although there is no provision in the Convention that explicitly protects these rights. A significant portion of these cases (80 percent) invoke the right to property (P1-1), which entered into force in 1954 as an optional protocol and has become the second most invoked provision in all labor judgments (Figure 4.2). There is now a fairly developed case law where the ECtHR recognizes restrictions on access to disability pensions (*Kjartan Ásmundsson v. Iceland* 2004) or the reduction of benefits acquired in a previous collective bargaining agreement (*Aizpurua Ortiz and Others v. Spain* 2010) and the confiscation of wages obtained through work using a false passport (*Paulet v. the United Kingdom* 2014) as violations of property rights. However, the Court is generally reluctant to engage in any substantive debates about minimum or living wage calculations. For example, in cases regarding the inclusion of tips as part of salary calculations in the restaurant industry (*Nerva and Others v. the United Kingdom* 2002) or salary cuts introduced as part of austerity measures (*Koufaki and ADEDY v. Greece* 2013) the Court found no violations. The Court found a violation only in extreme cases, such as the imposition of a 98 percent tax on a portion of an applicant's severance payment (*N. K. M. v. Hungary* 2013). In general, the ECtHR leaves a wide margin of appreciation for domestic authorities in these types of cases (Sychenko 2017: 191; see also Herzfeld Olsson 2013).[16]

The second category with the highest number of cases is *workplace discrimination*, where the ECtHR has addressed a wide range of matters, including discrimination based on age, ethnicity, race, nationality (including stateless people), immigration status, gender, sexual orientation, disability, and criminal background, among others, mainly under Article 14. One of the most consequential cases in this area is undoubtedly *Konstantin Markin v. Russia* (2012), where the Court departed from its previous jurisprudence (*Petrovic v. Austria* 1998) and found that the Russian government's legal provision regarding parental leave, which excluded fathers, constituted gender discrimination (Article 14 taken together with Article 8).[17] While the judgment did not explicitly affirm

---

[16] Margin of appreciation is an established doctrine of the ECtHR and refers to the leeway given to states in applying the Convention provisions at the domestic level. It recognizes that there can be reasonable differences in the domestic applicant of human rights laws.

[17] See also *Hulea v. Romania* (2012).

a general right to parental leave under Article 8, the Court noted that when this right is provided, the state cannot discriminate based on gender. Some of the claims regarding dismissals, differential treatment in access to pensions (*Stummer v. Austria* 2011) as well as working time arrangements (*Garcia Mateos v. Spain* 2013) also fall under Court's case law on discrimination. However, the Court imposes stringent standards when assessing Article 14 claims (e.g. *Fábián v. Hungary* 2017). In only 5 percent of claims invoking Article 14 did the Court find a violation. Part of the reason behind the Court's restrictive interpretation stems from Article 14's framing, which is not designed to eliminate all forms of discrimination, but rather to ensure the enjoyment of the rights and freedoms set forth in the Convention without discrimination. Efforts to expand the Court's interpretation of discrimination resulted in the adoption of Protocol 12, but the progress on its ratification has been slow; therefore, the case law on this protocol is underdeveloped.[18]

Freedom of expression (Article 10) claims constitute the third largest category of cases but rank highest in terms of the Court's responsiveness to alleged violations. In nearly half of the cases (46 percent) where the applicant makes an Article 10 claim, the ECtHR finds a violation. A big portion of freedom of expression cases in StrasLab concern the freedom of journalists, or press workers broadly construed, where applicants complain about facing criminal charges or censorship because of their publications. Within the past decade, the Court started to apply these principles to other types of workers' claims and recognized the inherently vulnerable position of workers relative to their employers in the workplace. Most prominently, in a series of landmark judgments on whistleblowing, the Court ruled that dismissing public sector workers – including intelligence service members – due to their public disclosure of illegal conduct by state representatives (*Guja v. Moldova* 2008; *Bucur and Toma v. Romania* 2013) and terminating private sector workers who blew the whistle on the incriminating behavior of their employers (*Heinisch v. Germany* 2011) constituted violations of freedom of expression. In cases where the leaks served no public interest but instead caused harm to individuals, such as the case brought by a prison officer who leaked information to a tabloid (*Norman v. the United Kingdom* 2021), the Court found no violation. More recently, the Court has addressed the growing use of censorship and repression tactics by

---

[18] See Bruun (2014) for a more detailed discussion on workplace discrimination cases at the ECtHR.

governments. For example, in Turkey, a cleaner was dismissed by the Ministry of National Education for having clicked the "Like" button on various Facebook posts (*Melike v. Turkey* 2021), which the Court deemed a violation of freedom of expression.

The category with the fourth highest number of cases contains a broad range of disputes concerning *job access and security*, including claims regarding unfair dismissals as well as workers who have been denied promotion or a license to work. There are no Convention articles that directly protect employment access or job security, but the Court's most notable case law in this area has developed through its interpretation of civil liberties, including alleged violations of freedom of expression (Article 10), the right to private life (Article 8), freedom of religion and conscience (Article 9), freedom of association (Article 11), and various forms of discrimination (Article 14) in unfair dismissal claims. In response to these cases, the Court has emphasized that "business necessity" or "national security" are not sufficient reasons to deny work to disadvantaged groups. In cases concerning the prohibition of former KGB (Committee for State Security, Soviet Union) officers from finding employment in the private sector (*Sidabras and Džiautas v. Lithuania* 2004), dismissal of a security officer on the grounds that night shifts and physically demanding work were unfit for women (*Emel Boyraz v. Turkey* 2014), and the dismissal of a worker simply because he was HIV positive (*I. B. v. Greece* 2013), the Court found violations of Article 8 in conjunction with Article 14. Noting that "the hallmarks of a 'democratic society' include pluralism, tolerance and broadmindedness," the Court decided that discharging members of the armed forces due to sexual orientation also constituted violations of Article 8 (*Beck, Copp and Bazeley v. the United Kingdom* 2002; *Lustig-Prean and Beckett v. the United Kingdom* 1999; *Perkins and R. v. the United Kingdom* 2002; *Smith and Grady v. the United Kingdom* 1999: para. 87). Additionally, the Court ruled that the dismissal of a driver transporting a group of mostly Asian people with disabilities due to his membership to an allegedly white-supremacist political party violated Article 11 (*Redfearn v. the United Kingdom* 2012). Conversely, in *Pay v. the United Kingdom* (2008), the Court dismissed a case regarding the discharge of a probation officer who engaged in BDSM activities due to the sensitive nature of the applicant's work involving sex offenders.[19]

---

[19] BDSM refers to a wide range of activities including bondage and discipline, dominance and submission, and sadism and masochism.

The *forced labor* category is composed of claims on Article 4 (prohibition of slavery, servitude, and forced labor), which is one of the two articles that explicitly protect labor rights and is a non-derogable right. As with most other labor rights cases, the Court dismissed all Article 4 claims during the first four decades of its existence. But since 2005, the Court's rulings in this area have been pivotal as it started to consider the precarious working conditions of immigrants when interpreting the meaning of forced labor and slavery in contemporary Europe. The first landmark case, *Siliadin v. France* (2005) concerned a Togolese national who was brought to France when she was fifteen under false pretenses and was forced to become an unpaid domestic worker. In finding the applicant's work conditions and her deprivation of liberty to amounted to servitude, the Court acknowledged that victims whose passports have been confiscated find themselves "in a situation of total vulnerability with regard to their employers" and experience "physical and emotional isolation" (para. 49). The Court also referenced Recommendation 1523 of the PACE, which noted that "a new form of slavery has appeared in Europe," but found that the circumstances of the case did not amount to slavery, which according to the Court would require proof of legal ownership of the worker.[20]

Siliadin led to a rapid development of new case law (*C. N. v. the United Kingdom* 2012; *C. N. and V. v. France* 2012; *Kawogo v. the United Kingdom* 2013) where the Court identified the lack of legislation criminalizing domestic servitude as the cause of inadequate protections provided to victims at the domestic level. The Court further broadened the scope of Article 4 in *Rantsev v. Cyprus and Russia* (2010), concerning a woman who was trafficked from Russia to Cyprus for sex work. She tried to escape her exploitative work conditions but was returned to her employer by the police, only to be found dead after her release. The Court noted that labor exploitation constitutes the treatment of "human beings as commodities to be bought and sold" and went on to adopt the term "modern slavery," which, by then, had been widely used by human rights activists to describe human trafficking. In a series of cases following *Rantsev*, the Court specified the conditions under which expulsion may be permissible (*L. R. v. the United Kingdom* 2011) and outlined positive obligations of states regarding the prevention and investigation of human trafficking (*Chowdury and Others v. Greece*

---

[20] See Mantouvalou (2006, 2013) for a detailed discussion on the ECtHR's early case law on modern slavery under Article 4.

2017; *L. E. v. Greece* 2016; *S. M. v. Croatia* 2020; *V. C. L. and A. N. v. the United Kingdom* 2021).

These remarkable cases on modern slavery notwithstanding, the Court has adopted a narrow interpretation of slavery and forced labor in other issue areas. In accordance with the exceptions listed in Article 4(3) regarding work in military service, detention, and civic obligations, the Court ruled that the following claims did not constitute violations of Article 4: twenty-eight years of prison labor without access to pensions (*Stummer v Austria* 2011), requirement of pro bono work for lawyers (*X v. Federal Republic of Germany* 1974; see also *Van Der Mussele v. Belgium* 1983), and the requirement of a prisoner to work beyond the retirement age (*Meier v. Switzerland* 2016). Similarly, in *Eker v. Turkey* (1998) a seasonal farm worker claimed he worked without pay for months, but the Court upheld the national court's finding of insufficient evidence.

One issue area where the Court's approach has been the subject of controversy concerns *freedom of religion* in the workplace, composed of Article 9 (freedom of religion and conscience) claims. After Article 4 claims, this is the issue area in which the Court is least likely to rule a violation. In only 4 percent of Article 9 claims has the Court ruled in favor of applicants.[21] The Court's handling of cases involving religious symbols in the workplace has been especially contentious.[22] In *Eweida and others v. the United Kingdom* (2013), the Court held that a flight attendant's right to wear a cross fell under the right to manifest religious affiliation. By contrast, it held that dismissing a school teacher for wearing a headscarf (*Dahlab v. Switzerland* 2001) or refusing to renew the contract of a hospital social worker due to her decision to wear a veil (*Ebrahimian v. France* 2015) did not constitute a breach of Article 9. The Court reasoned that these Islamic religious symbols could have a "proselytizing effect" and risk compromising the neutrality of the services provided. These cases, along with a highly contentious case concerning the display of a cross in public schools in Italy – where the Court found the cross, as opposed to the headscarf, to be a "passive" religious symbol (*Lautsi and Others v. Italy* 2011) – led some scholars to raise the question of whether the ECtHR applies double standards

---

[21] This rate is 3 percent for Article 4 claims.
[22] There is also a fairly developed case law on dismissals (*Obst v. Germany* 2010; *Rommelfanger v. Germany* 1989; *Schuth v. Germany* 2010; *Siebanhaar v. Germany* 2011). See Vickers (2014) for a more detailed discussion.

when the rights of Muslim minorities in Europe are at stake (Danchin 2011; Elver 2014; cf. Joppke 2013; Koenig 2015).

Workers' health and safety is arguably the least developed yet one of the most critical areas of labor rights in ECtHR's case law. For many workers, the workplace is a dangerous environment; according to the ILO, every year over 2 million people die due to work, and millions more suffer lifelong impairments due to work-related diseases and injuries. The ECtHR identifies the right to life (Article 2) and the prohibition of torture and inhuman or degrading treatment (Article 3) as non-derogable rights and "as the most fundamental provisions of the Convention" (*Brincat and Others v. Malta* 2014: para. 59).[23] Yet until very recently the Court has paid little attention to workers' health and safety. This is in part due to the limited number of cases brought before it and in part due to the absence of robust provisions that address this issue in the Convention. In the few initial cases, applicants primarily challenged the fairness of domestic proceedings or the amount of compensation awarded under Article 6 and P1-1, but the Court quickly dismissed these claims, stating that it was not its role to act as "a court of appeal" and that domestic courts were best positioned to assess witness credibility and the relevance of evidence (*Dikici v. Turkey* 2009: para. 16).

The Court set a significant precedent on workers' health and safety in the 2013 case of *Vilnes and Others v. Norway* (2013) concerning the applicants who were divers and had been disabled due to their work in the North Sea during the pioneer period of oil exploration from 1965 to 1990. The Court ruled that as their employer, the Norwegian government's failure to provide essential information on the occupational risks amounted to a breach of Article 8. However, much to the disappointment of the applicants and pro-worker organizations, the Court dismissed claims that the government's failure to protect workers from health hazards amounted to violations under Articles 2 and 3. A year later, the Court for the first time found an Article 2 violation in *Brincat and Others v. Malta* (2014), a case concerning shipyard repair workers exposed to asbestos, which resulted in the death of one worker.[24] In addition to the Article 2 violation, the Court found that the

---

[23] Article 2 is a non-derogable right except in the context of lawful acts of war (Article 15).

[24] The Court referenced its developing case law on positive obligations of states under Article 2, particularly in socioeconomic rights cases (*L. C. B. v. the UK* 1998; *Öneryıldız v. Turkey* 2004).

authorities' failure to take preventive measures for other workers amounted to a violation of Article 8, given the availability of scientific knowledge on the threats posed by asbestos at the time. Although these two cases could have opened the door to a whole range of cases related to occupational health and safety to be brought before the ECtHR, many similar attempts failed. The primary reason is that the Court does not find violations in cases where domestic authorities have already provided some compensation (*Dikici v. Turkey* 2009). For example, in *Vilnes*, the Court dismissed the applicants' Article 3 claims because they were already receiving government pensions for their health conditions, and the ECtHR only awarded further compensation because the government had not informed the workers of the possible risks at the time (Article 8). Hence, many cases on occupational health and safety fail to reach the ECtHR's high standards for establishing a violation.

The ECtHR has also expanded the interpretation of Article 8 to address cases regarding *privacy and surveillance in the workplace*, which has become more complex as technological advancements enhance employers' monitoring capabilities. The Court strived to define what constitutes a legitimate aim to restrict workers' reasonable expectations on privacy. *Halford v. the United Kingdom* (1997) is an early example where the Court established that the interception of the applicant's phone calls without her knowledge violated Article 8. The applicant, who was the highest-ranking female police officer in the UK at the time, had an ongoing discrimination case against the police department regarding her being denied promotion, and she claimed that her calls had been intercepted to use the information against her during the proceedings. The Court applied the same reasoning in *Copland v. the United Kingdom* (2007), where the applicant's telephone, email, and internet usage had been monitored by her employer, a public university, without prior warning. In a case where university professors complained about the cameras installed in classrooms by the university administration for safety reasons, the Court contended that private life can include professional activities and found the video surveillance to constitute an Article 8 violation (*Antovic and Mirkovic v. Montenegro* 2017). On the other hand, the Court ruled that an employer, upon suspecting theft or misconduct by workers, can institute cameras to surveil the workplace (*Köpke v. Germany* 2010; *López Ribalda and Others v. Spain* 2019).[25]

---

[25] For a more detailed discussion on privacy in the workplace, see Hendrickx and Bever (2014).

4.4 EVOLVING TRADE UNIONS RIGHTS JURISPRUDENCE ACROSS THREE PHASES

The Court has issued its most influential cases on trade union rights by reversing its previous case law and adopting a new interpretation of Article 11.[26] Through landmark cases, brought primarily by unionists in Turkey and the UK, the Court recognized three core trade union rights as human rights: the right to unionize, the right to collective bargaining, and the right to take collective action. Below I examine the ECtHR's changing jurisprudence on trade union rights across three periods: an initial phase of doctrinal restraint, a period of expansive interpretation during the 2000s, and a more recent phase of judicial retrenchment in response to political backlash.

4.4.1 Initial Phase: The Conservative Approach to Trade Union Rights

For its first four decades, the ECtHR's rulings on trade union rights bore the imprint of its conservative origins. In *Swedish Engine Drivers' Union v. Sweden* (1976) and *National Union of Belgian Police v. Belgium* (1975), the Court decided that Article 11 did not impose any specific mechanisms on member states for the protection of trade union rights. Similarly, in *Schmidt and Dahlström v. Sweden* (1976: para. 36), while the Court recognized that "the Convention safeguards freedom to protect the occupational interests of trade union members by trade union action," it nevertheless granted a wide margin of appreciation to states by noting that they have "a free choice of the means to be used towards this end." These early judgments illustrate the Court's view that labor rights did not constitute a core area of human rights and hence could be relegated to the domestic level.

In the 1980s, the Court started to take a more active role in the adjudication of these claims but not in favor of trade unions. In *Young, James and Webster v. The United Kingdom* (1981), a case supported by a conservative British NGO, applicants challenged closed shop agreements, which are arrangements that require all employees at a workplace to be represented by a single trade union. The ECtHR found the agreements violated Article 11.[27] In *Council of Civil Service Unions et al.*

---

[26] Claims involving trade unions or their members that do not invoke Article 11, such as pension disputes or freedom of speech claims by union members, are excluded from this category.

[27] See the discussion in Chapter 3.

4.4 EVOLVING TRADE UNIONS RIGHTS

TABLE 4.1 Notable ECtHR rulings on trade union rights across three phases

Phase	Case name	Key contribution	A-11 Violation
Initial phase	*National Union of Belgian Police v. Belgium* (1975); *Schmidt and Dahlström v. Sweden* (1976); *Swedish Engine Drivers' Union v. Sweden* (1976)	Affirmed broad state discretion under margin of appreciation and denied positive obligations to protect union activity	No
	Young, James and Webster v. the United Kingdom (1981)	Invalidated closed shop agreements; narrowed scope of union freedom	Yes
	Council of Civil Service Unions et al. v. The United Kingdom (1987)	Dismissed union strike ban complaint; reaffirmed state's discretion	No
Expansion phase	*Wilson v. the UK* (2002)	Imposed positive obligation on states to protect union rights from employer interference	Yes
	Tüm Haber Sen and Çınar v. Turkey (2006)	Affirmed public sector workers' right to unionize	Yes
	ASLEF v. The United Kingdom (2007)	Upheld union autonomy in defining membership	Yes
	Demir and Baykara v. Turkey (2008)	Established collective bargaining as essential under A-11	Yes
	Enerji Yapi-Yol Sen v. Turkey (2009)	First ruling recognizing strike action under A-11	Yes
	Karaçay v. Turkey (2007); *Saime Özcan v. Turkey* (2009)	Sanctioning striking workers violates A-11	Yes
	Danilenkov and Others v. Russia (2009)	Recognized dismissal of striking workers as anti-union discrimination (A-14+11)	Yes

TABLE 4.1 (cont.)

Phase	Case name	Key contribution	A-11 Violation
Retrenchment phase	*Palomo Sánchez and Others v. Spain* (2011)	Upheld dismissals of unionists for offensive expression	No
	RMT v. The United Kingdom (2014)	Denied violation in sympathy strike ban case; affirmed accessory nature of strike rights	No
	Barış and Others v. Turkey (2021)	Narrowed A-11 protection by excluding wildcat strikes; upheld dismissals of workers protesting employer-aligned union	No
	Humpert and Others v. Germany (2023)	Upheld public sector workers' strike ban in Germany despite earlier precedent	No

v. The United Kingdom (1987), the Court rejected British public sector workers' complaints regarding the restrictions on the rights to unionize and strike. Although these cases arguably lacked the urgency of the blatant trade union rights violation claims that Turkish and British unionists brought before the Court a decade later, they still indicate the ECtHR's reluctance to move away from the narrow role defined for trade union rights by the original drafters of the Convention.

4.4.2 Expansion Phase: The Golden Years for Trade Unions at the ECtHR

The ECtHR's institutional empowerment and jurisprudential expansion throughout the 1990s yielded its first result in 1996 when the Court gestured toward a new interpretation of trade union rights. In *Gustafsson v. Sweden* (1996), the Court ruled that the trade union action aimed at pressuring an employer to sign a collective agreement did not infringe on his right to freedom of association or his property rights. While this case did not impose any positive duties on the state to protect collective action or the right to collective bargaining, it nevertheless was a rare case where the Court granted a margin of appreciation to states when issuing a judgment favorable to trade unions.

The real turning point was in 2002, when the Court held that states have a positive obligation to protect the right to unionize in a case from the UK. *Wilson. v. The United Kingdom* (2002) was a highly contentious case concerning whether employers offering better contracts to non-unionized workers constituted a violation of workers' right to unionize (see Chapter 5). Without the collective power of the trade unions, workers had no guarantee that they would be able to maintain their advantageous contracts in the long run. In a landmark judgment, the Court found the UK to be in violation of Article 11, noting the inadequacy of domestic protections, which made it "possible for an employer effectively to undermine or frustrate a trade union's ability to strive for the protection of its members' interests" (para. 48). This was the first time the ECtHR issued a pro-labor ruling in a case brought by a union. The Court further signaled its willingness to expand the meaning of Article 11 by noting that:

> it must be possible for a trade union which is not recognized by an employer to take steps including, if necessary, organizing industrial action, with a view to persuading the employer to enter into collective bargaining with it on those issues which the union believes are important for its members' interests ... If workers are prevented from so doing, their freedom to belong to a trade union, for the protection of their interests, becomes illusory. (*Wilson v. The United Kingdom* 2002: para 46)

Throughout the 2000s, the ECtHR continued to establish key precedents recognizing basic trade union rights. In *Tüm Haber Sen and Çınar v. Turkey* (2006), the Court recognized that the state has a positive obligation to ensure effective exercise of workers' right to establish and join unions in the public sector. A year later, in *ASLEF v. The United Kingdom* (2007), it affirmed a union's right to define its own membership, ruling in favor of a British union that had expelled a member of the far-right British National Party (BNP). The ruling explicitly recognized the political nature of trade unions, which are not merely service organizations, and hence acknowledged the collective dimension of labor rights (Ford and Hendy 2007). As the Court observed, unions are "commonly affiliated to political parties or movements, particularly those on the left" and are "often ideological, with strongly held views on social and political issues" (para. 50).

The most remarkable judgment came in *Demir and Baykara v. Turkey* (2008), in which the Grand Chamber unanimously reversed its earlier case law to establish collective bargaining as an integral part of freedom of association. The case emerged in 1993 when a Municipal Council in Turkey refused to honor its obligations under a collective agreement. The domestic courts dismissed the case brought by the union on the basis that no legal framework for collective bargaining agreements existed in the public sector. Departing from its earlier formalist approach, the ECtHR ruled that the absence of domestic legislation could not justify denying the union's rights under Article 11. A defining feature of the *Demir and Baykara* judgment was the Court's use of other international laws to interpret collective bargaining rights, given the absence of explicit protections in the Convention. Demonstrating its commitment to an "integrated approach" to human rights law, the Court referenced ILO Conventions, the ESC, and the EU Charter of Fundamental Rights to establish collective bargaining as a fundamental human right (Mantouvalou 2013). In doing so, the Court signaled its willingness to draw on instruments beyond the European Convention, even those not ratified by the respondent state. This "integrated approach" bolstered the authority of international labor standards while positioning the ECtHR as a leading venue for advancing trade union rights in Europe.[28]

Building on this precedent, the Court addressed the right to strike. Once again, cases from Turkey, where the government had a blanket ban on public sector workers' right to strike, were instrumental in building this case law. As discussed in the introduction, *Enerji Yapi-Yol Sen v. Turkey* (2009) marked the first time the ECtHR recognized strike action as a protected form of union activity under Article 11 (see also *Dilek and Others v. Turkey* 2007). While acknowledging that some limitations could be justified, an undifferentiated ban imposed on all public sector workers was incompatible with democratic principles.[29] Subsequent rulings extended this protection further as the Court found

---

[28] See Chapter 5 for a detailed discussion on the authority and impact of these international instruments.

[29] For example, in *Junta Rectora Del Ertzainen Nazional Elkartasuna (ER.N.E.) v. Spain* (2015), the Court found the limitations on the exercise of police officers' unions' right to strike to be justified, but found the absolute ban imposed on military personnel to join trade unions to constitute a violation of Article 11 (*Matelly v. France* 2014).

criminal and disciplinary sanctions imposed on workers who participated in collective action violated Article 11 (*Karaçay v. Turkey* 2007; *Saime Özcan v. Turkey* 2009). In *Danilenkov and Others v. Russia* (2009), which concerned dockworkers who were dismissed under the pretext of "structural reorganization" upon taking part in strike activity, the ECtHR found a rare Article 14 violation in conjunction with Article 11, widely referencing ILO and ESC standards on antiunion discrimination.

The Court, however, did not always adopt the ILO's principles on trade union rights in its rulings. In *Sørensen and Rasmussen v. Denmark* (2006), the Court rejected the argument that closed shop agreements could promote collective agreements within a global economy where trade union membership and collective bargaining are on a steady decline. Instead, the Court insisted that trade union membership and collective bargaining entry must remain strictly voluntary. This reasoning is consistent with earlier case law in which the Court found compulsory membership in trade unions (*Young, James, and Webster v. The United Kingdom* 1981) or professional associations (*Sigurður Sigurjónsson v. Iceland* 1993) to be in violation of Article 11.

4.4.3 Retrenchment Phase: Judicial Restraint at the ECtHR

The Court's expansive approach to labor rights emerged in a political environment where the ECtHR was gaining support and legitimacy. The tide, however, started to turn in the post-2010 period, as the Court faced mounting pressure from national governments. In the UK, ECtHR rulings that clashed with the government's policies on antiterrorism and immigration control became flashpoints, prompting Tory leaders to rally crowds with pledges to leave the ECtHR. Though the UK has been the most vocal critic among the liberal democracies, it is not the only one. In Denmark, the Netherlands, and Spain, political parties formally adopted agendas to leave the ECtHR or governments openly decried ECtHR rulings (Helfer and Voeten 2020; Madsen 2021; Stiansen and Voeten 2020; Voeten 2022). The first concerted effort to curb the ECtHR's authority came with the Brighton Declaration of 2012, when member states embedded the "margin of appreciation" to the Convention's preamble. Since the doctrine already existed in the jurisprudence of the Court, its inclusion in the preamble signaled an expectation for judges to apply it more broadly. The Copenhagen Declaration of 2018 reinforced this position by urging the Court to provide more leeway for states in its rulings. The UK and Denmark, albeit unsuccessfully, used their CM leaderships in these periods to campaign for even more severe limitations on the authority of the ECtHR (Glas 2020).

Recent studies indicate that the ECtHR has responded to this political pressure by exhibiting more restraint in its rulings. The judges have increasingly referenced margin of appreciation in the post-2010 rulings (Madsen 2018), particularly in cases brought against consolidated democracies, such as the UK (Stiansen and Voeten 2020). My findings from StrasLab confirm these general trends: The percentage of labor judgments where the Court found at least one violation declined from 93 percent in the 2000s to 78 percent in the 2010s. Notably, the ECtHR has not issued a single violation ruling on trade union cases brought by British workers in this period, despite the UK being the second most frequent litigant and the presence of well-orchestrated strategic litigation efforts led by experienced lawyers (Chapter 5). The Court's rejection of British unions' claims one after another prompted British lawyers Ewing and Hendy (2016: 416) to wryly suggest that there must be "a subliminal Article 11(3), visible only to Strasbourg (and British) judges, the subliminal paragraph providing explicitly that the '*The foregoing provisions of this article shall not apply to the United Kingdom.*'"

One concern is whether the ECtHR will start rolling back already established rights. In dissenting opinions, a growing minority of judges have expressed concern that the Court is reversing previous rulings in ways that favor the states (Helfer and Voeten 2020). While the ECtHR has not yet – at least overtly – overturned any of its pro-labor landmark rulings on trade union rights, my analysis of all ECtHR trade union rulings from 1960 to 2021 indicates a growing reluctance to expand protections.[30] At first glance, the ECtHR's overall finding of violation in trade union rights claims has actually increased from 23 percent in the 2000s to 39 percent in the 2010s.[31] However, nearly all of these violation judgments (33 out of 34) involved repetitive cases, where the

---

[30] The database includes trade union rights cases from all years (as referenced in Chapter 3), unlike the other types of labor rights cases analyzed above, which are from every other year.

[31] This calculation is based on cases where the ECtHR found Article 11 violation among all trade union rights *judgments and decisions* during the respective period. The ECtHR's finding of Article 11 violation among trade union rights *judgments* has increased from 41 to 69 percent during the same periods.

Court merely reaffirmed existing rights.[32] By contrast, the Court found no Article 11 violation in the six other high-importance cases, providing further support to the claim that the ECtHR is avoiding the recognition of new trade union rights claims.

The first indication of the ECtHR's retrenchment came in a 2011 Grand Chamber judgment where the Court ruled that the dismissal of two workers for publishing an offensive cartoon about their employer did not constitute a violation of Article 10 read in light of Article 11 (*Palomo Sánchez and Others v. Spain* 2011). The ruling illustrated a point of contention among the ECtHR judges regarding the interpretation of trade union rights. In a joint dissent, five judges criticized the majority opinion for disregarding the "social dimension of the situation," arguing that the applicants' freedom of expression should have been evaluated in the context of an ongoing industrial dispute. They further warned that the ruling could have a "chilling effect" on trade unionists and "encroach directly upon the raison d'être of a trade union."

Another important sign of the ECtHR's restraint is its narrow interpretation of the right to strike, which may be linked to the political pressure on the ILO. In 2012, the International Organization of Employers (IOE), which composes one leg of the tripartite supervisory body of the ILO alongside the states and the workers' association, challenged the Committee of Experts on the Application of Conventions and Recommendations' (CEACR) authority to interpret ILO Convention 87 as including a right to strike, citing the absence of explicit language.[33] Some observers viewed this move as a backlash against the ECtHR's earlier judgments where the Court had referenced the ILO in acknowledging basic trade union rights, including the right to strike (Ewing and Hendy 2014).

This controversy surfaced in *RMT v. The United Kingdom* (2014), which challenged Britain's ban on sympathy strikes (secondary action or solidarity action) and onerous pre-industrial action requirements.

---

[32] The only high-importance claim where the ECtHR found a violation was in Eğitim-Sen's case regarding the union's right to include a statement defending the right of individuals to receive education in their mother tongue (*Eğitim ve Bilim Emekçileri Sendikası v. Turkey* 2012; see discussion in Chapter 3).

[33] The CEACR is an independent body composed of legal experts that examines member states' implementation of ratified ILO Conventions and issues non-binding decisions. The case on the right to strike under Convention 87 is now referred to the International Court of Justice, which will have the final word on the matter.

The UK government urged the Court to reconsider its stance on the right to strike in light of the ongoing ILO dispute. While reaffirming that Article 11 protects the right to strike, the Court found no violation, reasoning that the union had ultimately been able to take collective action. It declined to view the ballot requirements as an interference, unlike its approach to financial inducements in *Wilson* (Bogg and Ewing 2014). However, the Court acknowledged that sympathy strikes constitute a form of trade union activity that warrants protection, albeit as an accessory rather than a core right. It also conceded that the UK's blanket ban on sympathy strikes could have "far-reaching, negative effects" (*Wilson v. The United Kingdom* 2002: para. 98) but avoided ruling on the issue, emphasizing that it does not review legislation in the abstract.

This rigid approach to the right to strike became entrenched in recent cases. *Barış and Others v. Turkey* (2021) concerned workers who were dismissed after participating in one of Turkey's largest strikes in decades. In 2015, thousands of Ford workers staged a wildcat strike to protest a collective bargaining agreement negotiated by Türk Metal, a yellowdog union with close ties to employers. About 4,000 workers resigned from Türk Metal, with some joining Birleşik Metal İş, a leftist union under DİSK. Subsequently, fifty workers who joined the strike were dismissed due to unexcused absence from work without excuse. The ECtHR rejected their case, interpreting Article 11 as protecting only union-organized strikes. In doing so, the ECtHR disregarded the vulnerable situation of the workers who were protesting against not just an automative industry giant but also against a yellowdog union, which they were pressured to join upon hiring (*Barış and Others v. Turkey* 2021: para. 12).

Moreover, despite the partial recognition of sympathy strikes in *RMT*, the Court sharply narrowed the range of protected collective actions in *Almaz and Others v. Turkey* (2024) and *Kaya v. Turkey* (2024) by holding that for a strike to merit protection under Article 11, its purpose must be directly tied to working conditions or the professional interests of workers. Actions motivated primarily by political protest, even when union-led and involving core economic concerns, was found to fall outside the scope of protection.

The ECtHR's deference to national restrictions was further underscored in *Humpert and Others v. Germany* (2023), where the Grand Chamber upheld Germany's blanket ban on civil servants' right to strike as compatible with Article 11 (*Humpert and Others v. Germany*

2023).³⁴ The case followed a Federal Constitutional Court ruling that extensively engaged with ECtHR case law on trade union rights. Given the Constitutional Court's prior assertion that it has the final say on interpreting the Convention, an ECtHR reversal risked Germany's non-compliance (Batura 2023). The ECtHR justified its ruling by distinguishing Germany's civil service governance structure from Turkey's, but in dissent, Judge Serghides called this a "double standard," as both countries imposed total bans. He also deemed it "paradoxical" to relegate the right to strike to a secondary status, contending that it is inseparable from collective bargaining and embedded in the "DNA" of freedom of association.

The ECtHR's recent case law suggests that the golden years of labor's legal mobilization at the ECtHR have come to an end. This period of judicial restraint is unlikely to be reversed in the near future, given that political pressure is piling up on the ECtHR and states appoint increasingly conservative judges to the ECtHR (Stiansen and Voeten 2020). It remains to be seen whether the Court will at least continue to uphold the pre-established protections on labor rights.

4.5 CONCLUSION

The 2000s marked the golden years for labor at the ECtHR. During this period, the Court has adopted a holistic approach to human rights, refuting a strict division between socioeconomic rights and civil and political rights. The Court overturned its earlier narrow jurisprudence to include a host of new labor rights claims from workers' health and safety to workplace surveillance. Some of its most remarkable rulings include granting state-sponsored parental leave for men in Russia, allowing public sector workers in Turkey to unionize, recognizing human trafficking as a form of modern slavery, banning discrimination in the UK military based on sexual orientation, and ordering the Maltese government to pay reparations for workers who have been exposed to asbestos. Nowhere was this transformation more profound than in trade union rights, where the Court has come to recognize some core trade union rights as human rights. Within a context of shrinking welfare states and declining trade union rights protection in Europe in

---

³⁴ Other similar recent examples include *LO and NTF v. Norway* (2021) and *Svenska Transportarbetareförbundet and Seko v Sweden* (2016).

the 1990s, the ECtHR emerged as one of the few institutional sites left at which organized labor could direct mobilization efforts.

This expansion of labor rights did not happen in isolation. It occurred during the height of the ECtHR's increased legitimacy and recognition as an important player in European politics. Throughout the 1990s, the Court gained new members, reformed its institutional structure to increase its effectiveness and oversight, and expanded its case law to new issue areas. However, as the ECtHR grew more assertive, it also faced growing political backlash. By the early 2010s, concerns over national sovereignty, migration policy, and judicial overreach fueled criticism from key member states, particularly the UK and Denmark. The Court's recent case law suggests that this pressure is shaping its jurisprudence. Though the Court has not overturned any of its established labor rights precedents, the period of expansion for trade union rights appears to have come to an end.

For British and Turkish unionists facing increasingly repressive labor regimes since the 1980s, the rise of the ECtHR to prominence offered a perfect opportunity to take their grievances to the international stage. But the emergence of a new opportunity for activists does not automatically translate into legal mobilization, unless activists identify it as such. Following the most recent developments on international human rights law, however, is far from a routine part of workers' daily struggles. How, then, did British and Turkish unionists come to see the ECtHR as a viable tool to challenge their governments' neoliberal policies?

CHAPTER 5

LAWYERS AS STRATEGISTS
Between the Local and the International

David Wilson was a journalist working for the *Daily Mail* in London in 1991 when he was offered a 4.5 percent increase in his salary. The increase was presented as a bonus unrelated to his performance that year. But there was a catch – he needed to give up his membership in the National Union of Journalists (NUJ). Wilson soon found out that he was not alone. From newsrooms to shipyards, employers in many industries in the UK were undertaking efforts to facilitate "union derecognition" by enticing workers with lucrative contracts in exchange for renouncing their union membership.[1] Trade unions perceived this practice as a full-on attack on their existence.

Together with his union, the NUJ, Wilson initiated a legal battle against the *Daily Mail*. Shipyard workers who refused to sign similar deals soon joined the battle by bringing lawsuits against their employers.[2] The cases drew national attention not only to the employers' efforts to dismantle unions by buying workers out, but also to the government's evident support for these actions. Mere days before the House of Lords – the highest British court available at the time – issued its final ruling, the Tories rushed through legislation that effectively

---

[1] See Bogg (2022) for a detailed genealogy of the *Wilson* case and its political-legal context. (See also Ewing 1993; Smith and Morton 1993).

[2] At the ECtHR, Wilson's case was merged together with the shipyard workers' case since both had similar facts.

legalized the practice.³ Both unions ultimately lost their cases and they were outraged. There seemed to be no way at the domestic level to stop employers from ousting unions from workplaces.

When Lord John Hendy (King's Counsel), then a barrister and standing counsel for the NUJ and RMT, advised the unions in 1996 to take their cases to the ECtHR, he had little reason for optimism. The ECtHR had not found any violations against states on cases brought by trade union activists. But the unions had no other choice; the state institutions had clearly sided with the employers by endorsing union derecognition practices. Hendy thought they had little to lose from trying the ECtHR, "even if the odds were low."⁴ To his surprise, the ECtHR found the practice violated workers' right to unionize under Article 11 (right to association). As discussed in the previous chapter, *Wilson, National Union of Journalists and Others v. The United Kingdom* (2002) marked the beginning of a new era of trade union rights at the ECtHR by becoming the Court's first pro-union ruling. Thereafter, Hendy carefully curated all trade union cases submitted to the ECtHR from his country.

While the *Wilson* case marked a turning point, the most sustained and transformative trade union rights litigation at the ECtHR came not from the UK, but from Turkey, particularly through the efforts of public sector unions organized under KESK. As discussed in the previous chapter, the ECtHR's labor case law grew at a time when the Court was expanding its legal authority and legitimacy in the 1990s. But this expansion was far from inevitable and would not have materialized had it not been for the initiative of *a committed group of lawyers*. In both countries, these lawyers helped workers overcome a key challenge: Local activists generally invest their energies on lobbying activities or rank-and-file mobilization and, while they may pursue litigation at domestic courts, they are often unaware of or misinformed about legal remedies available at international courts. Lawyers served as intermediaries between the international and local levels by identifying emerging legal opportunities and leading strategic litigation efforts.

---

³ The amendment allowed employers to undermine workers' right to join a trade union so long as the purpose of the employer was implementing a change in negotiating arrangements (see the discussion on Ullswater Amendment in Ewing 2003; and Kang 2012).

⁴ Interview with John Hendy, November 2014.

As a court that has mandatory jurisdiction on all member states and accepts individual petitions, the ECtHR is highly accessible. In the 1990s, it was gaining prominence in European politics, setting new precedents on contentious national issues and expanding its jurisprudence. Still, even seasoned labor lawyers like Hendy could not have predicted its receptiveness to trade union rights cases, since the ECtHR was designed to address civil and political rights. Aside from a vague reference to the right to unionize under the right to freedom of association, core labor standards were absent from the Convention. The lawyers initially turned to the ECtHR out of necessity – but it was not the only institution they probed. They had multiple options at the international level, including the ILO with a clearer mandate for protecting trade union rights and the European Court of Justice (ECJ), with its proclaimed supremacy over national law.[5] Eventually, they identified the ECtHR as the best target due to its strength in both *judicial responsiveness* and *judicial authority*. The lawyers' probing efforts, however, differed from forum shopping, which assumes that international legal remedies are fixed and predictable. Rather, the ECtHR's new jurisprudence on trade union rights emerged through an iterative process between the lawyers' strategic litigation efforts and the ECtHR's responsiveness to these claims.

Moreover, the variation in the severity of domestic-level violations in Turkey and the UK prompted lawyers to tailor their litigation strategies to these contextual differences. In order to account for these contingencies and explain why and how organized labor targeted the ECtHR, the chapter analyzes how lawyers developed their litigation strategies in two phases. The *probing phase* of the 1990s saw the ECtHR's rising prominence, signaling its growing authority. At the same time, uncertainty over the Court's responsiveness to trade union rights prompted lawyers to test multiple international institutions before settling on the ECtHR. During the *expansion phase* in the 2000s, the ECtHR demonstrated responsiveness to trade union rights while solidifying its judicial authority. This encouraged further litigation, as lawyers grew more confident in the Court's receptiveness and actively shaped its jurisprudence from below. Once they identified their target institution, British and Turkish lawyers devised litigation

---

[5] Most of the trade union rights cases are brought before the ECJ, part of the Court of Justice of the European Union, through the preliminary ruling procedure which allows national court judges to refer cases directly to the court.

strategies appropriate to the needs and expectations of unions in each country. In the UK, where violations were less pervasive, lawyers were more selective, taking cases only on issues they could use for domestic legal reforms. In Turkey, neoliberal transformation, compounded by weak democratic institutions, created a more hostile environment for workers, resulting in Turkish lawyers bringing more precedent-setting and repeat violation cases before the ECtHR. Because the vast majority of ECtHR trade union rights cases were brought by KESK unions, the chapter focuses primarily on the strategies and experiences of KESK and its legal advocates.

The chapter first introduces the lawyers as key agents of change. Distinct from human rights lawyers or legal counselors working at NGOs, the primary allegiance of these lawyers is first and foremost to the labor cause. It then examines how committed lawyers from Turkey and the UK spearheaded strategic litigation efforts, ultimately shaping the legal landscape for trade union rights.

5.1 COMMITTED LABOR LAWYERS IN STRASBOURG

Unlike most studies on international litigation, I find that a group of committed lawyers, rather than wealthy, transnationally connected NGOs, lead organized labor's litigation efforts at the ECtHR (Cichowski 2007, 2016; Engstrom and Low 2019; Okafor 2007; Sundstrom 2014; Van der Vet 2012). The focus on NGOs or legal advocacy groups grew out of studies based in the US, where financial and legal resources were key to developing a long-term litigation strategy and becoming "repeat players." Such groups craft more compelling legal arguments, and hence have greater success at influencing judicial outcomes than "one-shotters" seeking remedies on individual cases (Galanter 1974; see also Epp 1998). But when the cost of litigation is not exorbitant, access to "deep-pocketed" support structures may not be essential (Wilson 2009; see also Vanhala 2018). In addition to the cost of litigation, the institutional capacity of international courts can be an important factor in determining the need for support structures. NGOs play an especially important role when courts are underfunded or lack the institutional capacity to run effective investigations or manage caseloads (Haddad 2018). For example, only a fraction of cases before the ECtHR, a well-funded and effective court, are supported by NGOs, whereas almost 60 percent of cases before the Inter-American Court of Human Rights are backed by a single NGO

(Haddad 2018). While the legal advocacy involvement in high-importance cases at the ECtHR has increased in recent years, overall only 8 percent of cases at the ECtHR are supported by a legal advocacy organization (Cichowski and Chrun 2017).[6] By contrast, during the first few decades of the ECtHR, when its case law was small and legal knowledge about the Court was limited, legal advocacy groups were more prominent in leading litigation efforts. Harlow and Rawlings (1992) estimate that up until the 1980s, roughly half of the cases from the UK were brought by NGOs.

The trade union rights litigation at the ECtHR does not require substantial financial resources. The ECtHR does not request any fees from applicants, though the cost of litigation at the domestic level could potentially deter activists from pursuing litigation strategy, as the ECtHR requires exhaustion of domestic remedies. In Turkey, the cost of litigation at employment courts is negligible. When preparing the first set of cases regarding the public sector workers' right to unionize in Turkey in the 1990s, the unions had virtually no financial resources to support litigation efforts. Many labor lawyers worked pro bono, driven by their commitment to the labor cause. Over the years, the expertise in ECtHR litigation concentrated in the hands of in-house lawyers within KESK unions. In the UK, there are no fees for making a claim to the employment tribunals, but litigation means lawyers' fees.[7] Individuals supported by unions have higher success rates in employment tribunals (Pollert 2007). Overall, the British unions were better positioned than their Turkish counterparts to fund litigation efforts, but labor lawyers still provided pro bono support for ECtHR litigation where necessary.

The committed labor lawyers spearheaded international litigation not due to financial interests, but because of their shared commitment to the norms and values advocated by the unions. The role of these labor lawyers bears similarities to the "cause lawyers" in the civil rights movement (Scheingold 1974) and the pay equity movement (McCann 1994) in the US. They view the struggle "in much the same terms as the activists themselves," act "as collaborators, rather than directors,"

---

[6] This number excludes cases supported by state authorities, political parties, and third-party individuals.

[7] In an effort to further suppress employment claims in 2013, the Conservative government introduced fees for filing suits at employment tribunals. The fees indeed resulted in a significant fall in the number of claims the following year, but the Supreme Court overturned this legislation (R (UNISON) v Lord Chancellor 2017).

and do not position themselves at the "heart of the movement" (Hilbink 2006; see also Sarat and Scheingold 2006). The personal histories of lawyers shape their approach to litigation and their relationship with the activists (McCann and Silverstein 1998). Having worked with unions their entire careers, this small cadre of labor lawyers working on the ECtHR cases are ideologically committed to the labor cause, and they view themselves primarily as labor lawyers, rather than human rights activists.

In some cases, the relationship between the activists and lawyers who privilege litigation over other strategies may be fraught (Rosenberg 2008; Schmidt 2018; Tushnet 2000). As discussed in Chapter 2, labor activists have good reasons to be resistant to litigation. For example, some labor scholars are skeptical of litigation strategy as they argue that it undermines the collective nature of labor claims, and it detracts from the rank-and-file mobilization that unions have traditionally used (McCartin 2005; Savage and Smith 2017; but see Kahraman 2018; McCann 1994). Tensions are particularly pronounced when NGOs, which tend to be motivated to set precedents, lead international litigation, as their priorities may not always align with the expectations of the victims (Sundstrom 2014; Van der Vet 2012). Lawyers or activists working at international NGOs may "be distrusted, because their ultimate loyalties are ambiguous and they may be double agents" (Merry 2006: 40).

However, such tensions were largely absent in ECtHR trade union litigation. The lawyers were not viewed as "double agents" by trade unionists, because they were not trying to instill or impose a rights-consciousness among activists. Instead, they identified the legal opportunities, communicated them to activists, and developed a litigation strategy collaboratively. Having previously established trusted relationships with the unions, the lawyers' allegiances were unquestioned. They proposed litigation as a last resort to seek protections for basic union rights, rather than as a substitute for traditional forms of mobilization. Since ECtHR litigation does not put much financial burden on unions, it required little persuasion; lawyers simply drew attention to the potential remedies at the international level. I even found that the more radical, left-wing unions were more eager to use international law, corroborating existing theories that such unions are more open to try options outside of the domestic systems.[8]

---

[8] Based on his study of trade unions in Latin America, Anner (2009) similarly finds that left-wing unions are more likely to develop transnational ties.

5.2 THE UNITED KINGDOM

5.2.1 The Legal Culture and Organized Labor's Changing Attitudes toward Law

In 1965, Lord Wedderburn, an influential legal scholar and Labour life peer, famously described the attitudes of the British workers toward courts as follows: "Most workers want nothing more of the law than that it should leave them alone" (Wedderburn 1965: 9). For much of the twentieth century, trade unions solved employment disputes through a decentralized and largely unregulated system of collective bargaining, which was described as "collective laissez-faire" (Kahn-Freund 1972). Statutory provisions governing individual workers' rights were few and individual employment relationships were "marginal," hence courts were mostly "excluded" from the industrial relations system (Brown et al. 2000). Starting in the 1960s, successive governments undertook major reforms to formalize employment relations, triggering a process of judicialization of employment relations (Clark, Lewis, and Wedderburn 1983; McCarthy 1992). A host of issues previously negotiated in collective bargaining agreements have come to be governed by employment law. As labor contracts became more formalized, employment tribunals expanded their jurisdiction and assumed a more prominent role in adjudicating workplace disputes.[9]

Part of unions' historical skepticism of litigation stemmed from limited legal opportunities offered by domestic courts. The British courts have been characterized by judicial restraint and an unwillingness to diverge from precedents (Flanders 1974; Hyman 1988). Workers often had little success in pursuing their rights in courts (Brown et al. 2000).[10] Moreover, unions had a preference to resolve employment conflicts through traditional rank-and-file mobilization, rather than litigation. Unions wanted to be viewed as "successful negotiators," rather than law offices, in order to maintain both their

---

[9] Employment Tribunals were established in 1964 as "Industrial Tribunals" as the lowest level legal body, in order to adjudicate labor disputes. Colling (2006: 142) notes that the range of Employment Tribunals' jurisdictions grew from six in the 1970s to about eighty by the mid-2000s.

[10] The conservatism of judges has not been limited to labor issues but extends to civil liberties at large (Epp 1998). Harlow and Rawlings (1992) similarly argue that public interest litigation is much less common in the UK than in the US. Yet both studies point out that integration with Europe accelerated the judicialization of politics.

strength against the employers at the bargaining table and their status before the members (Evans, Goodman, and Hargreaves 1985: 98). Nonetheless, with the ascent of neoliberal policies and violations of even their basic rights under Tory rule, the workers had little option but to turn to courts. Though the upswing in claims before employment tribunals started in the 1970s, there is a clear correlation between the decline in union power and the rise in employment tribunal cases in the post-1980 period (Burgess, Propper, and Wilson 2001; Kelly 1998). The number of claims to employment tribunals more than doubled from the early 1980s to early 2000s and continued to increase steadily thereafter.[11] Unable to negotiate workers' rights collectively, trade unions started to gain expertise and knowledge in employment law, albeit unwillingly.

The introduction of new employment regulations as part of European integration accelerated the judicialization of labor relations. In the 1990s, a host of new regulations on anti-discrimination law, working time, minimum wage, and subcontracted work was introduced, mostly by the Labour government. The changes produced mixed results for workers. On the one hand, trade unions' lobbying powers and ability to influence New Labour's policies had already been diminished, so the new regulations put in place responded much more to the flexibility demands of employers, rather than to workers' demands for security (Clark and Hall 1992; Davies and Freedland 2007; Dickens and Hall 2010; Smith and Morton 2009). At the same time, the judicialization of employment relations presented some new opportunities for individual workers to advocate for issues that trade unions had been reluctant to take up – in particular, racial and gender discrimination in the workplace. The pay equity movement quickly became a highly influential litigation campaign at the national and international level, and the ECJ set numerous precedents on this issue. Gradually, trade unions, as well as labor lawyers, have come to play central roles in leading litigation efforts, with the increase in litigation being principally concentrated in the public sector (Colling 2006; Deakin et al. 2015; Guillaume 2015).

By the 1990s, the unions had already gained expertise in ECJ litigation and had started to use litigation as leverage to recruit members in an economy with growing female labor participation (Howell 1996).

---

[11] The number of claims rose from 41,424 in 1980 to 103,935 in the 1999–2000 period and reached 186,300 in 2011–2012.

At the domestic level, employment tribunals eventually became more attentive to discrimination claims after decades-long litigation campaigns, but not to trade union rights claims. The fulfillment of complex ballot requirements by trade unions before taking industrial action, restrictions on collective bargaining, and a judicial system unresponsive to employers' attack against unionization in the workplace had left labor activists without remedies. The unionists were ready to try new options.

The lawyers I interviewed confirmed that they started to look for remedies at the international level because organized labor's ability to influence policy change through domestic channels had been hampered. Keith Ewing, a prominent legal scholar who advised on most ECtHR cases remarked: "in the [19]70s there was no need for human rights in labor issues because people were better organized [...] But, in the post-1980 period, the labor movement shrunk by half in the UK [...] [Now], labor is weak, it has to make use of whatever method is available."[12] Faced with increased state repression, labor activists sought alternative legal avenues to justify their basic right to unionize. John Hendy offered a similar perspective in 2014, when the Conservative government was in office: "We've got nowhere to go. You know, the Labour Party does nothing for the trade union rights, there's no effective opposition to the government. So where can we go? Naturally, we've looked at the international institutions."[13]

Victoria Phillips, a solicitor at Thompsons Solicitors – a firm with deep ties to unions – pointed out that the unions increasingly felt that they had "hit a roadblock in terms of pursuing cases in Great Britain. Is Strasbourg an alternative? Is Luxembourg an alternative? They're keen to explore all possible options."[14] She was the acting solicitor in *ASLEF v. The United Kingdom* (2007), a landmark ECtHR ruling concerning the union that expelled a member belonging to the far-right BNP. The case carried particular significance for unions since, at the time, the BNP had called on its members to infiltrate left-wing trade unions in order to have themselves be expelled and receive a five-figure compensation fee (Hendy and Ewing 2005: 198–199). When I asked her whether convincing union leaders to pursue the ECtHR route was difficult, she responded, "[After losing the case in domestic

---

[12] Interview with Keith Ewing, July 2013.
[13] Interview with John Hendy, November 2014.
[14] Interview with Victoria Phillips, November 2014.

courts], the union [leaders] were incensed – I think that's a fair word to use. They were furious. They felt so helpless."[15] The union had to pay substantial compensation to an expelled member they considered a Nazi. When Hendy suggested taking the case to the ECtHR, Associated Society of Locomotive Engineers and Firemen (ASLEF) leaders had no qualms.

The unions wanted to find a way to fight against the restrictions placed on union rights in the post-1980 period. The Human Rights Act of 1998, which brought the ECtHR into the spotlight, created new opportunities for workers to claim their rights as human rights (Chapter 3). But without the guidance of committed lawyers in identifying the ECtHR as a target institution and communicating this information to workers, the unions would not have considered the ECtHR as an option.

5.2.2 Probing Phase: Why British Labor Lawyers Turned to the ECtHR

The ECtHR was not an obvious choice for labor lawyers seeking legal remedies at the international level in the 1990s. On the one hand, the ECtHR's political influence was growing, as discussed in the previous chapter. Its membership almost doubled with the inclusion of Eastern European countries; its case law expanded rapidly; and it started to issue rulings in high-profile cases. Other international organizations, most notably the EU, increasingly referenced its judgments. Within the UK, prominent lawyers and civil society organizations turned to the ECtHR to challenge policies of the Conservative government, which had been in power since 1979. In particular, the National Council for Civil Liberties (NCCL), the predecessor of Liberty, was the leading organization on ECtHR litigation from the 1970s, advancing cases on Britain's anti-terrorism laws, disproportionate police violence against protestors, and government surveillance (Harlow and Rawlings 1992).[16] Following *Dudgeon v. the UK* (1981), in which the ECtHR ruled against the criminalization of homosexual conduct, the government eventually decriminalized same-sex relationships, signaling the Court's growing judicial authority.

---

[15] Interview with Victoria Phillips, November 2014.
[16] It is worth noting that hundreds of cases were filed from Northern Ireland, within the context of the ongoing civil war.

Yet, despite its expanding jurisprudence on civil and political rights, the ECtHR appeared largely unresponsive to trade union rights. The first case that drew British trade unions' attention to the Court, albeit in a negative light, was *Young, James and Webster v. The United Kingdom* (1981), brought by the conservative National Association for Freedom (later The Freedom Association), known for its anti-union campaigns. The case targeted closed shop agreements, which were still legal under the Labour government in the 1970s (Harlow and Rawlings 1992).[17] Wedderburn, who worked closely with unions and provided legal counsel to them, successfully petitioned the Court to make a third-party intervention for the Trades Union Congress (TUC) – the first time the ECtHR allowed such an intervention from an NGO – but the ruling ultimately favored the applicants. The disappointment deepened in yet another hotly debated case, *Council of Civil Service Unions et al. v. The United Kingdom* (1987), where the ECtHR dismissed public sector workers' challenge to the government's restrictions on their right to unionize and strike. In the 1990s, the Court did not have a single pro-union judgment (Chapter 4).

On the face of it, the most appropriate institution for claiming labor rights was the ILO. Trade unions in the UK and elsewhere have long turned to the ILO, the international institution with the strongest formal rights protections for workers, to garner international support for their claims. The ILO provides a special complaint mechanism for unions to bring their grievances regarding violations of freedom of association directly before the Committee on Freedom of Association (CFA). Although the CFA was not established as an adjudicative body empowered to issue binding rulings, over time it has come to function like one, settling disputes and issuing authoritative interpretations of ILO Conventions, which are legally binding on states once ratified (Weisband 2006: 124). Although activists and experts have long criticized its low compliance rate, CFA recommendations have nonetheless been referenced and adopted as labor standards by international organizations, national courts, and NGOs (Anner and Caraway 2010; Weisband 2006) signaling its extensive authority.

The first institution to which unions turned was the ILO, which, as expected, was highly responsive to the unions' complaints. After the famous miners' strike, Hendy filed the first petition: "Really, the first

---

[17] The closed shop agreements were banned altogether by the Conservative government in 1990.

real go was the case I drew up for the National Union of Mine Workers in 1988 to the ILO when we attacked every aspect of the anti-union legislation. We've been hammered away in the ILO ever since."[18] At the time, the recently enacted 1988 Employment Act had introduced ballot requirements that considerably limited strike action. As a result of the complaint filed by Hendy and other labor activists, the ILO's CFA condemned these restrictions, but to no avail. The Conservative government not only ignored the condemnation, but it also withdrew from thirteen previously ratified ILO Conventions (Kang 2012).

The famous *Wilson* case, mentioned in the introduction, fully demonstrates why British lawyers ultimately turned to the ECtHR. During the domestic proceedings, Hendy repeatedly invoked Article 11 in both written and oral submissions, but Hendy's pleas fell on deaf ears; the judges did not even address them (Bogg 2022: 226). Following an adverse ruling from the House of Lords in 1995, the unions initially sought remedy at the ILO. In a series of reports, the CFA and CEACR criticized the relevant legislation and domestic rulings. Next, the Committee on Economic, Social and Cultural Rights (CESCR) of the UN raised concerns about the government's refusal to comply with the ILO's recommendations and found that discouraging workers from joining a union through financial incentives violated Article 8 of the International Covenant on Economic, Social, and Cultural Rights (ICESCR). The CoE's Committee of Independent Experts similarly found that the current legislation and practice violated Article 5 (the right to organize) and Article 6 (the right to collective bargaining) of the ESC. However, complying with the judgments of international organizations with weak judicial authority was not a priority for the Tories, who had little regard for international law. The government stood its ground, disregarding all international pressure.

The ECJ might have been an appealing option for British labor activists – though it is no longer an option after Brexit – since it is a supranational court with strong judicial authority in Europe (Kelemen 2016).[19] Moreover, as noted above, British labor lawyers had gained considerable experience in EU law, having successfully litigated

---

[18] Interview with John Hendy, November 2014. The ILO CFA Complaint, The National Union of Mineworkers and the International Miners' Organisation 1988; Case No. 1439.

[19] The ECJ proclaimed its rulings to have direct effect at the domestic level.

numerous cases on gender discrimination in the workplace to the Luxemburg Court by the 1990s (Alter and Vargas 2000; Guillaume 2015).[20] However, until the 2000s, the EU legal instruments did not explicitly protect trade union rights of workers. While the so-called social dimension of the European integration was hotly debated in the 1990s, the EU member states, particularly the UK, opposed any binding legislation on collective labor rights (Ryan 1997). Notably, the 1992 Social Policy Agreement recognized a broad range of labor rights but explicitly excluded protections for the right to association, the right to strike, and the right to impose lockouts (Ryan 1997: 308). In the few cases that reached the ECJ during this period, the Court largely deferred to national political and judicial institutions, signaling a broader reluctance to intervene in collective labor law (Novitz 2007: 366–367). Given these limitations, the British labor lawyers did not consider the ECJ as a viable option to pursue a legal battle against domestic anti-union laws during this period.[21]

Hence, identifying the ECtHR as a target institution was not a straightforward process for the British labor lawyers. They first turned to the ILO, which was highly responsive but lacked the authority to compel compliance. The ECJ, by contrast, wielded strong judicial authority but showed little willingness to intervene in trade union rights. With no viable alternatives, the ECtHR emerged as a legal avenue of last resort. The ruling in *Wilson* came as a surprise to Hendy and the unions, as they had not expected it to be the first ECtHR case recognizing a violation of workers' right to unionize under Article 11.[22] This judgment marked a pivotal shift, demonstrating that, despite its earlier reluctance, the ECtHR could serve as a meaningful venue for contesting restrictive labor laws.

5.2.3 Expansion Phase: Strategic Litigation at the ECtHR

In the post-2000 period, the ECtHR became a clear target for British labor lawyers as the Court solidified its judicial authority and responsiveness. As Hendy observed, the *Wilson* case gave the unions "a real possibility for attacking anti-union legislation in the UK via the

---

[20] The CJEU has been a good option for workers to claim their rights on working time and holiday pay as well (Lubow and Schmidt 2021).
[21] Interview with John Hendy, February 2024 and Keith Ewing, March 2024.
[22] Interview with John Hendy, November 2014.

ECtHR."[23] Though the ruling came almost a decade after the initial application, the unions successfully leveraged it to pressure the government into passing the Employment Relations Act (2004), which protected workers from employer coercion to forgo union rights. Similarly, after *ASLEF v. the UK* (2007), the unions secured a legislative reform to give effect to the ECtHR ruling. While these policy changes were criticized for providing minimal protections (Bogg 2005; Ewing 2009b; see Chapter 6), they nevertheless demonstrate the ECtHR's judicial authority.

After *Wilson*, British labor lawyers increasingly viewed the ECtHR as the key international forum for defending trade union rights. Hendy affirmed the importance of judicial authority, stating: "The tradition has been that the members of the CoE, including the UK, abide by the ECtHR, whereas the decisions of the ILO, they just ignore them."[24] When the HRA came into effect in 1998, the ECtHR litigation gained even more significance. Comparing ECtHR judgments to other international legal remedies, Michael Ford KC, another well-known barrister who worked on the ECtHR cases, said:

> [When] the HRA came into effect [the European Convention] had been incorporated into domestic law. In a sense, that is precisely the same as the ILO Conventions, to which the UK is a signatory. But yet, those [...] have never been picked up that way. All the potential conventions, like the UN Covenant on socioeconomic rights [the ICESCR], all of those never fed into domestic law – other than in a very, very superficial way.[25]

While the ECtHR had become the dominant legal venue for trade union rights, the ILO's CFA remained an attractive option due to its norm-setting power and fast pace for delivering decisions, compared to the ECtHR's lengthy litigation process. Throughout the 2000s, the ECtHR routinely referenced the ILO, particularly when confronted with a new rights claim, reinforcing the latter's extensive authority (Ewing and Hendy 2010; Fudge 2015). Unlike the ECtHR, the CFA does not require exhaustion of all domestic remedies, allowing unions to file grievances earlier in the process.[26] In the 1990s, unions in

---

[23] Interview with John Hendy, February 2024.
[24] Interview with Hendy, November 2014.
[25] Interview with Michael Ford, November 2014.
[26] However, in a 2013 judgment, the ECtHR ruled that unions must choose between filing claims at the ILO or the ECtHR, deeming the applicant union POA's case inadmissible after it had first sought relief at the CFA.

mainland Britain filed five complaints against the government with the CFA and four petitions to the ECtHR.[27] In contrast, between 2000 and 2021, they submitted only three complaints to the CFA but seven petitions to the ECtHR, indicating that after 2000, lawyers increasingly turned to the ECtHR while continuing to use the CFA.[28]

Developments at the ECJ further cemented the ECtHR's position as the preferred legal avenue, as lawyers became increasingly disillusioned with the ECJ's approach to trade union rights. Explicit protections on core trade union rights, including the freedom of association (Article 12), the right to collective bargaining and the right to take collective action (Article 28) finally came under the Charter of Fundamental Rights of the European Union, which was drafted in 2000 and became legally binding in 2009. But despite its judicial authority and the de jure rights protection, the ECJ has become a court that trade unions avoided because of its narrow interpretation of trade union rights.

In two landmark cases, *Viking* and *Laval*, issued in 2007,[29] the ECJ judges prioritized the economic freedoms of corporations over trade union rights, intensifying broader debates regarding the role of European economic integration on dismantling welfare states, accelerating social dumping, and undermining organized labor (Davies 2008; Ewing and Hendy 2010; Fudge 2015).[30] Moreover, the court refrained from integrating ILO Conventions in its interpretation of union rights, in response to which the ILO's Committee of Experts expressed concern about the ECJ's restrictive rulings, especially on the right to

---

[27] Three other cases were from the Isle of Man, Bermuda, and Hong Kong, and a fourth was brought by US and Canadian unions against the British Embassy.

[28] The ILO, however, may be gaining more importance for unions within the past decade as the British unions started to lose their ECtHR cases in the "retrenchment phase" (Chapter 4). I address this issue in Chapter 9.

[29] Court of Justice of the European Union (CJEU). 2007. *International Transport Workers' Federation and Finnish Seamen's Union v Viking Line ABP and OÜ Viking Line Eesti (Viking)*, Case C-438/05, Judgment of 11 December 2007; Court of Justice of the European Union (CJEU). 2007. Laval un Partneri Ltd v Svenska Byggnadsarbetareförbundet and Others (Laval), Case C-341/05, Judgment of 18 December 2007

[30] Case C-438/05, *International Transport Workers' Federation (ITF) and Finnish Seamen's Union (FSU) v. Viking Line*, judgment of 11 December 2007, para 44; and Case C-341/05, *Laval un Partneri v. Svenska Byggnadsarbetareförbundet* [2007] ECR I-11767, para. 91.

strike.[31] During interviews, labor lawyers unanimously told me that after *Viking* and *Laval*, they deliberately avoided the ECJ. As Ewing put it, the ECJ "is a different kind of court: its priority is to protect business interests."[32] The ECtHR, by contrast, as a court not bound by the duty to uphold business interests, was in a much better position to protect trade union rights. When the Court issued its ground-breaking ruling on the right to collective bargaining in *Demir and Baykara v. Turkey* (2008), Ewing and Hendy (2010) noted that the ECtHR had the potential to "clean up the mess" created by the ECJ rulings on trade union rights.

Hence, in the 2000s, British labor lawyers came to see the ECtHR as the most viable international institution for litigating trade union rights, combining responsiveness with strong judicial authority.

5.2.4 Choosing Battles Wisely: The Legal Architects of ECtHR Litigation Strategy

A defining feature of trade union rights litigation before the ECtHR is that it is led by a small and coordinated network of lawyers who are committed to advancing workers' rights both inside and outside the courtroom. It would not be an exaggeration to say that since the 1990s, the ECtHR litigation has been organized and coordinated primarily by John Hendy, who is a leading barrister at the Old Square Chambers in London. He has dedicated his entire career to advancing workers' rights and trade unions' collective power through legal means. Over the past five decades, he has appeared in most major trade union rights cases at both domestic and international levels. Starting with *Wilson*, Hendy has either directly represented or provided legal advice on every trade union rights case submitted to the ECtHR.[33] In addition to his legal work, Hendy has also been active in labor policy, serving as an advisor to the Shadow Secretary of State for Employment Rights (2019–2021) and, since 2019, as a Labour peer in the House of Lords. As he put it, "I spend all my time thinking about devising ways that unions can move forward on the legal front."[34]

Hendy's closest collaborator in ECtHR litigation is Keith Ewing, who is a legal scholar at King's College London. Like Hendy, Ewing is

---

[31] Report of the Committee of Experts on the Application of Conventions and Recommendations, Ilolex No. 062010GBR087, 2010.
[32] Interview with Keith Ewing, July 2013.   [33] Hendy advised in nine cases in total.
[34] Interview with John Hendy, February 2024.

committed to advancing the labor cause through legal and political means. Since the early 1990s, they have worked together to develop an international litigation strategy at both the ECtHR and the ILO. They co-founded the Institute of Employment Rights (IER), an organization dedicated to informing public debates, analyzing labor law, and advocating for stronger trade union protections. The IER serves as both an intellectual hub and an influential advocacy organization for labor.

A key function of the IER is to equip unions with knowledge about labor rights under the European Convention. Through workshops and publications, the IER informs workers on ECtHR judgments covering issues such as workplace privacy and the right to strike. As will be discussed in Chapter 6, a report published by Ewing played a pivotal role in drawing blacklisted workers' attention to the ECtHR and ultimately led them to incorporate human rights language in their campaigns. Hendy and Ewing also use the IER to lobby the government and influence labor legislation. For example, IER's policy report, *A Manifesto for Labour Law*, which outlined a strategy for restoring collective bargaining in the UK, was adopted by all major trade unions and the Labour Party ahead of the 2015 general election.[35]

Having a long-established relationship with Hendy and Ewing, unions trust their legal representatives on strategy.[36] Hendy serves as standing counsel to several left-wing unions – including ASLEF, NUJ, RMT, Prison Officers' Association (POA), the University and College Union (UCU), and Unite The Union – which are more eager to pursue international litigation than other unions. These relationships mean that lawyers do not have to convince unions to take cases to the ECtHR – the main concern for unions is simply the cost of litigation. As Hendy explained, "We've been constantly saying to our pals in the movement, look there's a crock of gold here ... just give us the bowl, and we'll have it filled."[37] Unions are often relieved to learn that there are no legal fees involved in bringing cases to the ECtHR. Where necessary, labor lawyers also do pro bono work for individual workers' ECtHR cases, as in the case of the blacklisted workers (Chapter 7).

---

[35] The *Manifesto for Labour Law* was collectively authored by fifteen labour law experts and first launched in 2013. In 2018, it was expanded into an edited volume (Ewing, Hendy, and Jones 2016).

[36] Interview with Adrian Weir, Unite's Assistant Chief of Staff, December 2014.

[37] Interview with John Hendy, July 2013.

While Hendy and Ewing lead the legal strategy, a small group of barristers and solicitors collaborate on key ECtHR cases. One of the most prominent firms involved is Thompsons Solicitors, which has historically represented trade unions. Among the barristers working closely with Hendy is Michael Ford KC, a former barrister at Old Square Chambers and now a Deputy High Court Judge. Ford, like Hendy, has longstanding ties to unions and has one foot in academia, at the University of Bristol Law School. In addition to working on the ECtHR litigation, Ford has taken multiple cases on discrimination and working time to the ECJ.[38]

Rather than flooding the ECtHR with individual claims, labor lawyers approach the ECtHR strategically, selecting cases with the potential to set legal precedents or pressure the government into legislative change.[39] The limited number of lawyers working on the ECtHR cases has been an advantage in leading strategic litigation. As Hendy put it: "We have been very lucky [to be able to] preserve a monopoly [on taking cases to the ECtHR], which means that we have been able to devise the strategy."[40] The goal is not simply to win cases but to advance the collective power of organized labor. Out of the eleven trade union rights cases brought to the ECtHR from the UK since the 1990s, four set precedents. The strategy of careful case selection has been particularly evident in key rulings such as *ASLEF v. The United Kingdom* (2007), which followed the victory in *Wilson*, and *RMT v. The United Kingdom* (2014), which was specifically chosen to challenge restrictive laws on secondary action (sympathy strikes).[41] Hendy and RMT leader Bob Crow had long sought a strong case to contest the UK's onerous ballot requirements, but much to their disappointment, the ECtHR upheld the restrictions (see Chapter 4).

Legal advocacy groups and union confederations play a critical supporting role in the litigation strategy led by labor lawyers. Liberty, the UK's oldest civil liberties organization, is the only human rights group that has consistently been involved in trade union rights litigation at the ECtHR. Liberty has historically maintained close ties with

---

[38] Additionally, academics who work on labor law, such as Alan Bogg, Sandra Fredman, and Tonia Novitz, provide support in both preparing the initial applications and the third-party submissions.
[39] Interview with Keith Ewing, July 2013.
[40] Interview with John Hendy, November 2014.
[41] Interview with John Hendy, November 2014.

trade unions, initially through its predecessor NCCL (Harlow and Rawlings 1992; Madsen 2004). In the 1980s, the first labor cases brought to the ECtHR were coordinated by the NCCL lawyer Harriet Harman, who later became Deputy Leader of the Labour Party, Anthony Lester, a prominent human rights lawyer who had argued many leading cases at the ECtHR, and Wedderburn. None of these initial cases were successful, however.[42] Today, Liberty continues to support trade union rights cases, filing third-party interventions in notable cases such as *Wilson* (2002), *RMT* (2014), and the blacklisted workers' case (*Brough v. The United Kingdom* 2016).[43]

The TUC and European Trade Union Confederation (ETUC) also regularly submit third-party interventions to help demonstrate the broader implications of trade union cases for organized labor and to draw the Court's attention to other relevant international labor standards. The ETUC, in particular, highlights the consequences of an individual case for Europe at large. Its involvement increased after the major defeats unions suffered at the ECJ in the *Viking* and *Laval* cases and established its own Litigation Network in 2009 to counteract these decisions (Louis 2022).

***

Throughout the 1990s and 2000s, the ECtHR established its judicial authority and started accepting new rights claims, but the success of trade unions at the ECtHR was far from inevitable; it was carefully engineered by a small group of labor lawyers who saw international laws as a tool for advancing the collective power of organized labor at a time when unions were crushed under Thatcher's assault on labor. By coordinating strategy, selecting movement-wide cases, and working closely with unions, these lawyers helped turn a historically reluctant court into a key venue for trade union rights. Their legal victories not only shaped domestic labor protections but also influenced labor litigation across Europe.

The severity of the violations Turkish labor activists faced during that same period was even worse. As I show in the next section,

---

[42] In one case, Harman, together with the General Secretary of the NCCL Patricia Hewitt, successfully proved before the ECtHR that their activities at the NCCL were being intercepted by the intelligence services (*Harman and Hewitt v. the United Kingdom* 1992), though this was not a trade union rights case.

[43] Interview with Corrina Ferguson, December 2014.

Turkish labor lawyers, despite having no prior ECtHR experience, similarly used the Court to carve out new legal protections for unions.

5.3 TURKEY

Drafted in the aftermath of the 1980 military coup, the 1982 Constitution was much more regressive in terms of the rights and freedoms set out than its predecessor. And, it profoundly curtailed trade union activism, with two notable exceptions. First, unlike its predecessor, the 1982 Constitution did not preclude public sector workers from forming a union. Second, Article 90 of the Constitution introduced an important legal provision: "international treaties that are duly in force are directly applicable in domestic law. Their constitutionality cannot be challenged in the Constitutional Court." These two provisions granted a legal foothold for the eventual legal recognition of public sector unions. They provided a foundation for lawyers and activists to argue that international labor standards could be directly invoked to support unionization efforts. By relying on these international legal frameworks, particularly from the ILO and the ECtHR, labor activists established the first public sector unions in the early 1990s. These unions later united under the confederation KESK in 1995.

Between 1990, when Turkey accepted the jurisdiction of the ECtHR, and 2021, out of 97 trade union rights cases filed before the Court, 74 were submitted by KESK unions. While private sector unions also participated – DİSK unions, for instance, filed 10 cases – these efforts were largely uncoordinated.[44] KESK, by contrast, engaged in sustained legal mobilization. This section focuses on how KESK

---

[44] Private sector unions filed 19 cases, 10 of which were filed by the unions affiliated with DİSK. With the exception of the most recent case of *Barış and Others v. Turkey* (2021), discussed in the previous chapter, none of these 19 cases were of high importance. The ECtHR found a violation of Article 11 in only four cases, 3 of which were about the disproportionate use of violence against activists engaged in trade union activity. While state repression is a major problem for trade unions, these cases primarily concerned the civil liberties of union members, rather than rights intrinsic to union membership and activity. Some of the claims brought by private sector unions, such as challenges to the 10 percent threshold for establishing unions (*Dev Maden-Sen v. Turkey* 1999; see Chapter 3) or the right of retired workers to form trade unions (*Tüm Emekliler Sendikası v. Turkey* 2017), were more complex than the pressing and more straightforward claims advanced by public sector unions. Hence, the ECtHR dismissed these claims, leaving their resolution to domestic legal mechanisms.

identified and utilized international legal mechanisms and eventually concentrated its focus on the ECtHR due to its judicial authority and responsiveness.

5.3.1 Probing Phase: Why Turkish Labor Lawyers Turned to the ECtHR

When Turkish public sector workers set out to build their movement in the late 1980s, they sought to achieve three main goals: the right to establish and join unions, the right to engage in collective bargaining, and the right to take collective action. At the time, the Constitution safeguarded the right to form and join trade unions (Article 51) and the right to conclude collective bargaining agreements (Article 52) for "workers," but did not specify the status of *public sector workers*. The omission caused a major controversy among legal scholars and jurists. One group contended that public sector workers were "civil servants" and not "workers" under the Constitution, and therefore excluded from these protections (Koç and Koç 2009). A second group, led by two prominent labor law scholars, Alpaslan Işıklı and Mesut Gülmez, countered that the absence of a formal stipulation did not amount to prohibition. On the contrary, they argued that public sector workers retained these rights under both domestic and international law (Gülmez 1988; Işıklı 1986).

While the legal professionals fiercely debated the constitutionality of the right to unionize, the government made it clear that it had no intention of allowing public sector workers to unionize. Union publications were banned, public sector workers who tried to join trade unions received disciplinary punishments, the unions were folded, and attempts to march with union banners were blocked. Finally, in 1991, Vecdi Gönül, the Minister of Interior at the time, attempted to resolve the issue once and for all by issuing a circular that explicitly prohibited the establishment of trade unions in the public sector.[45]

Faced with escalating repression, labor lawyers and activists led by Gülmez and Işıklı decided to pursue international avenues. Like their British counterparts, Turkish labor lawyers first petitioned the ILO's CFA due to its strong de jure rights protections. In 1991, public sector workers filed two applications at the CFA: one regarding the closure of their unions, and the other concerning the inability to sign collective

---

[45] Circular No. 630, February 28, 1991 (for a discussion see Gülmez 1992 and 2002).

bargaining agreements. Although the CFA promptly urged the government to amend domestic legislation to recognize these rights, the government ignored the recommendations.

The closure of Tüm Haber Sen, the first media workers' union, became a defining moment in the early history of the public sector labor movement. The Istanbul Governor's Office suspended the union the same year it began operating. When the activists litigated the case in domestic courts in 1993, they were hopeful. The previous year, in separate cases, the First and Tenth Circuits of the Council of State (Danıştay), the highest administrative court, had ruled that public sector workers' right to unionize – and the relevant ILO conventions – did not conflict with the Constitution. That same year, the Turkish government had ratified two new ILO Conventions, Nos. 87 and 151, protecting the rights to unionize and to engage in collective bargaining. The Court of Cassation dashed these hopes by declaring that public sector workers could not legally establish trade unions and dismissed the claim regarding the applicability of the ratified ILO Conventions. By 1995, all branches of Tüm Haber Sen had been dissolved by order of the Ministry of Interior.

As was the case for British labor lawyers, the Turkish lawyers knew that the prospects of winning the case at the ECtHR looked dim. Moreover, in the early 1990s, virtually no labor lawyers had any experience of ECtHR litigation in the country. Naturally, the rulings of the Court were not available online at the time. After Turkey accepted the Court's jurisdiction, Gülmez decided to travel to Strasbourg in order to study its jurisprudence firsthand. "I stayed in Strasbourg for months. At the premises of the Court, I compiled all the [relevant] rulings [on Article 11]," he recalled.[46] After examining the trade union rights case law, Gülmez noticed that the Court had never considered a case involving a blanket ban on unionization for all public sector workers. The closure of Tüm Haber Sen provided a perfect opportunity to submit a test case. Indeed, *Tüm Haber Sen and Çınar v. Turkey* (2006), filed by the unions' legal team under Gülmez's direction, would become a major victory.

After filing their first case, the public sector unions turned their attention to a second key goal: securing the right to engage in collective bargaining.[47] The opportunity presented itself when one

---

[46] Interview with Mesut Gülmez, April 2015.
[47] Interview with Ayhan Erdoğan, April 2015.

municipality broke a collective bargaining agreement it had signed with KESK's municipal workers' union, Tüm Bel Sen (Union of All Municipality and Local Administration Services Employees). At the time, very few believed that public sector workers even had the legal right to unionize or sign collective agreements, and only left-wing municipalities were willing to enter into such contracts with Tüm Bel Sen. After signing such an agreement with Tüm Bel Sen in 1993, the Mayor of Gaziantep violated the terms of their agreement. Ayhan Erdoğan, a lawyer and a founding member of KESK, later explained that while the legal team did not engineer the breach deliberately, they saw the violation as a strategic chance to challenge the legal status of collective bargaining agreements for public sector unions:

> It was such a process that ... we did not sit and arrange a deal [with the Mayor so that he would violate the contract] like that. But it just happened to be that way ... I mean, we wouldn't go up and tell him [the Mayor], "Why did you implement it [the contract]?" [*Laughs*] But we seized on the opportunity.[48]

When the union brought the case through domestic channels, the Court of Cassation once again rejected their claim, dismissing the argument that Turkey's ratified ILO Conventions imposed binding obligations on the state.[49] When the application to the ECtHR was filed in 1996, the success and the international fame *Demir and Baykara v. Turkey* (2008) would bring was unbeknownst to the trade unionists and the legal team.[50] In an unexpected and innovative interpretation of the right to association (Article 11), the ECtHR affirmed that the right to unionize also included the right to collective bargaining. The Court heavily cited ILO Conventions, further strengthening the extensive authority of the ILO and its norm-setting role at the global level.

The Turkish labor activists achieved some of their goals without waiting for the final ruling of the ECtHR (see Chapter 8). The Court's

---

[48] Interview with Ayhan Erdoğan, April 2015.
[49] The Gaziantep District Court actually acknowledged the applicability of ratified ILO Conventions in this case and recognized public sector workers' rights to unionize and engage in collective bargaining despite the absence of explicit legal protections. The Court of Cassation, however, overturned the ruling, arguing that Tüm Bel Sen lacked legal personality, as public sector workers were not legally permitted to form unions.
[50] Interview with Sevgi Karaduman, May 2015.

slow timeline – it took nearly a decade to decide the *Demir and Baykara* case – did not prevent the unions and their lawyers from leveraging the *pending* cases to exert pressure on domestic lawmakers. This was a period of intense Europeanization in Turkey (see Chapter 3), and the combination of international litigation, references to international legal standards in domestic courts, and grassroots mobilization helped push significant reforms. In 1995, the Turkish parliament passed a new constitutional amendment recognizing public sector workers' right to establish and join trade unions. Then, in 2001, new legislation granted them the right to engage in collective bargaining, though these rights remained heavily circumscribed (Chapter 6).

By 2001, KESK unions had filed 17 cases at the ECtHR, but they only filed 3 petitions at the ILO throughout the 1990s. The ECtHR's judicial authority grew rapidly in the eyes of Turkish labor activists during this time. As Öztürk Türkdoğan, a legal advisor to the Healthcare Workers' Union (SES) and a founding member of KESK's executive board, put it, "if you're going to use international law, the ECtHR will be your first choice, undoubtedly."[51] This perspective reflected a broader shift. What began as a largely improvised recourse to international law in the face of domestic repression gradually gave way to a more strategic orientation, with the ECtHR emerging as the clear target institution for KESK lawyers.

5.3.2 The Legal Architects of ECtHR Litigation Strategy During the First Decade

During the initial years of KESK, the international litigation strategy on core trade union rights cases was spearheaded by a small group of committed lawyers. Of the 17 cases KESK unions filed at the ECtHR, 10 involved violations of both civil and political rights and trade union rights of Kurdish members. These cases, typically prepared by lawyers active in the Kurdish movement, emphasized civil liberties, with Article 11 claims playing a secondary role and ultimately failing to persuade the Court. By contrast, the remaining seven cases were prepared by a small core of labor lawyers who, like their British counterparts, were focused on using litigation to establish a legal foundation for KESK unions and secure basic collective rights. Of these seven, six

---

[51] Interview with Öztürk Türkdoğan, May 2015. In the 2023 general elections, Türkdoğan ran as a candidate for the pro-Kurdish Green Left Party (Yeşil Sol Parti, YSP).

were considered high-importance cases, and in four, the ECtHR found that Turkey had violated Article 11. These outcomes marked major legal victories for the public sector workers' movement in Turkey.

Two legal scholars, Alpaslan Işıklı and Mesut Gülmez, paved the way for international litigation by pointing out Turkey's obligations under international laws and offering legal advice to unionists during these foundational years. As İrfan Kaygısız, a union official involved in this work, explained:

> Now, a large amount of [legal] basis has accumulated. Five or ten years ago, it wasn't like this. But, this all happened little by little thanks to twenty-five years of effort ... Frankly, nobody believed us at the time ... There were two or three legal scholars who said that we had such a right. Alparslan *Hoca* [Işıklı] was the first to find out [that we have such a right].[52]

Working closely with these scholars, a small group of KESK lawyers devised a careful litigation strategy for international courts. According to Gülmez, the team needed to proceed incrementally due to ongoing disputes among legal experts over whether public sector workers had a constitutional right to unionize and whether international treaties could be directly applied:

> Our concern in those years was first to establish the right to unionize [for public sector workers], so that we could establish trade unions ... Because, when you said there is also a right to strike [and] a right to engage in collective bargaining agreements, it raised goosebumps on people's skin.[53]

Much like in the British experience, the legal team did not have to do much convincing with union activists. The grievances of the Turkish public sector unions were pressing and foundational. They were ready to try all options.

Gökhan Candoğan, the lawyer who represented and advised Yapı-Yol-Sen in a trio of cases on collective action (*Dilek and Others v. Turkey* 2007; *Enerji Yapı-Yol-Sen v. Turkey* 2009; *Karaçay v. Turkey* 2007), explained that the team deliberately selected cases to push the boundaries of ECtHR jurisprudence. At the time, domestic courts did not recognize public sector workers' right to take collective action,

---

[52] Interview with İrfan Kaygısız, April 2015.
[53] Interview with Mesut Gülmez, April 2015.

let alone their right to strike. As a result, when workers were punished for protesting or demonstrating, they rarely pursued legal recourse. But in these three cases, the unions and their lawyers decided to pursue litigation precisely to exhaust domestic remedies and bring their claims before the ECtHR. The *Enerji Yapı-Yol-Sen* ruling became the first ECtHR case to recognize the right to strike under Article 11.

Since Turkey had only accepted the jurisprudence of the ECtHR in 1990 and was not an EU member, Turkish labor lawyers had little experience with international litigation and lacked access to the resources enjoyed by their counterparts in Western Europe. As noted above, Gülmez had to visit Strasbourg to compile rulings manually. This kind of commitment was typical among the early architects of the litigation strategy. Most of the legal professionals and scholars who worked on these cases did so without compensation, due to the limited financial resources of the public sector unions at the time. As Erhan Karaçay, then president of Enerji Yapı-Yol-Sen, explained, "our unions did not have much money at the time," so their lawyer, Gökhan Candoğan represented the union's cases without receiving payment.[54] Similar accounts emerged from others involved in the early ECtHR efforts. İrfan Kaygısız, who conducted the legal research for *Demir and Baykara*, emphasized the sense of commitment that drove their work: "Nobody works on these kinds of issues [on human rights law] unless you have a motivation other than being a paid employee of a union. When we were working there [at Tüm Bel Sen], it wasn't like this," he said, pointing out his current office at Birleşik Metal İş. "During the first years of KESK, there was no money. [...] I would stay up all night working. There was a time I did not get paid for three months." He was not, however, resentful. "It was a different kind of excitement," he explained.[55] The dedication of these lawyers (and activists) to claiming labor rights as human rights was key to the successful litigation efforts at the ECtHR.

5.3.3 Parallel Pathways: Kurdish Unionists and the Civil–Political Rights Frame

In parallel to the legal strategy of these committed labor lawyers, another set of legal mobilization emerged from within the Kurdish movement. These lawyers filed ten ECtHR cases concerning the dual

---

[54] Interviews with Erhan Karaçay, April 2015 and Gökhan Candoğan, May 2015.
[55] Interview with İrfan Kaygısız, April 2015.

repression Kurdish trade unionists faced due to their union activity and their involvement in the broader Kurdish movement. Unlike the core KESK cases, however, there was no coordination between these lawyers and the labor-focused legal teams.[56] As a result, while trade union rights claims were raised under Article 11 in these Kurdish cases, the ECtHR dismissed them all. Instead, the Court often found violations of civil and political rights, reflecting the legal priorities and expertise of the lawyers involved.

Since its inception, KESK maintained close ties with the Kurdish movement. Many of its most active members organized in the Kurdish region in Southeastern Turkey. In 1992, Kurdish public sector workers established an association called Yurtsever Emekçiler (Patriotic Workers), which later formed a core constituency of KESK. Activists from this association became leading figures in establishing several KESK-affiliated unions such as Office Workers' Union (BES), Education and Science Workers' Union (Eğitim-Sen), SES, and Tüm Bel Sen, among others (Özdoğan 2015).[57] These unionists faced some of the worst forms of abuse and oppression, primarily for being active in the Kurdish movement, which the Turkish state perceived as an existential threat. According to a report by the Diyarbakır branch of Eğitim-Sen, thirty-six trade unionists had been killed between 1992 and 1999, including Necati Aydın, Zübeyyir Akkoç, and Hamit Pamuk, who were among the founders of Yurtsever Emekçiler.

Soon after Turkey accepted the jurisdiction of the ECtHR, Kurdish lawyers began filing hundreds of applications at the Court. The first wave of cases regarding the rights of the Kurdish minority was made possible through a collaboration between Kurdish lawyers from the region and transnational human rights lawyers based in the UK (Çalı 2010; Hodson 2014; Kurban 2020). The London-based advocacy group, the Kurdish Human Rights Project (KHRP), served as a liaison between the local Kurdish lawyers and the British lawyers and legal scholars. A series of landmark judgments issued by the ECtHR were highly influential in documenting widespread and systematic state violence in the Kurdish region, including village burnings, extrajudicial killings, torture, and the criminalization of expressions of Kurdish identity.

---

[56] Interviews with Gökhan Candoğan (May 2015), Ayhan Erdoğan (April 2015), Mesut Gülmez (April 2015), İrfan Kaygısız (April 2015).

[57] In particular, Kurdish unionists were active in founding Eğit-Sen, which later merged with Eğitim-İş to form Eğitim-Sen (see Chapter 8).

Some of these cases brought by this network involved Kurdish activists who were members of KESK unions. However, the primary focus of these cases was civil and political rights violations. This orientation reflected both the expertise and strategic priorities of the legal teams involved. Given the severity of the abuses Kurdish activists suffered, ranging from torture in police custody and arbitrary detention to state-sponsored killings, it is not surprising that the human rights lawyers prioritized these issues over trade union rights (see for example, *Akkoç v. Turkey* 2000). In one such case, the Court dismissed the claim under Article 11, reasoning that the applicant's trade union activities "were of no interest to the authorities and that they were only investigated in relation to their alleged links with the PKK" (*Süheyla Aydın v. Turkey* 2005: para. 202).[58]

The case of *Zengin v. Turkey* (1997) further illustrates the legal limits of the transnational advocacy network's approach to union rights. The applicant, a teacher and the secretary of Eğitimciler Sendikası (Eğit-Sen) Diyarbakır branch, was denied a promotion after releasing a press statement. The legal team litigated the case primarily as a trade union case, arguing that both the denial of legal status to the applicant's trade union, Eğit-Sen, and the disciplinary sanctions imposed on the applicant violated her rights to freedom of association (Article 11) and freedom of speech (Article 10). However, the case was dismissed due to non-exhaustion of domestic remedies. In particular, the Court noted that the applicant had never challenged the legal status of her union before a domestic court, nor did she frame her case in terms of Convention rights before national judges or appeal her case to the highest administrative court in Turkey.[59]

This case brings into sharp relief the differences in legal approach between those who represented the Kurdish cases and the core group of KESK's labor lawyers. The latter consistently framed their arguments in

---

[58] The PKK (Partiya Karkerên Kurdistanê, Kurdistan Workers' Party) is the Kurdish guerilla organization that has been leading an armed struggle against the Turkish state since the 1980s.

[59] One possibility is that the lawyers filed this case at the ECtHR before exhausting domestic remedies due to the persistent non-cooperation of Turkish legal authorities in the Kurdish cases during those years. In recognition of this, the Court in *Akdıvar and Others v. Turkey* (1996) lifted the exhaustion requirement, accepting the applicants' argument that domestic remedies would be "illusory, inadequate, and ineffective," in light of the state's condonement of, or complicity in, the crimes committed against the applicants (Çalı 2010; Kurban 2020).

terms of international obligations, invoked trade union rights under domestic and international law, and ensured that all domestic remedies were exhausted prior to approaching the ECtHR. The Kurdish cases, while crucial in advancing civil and political rights protections for one of Turkey's most marginalized populations, were not structured with the same level of procedural preparation or strategic focus on labor rights. As a result, in these initial years, they did not contribute to the ECtHR's growing jurisprudence on Article 11 in the same way as the foundational KESK cases did.

5.3.4 Expansion Phase: Flooding the ECtHR with Repeat and Leading Cases

In the years following 2001, as ties between the Kurdish movement and KESK deepened, Kurdish lawyers with expertise in labor law increasingly took on leadership roles in litigating trade union rights cases at KESK unions. This growing alliance diversified the trade union rights cases before the ECtHR, bringing issues at the intersection of class and ethnic identity into the legal spotlight. During this expansion phase, KESK unions continued to set important precedents, even as their litigation strategy changed from filing only carefully selected cases to flooding the Court with many repeat cases.

The transformation is reflected in the numbers: KESK unions filed 17 trade union rights cases between 1992 and 2001, and 58 between 2002 and 2011 – a more than threefold increase. In this second phase of litigation, KESK unions began taking nearly every case lost at domestic courts to the ECtHR, signaling a move from strategic litigation to routine recourse. As discussed in Chapter 8, this change in approach stemmed largely from the changing nature of public sector unionism in Turkey and the unions' growing frustration with the government's refusal to implement ECtHR judgments.

A similar shift occurred within the Kurdish legal community. The Kurdish movement adopted a comparable strategy of flooding the Court with thousands of cases. Given the sheer scale of rights violations experienced by the Kurdish population, as well as the depth of legal expertise among Kurdish human rights lawyers, the ECtHR has become a regular destination for both individual and collective grievances. Today, many experienced human rights lawyers litigate both types of claims – those related to trade union rights and those focused on civil and political rights.

Roughly one third of all trade union rights cases from Turkey involve Kurdish minority rights claims, the majority of which were filed after

2001. One prominent case in this period was the government's attempt to dissolve Eğitim-Sen in 2004, due to the union's decision to include in its constitution a provision affirming the right to education in one's mother tongue (*Eğitim ve Bilim Emekçileri Sendikası v. Turkey* 2012). Many others concern KESK members, primarily teachers, who were reassigned from their posts in Kurdish-majority cities to distant parts of the country due to their union activities. Lawyers refer to these cases as *sürgün davaları* (forced relocation or exile cases), since trade union members were reassigned outside the Kurdish region as a punitive measure, forced to leave their homes, families, and communities. Still other cases involve trade unionists facing disciplinary or criminal proceedings for participating in otherwise lawful labor organizing activities – distributing leaflets, joining rallies, or issuing press statements that denounce state repression of Kurds. These cases illustrate not only the persistence of anti-union practices, but also how state repression of Kurdish identity and labor rights have become deeply intertwined.

5.4 CONCLUSION

This chapter has explored the central role of lawyers in initiating and sustaining litigation efforts at the ECtHR. I have argued that legal advocacy groups perform vital functions within a field of international legal pluralism: They identify strategic venues, develop targeted litigation strategies, and draw unions' attention to these legal opportunities. In both the UK and Turkey, lawyers played a key role in transforming the ECtHR – initially an institution with weak de jure protections for labor rights – into a viable forum for advancing trade union rights. Their efforts offer important insight into how international legal institutions can be shaped from below.

   While lawyers in both countries pursued strategic litigation, the form and evolution of their approaches diverged. In the UK, a small and tightly coordinated group of labor lawyers and scholars carefully selected test cases, working in close alignment with trade unions as restrictive domestic laws mounted. In Turkey, public sector unions organized under KESK followed a similar strategy in the 1990s, carefully crafting test cases to push for foundational rights. But as KESK's capacity to influence domestic legal and political outcomes diminished in the 2000s, its litigation strategy shifted. Lawyers began to flood the ECtHR with repeat claims, seeking not only precedent but also

5.4 CONCLUSION

individual remedies for their members. As Chapter 3 demonstrated, Turkey now accounts for more trade union rights cases at the ECtHR than any other country, comprising more than half of the total. While Turkey and the UK produced a comparable number of high-importance rulings, a large majority of Turkey's cases consist of repeat or follow-up petitions. By tracing these divergent paths, the chapter has shown how lawyers in each country recalibrated their litigation strategies in response to changing political opportunity structures.

In both countries, litigation efforts were led by a small number of committed lawyers who worked in tandem with trade unions. In Turkey, in particular, the commitment of lawyers made up for the lack of institutional resources and helped sustain long-term legal mobilization. These lawyers not only brought cases to the ECtHR; they also acted as bridges between local activism and international law, translating complex legal norms into accessible tools for organizing. Hence, they acted as agents of legal and political change, helping expand the scope of human rights law and making it accessible for labor movements on the ground.

The first part of this book has focused on explaining why and how workers came to mobilize international law. As shown, the push from hostile domestic regimes combined with the pull from the ECtHR's growing responsiveness created the conditions for this turn to international litigation. Lawyers played a central role in guiding workers through these processes and helped translate grievances into legal claims that, over time, contributed to the expansion of human rights jurisprudence.

But legal victories at the ECtHR raise a new set of questions that go beyond claims-making to the politics of impact. What happens after a favorable ruling? Do states comply with the Court's rulings? And if the enforcement powers of the ECtHR are limited, how can grassroots actors push for change? The second part of this book turns to these urgent questions, tracing the afterlife of ECtHR rulings and the political struggles they set in motion.

PART II

WHAT IS THE IMPACT OF LITIGATION AT THE EUROPEAN COURT OF HUMAN RIGHTS?

CHAPTER 6

DIRECT REMEDIES
Limits of Compliance with European Court of Human Rights Rulings

The first part of the book traced the story of why and how the ECtHR became a strategic resource for labor activists at a time when domestic governments were adopting anti-union policies. The ECtHR issued some landmark rulings in cases brought by Turkish and British labor activists and recognized the right to unionize, the right to collective bargaining, and the right to strike as human rights. The new approach of the Court, abandoning its previous narrow interpretation of trade union rights, augured new hope for labor activists, who have begun taking cases to the ECtHR in order to challenge repressive national policies.

Before delving into the labor struggles that took root in the shadow of these rulings, this chapter takes a more conventional, compliance-focused lens to analyze the direct impact of these judgments on state behavior. Focusing on the Court's most transformative trade union rights judgments involving Turkey and the UK (discussed in Chapter 4), I assess not only the Council of Europe's formal oversight process, but also the actual implementation of reforms from the perspective of trade unions and workers.

The analysis shows that both governments maintain a high compliance rate on trade union rights rulings, underscoring the ECtHR's authority and influence within the European legal order. In many cases, the rulings triggered significant structural reforms. Since Turkish labor activists faced more severe and recurring rights violations, the executive body of the CoE, the Committee of Ministers (CM) requested more extensive measures from Turkey than from the UK.

A closer examination, however, demonstrates that both states, the differing political contexts notwithstanding, do the bare minimum necessary to finalize the compliance negotiations with the CM on the execution of judgments. While the ECtHR is a strong human rights court with a high compliance rate, formal compliance does not necessarily translate into meaningful change. Often, domestic reforms fail to reflect the spirit of the ECtHR judgments to prevent future violations.

These findings suggest that while ECtHR judgments can pressure states to alter specific laws or practices, they rarely produce deep or lasting reforms in the absence of powerful mobilization from below. This chapter, therefore, shows that a singular focus on formal compliance measures ultimately supports realist and critical accounts that question the transformative power of international legal institutions.

6.1 EXECUTION OF ECTHR RULINGS

The ECtHR is often singled out among international human rights courts for its effectiveness and ability to influence policies in high-stakes issue areas (Alter, Helfer, and Madsen 2016; Helfer and Voeten 2014; Hillebrecht 2014; Stiansen 2019; Stone Sweet and Keller 2008). Scholars have pointed to several factors behind the Court's relatively high compliance rate. Some emphasize the strength of the ECtHR's institutional enforcement mechanisms, notably the CM, which oversees the implementation of judgments on behalf of the CoE (Çalı and Koch 2014; Hafner-Burton and Tsutsui 2005). Composed of the foreign affairs ministers of the member states or their permanent representatives in Strasbourg, the CM creates peer pressure on states for compliance. Much of the bureaucratic and legal work, however, is carried out by the Department for the Execution of Judgments (the Secretariat), which conducts detailed reviews of state compliance and recommends whether cases should be closed. The Secretariat, therefore, places institutional constraints on the CM's political discretion and promotes uniform applications of standards in order to ensure that enforcement does not become a topic of political bargaining among members (Çalı and Koch 2014).[1]

---

[1] Despite the importance of the behind-the-scenes work undertaken by the Secretariat, in this chapter I'll refer to the CM as the authoritative body that monitors compliance.

Others attribute the ECtHR's authority to broader cultural and normative factors. Some scholars point to the liberal-democratic traditions and rights-conscious political cultures of many member states (Moravcsik 2000), while others emphasize the reputational and socializing effects of belonging to the CoE system (Helfer and Slaughter 1997). In this view, compliance stems less from coercion than from persuasion and norm internalization. As Helfer (2008b: 135) puts it, the Court's influence lies in "the skillful use of persuasion to realign the interests and incentives of decision-makers in favor of compliance with the tribunals' judgments." The ECtHR thus operates through soft power: It has no means of direct enforcement beyond the symbolic weight of its rulings and the threat – seldom used – of political sanctions. The weakness of the ECtHR's hard power came into stark relief with Russia's 2022 expulsion from the CoE following its invasion of Ukraine. When coercive tools are invoked, they may undermine the Court's legitimacy more than they constrain abusive governments. In most cases, compliance is driven less by external enforcement than by states' concern for their international standing and their habituation to rights-based norms (Helfer 2008; Koh 2005).

What, then, happens when the ECtHR finds a violation? The Court itself does prescribe specific implementation measures beyond determining financial compensation, "just satisfaction," owed to the applicant. The CM works with the responding states to determine the necessary steps for implementation (Article 46(2)).[2] These steps fall into two categories: individual measures, which address specific violation(s) suffered by the applicant, such as reopening proceedings at the domestic level or punishing perpetrators; and general measures, which aim at preventing future violations through structural reforms. For instance, a state may be required to amend its employment laws to protect trade union members from discriminatory treatment or to submit data showing that unionized workers can lawfully take industrial action. Domestic courts' compliance with the ECtHR rulings and the Convention in similar cases is also part of the general measures. Hence, the ECtHR monitors compliance by analyzing the behavior of executive, legislative, and judicial branches.

Given that undertaking structural changes frequently carries heavy political and financial costs for states, states are generally more willing to pay the compensation award than implement general measures

---

[2] In exceptional cases, the Court may indicate specific measures to be adopted.

(Hawkins and Jacoby 2010; Hillebrecht 2014). Nevertheless, in most cases, governments eventually carry out legislative or policy reforms, even if implementation is slow and uneven (Stiansen 2019). The policy effects of the ECtHR's rulings often reach beyond the respondent state: A violation ruling against one state can prompt legislative changes in others, as domestic courts reference the ECtHR jurisprudence in their own decisions (Helfer and Voeten 2014).

However, as with most international human rights courts, compliance varies by member state. Either due to lack of political will or state capacity, repeat offenders often fail to undertake measures that would prevent the same type of cases from being brought before the court (Anagnostou 2013; Kurban 2020). Newer democracies initially respond to ECtHR rulings quickly, but their record worsens on more complex or politically sensitive issues (Grewal and Voeten 2015).[3] Most notable and recent examples of these are Turkey's refusal to release its political opponents from prison, despite ECtHR rulings and mounting pressure from the CoE (*Kavala v. Turkey* 2022; *Selahattin Demirtaş v. Turkey* No. 2 2020). Conversely, established democracies, where institutional checks and balances are stronger, may take longer, but eventually implement the compliance measures. For example, the UK's long-standing resistance to the ECtHR ruling on prisoner voting rights eventually gave way to compliance (*Hirst v. the United Kingdom* 2005). UK's response exemplifies what Hillebrecht (2014) calls a broader pattern of "begrudging compliance," where judgments are taken seriously not because of enthusiasm for international oversight, but because of deeply rooted political institutions and traditions of rule of law.

6.2 LIMITS OF COMPLIANCE WITH COURT RULINGS

An overwhelming majority of studies on compliance with ECtHR judgments utilize the Court's online database on the execution of judgments. These studies help us understand some of the general patterns of compliance across states. Yet relying on an international court's own assessment may provide an incomplete or even misleading picture of the real-world impact of its judgments. While the CM makes an effort to conduct a thorough analysis of implementation by

---

[3] For the transitioning democracies of Europe, joining the EU constitutes a significant pressure mechanism for compliance with the ECtHR rulings (Holzhacker 2013; Kochenov 2008; Schimmelfennig and Sedelmeier 2005).

reviewing reports from NGOs and the judicial practices on similar cases at the domestic level, it is not always the most reliable arbiter of compliance. Assessing on-the-ground impact requires a closer look at domestic practices and attention to voices from below.

Since 2006, the CM accepts reports from civil society organizations regarding states' compliance (Rule 9.2).[4] These submissions are intended to serve as a check on the self-reporting of states as they provide vital information about whether legislative reforms reflect the spirit of the ECtHR's judgments, how those reforms are implemented in practice, and whether domestic courts are applying Strasbourg case law. However, such reports are based on the voluntary initiatives of domestic NGOs, rather than a required or routine part of the Court's monitoring process. Participation by NGOs has been sporadic and sparse, not just in trade union rights cases, but across issue areas, due to lack of knowledge among civil society organizations about the Rule 9.2 procedures (Erken 2021; Küçüksu 2022).[5]

Case studies that go beyond the Court's own execution database confirm that states often find ways to sidestep meaningful reform, even in cases the CM formally closes as fully compliant (Anagnostou 2013; Búzás 2021; Kurban 2020; Von Staden 2018). A comparative study of France and the Czech Republic's compliance with ECtHR and EU rulings on racial equality finds that states frequently adopt minimal reforms while continuing to violate rights "under the cover of technical legality" (Búzás 2021: 5). Similarly, even liberal democracies such as the UK have been shown to make only half-hearted changes aimed primarily at ending CM supervision, rather than preventing future violations (Von Staden 2018). These findings reinforce a broader point: International courts alone cannot compel states to internalize the deeper commitments embedded in human rights norms.

My analysis of trade union rights cases in Turkey and the UK confirms this pattern. Both states appear to take ECtHR rulings

---

[4] Committee of Ministers, Appendix 4: Rules of the Committee of Ministers for the supervision of the execution of judgments and of the terms of friendly settlement, Rule 9.2 (2006).

[5] One study found that overall, NGOs make submissions in 5 percent of leading cases (Donald, Long, and Speck 2020). (See the discussion on leading cases in the next section.) One Europe-wide NGO, European Implementation Network (EIN), was recently established in order to raise awareness about the execution process and facilitate meetings among the CM and civil society actors. Erken (2021) finds that EIN's efforts resulted in an increase in NGO submissions to the CM.

seriously and undertake reforms accordingly. But international judges and bureaucrats sitting at a distant international institution cannot fully observe the practical consequences of legislative changes undertaken by member states. Moreover, the ECtHR does not provide adequate incentives for states to address the structural roots of labor rights violations. The reluctant reforms introduced to satisfy CM requirements often fall short of what trade unionists actually demand.

The length of proceedings also poses a major challenge for the reform process. The time it takes to exhaust domestic remedies, litigate in Strasbourg, and complete post-judgment communications with the CM easily add up to more than a decade. In the best cases, states undertake legislative reforms prior to the ECtHR judgment due to pressure from below and not as a result of pressure from the CM, as later chapters will show.

The number of judgments against Turkey is markedly higher than those against the UK, reflecting both more repressive labor policies and more frequent rights violations. In contrast to their British counterparts, Turkish legal advocates pursued a high-volume litigation strategy (as discussed in Chapter 5), but the Turkish government's failure to prevent further violations also contributed to the caseload. These failures are rarely the result of limited state capacity; rather, they are symptomatic of a political unwillingness to make concessions to trade unions. Yet, despite the difference in volume and severity, in both countries governments tend to do the absolute minimum in order to comply with the rulings of the Court and close the case. The only partial exception is found in Turkey's first wave of landmark trade union cases, where legislative change preceded the final ruling due to sustained pressure from activists. These rare instances highlight the importance of domestic mobilization in achieving substantive outcomes. Overall, the pattern across both countries is one of "begrudging compliance" (Hillebrecht 2014), which often amounts to a form of "evasion" (Búzás 2021) – a mode of engagement with the ECtHR that avoids confronting the structural causes of labor rights violations.

6.3 METHODOLOGICAL APPROACH TO ANALYZING COMPLIANCE WITH THE ECTHR'S TRADE UNION RIGHTS JUDGMENTS

By compliance, I refer to the measures undertaken by states to conform to a ruling. I compare the ECtHR's standards for satisfactory compliance to close a case with the actual effect of these judgments on the ground. To do so, I draw on a range of sources including the publicly available legal documents from Turkey and the UK, reports by domestic advocacy organizations, statements from international bodies such as the ILO and the EU, and publications by local labor scholars and trade unions. These diverse monitoring materials are essential for assessing the real-world impact of trade union rights cases, given that trade unions do not typically participate in the ECtHR's supervision process. Among the sixteen lead cases examined here, civil society groups submitted a Rule 9.2 communication in only one case from Turkey on disproportionate police violence – an issue that concerns not just trade unionists but all activists participating in demonstrations.

This chapter analyzes judgments in which the applicants – as trade unions or union members – invoked Article 11 (freedom of association) regardless of the Court's finding a violation regarding this provision.[6] In some of these cases, the Court found violations instead under ill-treatment (Article 3), freedom of speech (Article 10), or the right to effective remedy (Article 13) in complaints brought by trade union members.

Once the ECtHR judgments are transferred to the CM, they are categorized as leading or repetitive cases.[7] Leading cases raise new legal issues or require structural reforms by the respondent state. In 2024, 22 percent of all pending cases under supervision were classified as leading cases.[8] Repetitive cases are grouped under an existing leading case, and require the same general measures already identified by the CM. The progress on the execution – including states' action plans on compliance, CM decisions, and NGO submissions – is publicly available through the HUDOC.EXEC database. Table 6.1 presents the execution status of all leading trade union rights cases from Turkey and the UK, along with the related repetitive cases.

---

[6] Unlike in Chapter 4, which demonstrated the ECtHR's evolving jurisprudence on trade union rights, decisions on admissibility are not included in the analysis here because those do not go into supervision by the CM.

[7] This categorization often mirrors the ECtHR's assignment of importance level, with a few exceptions; cases with high importance level often end up being categorized as leading cases by the Secretariat.

[8] Eighteenth Annual Report of the CM, www.coe.int/en/web/execution/annual-report-2024.

TABLE 6.1 Execution of ECtHR's trade union rights cases from Turkey and the UK, 1960–2021

Issue	Leading cases	Repetitive cases #	Status	Just satisfaction	Individual measures	General measures	Union
Turkey							
Right to unionize							
Ban on public sector workers' right to unionize	Tüm Haber Sen and Çınar v. Turkey (2006)	0	closed	n/a	yes	yes	KESK/Tüm Haber Sen
Relocation of a worker due to trade union activities (sürgün)	Metin Turan v. Turkey (2006) Müslüm Çiftçi v. Turkey (2010)	1 1	closed pending	yes yes	yes pending	yes yes	KESK/Various KESK/Eğitim-Sen
Lack of effective remedy for relocation of a union member (sürgün)	N/A*	10	closed	yes	yes	yes	KESK/Various
Closure of a union for supporting right to education in a mother tongue	Eğitim-Sen v. Turkey (2012)	0	closed	yes	yes	yes	KESK/Eğitim-Sen
Dismissal of workers due to trade union membership	Tek Gıda İş Sendikası v. Turkey (2017)	0	pending	yes	yes	partial	Türk-İş/Tek Gıda İş

146

TABLE 6.1 (cont.)

Issue	Leading cases	Repetitive cases #	Status	Just satisfaction	Individual measures	General measures	Union
Turkey							
Collective bargaining							
Ban on public sector workers' right to collective bargaining	*Demir and Baykara v. Turkey* (2008)	1	closed	yes	yes	yes	KESK/Tüm Bel Sen
Turkey							
Collective action/strike							
Ban on public sector workers' right to strike	*Enerji Yapı-Yol Sen v. Turkey* (2009)	0	closed	yes	yes	yes	KESK/Enerji Yapı-Yol Sen
Criminal charges against union members for joining collective action/reading public statement	*Karademirci and Others v. Turkey* (2005) *H. M. v. Turkey* (2006)	0	closed	yes	yes	yes	KESK/Various
Criminal charges against union members for joining collective action	N/A*	2	closed	yes	yes	yes	KESK/Various
Disciplinary sanctions against union members for joining collective action	*Karaçay v. Turkey* (2007)	6	closed	yes	yes	yes	KESK/Various
Disciplinary sanctions against union members for joining collective action	*Dilek and Others v. Turkey* (2007) *Kaya and Seyhan v. Turkey* (2009)	5	pending	yes	yes	partial	KESK/Various

147

TABLE 6.1 (cont.)

Issue	Leading cases	Repetitive cases #	Status	Just satisfaction	Individual measures	General measures	Union
Criminal charges against union members for joining strike	*Urcan and Others v. Turkey* (2008)	1	pending	yes	yes	partial	KESK/Eğitim-Sen
Use of force against union members for joining peaceful protest	*Akarsubaşı v. Turkey* (2015)	4	pending	yes	yes	partial	KESK/Various
Use of force against union members for joining peaceful protest	N/A*	15	pending	yes	yes	partial	KESK/Various
UK							
Preferential contracts offered to non-unionized workers	*Wilson, National Union of Journalists and Others v. The United Kingdom* (2002)	0	closed	yes	yes	yes	NUJ and RMT
Trade union's right to dismiss members	*ASLEF v. The United Kingdom* (2007)	0	closed	yes	yes	yes	ASLEF

Data collected by the author from HUDOC-EXE.
* The leading case is not a trade union rights case.

6.4 COMPLIANCE WITH ECtHR RULINGS IN THE UNITED KINGDOM

The ECtHR found Article 11 violations in two leading cases from the UK, both of which were discussed in detail in Chapter 4 and are listed in Table 6.1. Despite being few in number, both were designated as "key cases" within the Court's jurisprudence and have since become important precedents in the ECtHR's evolving approach to trade union rights. Unlike in Turkey, these cases did not generate repetitive applications, which reflects both the narrower scope of labor-related litigation and the more stable institutional environment in the UK. In both cases, the UK adopted the required individual and general measures, and the CM closed supervision. Although the legislative reforms introduced some important protections for trade unionists, the reforms largely failed to satisfy the expectations of the trade unions and reflect the essence of the ECtHR rulings.

6.4.1 Rights to Unionize and Collective Bargaining

(1) **Reforms and glimmers of hope.** *Wilson, National Union of Journalists and Others v. The United Kingdom* (2002) addressed whether a company can offer favorable contracts to workers who opted out of collective bargaining. The applicants refused to sign individual contracts with their employers, and hence received less pay. The case was highly politicized at the domestic level, both in parliament and in the media, as the legal battle became a flashpoint in union's struggle against the derecognition that was going on in many sectors. Mere days before the final ruling was issued by the House of Lords, the highest court of appeal at the time, the Conservative-majority parliament passed the Ullswater Amendment which ensured a favorable decision for the employers. The ECtHR, however, in a landmark judgment, decisively precluded such acts as attacks on trade unions, reasoning that the practice aimed at persuading workers to forgo their trade union rights by offering short-term financial benefits.

The new government, led by Tony Blair's Labour Party, enacted the Employment Relations Act (ERA) of 2004 in order to bring British law in line with the ECtHR judgment. Most notably, the Act repealed the Ullswater Amendment and amended the Trade Union and Labour Relations (Consolidation) Act (TULRCA) of 1992 to strengthen protections against employer pressure. Section 145A of the amended Act prohibits offers made with "the sole or main purpose of inducing the worker" not to join an independent union, engage in union activities, or use "trade union services." Sections 146 and 152 also protect workers from being subjected to detriment or dismissal for exercising those rights. Workers who receive such offers or face retaliation for using union services may file a complaint with an employment tribunal. Upon finding these new protections satisfactory, the CM decided to close the case in 2011.[9]

(2) **Limitations and persistent violations.** A closer inspection of the legislative changes uncovers a more complicated picture. The government largely disregarded the calls by pro-labor institutions and trade unions to overhaul employment law to give effect to the ECtHR's judgment and instead opted for a narrow interpretation of the legal requirements of *Wilson*. The two leading architects of British trade union cases at the ECtHR, Keith Ewing and John Hendy, had called for comprehensive revisions, including prohibition of any attempt by employers to deter or prevent workers from joining a trade union or participating in its activities, as well as clarifications to broad definitions contained in TULRCA in order to prevent similar issues from arising (Bogg 2022; Ewing 2003). But labor scholars and lawyers identified numerous shortcomings in the amended legislation (Bogg 2005; Collins, Ewing, and McColgan 2012; Smith 2009). The Joint Committee on Human Rights (JCHR), a parliamentary committee responsible for preparing reports on the general measures that need to be undertaken in order to comply with ECtHR rulings, also concluded that the Act fell short of providing adequate protections for workers' trade union rights (Joint Committee on Human Rights 2004).

One major problem with the reform concerns the term "union services," which is imprecise and does not explicitly include collective bargaining (section 145B). This omission directly contradicts the ECtHR's finding in *Wilson*, where the denial of collective bargaining was central to the violation. While Bogg (2005: 75) notes that it was still possible for British judges to interpret the act to read collective bargaining into trade union membership or activities, he emphasizes

---

[9] The process of closing a case can exceed reasonable expectations, either because the CM delays in order to observe further developments in domestic case law or because the execution process becomes protracted for reasons unrelated to the state's behavior. In *Wilson*, the UK appears to have fulfilled all compliance measures by 2004, yet the CM's 2011 resolution includes no reference to additional domestic rulings.

that "reliance on the interpretative obligation does not ensure sufficiently certain protection for it to be considered effective, and it is shocking that this is even necessary," given the unambiguous Strasbourg ruling.

A second flaw is the restriction on legal standing: Under the new law, only individual workers, and not unions, have the right to bring claims against employers. This exclusion weakens collective protections. Workers may accept inducements out of immediate need or self-interest, while unions are positioned to defend collective, long-term interests. Furthermore, under the new law, deterring a worker from joining a union or participating in trade union services must be the employers' "sole or main purpose" for the offer to constitute a violation. This high evidentiary bar enables employers to argue alternative motives – such as business restructuring – thus sidestepping liability for dismissing workers or engaging in action short of dismissal.

Finally, the limited compensation available to workers has been criticized for offering little deterrence. Employers may simply absorb the cost as a price worth paying to undermine union power. In short, the reforms failed to unequivocally prohibit employers from deterring union membership or collective bargaining.[10]

6.4.2 Right of Unions to Choose Their Members

(1) **Reforms and glimmers of hope.** The second landmark case from the UK, *ASLEF v. The United Kingdom* (2007), concerned the right of unions to exclude individuals from membership based on political affiliation. ASLEF terminated a worker's membership due to his membership to an extreme right-wing party, the BNP. During the domestic procedures, the Employment Appeal Tribunal upheld the worker's complaint by relying on section 174 of the TULRCA 1992, which prohibited expulsion from a union on the basis of political party membership. The case carried significant weight for unions, in part because the BNP had deliberately encouraged its members to join trade unions to provoke expulsions and pursue compensation claims (Hendy and Ewing 2005: 198–199). In a highly significant judgment, the Court recognized the autonomous political identity of unions and their right to grant membership to those workers whose values and views align with the collective objectives of unions.

---

[10] See Bogg (2022) and Bogg and Ewing (2021) for an application of changes prompted by *Wilson* in recent case in domestic courts.

Before the case reached Strasbourg, the government changed section 174 of the TULRCA 1992 in response to trade union pressure. The new amendment introduced under the ERA 2004, permitted trade unions to exclude and expel individuals not based on political party membership, but due to *participation in party activities*. The reform, however, did not allay the concerns and complaints of unions. A year after the ECtHR's final judgment, the government, led by Tony Blair's Labour Party, undertook more stringent measures to remedy the issue. The ERA 2008 amended section 174 of TULRCA 1992 to give effect to the ECtHR ruling. The new Act permits trade unions to expel or exclude individuals due to their political party membership if:

- their party membership conflicts with a union rule or objective (provided the objective is sufficiently clear);
- proper procedures are followed in accordance with union rules and the individual's representations are fairly considered; and
- the exclusion does not result in loss of livelihood or other exceptional hardship.

In the event that a trade union excludes or expels a member unlawfully, it will be required to pay a compensation award to the affected individual. After examining the general and individual measures taken by the government, the CM decided to close the case in 2011.

(2) **Limitations and persistent violations.** Once again, however, the legislative response was limited in scope. The legal changes were designed to make it lawful for unions to expel their members based on political party membership, yet, under pressure from the House of Lords, the complex conditions brought under ERA 2008 made it practically difficult, if not impossible, for unions to expel such members.

In the wake of the *ASLEF* decision, the UK government initially proposed a pro-union remedy to the problem raised by the ECtHR. The draft legislation avoided any special treatment of political party membership or activities and allowed unions to expel or exclude individuals whose affiliations were deemed "unacceptable" to the union.[11] The government defended the draft legislation on the grounds of clarity

---

[11] Department for Business, Enterprise and Regulatory Reform ECHR Judgment in the *ASLEF v. UK* Case – Implications for Trade Union Law, Government Response to Public Consultation (November 2007), para. 3.9.

and ease of application. In response to the concerns about possible abuse by unions and the rights of individuals who are excluded, the government noted that the Certification Officer has the power to arbitrate on complaints about the breach and is able to offer quicker and more informal decisions than courts (para. 3.9).

These assurances, however, did not put to rest the concerns raised by the House of Lords, which pushed for stronger protections for individuals like the BNP member in *ASLEF*.[12] In a reversal of its approach after *Wilson*, the JCHR shifted its focus from the associational rights of trade unions to the protection of individual rights, even though the ECtHR had emphasized unions' autonomy to determine their membership. The resulting legislation, therefore, imposed several hurdles: political party membership must be shown to conflict with a union's objective or rule; the union must follow specific procedural obligations; and the expulsion must not result in "exceptional hardship" to the individual.

Critics have pointed out that these constraints are rooted in outdated anxieties – remnants of the 1970s, when expulsion or exclusion could mean the dismissal of a worker under closed shop agreements (Ewing 2009b). Today, however, not only are closed shop agreements abolished, but legal protections prohibit making hiring and firing decisions based on trade union membership. Indeed, both of these principles are well established in ECtHR case law, as demonstrated by the above-mentioned *Wilson* case and *Young, James and Webster v. The United Kingdom* (1981), the latter discussed in Chapter 5. The new requirements therefore impose unnecessary burdens on unions seeking to exercise a basic right.

Ewing, who served as a counsel to ASLEF before the ECtHR, questioned whether the union could now legally expel the same BNP member under the "over-prescriptive new regime, despite the fact that the new regime was passed purportedly to give effect to the *ASLEF* decision" (Ewing 2009b: 54). Once again, the legislative changes undertaken by the state fulfilled the requirements of the CM while failing to take effective measures that would prevent future violations.

---

[12] See Ewing (2009b) for a discussion on the different legislative options that were considered and the pressure from the House of Lords to implement the legislation with the most constraints on trade unions' freedom to choose their members.

6.4.3 Right to Strike

(1) **Reforms and glimmers of hope.** British labor lawyers and activists have not been able to bring a successful claim under the right to strike before the ECtHR. Two cases in which they had placed high hopes, *RMT v. The United Kingdom* (2014) and *POA and Others v. The United Kingdom* (2011), were dismissed by the Court. Nonetheless, both the reasoning of the Court on the substantive aspect of *RMT* and its broader case law on the right to strike – particularly in cases from Turkey – have influenced the legislative and judicial practices at British courts.

The right to strike has traditionally been construed narrowly in British law. In a 2009 case, Lord Justice Maurice Kay famously noted that "[i]n this country, the right to strike has never been much more than a slogan or a legal metaphor. Such a right has not been bestowed by statute" (*Metrobus Ltd v. Unite the Union* 2009).[13] As discussed in previous chapters, restrictions on the right to strike include complex requirements for conducting ballots, calculating results, and notifying employers – both about holding a ballot and about proceeding with strike action. Failure to comply with these procedural steps can result in legal liability, with unions held responsible for inducing workers to breach their contracts (Dukes 2011). Furthermore, as the ECtHR recognized in *RMT*, the UK is one of the few European countries with a blanket ban on all solidarity action. As a result, domestic case law is full of decisions upholding injunctions against strike activity (Dukes 2011; Ewing and Hendy 2010; Bogg and Ewing 2014).

Yet in the early 2010s, the ECtHR's pro-union judgments on the right to strike slowly came onto the radar of British judges. In *Serco Ltd. v. RMT* (2011), the Court of Appeal recognized the growing body of case law on the right to strike under Article 11, noting that this right forms part of the broader freedom of association guaranteed by the Convention and incorporated into UK law through the HRA. Another case the same year reiterated that while UK law does not explicitly grant a right to strike, ECtHR jurisprudence recognizes such a right as an integral part of trade union freedoms (*RMT v Serco Ltd; ASLEF v. London and Birmingham Railway Ltd* 2011). Commenting on the importance of these cases, Ewing (2011: 250) argued that "*RMT v Serco Ltd and ASLEF v London and Birmingham Railway Ltd* represent

---

[13] Cited in Ewing and Hendy (2010).

a seismic shift in English law and mean that trade union action will not be quite so easily restrained in the future."

A definitive victory for unions came in *Secretary of State for Business and Trade v. Mercer* (2024) as the UK Supreme Court reversed the Court of Appeal's ruling and unanimously concluded that the lack of protection provided to workers who joined lawful strikes violated Article 11 of the Convention. The ruling pointed out a key gap in section 146 of the TULRCA 1992, as amended after *Wilson*, which protected workers from detriment for engaging in trade union activities but did not include strike action in that definition. This omission, the ruling concluded, effectively "nullifies the right to take lawful strike action." Using the powers vested in UK judges with the HRA, the Supreme Court declared section 146 incompatible with Article 11, since the ECtHR firmly establishes the right to strike as a core component of trade union rights.

(2) **Limitations and persistent violations.** The tide did not turn around so quickly on the right to strike, however. Limitations persisted on two fronts: from the state and from the ECtHR itself. First, despite the gradual incorporation of some ECtHR principles into domestic law, the ballot requirements still pose serious practical and judicial barriers to industrial action. Ewing (2011: 244) notes that in the two-year period following the *Metrobus* case, at least eight legal challenges were brought that restricted the right to strike; four of these were eventually overturned by the Court of Appeal. Even in cases where the unions prevail, the countless litigation and injunction attempts by the employers pose great practical difficulties for unions. In at least one case ultimately won by workers, the union decided to hold the ballot again rather than wait for the outcome of a lengthy trial.[14]

The second constraint comes from the ECtHR itself. As discussed in Chapter 5, the Court has taken a narrower approach in recent years, dismissing multiple trade union rights claims particularly from the UK. The Court's inadmissibility decision in *RMT* is a case in point, given that another CoE body, the ECSR, had already found these ballot requirements on trade unions onerous. In its 2010 report, the ECSR noted that the requirement to notify the employer when trade unions are holding a ballot, in addition to the obligation to give a strike notice,

---

[14] *Milford Haven Port Authority v. Unite* [2010] EWCA Civ 400 (see Ewing 2011).

is excessive and incompatible with freedom of association. The ECtHR, however, dismissed this part of the *RMT* claim on procedural grounds since the union was able to take collective action eventually, even if delayed due to employer interference. The Court also did not find a violation regarding the UK's blanket ban on sympathy strikes, although it did not preclude the possibility that such a case could succeed under different circumstances.

The ECtHR's increasingly restrictive posture since the early 2010s has had ripple effects beyond the courtroom. Emboldened by the ECtHR judgments against the UK, the Conservative government introduced even further constraints to the right to strike during its uninterrupted rule from 2010 to 2024.[15] The Trade Union Act of 2016 added even more demanding ballot thresholds and notification procedures.[16] The government produced a special memorandum justifying the new amendments under ECtHR law, relying heavily on the Court's wide margin of appreciation to the UK in *RMT* and not once engaging with the ECtHR's broader case law recognizing the right to strike as a core element of trade union freedom. More recently, the Strikes (Minimum Service Requirements) Act of 2023 imposed additional restrictions, requiring workers in key public sectors – such as health, education, and transportation – to maintain minimum service levels during strike action. The law has limited the ability of unions, including ASLEF, to organize effective strikes. Despite strong opposition from trade unions and labor law scholars, the Act passed into law, raising serious concerns about the UK's ongoing compliance with its obligations under international human rights law, including Article 11 of the Convention.

6.5 COMPLIANCE WITH ECTHR RULINGS IN TURKEY

As noted in Chapter 2, the 1982 Constitution gave direct effect to international law, stating that "international treaties that are duly in force are directly applicable in domestic law. Their constitutionality cannot be challenged in the Constitutional Court" (Article 90). For years, however, jurists debated whether international law takes precedence in the case of a conflict with domestic legislation.

---

[15] For a discussion of the resulting decline in industrial action in the UK see Ewing (2021).

[16] See Ewing and Hendy (2016) for a detailed discussion on this Act.

A constitutional amendment in 2004 resolved this debate by explicitly establishing that international agreements on fundamental rights have supremacy over domestic law, thereby confirming the direct effect of ECtHR judgments and placing the Convention at the top of Turkey's legal hierarchy.

Trade union rights violations in Turkey have clustered around three core issues: the right to establish trade unions, the right to enter into collective bargaining agreements, and the right to take collective action, including strikes. As shown in Table 6.1, Turkey has fourteen leading cases and forty-six repetitive cases. With the exception of one, all were brought by KESK, the confederation representing left-wing public sector unions discussed in earlier chapters. The high number of both leading and repetitive cases highlights the extent of structural reforms required to address persistent violations. According to the CM's official data, the Turkish government has made significant progress on this front. As of 2023, the Turkish government managed to close nine of the fourteen leading cases, as well as the associated repeat cases under these nine cases. The Turkish government's action reports indicate that it has undertaken substantive measures regarding the remaining leading cases, except one case on disproportionate police violence against peaceful protestors (*Akarsubaşı v. Turkey* 2015).

Yet formal compliance tells only part of the story. In most of the closed cases, the legislative reforms undertaken by the Turkish government have fallen well short of trade unionists' expectations. The delays and shortcomings in execution cannot be attributed to a lack of state capacity or resources. Rather, they stem from deliberate evasion by the state, complying just enough to satisfy the CM without addressing the deeper structural causes of rights violations. Compared to their counterparts in the UK, Turkish labor activists have faced far more dire labor conditions, including blanket bans on basic trade union rights. As will be discussed in Chapter 8, the workers' biggest achievement was the legal recognition of the right to establish and join public sector trade unions, which was achieved thanks to grassroots mobilization in the shadow of international laws.

6.5.1 Right to Unionize

(1) **Reforms and glimmers of hope.** The right to unionize is an issue where, according to the CM reports, the government has made remarkable progress. Table 6.1 shows that the supervision of all leading cases brought by KESK unions on this issue – except the one case that was

brough by a private sector union (*Tek Gıda İş Sendikası v. Turkey* 2017) – is closed.

Up until 1995, the most pressing issue for public sector workers was the lack of legislation that explicitly recognized public sector workers' right to unionize. The communication workers' union, Tüm Haber Sen, was shut down just four days after its establishment in 1992. In response to the case brought by the union, the ECtHR issued a landmark ruling acknowledging the right to establish and join unions under Article 11 for the first time (*Tüm Haber Sen and Çınar v. Turkey* 2006). The ECtHR, however, took eleven years to issue its final ruling on this case. By then, thanks to the sustained mobilization efforts of labor activists and legal pressure, key reforms had already been implemented (Chapter 8).

A few months after Tüm Haber Sen petitioned the ECtHR in 1995, the parliament amended the Constitution to expressly allow public sector workers to establish and join trade unions.[17] Another constitutional amendment in 2001 guaranteed all workers' right to unionize in order to advance "their economic and social rights and the interests of their members in their labor relations" (Article 51 as amended in October 2001). This paved the way for the enactment of Law No. 4688 on Public Servants' Trade Unions (hereafter, Law No. 4688), which regulates trade union relations in the public sector.[18] Importantly, the law prohibits discriminatory treatment based on trade union membership (Article 18). Taking all these reforms into account, the CM decided to close the case in 2010.

Despite these legislative advances, however, the state's repression of unionized public sector workers, especially the leftist KESK members, did not cease. As the Kurdish movement's ties with KESK solidified, the government identified KESK as a target institution in its broader "war on terror." One of the first major incidents was the government's attempt to shut down Eğitim-Sen, KESK's largest affiliate representing education workers, due to a clause in its constitution affirming the right of all persons to receive education in their mother tongue (Article 2(b)). The implication that Eğitim-Sen defended the right to education in Kurdish was perceived as a threat against the unity and territorial integrity of the Turkish state. The Court of Cassation (Yargıtay)

---

[17] Article 53 of the Constitution, as amended by Law No. 4121 of 23/07/1995.
[18] A new amendment introduced under Law No. 6289 in 2012 changed its name to the Law on Public Servants' Trade Unions and Collective Agreement.

ruled that in this case, restrictions on Articles 10 and 11 of the Convention could be justified as necessary in a democratic society because Eğitim-Sen's call for education in a mother tongue posed a threat to public order (*Eğitim ve Bilim Emekçileri Sendikası v. Turkey* 2012: para. 24). After the decision of the Court of Cassation, Eğitim-Sen temporarily amended its constitution to remove the controversial clause and petitioned the ECtHR in 2005. The union then reintroduced the clause in 2011, prior to the ECtHR's final judgment, which came the following year and found Turkey in violation of both Article 11 and 10.

The implementation of this judgment demonstrates the ECtHR's indirect influence on the Turkish judiciary. The CM did not require any general measures from the Turkish state because the violation did not stem from faulty legislation but from the Court of Cassation's misinterpretation of the Convention. In its 2013 action report, the government states that it undertook several training programs to increase awareness of ECtHR case law among judges and prosecutor.[19] These included the Project on Freedom of Expression and Media in Turkey and the Project on Enhancing the Role of the Supreme Judicial Authorities in Respect of European Standards, both of which were initiated jointly by the EU and the CoE in order to promote judicial commitment to European standards. As a result, in 2020, the CM decided to close the case.

(2) **Limitations and persistent violations.** The lifting of the ban on public sector workers' right to unionize and the establishment of KESK were major victories, and the importance of the ECtHR could not be overstated in labor activists' struggle. Yet even after the CM closed supervision of key cases related to union repression, the Turkish government continued to find ways to undermine KESK's power and criminalize its members.

As noted in the previous chapter, *sürgün* (forced relocation or exile) has been a systematic anti-union tactic that the government has used to reappoint KESK-affiliated public sector workers, especially those vocal on Kurdish issues, from urban centers to remote regions. This practice at once aimed at weakening KESK's organizing power and depoliticizing

---

[19] Action report – Communication from Turkey concerning the case of *Eğitim ve Bilim Emekçileri Sendikası v. Turkey* (Application No. 20641/05) [Anglais uniquement] [DH-DD(2014)74].

the Kurdish region by scattering activists across the country. It can be viewed as part of the government's broader assimilation policy, under which thousands of Kurds have been displaced since the 1990s (Human Rights Watch 2004; Kurban, Yükseker, and Çelik 2006; Özerdem and Jacoby 2007).[20] Table 6.1 shows two leading and twelve repetitive ECtHR cases related to *sürgün*, all of which have now been closed.

In its early judgments, the ECtHR limited its findings to procedural violations regarding the lack of access to judicial review under the state of emergency in the Kurdish provinces (Article 13) without establishing a link between the *sürgün* of the applicants and their trade union activities (Article 11).[21] A turning point came in *Metin Turan v. Turkey* (2006), where the applicant was reassigned from a Kurdish city to a small Anatolian province by the decision of a state of emergency governor on the grounds that the applicant's participation in KESK activities posed a threat to public order and safety. For the first time, the ECtHR recognized that the applicant's *sürgün* was due to his trade union activities, and hence constituted a violation of Article 11. The CM hastily closed the case in 2009, reasoning that the state of emergency had already been lifted in 2002 and that there was no legal framework in place that would cause further violations. The CM closed the supervision of ten procedural rights cases as well on the same basis.[22]

That the end of the state of emergency did not provide sufficient safeguards against the government's crackdown on trade unionists in the Kurdish provinces was evidenced by the continued *sürgün* cases brought before the Court after 2002. In two other judgments, the ECtHR once again found Article 11 violations regarding the forced relocation of KESK members due to their trade union activities (*Dedecan and Ok v. Turkey* 2015; *Müslüm Çiftçi v. Turkey* 2010).

---

[20] The first ECtHR case on forced displacement was *Akdıvar and Others v. Turkey* (1996). See Çalı (2010) and Kurban (2020) for an analysis of the ECtHR case law on this issue.

[21] See, for instance, *Ertaş Aydın and Others v. Turkey* (2005). Of the twelve repetitive *sürgün* cases listed in Table 6.1, the Court did not find any Article 11 violations in ten. These ten cases fall under the leading case *Güneri and Others v. Turkey* (2005), which is not included in the table because it does not concern trade union rights. There are other repetitive cases under *Güneri*, some involving *sürgün* decisions during the state of emergency but unrelated to trade union activity.

[22] See Case of Güneri and Others and Five Other Cases Against Turkey [CM/Resdh (2007)97].

In its 2012 action report on the execution of these judgments, the government referenced a decision by the Council of State, the highest administrative court, which held that the transfer of trade union officials due to their trade union activities was incompatible with Turkey's obligations under Article 11. This time, the CM did not rush to close the case. While taking note of the judicial compliance, the CM stated that to ensure the full execution of the judgment, a legislative amendment was necessary in Article 18 of Law No. 4688. This article prohibited dismissing public sector workers due to their trade union membership and activities, but did not protect against forced reassignments.

The government did not amend the legislation. Instead, in its subsequent action reports in 2019, it continued to argue that the violations stemmed from misapplication of existing laws, not legal gaps, and listed similar domestic rulings where courts had upheld union rights under Law 4688.[23] In a brief resolution in 2020, the CM decided that the measures undertaken by the government were sufficient to prevent further violations and closed the case.[24] The Committee did not explain why it abandoned its earlier demand for legislative amendment. Perhaps not surprisingly, three years later, the ECtHR issued yet another repetitive case of *sürgün* ruling (*Erenler and Others v. Turkey* 2023).

On the bright side, a growing number of domestic court rulings are reversing *sürgün* decisions with references to the Convention and ECtHR rulings. But the constant flow of repetitive cases despite the closure of the supervision of the leading case points to a systemic problem.[25] The ECtHR and the CM could take a stronger stance against the targeting of union members. Yet, despite the volume of similar complaints, the Court has not recognized the structural nature of state repression and discrimination against KESK members, whether based on their union activities or their Kurdish identity. This reluctance is consistent with the Court's broader approach to Kurdish claims. Even in the thousands of cases involving grave human rights abuses – including extrajudicial killings, torture, sexual abuse,

---

[23] 1362nd meeting (December 2019) (DH) – Action report (28/10/2019) – Communication from Turkey concerning the Case of Müslüm Çiftçi v. Turkey (Application No. 30307/03) [Anglais uniquement].
[24] Case of Müslüm Çiftçi Against Turkey and 1 Other Case [CM/ResDH(2020)152].
[25] See Action report 2019, cited above.

forced displacement, village burnings, and obstruction of justice – the ECtHR treated each case as a matter of individual rights and has not recognized this repression as discriminatory under Article 14 (Çalı 2010; Kurban 2020).[26]

More importantly, however, the Turkish state finds ways to evade implementation of ECtHR rulings in thorny issues. In the 1990s, the government agreed to allow public sector workers to unionize, but it did not want an oppositional union, especially one that is vocal on the Kurdish issue, to become a strong union. The administrative and judicial authorities consistently interpret the KESK members' union activities as support for the PKK, and hence a threat to national security. Even where legislative reforms are adopted, the state continues to criminalize KESK members under the pretext of counterterrorism.

This trend escalated during the second term of the AKP government, led by Erdoğan, toward the end of the 2000s. In 2009, a wave of arrests targeted hundreds of pro-Kurdish lawyers, politicians, academics, journalists, activists – and trade unionists – under the sweeping "KCK" trials.[27] KESK members were among those detained, with police raiding union offices and homes and subjecting members to violence and harassment.[28] Those detained included the head of KESK, Lami Özgen, and former president Mustafa Avcı. While Özgen was later released, Avcı was tried under twelve separate charges, mostly of them tied to organizing and participating in peaceful protests and seminars. The ECtHR found that his pretrial detention violated his right to liberty (Article 5), affirming that his peaceful activities could not justify such punitive treatment (*Mustafa Avcı v. Turkey* 2017).[29] These cases, along with the *sürgün* rulings, illustrate the persistence and the extent of the government's crackdown on KESK and Kurdish activists.

---

[26] As discussed in Chapter 4, the ECtHR has a very narrow interpretation of Article 14 on prohibition of discrimination.

[27] The KCK (*Koma Civakên Kurdistan*, or Kurdistan Communities Union) is described by the Turkish state as the "urban branch" of the PKK and has been prosecuted as a terrorist organization.

[28] International Labour Organization. 2012. *Committee of Experts on the Applications of Conventions and Recommendations* (CEACR). Report III (Part 1A). International Labour Conference, 101st Session.

[29] See also *İşçi and Others v. Turkey* (67483/12). These cases are not included in Table 6.1 because the ECtHR did not find Article 11 violations.

6.5.2 Right to Engage in Collective Bargaining

(1) **Reforms and glimmers of hope.** The right to establish and join trade unions is devoid of meaning if workers are not also able to reach collective bargaining agreements with their employers. According to the CM reports, the Turkish government fulfilled its obligations on this front by lifting the ban on public sector workers' right to engage in collective bargaining and regulating the practice with new legislation.

As discussed in Chapter 4, *Demir and Baykara v. Turkey* (2008) marked the height of the ECtHR's expansion of trade union rights and had far-reaching implications for union protections across Europe. In a Grand Chamber ruling issued twelve years after the application was lodged, the Court deemed the right to collective bargaining "an essential element" of trade union freedom Yet, as with earlier cases, many key reforms were enacted before the Court issued its final judgment. In the early 1990s, most state authorities and jurists assumed that public sector workers could not engage in collective bargaining because of the lack of legal regulations on this issue. In 1995, the Court of Cassation voided the collective bargaining agreement signed by the Gaziantep Municipality and the municipal workers' union, Tüm Bel Sen, on those grounds. In a separate ruling, the Audit Court (Sayıştay) even ordered that the difference in payments between what had been granted through collective bargaining and what was legally mandated be returned to the state budget.[30]

Simultaneous with the ECtHR applications, public sector workers launched a wave of grassroots mobilization, as will be shown in Chapter 8. In response, just months after the court decisions in 1995, the government amended the Constitution to allow public sector workers to establish trade unions and to engage in collective bargaining.[31] The abovementioned Law No. 4688, enacted in 2001, set out the legal framework governing how public sector workers could enter into and conclude collective bargaining agreements. The Constitution (Article 53) was later amended in 2010 to reflect these changes.[32]

---

[30] The Audit Court, also known as the Court of Accounts, is responsible for auditing all accounts relating to the revenue, expenditure, and property of government departments financed by the state budget. Although the Constitution does not list the Audit Court as one of the supreme courts (as are the Constitutional Court, the Court of Cassation, and the Council of State), the decisions of the Audit Court are not subject to judicial review.

[31] Article 53 § 3 of the Constitution, as amended by Law No. 4121 of 23/07/1995.

[32] Article 53 § 3 of the Constitution, as amended by Law No. 5982 of 07/05/2010.

Based on these legislative steps, the CM closed the *Demir and Baykara* case in 2011, just one year after the final ruling, having concluded that the necessary general measures were already in place.

These legislative changes allowed public sector unions to negotiate biennial collective agreements with the state, represented by a committee, to determine salaries for all public sector workers. They did not, however, permit unions to conclude separate agreements with employers in specific workplaces. This created continued legal uncertainty for unions like Tüm Bel Sen, which had negotiated directly with sympathetic municipal administrations. The problem for Tüm Bel Sen, therefore, was not resolved after *Demir and Baykara*. In 2010, a year before the CM decided to close *Demir and Baykara*, Tüm Bel Sen filed two new petitions to the ECtHR again alleging violations of its right to engage in collective bargaining (*Tüm Bel Sen v. Turkey* 2014).[33] The Audit Court had again ruled that such agreements were invalid and requested the extra payments municipal workers received. In response, the ECtHR reiterated its findings in *Demir and Baykara* and found Turkey to be in violation of Article 11.

Two months after Tüm Bel Sen filed its petitions in 2010, the government started to undertake reforms to accommodate the ongoing municipal bargaining practice. A new amendment to Law No. 6009 stipulated that additional payments workers gained as "social aid" from the administration need not be returned to the state budget. In 2012, further amendments were introduced to Law No. 4688 authorizing municipalities and provincial workers' unions to negotiate higher pay for workers under "social welfare" (*sosyal denge*) agreements, provided the local administration consented to it (Article 32 of Law No. 6289). The ECtHR acknowledged these reforms in its 2014 judgment, but nonetheless found Turkey in violation due to its failure to retrospectively apply these changes to Tüm Bel Sen. In 2019, the CM closed the supervision of the case, noting both the legislative reforms and the individual remedies provided to the applicant.

(2) **Limitations and persistent violations.** A closer look at the legislative changes and their implementation shows that it is not possible to speak of a right to enter into collective bargaining agreements for

---

[33] The Court joined the two applications in one case since the alleged violations were essentially on the same issue (para. 14).

public sector workers in real terms. The 2012 reforms introduced under Law No. 6289 have not altered the essential problem at the heart of the right to collective bargaining and, in some respects, have made it even worse. The collective agreements governing all public sector workers' "financial and social rights" are signed biennially by the Collective Agreement Committee (formerly the Collective Consultation Committee), which is composed of fifteen members of the Public Employers' Committee and fifteen members of the Public Employees' Unions Committee, all of whom may join the collective agreement meetings. However, only the heads of each committee are authorized to sign on behalf of 3.5 million public sector workers and 2 million pensioners. The head of the Public Employees' Unions Committee is determined by the trade union with the highest representation in civil service – currently Memur-Sen (Memur Sendikaları Konfederasyonu, Confederation of Civil Servants' Unions), which developed corporatist-clientelist ties with the AKP government in the post-2000 period (see Chapter 8). Under the previous system, a majority of votes in each group was required to finalize agreements. Hence, the current system eliminates KESK's influence completely.

The right to strike is also effectively nullified under Law No. 4688, and the 2012 changes did nothing to alter this situation. If the parties fail to reach an agreement within fifteen days, the dispute may be referred to the Public Workers Arbitration Board (PWAB, Kamu Görevlileri Hakem Kurulu), a body composed mainly of government-appointed state officials and jurists, with minimal trade union oversight. The decisions of the PWAB are final and are not subject to judicial review. Critics describe this system as a form of compulsory arbitration designed to prevent strikes by public sector workers during negotiations (Çelik 2010; Gülmez 2013: 86; Kutal 2015: 174; Uçkan 2013: 91). Even the 2013 EU–Turkey Joint Report noted that "it is not correct to call the salary fixing system in the public sector collective bargaining" as the current system merely involves "consultation" rather than actual "negotiation."[34]

As is evident from this description, public sector workers are barred from signing collective bargaining agreements directly with their employers in individual workplaces or different branches of public

---

[34] EU–Turkey Joint Consultative Committee. 2013. *Joint Report: Trade Union Rights Situation in Turkey*. Brusells (p. 7).

work, except for municipal and provincial workers. In essence, this exception reduces the right to collective bargaining from a core element of trade union rights to a special right reserved only for municipal workers. Even for municipal workers, it is hard to regard the narrowly defined "salary fixing" scheme under "social welfare" agreements, with no right to strike, as genuine collective bargaining agreements. These agreements depend entirely on the goodwill of local administrations: workers have no legal mechanism to compel employers to negotiate, let alone to conclude agreements. It appears that the 2012 reforms primarily aimed at putting an end to Tüm Bel Sen's repeated applications to the ECtHR without meaningfully expanding the right to collective bargaining for all public sector workers.

6.5.3 Right to Engage in Collective Action

(1) **Reforms and glimmers of hope.** Among the three core trade union rights, the right of public sector workers to participate in collective action is the least secure. Nonetheless, according to the CM reports, the Turkish government has made notable progress on this issue.

Currently, there are seven leading cases – all brought by KESK unions or members – before the ECtHR, regarding criminal or disciplinary reprisals meted out to members for participating in strikes or other collective action activities and the lack of judicial review for disciplinary sanctions against public sector workers (Table 6.1). In response to these cases, the ECtHR affirmed that public sector workers have the right to participate in peaceful union-organized protests under Article 11, and explicitly recognized the right to strike as an integral part of trade union rights (*Enerji Yapı-Yol Sen v. Turkey* 2009). The CM has closed supervision in four of these leading cases and eight associated repetitive cases. For the remaining three, the Committee found legislative reforms to be sufficient but requested further evidence of implementation.

One significant reform on the right to strike occurred, once again, before the ECtHR issued its final ruling. The 1996 Prime Ministry Circular (No. 1996/21) banning all strike action for public sector workers was at the origin of the violation in *Enerji Yapı-Yol Sen*. In 2007, six years after the union submitted its case to the ECtHR, the government repealed the circular. While the CM initially called for additional reforms to ensure that workers would not face sanctions for participating in strike action, it later accepted the government's position that such issues were being supervised under other cases, and closed supervision in 2017.[35]

In response to the rest of the ECtHR judgments on the right to engage in collective bargaining, the Turkish government undertook a series of reforms. First, in terms of access to justice, a Constitutional amendment in 2010 (Article 129/3) granted public sector workers the right to challenge disciplinary sanctions at administrative courts and Law No. 657 was amended accordingly. This marked an important step in ensuring access to effective remedies at the domestic level. Next, the government provided new legal protections on the right to strike and the right to take collective action (*Dilek and Others v. Turkey* 2007; *Enerji Yapı-Yol Sen v. Turkey* 2009; *Karaçay v. Turkey* 2007; *Urcan and Others v. Turkey* 2008). The CM acknowledged the 2012 Law on Trade Unions and Collective Agreement (Law No. 6356) which guaranteed all workers' right to freedom of assembly and participation in union activities (Articles 25/3 and 66). But the Public Servants Act (Law No. 657) still imposes restrictions: Article 26 limits go-slow and no-show actions, and Article 27 prohibits strike-related activities.

Despite these bans, the CM welcomed the examples of jurisprudence provided by the government, signaling that Turkey's supreme courts have aligned their interpretations of these laws with ECtHR requirements.[36] Notably, supreme courts eschewed these restrictions by relying on the supremacy of the ECtHR's case law. In its 2013 decision, the Council of State explicitly referred to the ECtHR in overturning disciplinary sanctions imposed on an Eğitim-Sen member for joining a trade union protest and missing one day of work.[37] Gülmez (2014) observes that the Council of State's decision, which ignored the relevant strike bans, effectively established a limited right to collective action. In 2016, the Constitutional Court similarly lifted a disciplinary sanction imposed on a teacher who had participated in a strike,

---

[35] Resolution CM/ResDH(2017)374 Execution of the judgment of the European Court of Human Rights Enerji Yapı-Yol Sen against Turkey (Adopted by the Committee of Ministers on 25 October 2017 at the 1298th meeting of the Ministers' Deputies).

[36] This development is noteworthy, because the ECtHR had found that Law No. 657 was interpreted in such a way by domestic courts that even peaceful protests organized by trade unions were deemed illegal (*Dilek and Others v. Turkey* 2007).

[37] Council of State, Grand Chamber, Docket No. 2009/1063, Decision No. 2013/1998. See also Docket No. 2015/538, Decision No. 2016/3336.

referencing both the right to unionize under the Constitution (Article 51) and ECtHR rulings such as *Karaçay v. Turkey* (2007) and *Kaya and Seyhan v. Turkey* (2009).

After examining sample cases where Turkish courts interpreted Law No. 657 in light of Article 11, the CM decided to close *Karaçay v. Turkey* (2007) and the six repetitive cases associated with it in 2020. The CM accepted the government's argument that problems arose from the implementation of existing laws, not the legal framework itself. Yet, before closing *Kaya and Seyhan* (2009) and *Dilek and Others* (2007), the Committee requested further examples of domestic court decisions because three more cases have been submitted to the ECtHR since 2018.[38]

In its observations on the execution of *Urcan and Others v. Turkey* (2008), which concerned criminal charges brought against public sector workers for participating in collective action, the CM welcomed the 2004 changes to the Criminal Code, pursuant to the applicants filing their case to the ECtHR the same year. The new amendment (Article 236) still criminalizes collectively abandoning or slowing down work. Nevertheless, the CM found it promising that the second section of the same article allows for reduced or waived penalties provided that the discontinuance of work is short-term, aimed at professional or social goals, and does not disrupt essential public services. The CM concluded that the new code gives judges some discretion by not automatically criminalizing all collective action of public sector workers. The government presented sample cases where lower court judges had exercised this discretion by declining to prosecute or penalize strike activity or collective action led by unions. After reviewing these cases, the CM did not request any more legislative reforms, but did request more information on the implementation of the law by domestic courts, awareness-raising activities undertaken within the judiciary, and data on industrial action taken by public sector workers.[39]

---

[38] These three cases are not included in Table 6.1 because two of them are pending as communicated cases (*Yılmaz v. Turkey* and *Zengin v. Turkey*). The ECtHR issued a violation judgment on the third case, but it was not yet in the HUDOC-EXE system as of July 2023 (*Kaymak and Others v. Türkiye* 2023)

[39] The last government action report, where the government responded to these requests, was submitted on 2021, but the CM has not yet issued a resolution on this report.

There are four other cases where public sector workers faced criminal charges, illegal house arrests, or unlawful detention as a result of participating in collective action organized by their union or reading a public statement. The ECtHR found an Article 11 violation in only one of these cases, while identifying other human rights violations in the remaining cases. The CM also did not regard these incidents as evidence of systemic criminalization of KESK members. After reviewing the Criminal Code amendments and domestic jurisprudence, the CM closed supervision of these cases (*Fatma Akaltun Fırat v. Turkey* 2013; *Gül and Others* 2010; *H. M. v. Turkey* 2006; *Karademirci and Others v. Turkey* 2005).

(2) **Limitations and persistent violations.** Public sector workers in Turkey still lack a meaningful right to engage in collective action, as legal prohibitions and restrictive practices continue to undermine their ability to organize and protest effectively. Some of the problems are already recognized in CM's evaluation of the pending cases. Yet, given the ongoing violations and repetitive cases that keep coming before the ECtHR, it is surprising that the CM agreed to close any of these cases.

Numerous legal restrictions on collective action by public sector workers have gone largely unaddressed by the CM. Although the CM acknowledged that the Law on Trade Unions and Collective Agreement (Law No. 6356) of 2012 provides certain safeguards for workers' right to participate in industrial action, these provisions do not extend to public sector workers.[40] The Turkish state has never considered public sector workers as "workers" per se, and domestic laws always refer to public sector workers as "civil servants" or "public servants" (*memur* or *kamu görevlisi*).[41] In practice, the limited safeguards provided for workers in Law No. 6356 do not apply to public sector workers.

Three key legal instruments govern public sector workers' union activities, all of which restrict or prohibit strike action. First, and most

---

[40] This law was amended in 2017, but the changes do not apply to public sector workers due to abovementioned reasons.

[41] This distinction is reflected even in the names of the public sector unions; KESK explicitly uses the word "emekçi" (laborer or worker) in its name, while Memur Sen – the union with close ties to the government – adopted the name "civil servants' union."

importantly, the Public Servants Act (Law No. 657, Article 27) explicitly bans public sector workers from joining strikes and mandates disciplinary measures against public sector workers who are absent without leave (Article 125). Second, the Law on Public Servants' Trade Unions and Collective Agreement (Law No. 4688), permits union activity only outside working hours or, with employer permission, during work hours (Article 18). The law in effect undermines the purpose of collective action by requiring the employer's consent for activities meant to create hardship for the employer to gain benefits for workers. More importantly, strike action during collective bargaining is also effectively illegal because Law No. 4688 states that unresolved disputes in collective bargaining have to be appealed to the PWAB. As mentioned above, this forced arbitration undermines the unions' bargaining power against the state.

Third, the Turkish Criminal Code stipulates that public sector workers may be charged with prison sentences if they collectively abandon or slow down work. Although a second clause permits reduced or waived penalties if the action is short, limited in disruption, and aimed at protecting workers' rights, the vague language – particularly the condition that "public service must not be jeopardized" – conflicts with the very purpose of collective action. While the ECtHR has recognized that public sector workers' right to strike is not absolute, and in certain cases may be restricted, the lack of legal clarity regarding what those conditions are casts serious doubt on the effective protection of this right.

The main source of optimism in CM's decision to close some of these cases stems from the favorable domestic rulings referencing ECtHR rulings. While the CM acknowledged the discrepancy between the current legislation and judicial practice in its supervision of *Karaçay*, it ultimately found that the examples of pro-union decisions from Turkish courts constituted sufficient evidence of progress. However, legislative prohibitions place significant disincentives on collective action, with workers facing salary cuts or even prison time. Although they may now challenge sanctions in court, this post hoc remedy is no substitute for legal guarantees. Perhaps more surprisingly, the CM did not even address the forced arbitration process which clearly infringes upon workers' right to strike and to bargain collectively. Given that the conflict between these legal restrictions and Turkey's international legal obligations is plainly recognized by the ILO, ECSR, and EU, the CM's failure to take these practical and legal impediments into account in its supervision of this group of cases is striking.[42]

The final set of cases pending before the CM deals with excessive use of force by police against trade unionists participating in peaceful protests, where the Court found violations of Article 11 in conjunction with Article 3 (prohibition of torture and ill-treatment). The government's performance in this area has been particularly poor, and the CM considers this one of the most urgent human rights concerns in Turkey. As of 2025, there are eighty-two cases on police violence against protestors, twenty of which are brought solely by trade unionists (KESK) (Table 6.1).[43] These cases are labeled for "enhanced supervision," meaning that the issue constitutes a high priority for the CM and Turkey is expected to undertake immediate measures to stop violations.

Police violence has become a defining feature of the government's crackdown not only on trade unionists but also on all dissidents. Since the 2010s, as the Turkish government consolidated power and abandoned its earlier liberalization promises made during EU accession talks, the use of force to suppress peaceful protest has escalated. ECtHR judgments showcase the violent conditions trade unionists face when demonstrating, adding another layer to the legal restrictions described earlier.

The CM singled out the case brought by DİSK and KESK (2012) regarding the use of tear gas, pressurized water, and paint sprays – including a gas bomb deployed on hospital grounds – during May Day protests. For the first time, the Committee emphasized "the systematic nature of the problem" in reference to the case brought by the president of DİSK (*Süleyman Çelebi and Others v. Turkey* 2016), and "strongly urged" the government to take immediate measures to ensure that members of the public are able to participate in peaceful demonstrations without fear of violence or retaliation. Notably, national and international NGOs have made submissions to the CM regarding the

---

[42] European Committee of Social Rights, November 2022, Draft Third Report on the Non-Accepted Provisions of the European Social Charter Turkiye, https://rm.coe.int/turkiye-report-on-non-accepted-provisions-november-2022-/1680aa0bfc. EU progress report 2015, www.ab.gov.tr/files/5%20Ekim/2015_turkey_report.pdf.

[43] The leading case *Oya Ataman v. Turkey* (2006) was not brought by trade unionists. *Akarsubaşı* is the leading case among those cases brought by KESK activists.

supervision of these group cases, highlighting the urgency and gravity of the problem. Also noteworthy is that, unlike in other cases, the CM is not willing to overlook the explicit bans and restrictions on this issue simply because the domestic courts provide remedies to victims after they suffer the violation:

> [T]he continuing positive developments as regards the Constitutional Court's case-law and the improvement in the domestic courts' interpretation and application of the domestic law cannot alleviate the need for the legislative amendments required in this group of cases, as recent domestic judgments show that the legislation allows the authorities to continue their practice of declaring blanket bans on peaceful meetings and demonstrations.[44]

The urgency with which the CM is requesting government action on this issue may be attributed to both the seriousness of state violence and sustained pressure from civil society organizations. Yet, despite the priority status of these cases, the Turkish government has made little progress in nearly two decades. The CM's limited ability to compel change, even in the face of systemic violations, points to the limits of international pressure in the absence of domestic political will.

6.6 CONCLUSION

The analysis of the measures undertaken by the Turkish and UK governments on trade union rights cases shows that the slow incorporation of Convention rights into legislation and domestic judicial systems – albeit non-systematic – is promising and significant. That said, close inspection of the actual practices on the ground demonstrates that the reluctant reforms undertaken to comply with ECtHR judgments often fall short of securing the core protections identified by the ECtHR and preventing future violations. While the argument that human rights regimes merely serve as window dressing may be overblown, the findings in this chapter lend support to the realist position that such regimes provide meager incentives for meaningful state action.

---

[44] Interim Resolution CM/ResDH(2023)39. Execution of the judgments of the European Court of Human Rights Oya Ataman group v. Turkey (Adopted by the Committee of Ministers on 9 March 2023 at the 1459th meeting of the Ministers' Deputies).

6.6 CONCLUSION

Despite their clear differences in regime type and the severity of repression faced by unions, Turkey and the UK display a similar pattern of doing the bare minimum to comply with ECtHR rulings. The problems in Turkey are more fundamental, ranging from bans on basic trade union rights to violent repression and the criminalization of union activity – all of which are exacerbated for Kurdish unionists. Unsurprisingly, there are more leading and repeat cases from Turkey before the Court. Yet none of the problems, except for police violence against protestors, are issues that could not be resolved through legislative reforms allowing public sector unions to exercise basic trade union freedoms. Hence, the primary reason behind the continued violations in Turkey and the half-hearted reforms in the UK is not state capacity, but a lack of political will. Rectifying persistent trade union rights violations does not require many resources from the state, such as building new infrastructure or providing expensive services, but political will to pass strong legislation that allows workers to organize, engage in collective bargaining, and take collective action.

As scholars have noted, states are not unitary actors and international human rights law can provide leverage for reform-minded domestic actors within the state apparatus (Alter 2014; Hillebrecht 2014; Simmons 2009). In Turkey, for example, the judiciary, including the Constitutional Court, have at times referenced ECtHR jurisprudence to offer legal remedies to unionists. But the government refuses to lift bans on trade union rights to align domestic laws with international standards. This disjuncture between judicial and legislative behavior has left Turkish unionists in limbo. Workers face sanctions for engaging in union activity, endure the consequences, and must then rely on the courts for eventual redress. Thus, participation in union activity is a risky business, requiring a level of legal knowledge, courage, and persistence that few can afford.

This chapter has focused deliberately on a conventional, state-centered analysis of compliance with ECtHR rulings to demonstrate what governments do in response to judgments and how formal legal reforms unfold. The findings support realist and critical accounts that caution against overestimating the reform potential of international courts when measured solely based on state behavior. But this is only part of the story. The following chapters take up a central question: Under what conditions can human rights law become a resource for labor activists? Answering this question requires paying closer attention to the voices and mobilization from below. As this chapter has shown, in the best cases, reforms were already underway by the time the ECtHR issued its judgment, often nearly a decade after the application. The next two chapters zoom in on the labor struggles that made these changes possible in the shadow of international litigation.

CHAPTER 7

ON-STAGE AND OFF-STAGE MOBILIZATION
Blacklisted Workers in the United Kingdom

The previous chapter examined how the British and Turkish governments have responded to ECtHR rulings on trade union rights. While compliance was often formal, policy changes tended to follow the letter rather than the spirit of the law. In both countries, measures adopted in response to ECtHR judgments frequently fell short of the expectations and demands of trade union activists. This chapter switches focus to indirect effects of international litigation: the ways in which ECtHR cases can catalyze grassroots mobilization. Even in the absence of favorable rulings, or before any judgment is issued, activists can leverage human rights litigation to amplify their claims, generate public support, and exert political pressure.

This chapter illustrates that dynamic through the case of the Blacklist Support Group (BSG), a grassroots network of construction workers in the United Kingdom who were blacklisted for their trade union activism. The next chapter turns to KESK, a major public sector union confederation in Turkey. While both movements turned to the ECtHR in contexts where domestic legal avenues were inadequate, they did so under very different political and legal conditions. The BSG operated in a liberal democratic setting where trade union rights were nominally protected but routinely undermined in practice; KESK faced overt repression and legal exclusion in an increasingly authoritarian regime. Despite these contrasts, both groups used the prospect of ECtHR litigation to mobilize at the grassroots level, relying on human rights frameworks not only to seek justice through courts, but also to strengthen their collective voice, build alliances, and push for change on the ground.

The two movements incorporated human rights into their mobilization efforts in distinct ways, shaped by the institutional and discursive environments in which they operated. By the time the BSG formed in 2009, the ECtHR had already developed a robust body of case law on trade union rights, giving the Court both legal authority and symbolic resonance in the UK context. The BSG drew on this framework in its public campaigns, where human rights served as a strategic language to counter negative portrayals of trade unionists. But in internal organizing, activists continued to be anchored in class-based solidarity and identity. In contrast, during KESK's formative years in the early 1990s, human rights had not yet gained broad traction in Turkish labor or civil society movements. As a result, KESK did not foreground rights language in its public messaging, but activists did use the ECtHR's growing authority – and Turkey's EU aspirations – as a legal foundation to overcome workers' fears, contest state repression, and carve out space for organizing.

7.1 THE CASE OF BLACKLISTED WORKERS

Steve Acheson's story was similar to that of Dave Smith, mentioned in the opening of Chapter 1. Like Smith, Acheson was tired of not being able to find jobs in the construction industry in which he had devoted years to become a skilled electrician. Acheson, a trade union representative, was sure that he was on the blacklist. In 2006, he took the latest company that denied him a job to an employment tribunal. To his surprise, a whistleblower, who worked in the human resources department, came forward to testify on his role in blacklisting. The tribunal concluded: "Disgraceful though it is, the tribunal concludes that a blacklist exists in relation to certain workers in the industry in which the claimants work and that the claimants are all on that blacklist."[1] Acheson's case, along with two other electricians, represented the first legal document that acknowledged the existence of a blacklist in the construction industry.

The tribunal ruling helped prompt a series of official investigations, during which the vast scope of the blacklisting operation involving

---

[1] Phil Chamberlain, "Enemy at the Gates," *The Guardian*, June 28, 2008, www.theguardian.com/money/2008/jun/28/workandcareers.

construction firms and police collaboration surfaced. The blacklist, managed by the Consulting Association, included information about more than 3,200 individuals. One example from the activities of the Consulting Association illustrates the magnitude of the practice: Evidence from the data protection agency ICO's 2009 investigation showed that, during the construction of the London Olympic Park from July to September 2012, the multinational corporations responsible for building the Olympic media center and the Olympic stadium were invoiced for nearly £13,000 and £28,000 respectively, equating to more than 5,000 individual name checks (Smith 2014). Needless to say, those whose names appeared on the blacklist were not recruited for these jobs.

What is perhaps more troubling is that court hearings later documented that for decades, undercover police officers, posing as activists, had infiltrated leftist groups and routinely provided information about the political activities of some of the workers to the Consulting Association. The blacklist devastated the lives of many workers who lost their livelihoods.

Upon losing hope in the British justice system, two blacklisted workers, with the help of experienced lawyers, took their cases to the ECtHR (*Brough v. the United Kingdom* 2016; *Smith v. the United Kingdom* 2017). These were neither the first nor the most consequential cases brought by British trade unionists to the ECtHR (see Chapter 5). But they were the first to catalyze grassroots mobilization. In a legal context where domestic avenues for redress appeared blocked, the ECtHR offered hope not just for legal recognition, but for political traction. Workers believed that the litigation could amplify their cause, pressure the government to respond to their demands, and attract public support by framing their grievances in human rights terms. Mobilized by this sense of possibility, workers responded to the blacklisting scandal by forming the BSG, a grassroots organization committed to exposing blacklisting as a violation of human rights.

This chapter shows that despite the limitations of direct policy outcomes resulting from ECtHR rulings, human rights litigation can reshape the dynamics of social movements and yield material gains for activists. In the case of the BSG, workers built a movement around their ECtHR claims and strategically deployed human rights language in public campaigns. As a result, they achieved some of their most concrete victories even before the Court delivered its final (and ultimately adverse) judgments.

The BSG activists have made a conscious effort to incorporate human rights discourse in their campaigns and media statements, but it has not become a central reference point within the movement itself. In other words, BSG's mobilization displays a dual character: *On-stage*, human rights serve as a framing device to attract national attention and counter prevailing negative portrayals of trade unionists; *off-stage*, when they are away from the spotlight, activists continue to rely on a traditional class-based language that underpins their solidarity and political identity.

The chapter draws on rich qualitative data, including interviews I conducted with lawyers and blacklisted workers; participant observation from BSG meetings, campaigns, and domestic court proceedings; social media analysis of BSG's Facebook page; media coverage of the blacklisting scandal; and House of Commons minutes on the issue (see Appendix II). These data demonstrate how the ECtHR litigation transformed the terrain of grassroots mobilization. To assess the broader impact of the blacklisted workers' campaign, I also examine policy reforms prompted by their activism and the remedies they secured in domestic courts.

7.2 DOMESTIC ORIGINS OF THE BLACKLIST SUPPORT GROUP

The employment tribunal case in 2006 involving Acheson, who would later become the chair of the BSG, and two of his colleagues constituted a critical juncture. It was the first time evidence of ongoing blacklisting practices was documented and acknowledged in court. The practice has a long history in the UK, stretching back to the early twentieth century. In the 1990s, a parliamentary inquiry initiated at the request of the TUC documented that the Economic League, a now defunct organization, had collected information about political activists, as well as trade unionists, and shared them with employers. When the League was shut down in 1993, the Conservative government at the time declined to pass a separate piece of legislation banning or criminalizing blacklisting, despite pressure from the ILO (Case No. 1618). A few years later, in 1999, the Labour government under Blair came close to enacting such legislation but ultimately backed down on the grounds that there was no evidence that blacklisting was still going on.

The tribunal's findings in Acheson's case therefore confirmed what many in the industry already suspected: Skilled, experienced workers could not find jobs for years because they were blacklisted. Workers were aware that the blacklist only needed to be suspected – not seen – to be effective.[2] It functioned as a form of discipline, a scare tactic aimed at deterring workers from joining trade unions or speaking out about the rights violations they experienced in the workplace. After the tribunal's findings were publicized in the media, the ICO launched a formal investigation into blacklisting in the construction industry. In 2009, the ICO raided the offices of the Consulting Association, seized its documents, and immediately shut it down.

In response, blacklisted workers established the BSG as a solidarity network to voice their demands. When they began mobilizing in 2009, they had three main goals: (1) "blacklisting the blacklisters" by pressuring local authorities to deny public contracts to offending construction firms, (2) criminalizing the practice of blacklisting, and (3) increasing transparency in construction industry practices, including exposing police collusion in blacklisting.

The primary site of organizing for the BSG soon became a major group litigation that the blacklisted workers, guided by their lawyers, initiated against the companies involved. The BSG activists reached out to workers whose names appeared on the blacklist and encouraged them to join the lawsuit. Hundreds of workers came together to bring a collective claim against thirty-seven firms at the High Court. For many, participation in the trial offered not only the prospect of financial compensation but also the chance to have their day in court after being shunned by the construction industry. Appearances before the High Court were instrumental in assembling activists regularly and maintaining cohesion among the group. After the hearings, the BSG often held debrief meetings, sometimes joined by their lawyers, at the nearby pub, the Seven Stars. The litigation brought blacklisted workers together for the common cause of seeking justice.

While the High Court case helped expose the scale of blacklisting and lay the foundation for organizing, it soon became clear that domestic litigation would not be enough to achieve the BSG's goals due to limitations of existing laws. The ICO's prosecution of the CA's director, for example, was confined to a breach of the Data Protection Act, and the small fine he received was ultimately paid by one of the construction firms. Following the ICO revelations, the government

---

[2] Conversations with blacklisted workers, October and November 2014, and interview with Dave Smith, October 2014.

passed new blacklisting regulations under the Employment Relations Act 2010, drawing on the draft legislation that had failed in 1999. Though the new legislation made blacklisting unlawful, there were still several loopholes within the Act: Compensation for blacklisted workers remained vague, no clear procedures were outlined for destroying existing blacklists, and, crucially, blacklisting was not criminalized (Ewing 2009a). Because blacklisting was not a criminal offense, the workers' lawsuit at the High Court was a civil claim for damages, despite the extensive evidence collected on systematic discrimination efforts organized by the construction companies and the devastating effects on workers' lives.

To escalate their demands, workers needed to raise public awareness about the scandal and increase pressure on the government. The possibility of bringing their cases to the European Court of Human Rights opened up a new front in their struggle. ECtHR litigation offered an avenue not only for legal recognition but also for public visibility. Framing blacklisting as a human rights violation allowed workers to shift the conversation from industrial relations to human rights, potentially resonating with wider audiences and generating political momentum. This strategic turn was shaped in close collaboration with labor lawyers, who guided the BSG in devising a litigation approach aimed at both legal and political traction. The ECtHR litigation thus became not just a legal effort, but a way to reassert the validity of workers' claims in a context where domestic institutions had failed them.

7.3 HUMAN RIGHTS LITIGATION STRATEGY

The lawyers who identified the ECtHR as a target institution and led the strategic litigation efforts were the same group discussed in Chapter 5. Led by John Hendy and Keith Ewing, this small team had a wealth of experience in litigating labor rights before the ECtHR. When the blacklisting scandal broke in 2009, they knew that the ultimate destination needed to be Strasbourg. Just a year earlier, the ECtHR had issued its landmark ruling in *Demir and Baykara v. Turkey* (2008), and the lawyers were hopeful that they could build on this momentum to establish new precedents around blacklisting.

The first formal articulation of a human rights-based litigation strategy came in 2009, following the ICO raid. In a report commissioned by the construction union, Union of Construction, Allied Trades and

Technicians (UCATT), Ewing reviewed the draft legislation on blacklisting, which would later be enacted that same year, and identified its core weaknesses, mentioned above (Ewing 2009a).[3] Framing blacklisting as a serious human rights violation, Ewing argued that if domestic remedies failed, the ECtHR should be pursued as the final legal forum. The report also situated the issue in a longer history of governmental inaction: Despite the ILO's criticism and a complaint filed with the CFA in 1992, successive UK governments had refused to take meaningful steps to address blacklisting.

Human rights arguments soon began to appear in individual Employment Tribunal claims filed after Acheson's legal victory. Later, in the group litigation at the High Court, Hendy and other members of the legal team explicitly referenced the UK's obligations under Article 11 (freedom of association) of the European Convention. Before that case concluded, the lawyers strategically selected two applications to bring before the ECtHR, knowing that some BSG members were unable to succeed under domestic law due to legal technicalities.

The first case, brought by Terence Brough in 2011, concerned his blacklisting in 1988 (*Brough v. the United Kingdom* 2016). Brough had been labeled a "militant troublemaker" in the blacklist report due to his trade union activities, and there was clear evidence that he was denied work by a firm which checked his details with the Consulting Association. Because blacklisting on the basis of union membership was not unlawful in the UK until 1992, his domestic appeals were dismissed. His ECtHR application argued that the lack of legal protection against blacklisting at the time of his blacklisting violated Article 11 and Article 14 (prohibition of discrimination).

The second case was brought by Dave Smith, whose thirty-six-page Consulting Association file detailed years of trade union activity, including his work as an elected health and safety representative. As a result of his futile attempts to find work in construction sites starting in 1999, he was forced to look for employment elsewhere and later became the secretary of the BSG. When Hendy, along with David Renton and Declan Owens, approached him to represent his case, they were clear: They expected to lose in domestic courts but saw strategic value in taking his case to Strasbourg.[4] As discussed in Chapter 5, the British lawyers pursued only those cases they believed could set

---

[3] UCATT merged into Unite in 2017.
[4] Interview with Dave Smith, October 2014.

precedent or support legislative reform, in contrast to the mass-filing approach adopted by Turkish lawyers in the 2000s.

By the time Smith exhausted domestic remedies in 2015, the ECtHR had already started to show signs of restraint on trade union rights, notably in *RMT v. The United Kingdom* (2014), which rejected a claim on the right to strike (see Chapter 4). Nevertheless, the legal team believed his case was still worth pursuing. In the ECtHR application, Smith's lawyers argued that his blacklisting violated Article 8 (right to private life), due to the secret collection and storage of personal data about his trade union activities, and Article 11, due to the obstruction of his activities as a trade union member.

The BSG was established as a grassroots mobilization group, and the activists did not wait for the High Court or the ECtHR rulings to launch a public campaign. But the ECtHR litigation changed the dynamics of BSG's mobilization. The possibility of remedy under human rights law gave the BSG activists renewed hope that they can hold blacklisting companies accountable and push for stronger protections on blacklisting. For the first time, trade union activists framed their struggle not only as a fight for labor rights but as a broader human rights issue that exposed state and corporate collusion and demanded accountability on the public stage. This shift opened up new political possibilities, allowing the BSG to expand its audience, strengthen its moral authority, and pressure institutions that had long refused to act.

7.4 ADOPTING HUMAN RIGHTS LANGUAGE IN THE SHADOW OF INTERNATIONAL LITIGATION

Lawyers played an essential role in facilitating BSG's adoption of human rights language by translating human rights law to workers through various mediums. As discussed in Chapter 4, the Institute of Employment Rights, led by Ewing and Hendy, regularly holds workshops and issues publications to inform trade unions about their rights under international law. These lawyers developed the litigation strategy around human rights while simultaneously communicating its political potential to the workers.

The lawyers' purpose here was not raising awareness among the workers about the abuses in the workplace or encouraging workers to articulate their grievances through human rights language. Most of these workers were blacklisted due to their trade union activism in the workplace, so they were well aware that they were wronged.

Instead, the lawyers' aim was to point out that international law could offer a form of redress where domestic legal institutions had fallen short. But the decision to incorporate human rights language into BSG campaigns was ultimately made by the activists themselves.

This raises a key question: Why did the BSG adopt human rights language when these pro-labor institutions and lawyers had long promoted human rights law to trade unions? Ewing and Hendy had worked with unions since the 1990s to develop strategies based on international legal norms. Yet until the BSG, there had been no sustained movement organized around the "human rights" of workers, except occasional references in events and publications.

The BSG held a distinctive position within the trade union movement. The group emerged as an independent, grassroots formation. Though the workers were blacklisted due to their trade union activism, the BSG activists had a complicated relationship with the unions. Some blacklisted workers resented the unions for their earlier inaction,[5] and for good reason: During the High Court proceedings, evidence emerged that officials from Unite, Britain's largest construction union, had colluded with employers by sharing information about "troublemakers" on site.[6] In response, Unite initiated an inquiry into the allegations in 2019.[7] And, since the beginning of the group litigation, the unions provided legal and financial support to the claimants at the High Court.

The gravity of the blacklisting scandal demanded a strategy that could break through political inertia. Unlike conventional union struggles for better pay or protections during strikes, this was about systematic and institutionalized exclusion – enabled by both corporate power and state surveillance. BSG activists sought retribution, safeguards, and structural change. Framing their demands as human rights violations allowed them to cast blacklisting not simply as a labor dispute, but as a moral and legal outrage. It gave them a language with

---

[5] Conversations with two blacklisted workers, October and November 2014, and participant observation data.

[6] Unite is the second largest union in the country with over a million members. Allegations were raised against UCATT as well, but UCATT merged into Unite in 2016.

[7] Rob Evans, "Unite to Investigate Claims of Collusion with Construction Blacklist," *The Guardian*, July 14, 2019, www.theguardian.com/business/2019/jul/14/unite-to-investigate-claims-of-collusion-with-construction-blacklist.

broad public resonance and forced political actors to reckon with their obligations under international law.

One of the key figures to pioneer this strategy was Dave Smith, the BSG's secretary and one of its ECtHR applicants. Smith collaborated closely with the IER and other pro-labor organizations in efforts to spread information on blacklisted workers and international human rights law. He is often featured as a speaker, alongside lawyers like Ewing and Hendy, at public events, and he contributed to publications that linked blacklisting to international legal norms.[8]

Smith had worked as an engineer and an elected safety representative for his union on construction sites in East London before he was blacklisted. A committed activist since the age of eighteen, he never shied away from contentious action.[9] After being ousted from the construction industry, he continued to campaign on trade union rights and became an educator and researcher. Upon joining the BSG, he pursued a doctoral degree at the University of the West of England to study union organizing. In 2015, he co-authored *Blacklisted: The Secret War Between Big Business and Union Activists* with journalist Phil Chamberlain, who wrote the breaking story on blacklisting in *The Guardian* in 2009 (Smith and Chamberlain 2016). Smith's growing knowledge, especially of the history of blacklisting, the extent of police collusion, and the weaknesses of legal protections, convinced him that the BSG needed to pursue legal and disruptive tactics together in the fight against the state and big business.

Reading Ewing's report (2009a), which identified the ECtHR as the target institution, Smith recalled having a strategic breakthrough and thinking: "Now we know what to do!"[10] The report helped explain why unions had struggled to take meaningful legal action for so long: Protections under the Data Protection Act were weak, and subcontracted workers like Smith often had no clear legal relationship with the construction giants controlling the blacklist. Even with union

---

[8] See for example his publication in the special issue of *International Union Rights*, a journal published by the pro-labor organization International Center for Trade Union Rights (ICTUR), on blacklisting. The issue aims to inform workers and lawyers on national and international struggles against blacklisting and discusses the importance of legal protections against blacklisting. Similarly, in 2015, he participated in a conference featuring his book, *Blacklisted*, jointly held by the IER and the Haldane Society of Socialist Lawyers.
[9] Interview with Dave Smith, October 2014.
[10] Interview with Dave Smith, October 2014.

support, cases brought to employment tribunals often failed or yielded only modest compensation.

For Smith, the ECtHR was not just a court of last resort, it was also a political tool. He recognized that achieving their goals required creating pressure from multiple angles: legal, political, and social. Even the pending cases at the ECtHR gave the BSG greater leverage to push for structural reforms. A judgment from Strasbourg condemning blacklisting could discredit the firms involved and strengthen the BSG campaign to "blacklist the blacklisters" both domestically and internationally. As Smith put it: "They could end up losing UN contracts or World Bank contracts because of human rights violations," or find themselves excluded from major contracts like building the London Olympic Park.[11]

Through their close relations with the lawyers, BSG activists were prompted to incorporate human rights language into their campaigns. Smith explained the influence of this relationship and the deliberate decision made on adopting human rights language as follows:

> I can stand up and talk about socialism; bang the table and talk about a new world ... But if I just stand up and talk about, "I want more money for builders," it's very easy to be painted as ... It's about how you frame the argument. We're using the human rights stuff that we've really heard the lawyers say, and then, we're just putting it into our own propaganda. We virtually never put stuff out without mentioning human rights now.[12]

For Smith and other activists, human rights framing wasn't just about legal arguments; it was about media strategy. Stories framed as violations of "human rights" carried far more weight in the public imagination than technical claims of trade union victimization. As Smith explained: "the only claim you can take to the employment tribunals is victimization for trade union activities ... That's the bit of [employment] law that you have to use. But the newspapers aren't interested in that. They are interested in human rights violations at Crossrail."[13] He was referring to the revelation that a senior manager at London's major rail project at Crossrail checked the names of workers on the blacklist more than 900 times with the Consulting Association in

---

[11] Interview with Dave Smith, October 2014.
[12] Interview with Dave Smith, October 2014.
[13] Interview with Dave Smith, October 2014.

2007.¹⁴ Framing such practices as human rights violations made them legible and urgent in ways that domestic labor law could not.

The BSG's decision to reference the ECtHR and human rights in its campaigns might seem questionable given the growing backlash against European institutions in the UK since the early 2000s. ECtHR judgments on prisoners' right to vote and migrants' rights had drawn harsh criticism from the right and fueled debates over judicial overreach and national sovereignty. The backlash intensified in 2015, when the Conservative Party pledged to repeal the HRA, and again in 2022, following the ECtHR's intervention in deportation flights to Rwanda.¹⁵ Yet despite political posturing, the UK continued to comply with ECtHR rulings, as discussed in Chapter 6. Even in *Hirst v. the United Kingdom* (2006) – one of the most publicly maligned decisions – the government ultimately made the required changes, albeit "begrudgingly" (Hillebrecht 2014). Therefore, ECtHR litigation still presented legal and political opportunities for the BSG to pressure the government.

In this context, the BSG's embrace of human rights discourse points to the contested but enduring power of rights-based claims. Political outrage over *court rulings* does not mean that *human rights discourse* has lost its normative power or public legitimacy; if anything, the intensity of political response and media coverage validates their continued salience. Human rights have become such a globally resonant framework for articulating social injustice that even the Tories do not reject them outright. Instead, they dispute what qualifies as a human right and who has the authority to define it. As the former Prime Minister David Cameron remarked ahead of the 2015 elections, referring to the Convention: "When that charter was written, in the aftermath of the second world war, it set out the basic rights we should respect. But since

---

[14] Daniel Boffey, "Crossrail Project Dragged into Blacklist Scandal," *The Guardian*, December 2, 2012, www.theguardian.com/uk/2012/dec/02/crossrail-blacklisting-scandal.

[15] The repeal plan, which was met with strong opposition from civil society organizations and human rights advocates across the country, would enable the government to limit implementation to only the "most serious cases" and ensure that "the rulings of Strasbourg will not have legal effect in the UK without the consent of parliament." Nicholas Watt and Owen Bowcott, "Tories Plan to Withdraw UK from European Convention on Human Rights," *The Guardian*, October 3, 2014, www.theguardian.com/politics/2014/oct/03/tories-plan-uk-withdrawal-european-convention-on-human-rights. The Conservative government abandoned its plans to repeal the HRA in 2023, and it is unlikely that the current Labour government will revive them.

then, interpretations of that charter have led to a whole lot of things that are frankly wrong."[16] When the government proposed repealing the Human Rights Act, it simultaneously pledged to replace it with a British Bill of Rights, signaling that the objection lay not with human rights per se, but with the perceived erosion of national sovereignty. The BSG specifically seized on this contested terrain to position trade unionists as bearers of human rights.

7.5 WORKERS' ON-STAGE MOBILIZATION: FRAMING BLACKLISTING AS A HUMAN RIGHTS ISSUE

Human rights language became a prominent frame that the BSG frequently used in demonstrations, social media activism, press statements, and lobbying efforts. I refer to the totality of these campaign activities aimed at a broader national audience as the BSG's *on-stage mobilization*.[17] The group consciously framed blacklisting as a human rights violation, using this discourse to increase the visibility and perceived gravity of its claims and to gain political traction.

Among the most visible sites of this on-stage mobilization were the High Court hearings, which became rallying points for strategic protest and public messaging. BSG activists planned demonstrations to coincide with hearing dates and used them to gain media visibility. Workers wore black and white "blacklisted" t-shirts and flooded the courtroom, creating a visual spectacle. Throughout the proceedings, lawyers representing the blacklisted workers repeatedly cited the UK's obligations under the Convention and drew on ECtHR case law protecting trade union rights under Article 11. BSG activists amplified these legal arguments through social media. For instance, one post on the BSG's Facebook page summarized courtroom proceedings and emphasized human rights language:

---

[16] Owen Bowcott, "Cameron's Pledge to Scrap Human Rights Act Angers Civil Rights Groups," *The Guardian*, October 1, 2014, www.theguardian.com/politics/2014/oct/01/cameron-pledge-scrap-human-rights-act-civil-rights-groups.

[17] This theorization draws on Goffman's (2007) concepts of "frontstage" and "backstage," which describe people's presentation of themselves in public versus private settings. While Goffman emphasizes private backstage behavior, in the context of grassroots activism, the backstage is not hidden but rather a semi-private space where activists lower their guard among trusted peers. Their frontstage performance, by contrast, is deliberate and planned; activists deploy human rights language to frame their grievances and appeal to broader audiences.

John Hendy QC representing also underlines the importance of the Human Rights legislation and gives previous cases and law that is now set in stone. He then reminds the court of its duty and its obligation to the state regarding everybody's right freedom [sic] to join a trade union under article 11 and article 14 which covers discrimination also.[18]

Human rights also served as a salient framework for *tactical innovation* in the BSG's campaigns and demonstrations. One such example was the series of "citizens' arrest" activists organized to highlight the lack of criminal accountability for blacklisters. During these events, BSG activists visited the offices of construction companies to symbolically arrest those responsible, often the CEOs or senior managers. The "arrest warrants," deliberately designed as large protest signs, cited a breach of Article 11 of the Convention, signaling the BSG's effort to cast blacklisting as a human rights violation.[19]

In another campaign event, the activists organized a series of protest tours called "crocodile tears," aimed at naming and shaming managers of construction firms by either raiding their offices or protesting outside them. At these events, activists held banners and chanted slogans such as "Nuremberg defense on blacklisting won't wash." This slogan referenced the Nazi soldiers' defense during the Nuremberg trials that they were merely following orders. The same framing appeared in the legal team's submission to the ECtHR, where they reminded the Court that the European Convention was drafted in the aftermath of the Holocaust to prevent the rise of totalitarian regimes.[20] Smith's lawyers, John Hendy and David Renton, reiterated this framing in media reports to emphasize the human rights dimensions of blacklisting.[21]

The BSG also expanded its reach by *forming alliances* with other human rights-focused groups, most notably the Campaign Opposing Police

---

[18] Royston Bentham, "Blacklist Support Group Facebook Page," posted December 17, 2014, www.facebook.com/groups/blacklistSG/posts/10152598879057428/.

[19] See images of the "arrest warrant" used during the citizens' arrest protest at the offices of construction giant Sir Robert McAlpine, targeting Cullum McAlpine, who had admitted during a parliamentary investigation that he was the first chairman of the Consulting Association. "Blacklisted Workers Serve Arrest Warrant on Cullum McAlpine," Reelnews, February 21, 2014, https://reelnews.co.uk/2014/02/21/all-reelnews-campaigns/workplace-struggles/blacklisted-workers-serve-arrest-warrant-on-cullum-mcalpine/.

[20] *Brough v. the United Kingdom*, Reply on Behalf of the Applicant. This is not a public document, I obtained it through the lawyers who made the submission.

[21] "Smith v Carillion Case at Court of Appeal," Institute of Employment Rights, February 5, 2015, www.ier.org.uk/news/smith-v-carillion-case-court-appeal/.

Surveillance (COPS). Together, the BSG and COPS worked closely to expose the broader implications of blacklisting and police collusion. The ICO raid of the Consulting Association revealed that the blacklist included not only construction workers but also academics, journalists, environmentalists, and other leftist activists, raising early suspicions about the role of police surveillance. These suspicions were confirmed when a former undercover officer publicly admitted to spying on trade union activists, and ICO evidence showed that police officers attended secret Consulting Association meetings (Smith and Chamberlain 2016).[22] Further revelations exposed that some of the undercover police officers had formed long-term romantic relationships with women activists under false identities, and in some cases even conceived children.[23] The COPS aimed to expose the depth of this surveillance and demand accountability. Human rights language was a salient feature of their joint events, including co-organized demonstrations and media briefings. Notably, the citizens' arrest protest was a BSG–COPS collaboration.

The 2015 launch of a public inquiry into police surveillance deepened BSG's alliances with other activist groups, including environmental campaigners and anti-racist organizers. Prominent human rights lawyer Imran Khan is representing both the BSG and the family of Stephen Lawrance, a young black man killed in a racially motivated attack, underscoring the shared stakes in this national investigation of human rights abuses. In his opening statement to the inquiry, Dave Smith stressed how infiltration into unions by undercover officers disrupted the internal democratic processes of independent trade unions and constituted a violation of Article 11.[24]

---

[22] Scottish Affairs Committee, "Blacklisting in Employment: Final Report Seventh Report of Session 2014–15," House of Commons, March 27, 2015. Rob Evans, "Covert Police Unit Spied on Trade Union Members, Whistleblower Reveals," *The Guardian*, March 13, 2015, www.theguardian.com/uk-news/undercover-with-paul-lewis-and-rob-evans/2015/mar/13/covert-police-unit-spied-on-trade-union-members-whistleblower-reveals.

[23] "New Blacklisting Evidence of Police Collusion Heightens Need for Public Inquiry," Unite The Union, March 6, 2019, www.unitetheunion.org/news-events/news/2019/march/new-blacklisting-evidence-of-police-collusion-heightens-need-for-public-inquiry; Rob Evans, "Police Spies May Have Had No Choice Over Sexual Relationships, Officer Claims," *The Guardian*, November 19, 2020, www.theguardian.com/uk-news/2020/nov/19/police-spies-may-have-had-no-choice-over-sexual-relationships-officer-claims.

[24] Dave Smith, "Opening Statement," published November 5, 2020, https://unitedleft.org.uk/wp-content/uploads/2020/11/Blacklist-Support-Group-UPCI-Opening-Statement-002.pdf.

BSG activists consistently framed their grievances as human rights violations in the media, frequently referring to the ECtHR. My analysis of *The Guardian* articles on blacklisting from 2011 to 2019 shows that out of seventy-four articles, fourteen made explicit references to human rights. Six of these were opinion pieces written by BSG activists and eight were news articles. The human rights framing was particularly driven by the BSG leadership: Dave Smith authored or co-authored four of the opinion pieces, including one titled, "Blacklisting activists is a *human rights scandal*. An inquiry is overdue."[25] In another, BSG activist Ricky Tomlinson wrote, "There is no place for blacklisting in the UK; standing up for your conditions at work is a *basic human right*."[26]

In the news coverage, human rights references appeared almost exclusively in quotes from BSG activists.[27] For example, after the High Court proceedings, BSG chair Steve Acheson told reporters: "Until such time that the full conspiracy is exposed and those responsible for the *human rights abuse* are called to account in a court of law, we will never stop fighting."[28] Another article similarly referenced anonymous blacklisted workers: "The workers have said they intend to continue their legal claim at the high court ... as well as their campaign for a public inquiry 'to expose everyone involved in this *human rights conspiracy*.'"[29] Even prominent trade union leaders adopted the language. Len McCluskey, then general secretary of Unite, said: "Lives have been ruined and families have been torn apart just because workers have raised safety concerns in Britain's most dangerous industry, or just because they exercised their *human rights* to belong to a trade

---

[25] Dave Smith, "Blacklisting Activists Is a Human Rights Scandal. An Inquiry Is Overdue," *The Guardian*, August 20, 2013, www.theguardian.com/commentisfree/2013/aug/20/blacklisting-activists-human-rights-inquiry (emphasis added).

[26] Ricky Tomlinson, "Are Bosses Still Blacklisting Trade Unionists?," *The Guardian*, June 12, 2013, www.theguardian.com/commentisfree/2013/jun/12/bosses-blacklisting-trade-unions-shrewsbury-24 (emphasis added).

[27] Except one article which referenced a human rights lawyer.

[28] Rob Evans, "Blacklisted Workers Win Compensation from Big Construction Firms," *The Guardian*, April 29, 2016, www.theguardian.com/business/2016/apr/29/blacklisted-workers-secure-compensation-construction-firms (emphasis added).

[29] Rob Evans, "Construction Firms to Compensate Unlawfully Blacklisted Workers," *The Guardian*, October 10, 2013, www.theguardian.com/business/2013/oct/10/construction-firms-compensate-workers-blacklist (emphasis added).

union."³⁰ While the media analysis indicates a deliberate effort by BSG activists to frame blacklisting as a human rights issue, it does not show that this framing shifted public opinion or was widely adopted by the media. Human rights language appeared mainly in activist quotes and opinion pieces, rather than standing out as a salient feature of the overall coverage. Still, its consistent use underscores the BSG's strategic attempt to recast trade union repression in a more resonant legal and moral frame.

Parliamentary advocacy offered another important avenue through which the BSG mobilized human rights. Despite the often fraught relationship between the Labour Party and the trade union movement since Tony Blair's leadership, lobbying has been a central pillar of BSG's campaign strategy. Since 2009, Labour MPs have attended BSG meetings, demonstrations, and court hearings. Jeremy Corbyn's rise to the party leadership in 2015 was welcomed by the group, which praised his longstanding support: "Jeremy has always supported blacklisted workers, signing Early Day Motions (when most Labour MPs didn't), attending BSG meetings in parliament and in his Islington constituency and over the years has stood next to us on picket lines outside building sites."³¹ John McDonnell, who was Shadow Chancellor, chaired the BSG's foundational meeting and is considered a founding member. The Scottish National Party (SNP) has also backed the campaign and spearheaded the first parliamentary inquiry into blacklisting.³²

Labour MPs, in particular, invoked human rights language to emphasize the gravity of the issue and the UK's obligations under international law. My analysis of House of Commons debates on blacklisting from 2009 to 2020 shows that these MPs regularly used human rights frames in parliamentary discussions. One MP stated, "This is not just an issue of data protection; it is *an issue of human rights*

---

[30] Matthew Taylor, "Blacklist Used by Construction Firms to Disrupt Environmental Protests," *The Guardian*, January 28, 2013, www.theguardian.com/business/2013/jan/28/blacklist-construction-firms-environmental-protests (emphasis added).

[31] "Blacklist Group Welcomes Jeremy Corbyn," *Northern Voices*, September 14, 2015, http://northernvoicesmag.blogspot.com/2015/09/blacklist-group-welcome-jeremy-corbyn.html.

[32] Scottish Affairs Committee, "Blacklisting in Employment: Final Report, Seventh Report of Session 2014–15," House of Commons, March 27, 2015, https://publications.parliament.uk/pa/cm201415/cmselect/cmscotaf/272/272.pdf.

and employment law,"³³ while another called for action to "eradicate this *appalling abuse of people's human rights* at work once and for all."³⁴ One MP cited Keith Ewing to describe blacklisting as "*the worst human rights abuse* in relation to workers in Britain in half a century."³⁵ In response to evidence of police collusion, Labour MPs introduced a motion urging parliament to support "calls by the Blacklisting Support Group and other campaigners for a full public inquiry into this *human rights injustice*."³⁶ The ECtHR cases gave Labour MPs a concrete legal framework for their advocacy. They cited Article 8 and Article 11 of the Convention in debates on police surveillance legislation,³⁷ and drew on legal reports by Liberty and labor lawyer Michael Ford QC during discussions of proposed reforms to trade union law.³⁸ These references allowed MPs to connect domestic legal reform efforts to the UK's obligations under international human rights law.

7.6 WORKERS' OFF-STAGE MOBILIZATION: CLASS SOLIDARITY OVER HUMAN RIGHTS

Since BSG activists made a conscious effort to use human rights language in their campaigns, one might expect the same framing to feature prominently in their internal meetings. Yet during *off-stage mobilization*, which includes internal strategizing and information discussions where activists are not performing for the media – references to human rights were largely absent. These internal discussions regarding how to compel trade unions to pay more attention to blacklisting, how to support a BSG candidate for a union's executive position, or how to reduce wage disparities between agency workers and permanent staff hardly ever included human rights language.

Instead, off-stage BSG discussions centered on traditional forms of workers' mobilization, such as class struggle or solidarity. When they shared personal stories of their victimization, such as the humiliation of seeking unskilled work after years in skilled trades or the shame they

---

[33] Chuka Umunna, House of Commons, 23 January 2013 (emphasis added).
[34] Margot James, House of Commons, 5 September 2017 (emphasis added).
[35] Jack Dromey, 5 September 2017 (emphasis added).
[36] House of Commons, Motion, 14 March 2019 (emphasis added).
[37] Discussions on "Covert Human Intelligence Sources (Criminal Conduct) Bill," House of Commons, October 5, 2020 and October 15, 2020.
[38] Discussions on "Transparency of Lobbying, Non-Party Campaigning and Trade Union Administration Bill," House of Commons, September 11, 2013.

faced in their families for being unemployed, they made no references to human rights. During one of the meetings, a BSG activist referred to the blacklisters as "fat, greedy" employers, a trope that resonates with the traditional class-based descriptions of big business bosses, but they reserve remarks such as "human rights abusing wretches" for when they are in front of cameras.[39]

The BSG is a grassroots activist network, organized in a non-hierarchical way and its decision-making processes are democratic. But some members, such as the secretary or the chairman, make more appearances in the media than others. These prominent figures put a special effort into deploying human rights language. As shown in the media analysis above, most of *The Guardian* articles came either from opinion pieces written by BSG leaders or from news articles quoting them. Social media analysis corroborates this pattern. An examination of BSG's public Facebook group from 2010 to 2019 indicates that 294 entries included references to human rights. More than half of these entries were posted by Dave Smith, who is one of the administrators of the Facebook group.[40] Six other BSG members who took leadership in campaign coordination and lobbying work, each posted between six and fifteen entries. For example, Stewart Hume and Greig McArthur, both of whom led lobbying efforts with the SNP, posted fifteen and seven entries, respectively.[41] Lee James Fowler and Royston Bentham, also Facebook group administrators, posted eight and seven entries. There are forty-eight other individuals who posted one or two human rights-related posts, often blending them with more familiar language rooted in working class identity.[42]

The primacy of class-based identity was also evident in how BSG members described themselves. None of the activists I interviewed – leaders or rank-and-file – identified as human rights activists. Instead, in unprompted conversations, activists often referred to themselves as "socialists" or praised one another as "working-class heroes." Discussions among workers made frequent references to their worker

---

[39] Other descriptions to the blacklisters include "horrible bastards," "the wretches," and "criminals," among others.

[40] Out of a total of 294 entries, 178 were posted by Smith.

[41] "Blacklisting," Scottish Parliament, debated May 2, 2013, www.theyworkforyou.com/sp/?id=2013-05-02.17.0#g17.4.

[42] Some of these include posts by journalists or supporters of the BSG as well as blacklisted workers. It is not possible for me to verify which of these individuals are BSG members since they were posting in a public Facebook group.

or class identity. For example, in response to an initial offer from the blacklisting companies in return for blacklisted workers' agreement to drop their charges at the High Court, a discussion among BSG activists ensued where they discouraged each other from accepting the offer with statements like "the fight is against capital," "it's another form of exploitation," "blood money is on offer."[43] One member added: "If we sell out, what message does that give to every *working class man and woman* in the UK who is getting victimized by their employer for speaking out about health and safety or their working terms and conditions?"[44] Overall, the social media analysis and the participant observation data indicate that the BSG's effort to use human rights language on-stage is led by the public-facing BSG leaders whereas off-stage discussions exhibit the primacy of class solidarity for workers.

This divide shows how the group balanced outward strategy with inward conviction. While prominent BSG leaders consciously deployed human rights language in public campaigns, many rank-and-file members were largely indifferent to rights-based framing. Even the leaders' engagement with human rights language was instrumental, rather than a sign of deep ideological commitment. Their political consciousness remained rooted in class, and they did not embrace human rights discourse without hesitation or critique. Smith made this clear in a 2014 interview: "It's not a case of, 'oh we'll give it to the lawyers and the lawyers are going to do it for us.' That's not what any of us think. We all think, 'it's about us fighting our fight, but we have used some of their language.' There's no question about that."[45] After losing his ECtHR case in 2017, he reiterated this point in an article addressed to trade unionists. He wrote that he had "no illusions that the law alone would provide justice," and emphasized that the primary purpose of his case was "to generate publicity as part of the wider political campaign waged by the Blacklist Support Group and the

---

[43] Various posts by BSG members on the Blacklist Support Group's Facebook page in response to the announcement Smith made regarding the compensation offer, June 9, 2015.

[44] Posted on Blacklist Support Group's Facebook page by Lee James Fowler, June 9, 2015 (emphasis added, edited for grammar and spelling).

[45] Interview with Dave Smith, October 2014.

construction unions." He urged fellow workers not to feel sorry for him but to "feel angry."[46]

In meetings, activists regularly expressed their frustration with a legal system that does not "lock up" the blacklisters who ruined their lives and lamented the slow pace of proceedings. One activist referred to the litigation efforts as "little more than a cover," asserting that rank-and-file mobilization remained the most meaningful form of resistance.[47]

The legal professionals working with the BSG shared this pragmatic view and exhibited caution about the promises of human rights litigation. Declan Owens, one of the lawyers who represented Smith at the ECtHR, described human rights law as a "Trojan horse" – a way to gain attention for labor issues and, ultimately, push broader political goals.[48] He emphasized that the aim of ECtHR litigation was not just about getting a compensation award and setting a precedent, but also gaining more advantage in lobbying efforts and raising labor issues, once again, to the top of national agenda. Hendy affirmed this logic by stating that: "As Dave Smith's [ECtHR] case shows, these problems cannot be left to the courts. They require urgent and fundamental legislation" (Smith 2017). Victoria Philipps, the solicitor in the *ASLEF* case, likewise noted that litigation at the ECtHR is "just another weapon in the armory" for workers. For these lawyers who viewed themselves as the "legal arm" of a broader labor movement, legal action served the political struggle, rather than defining it.[49]

These overlapping doubts among activists and their legal allies point to a shared understanding of the limits of legal redress. McCann (1994) refers to this orientation as "double consciousness": the ability to use legal discourse as a tactical tool while simultaneously recognizing its constraints (see also Matsuda 1987; Mehta 2024). In most legal mobilization campaigns, such pragmatic legal approaches are often accompanied by the formation of a group identity around rights or human rights (Chua 2012; McCann 1994). Often, lawyers play a key role in cultivating this new identity by encouraging members to view their

---

[46] Dave Smith and Phil Chamberlain, "No Blacklist Justice for Britain's Agency Staff," *Morning Star*, May 2, 2017, https://morningstaronline.co.uk/a-dc1a-no-blacklist-justice-for-britains-agency-staff-1.
[47] Conversation with a blacklisted worker, October 2014.
[48] Interview with Declan Owens, November 2014.
[49] Interview with Victoria Philipps, November 2014.

grievances through a human rights lens (Chua 2012; Merry 2006). What sets the BSG apart is that the lawyers working with the blacklisted workers did not pursue such endeavors; instead, their efforts were focused exclusively on advancing workers' claims through legal channels as part of a broader struggle for justice. The BSG's solidarity ties and group identity remained anchored in class-based themes, underscoring the movement's grounding in working-class politics rather than professionalized human-rights advocacy.

One possible explanation for this divergence lies in the preexisting solidarity among BSG members. Unlike in movements where legal discourse helps generate group identity, blacklisted workers were already bound by class-based ties forged through trade union activism. While the British trade unions no longer enjoy the glory they did before the 1980s, the BSG activists continued to draw on that shared history to encourage each other to step forward and mobilize again. In contrast to movements centered on violence against women (Merry 2006) or LGBTQ rights (Chua 2012), where instilling a rights-consciousness was integral to the aim of building a movement, the BSG did not require a new rights-consciousness to mobilize. Class identity remained the primary source of group affiliation and potent motivation for activism, even as human rights provided new political strategies for the movement.

7.7 BEYOND LITIGATION: THE MATERIAL IMPACT OF HUMAN RIGHTS MOBILIZATION

The analysis thus far has shown that the BSG activists made the strategic decision to articulate their grievances as human rights abuses in their public campaigns. But what was the material impact of mobilizing human rights law? In other words, did the BSG's efforts yield any tangible gains for the movement?

At first glance, the outcomes of the ECtHR litigation suggest limited success. The workers eventually lost both of the cases brought to Strasbourg, primarily on procedural grounds regarding time limitations and the non-exhaustion of domestic remedies. The Court noted that the group litigation at the High Court indicated domestic responsiveness to the workers' claims and therefore left the issue to be settled by domestic courts (*Smith v. the United Kingdom* 2017: paras. 40, 55). However, by the time the ECtHR issued its final rulings, the BSG activists had already launched their grassroots mobilization campaign.

Despite ultimately losing these cases, the group's strategic use of human rights helped it achieve meaningful advances.

The BSG's strategic mobilization of human rights resulted in material gains on three major fronts. First, one of the group's core demands – "blacklisting the blacklisters" – was partly realized through lobbying with Labour and SNP MPs. In an official statement, the House of Commons Scottish Affairs Committee (2014) popularized this demand by calling for disqualifying the blacklisting firms from all publicly funded work, leading the Scottish government to exclude all implicated companies from public contracts. The Welsh government, the Northern Ireland Assembly, and various local authorities followed suit by revising their procurement policies (Smith 2014).[50] Moreover, the Labour Party under Corbyn's leadership introduced ethical guidelines in order to ban all Labour-run councils from entering into public contracts with blacklisting firms.[51]

Second, in May 2016, the group litigation at the High Court was settled out of court in a deal deemed a major victory by the BSG. The companies involved issued a public apology and agreed to pay multimillion-pound compensation to 250 blacklisted workers. Following this outcome, Unite initiated a second round of group litigation. In total, the blacklisting firms were compelled to pay approximately £35 million in compensation to more than 1,200 blacklisted workers.[52] Commenting on the settlements, BSG co-secretary Roy Bentham stated: "Blacklisting of union members and those prepared to stand up for basic legal entitlements is not just a breach of the law, it is a violation of human rights."[53] As discussed above, the

---

[50] Matthew Taylor and Will Hurst, "Companies That Blacklist Workers Face Ban from Public Contracts in Wales," *The Guardian*, September 11, 2013, www.theguardian.com/politics/2013/sep/11/companies-blacklist-workers-public-contracts-wales.

[51] Jack Simpson, "Labour Plans Council Anti-Blacklisting Guide," January 21, 2016, www.constructionnews.co.uk/10001779.article?WT.tsrc5email&WT.mc_id5CN_Daily-Newsletter210116&cm_ven-ExactTarget&cm_cat5CN1Daily1News1%28R%29&cm_pla5Construction1News&cm_lm5gfr15%40dial.pipex.com.

[52] The initial deal included about 700 workers, but more workers joined in the following years, reaching up to 1,000 workers by 2019. Rob Evans, "50 Blacklisted Trade Unionists Win £1.9m from Building Firms," *The Guardian*, May 14, 2019, www.theguardian.com/business/2019/may/14/50-blacklisted-trade-unionists-win-19m-from-building-firms.

[53] The BSG statement sent in group email, December 4, 2017.

blacklisted workers' lawyers repeatedly reminded the High Court judges of the government's obligations under Article 11 of the Convention.

The third important goal of the BSG was exposing the full scale of blacklisting, particularly the extent of police collaboration with the Consulting Association. Their efforts paid off in May 2015 when Theresa May, then Home Secretary, ordered a public inquiry into undercover officers spying on political campaigners. The BSG was granted core participant status – an outcome the group described a once-in-a-generation opportunity. The first phase of the inquiry, which focused on the activities of the Metropolitan Police's special demonstration squad (SDS) between 1968 and 1982, concluded in 2023. The interim report found that many of the unit's surveillance practices, especially infiltration of left-wing groups and trade unions, were unlawful and unjustified. Had these practices been known at the time, the report indicated, "the SDS would have been brought to a rapid end."[54] The inquiry is, at the time of writing, proceeding to examine the post-1982 operations.

These developments show that even when activists ultimately obtain adverse rulings at the ECtHR, they can still leverage pending cases to pressure the government through grassroots mobilization. Indeed, in dismissing one of the applications, the ECtHR explicitly referenced the public inquiry and the High Court settlement as evidence that effective domestic remedies were available (*Smith v. the United Kingdom* 2017: paras. 39, 49, 54–55).[55] BSG activists have made significant progress in instigating structural reforms, securing compensation, and demanding accountability.

At the same time, these achievements do not suggest that the struggle is over. Blacklisting is still not a criminal offense, and the public inquiry continues to uncover deeper layers of state involvement.[56] Nor can the BSG's use of human rights be credited as the sole or even primary driver of success. As legal mobilization scholars have

---

[54] "Undercover Policing Inquiry Tranche 1 Interim Report," *Undercover Policing Inquiry*, June 2023, p. 96, www.ucpi.org.uk/wp-content/uploads/2023/06/Undercover-Policing-Inquiry-Tranche-1-Interim-Report.pdf.

[55] Although part of Smith's allegations in the ECtHR case were different than those addressed by the High Court settlement.

[56] Rob Evans, "Trade Unionist Was Refused Job after Police Gave Details to Blacklist," *The Guardian*, March 6, 2019, www.theguardian.com/uk-news/2019/mar/06/trade-unionist-refused-job-after-police-passed-details-to-blacklist.

long argued, outcomes depend on multiple factors: the responsiveness of political institutions, the judiciary's disposition, organizational capacity, and available resources (Arrington 2019; McCann 1994; Tarrow 2022). Still, given the centrality of human rights framing in the BSG's public campaigns, legal strategies, and political lobbying, it played a constitutive role in shaping the movement's trajectory and advancements. While litigation alone did not deliver victory, it helped launch a movement that made victory possible.

7.8 CONCLUSION

The case study of the BSG shows that the ECtHR litigation catalyzed and amplified grassroots mobilization in important ways. Activists strategically invoked human rights to shape public opinion and pressure the government. Even before the ECtHR's ultimate dismissal of the blacklisted workers' claims, the BSG's strategic mobilization of human rights helped secure tangible outcomes: disqualifying blacklisting firms from public contracts, initiating a public inquiry, and winning a major settlement in the High Court.

The analysis demonstrates a clear on-stage/off-stage dynamic in the way BSG members engaged with human rights language. On-stage, BSG activists used human rights strategically to gain visibility in a political environment where trade unions had long been marginalized. They used human rights strategically to cast themselves in a more sympathetic light and counter negative public perceptions of trade union activism. Off-stage, however, class-based language remained the primary vocabulary of solidarity. Internal discussions, identities, and motivations continued to be shaped by shared experiences of working-class struggle.

Throughout, neither the lawyers nor the BSG activists entertained any naive hopes about the scope of success in deploying human rights law and discourse. Their pragmatic approach means that they used human rights frameworks as a tool to protect basic trade union rights, but they did not view litigation as a replacement for rank-and-file mobilization. Their skepticism was well-founded, given that mobilizing trade union rights as human rights cannot resolve deeper structural problems facing labor today, such as the offshoring of manufacturing jobs or the expansion of the precarious, unorganized service sector. Nonetheless, the BSG case study indicates that activists can use human rights-based mobilization as a defensive strategy – fending off erosion of core protections and opening new political and legal opportunities in difficult terrain.

The next chapter analyzes another case study where the promise of human rights law helped catalyze grassroots mobilization: Turkish public sector workers' mobilization. While the political context differed significantly, marked by more severe and extensive repression, Turkish unionists, like their British counterparts, turned to international human rights law as a source of leverage. Once again, the language and institutions of human rights offered a framework of hope and a foothold for resistance.

CHAPTER 8

MOBILIZING TO UNIONIZE
Public Sector Workers in Turkey

When the Istanbul Governor's Office ordered the suspension of Tüm Haber Sen, Turkey's first press workers' union, four days after it was established in 1992, its president, İsmail Çınar, was not surprised. His union was one of the few public sector unions in the country that had been established and promptly shuttered within the past three years. As discussed in previous chapters, *Tüm Haber Sen and Çınar v. Turkey* (2006) would go on to become a landmark ECtHR ruling in the Court's growing jurisprudence on trade union rights in the 2000s. But for Çınar and his fellow activists, the real turning point came much earlier. Long before the ECtHR ruled in their favor, the mere act of filing the case and invoking international legal norms helped them rally new members, demand legal recognition, and lay the foundations for what would become the public sector confederation KESK.

Tüm Haber Sen's trajectory prompts a revaluation of how we measure the impact of international court rulings. Much like the blacklisted workers, Turkish public sector workers engaged in grassroots organizing in the shadow of ECtHR litigation, which helped them achieve core objectives – such as legal recognition and expanded membership – long before the Court handed down a final ruling. While BSG activists framed labor rights as human rights primarily to engage the general public and pressure political actors, Turkish public sector workers used international law to mobilize within their own ranks and claim legitimacy to state officials. During the first fifteen years, labor activists built the trade union movement from the bottom up by mobilizing international human rights law.

In response to the rising popularity and power of KESK in the post-2000 period, however, the government switched its repression tactic from outright bans and violence to coopting public sector workers by building a clientelist–corporatist relationship with a rival union. As KESK's capacity for rank-and-file mobilization declined, it started to rely heavily on ECtHR litigation. Yet in the absence of strong and sustained grassroots pressure, the legal victories provided at best limited relief to individual applicants, rather than bringing about structural change on the ground.

The chapter's main focus is on the formative years of the public sector trade union movement, when international human rights law played a constitutive role in building labor mobilization from the ground up. Drawing on interviews with KESK's founding members, lawyers, and current rank-and-file members; archival materials from the early organizing period, including internal reports, campaign material, and a journal published by the founding educators' union; media coverage from the late 1980s and 1990s; and documentary materials on post-2000 developments, such as government reports and KESK's yearly reports, the chapter examines how strategic appeals to human rights helped establish the first public sector unions in Turkey and why ECtHR litigation alone has been insufficient to sustain them in the absence of grassroots power (Appendix II).

8.1 FROM ASSOCIATIONS TO TRADE UNIONS: THE FORMATIVE YEARS OF PUBLIC SECTOR WORKERS' MOBILIZATION, 1980–2000

The concept of *hukuk mücadelesi* (legal struggle) entered the lexicon of Turkish trade unionists in large part due to the unionization efforts of public sector workers in the late 1980s. The first public sector unions were formed during this period through simultaneous grassroots mobilization and legal struggles, bearing all the qualifications of a robust legal mobilization. The unionists' legal struggle primarily rested on international human rights law due to restrictive domestic conditions.

The aftermath of the 1980 coup was devastating for organized labor, as discussed in Chapter 3. Leftist unions were closed down, their leaders were executed, and the most active trade unionists were either imprisoned or forced into exile. Concurrent with the implementation of neoliberal policies that undermined organized labor, the government started to undertake major reforms toward democratization and ratified new international treaties with the aim of integrating with Europe. By the end of the 1980s, workers were fed up with restrictions. "You are in the aftermath of September 12 [1980 coup], there was a burgeoning desire among the people to become free again and to organize," recalled Mesut Gülmez, a leading legal scholar who initiated some of Turkey's earliest ECtHR cases on trade union rights. The spring of 1989 marked the revival of organized labor, which had slipped into dormancy after the coup. When collective bargaining negotiations covering 600,000 blue-collar workers employed in state economic enterprises (SEEs) hit a deadlock, workers mounted a series of powerful protests, later remembered as *Bahar Eylemleri* (Spring Protests) (Çelik 1996; Doğan 2010). Following the protests, the workers were able to strike a lucrative deal with their employer and the governing party, ANAP (Anavatan Partisi, Motherland Party), which had overseen the neoliberal transformation in the post-coup period.

Bahar Eylemleri set a powerful example for white-collar public sector workers, who had never been able to establish successful unions before.[1] But their desire to unionize faced two main obstacles. The first was the lack of explicit language on public sector workers' right to unionize in the 1980 Constitution (see Chapter 3). The prevailing legal opinion held that this silence meant that these workers could not establish trade unions, let alone engage in collective bargaining agreements or collective action. The second challenge was persuading public sector workers to join the nascent trade union movement despite lingering fears. Most workers were still haunted by the images of workers arrested and tortured due to trade union activities. Activists had to find a way to assuage the fear that organizing would once again lead to arrest, torture, or dismissal. The legal basis provided by international law helped overcome both challenges by creating new legal opportunities for activists to pressure the government and to reassure

---

[1] Different than the blue-collared public sector workers who worked at the State Economic Enterprises (SEEs), white-collar public sector workers are often referred to as *memur* (civil servants). The SEE workers had been unionized under private sector unions due to the industries in which they worked. I refer to both groups as public sector workers, as this is the terminology used by KESK to underline that *memurs* are also workers. There was a brief five-year period in the 1960s when public sector workers were granted the right to unionize. But these unions operated more like associations, as they did not have the right to engage in collective bargaining or strike.

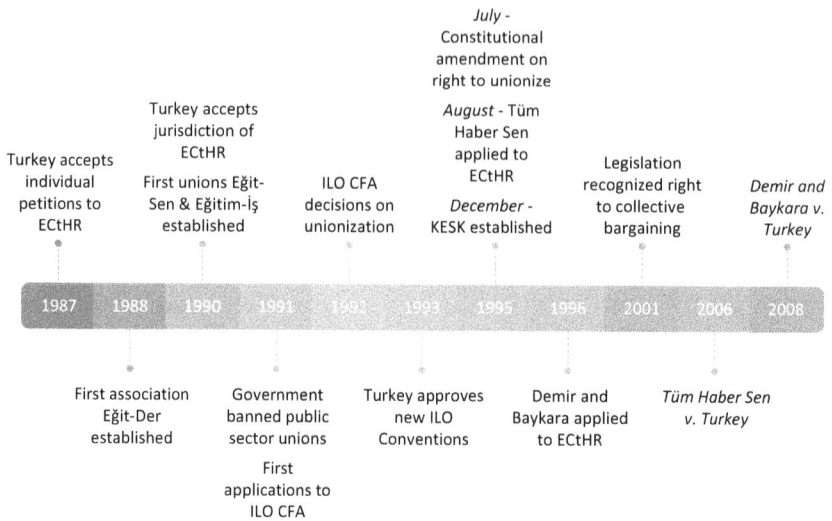

Figure 8.1 Key moments in Turkish public sector unionization and international legal mobilization

workers that unionization was not only legitimate but protected under binding legal norms.

Once again, lawyers played a central role. A handful of legal scholars, most prominently Alpaslan Işıklı and Mesut Gülmez, argued that the absence of explicit prohibitions in the Constitution created legal space for organizing. They further relied on Article 90 of the Constitution, which gave direct effect to ratified international treaties, to claim that public sector workers possessed the right to unionize, collectively bargain, and strike. The lawyers were well aware that international litigation was a long game. It took them until 1995 to find an appropriate case for the ECtHR and exhaust domestic remedies (*Tüm Haber Sen and Çınar v. Turkey* 2006). Complaints to the ILO's CFA moved more quickly, but the lawyers knew that they would have a much higher chance of obtaining a favorable decision if they could demonstrate actual violations, such as state sanctions against unionized workers, rather than file a complaint about abstract legal exclusions.[2]

---

[2] The criminal charges against trade union members constituted the subject matter of the first ILO CFA case submitted by the education workers' union, Eğitim-İş in 1991 (see discussion below). But, ultimately, the litigation at the ECtHR proved to be much more effective than filing complaints at the ILO CFA (Chapter 4).

Therefore, during the initial years, they used the power of ratified international treaties as well as the potential to petition the ILO and the ECtHR as tools to convince public sector workers that their demand for unionization was legal and that they could seek remedy at the international level.

In order to communicate this knowledge to workers more broadly and ease fears regarding repercussions, lawyers and activists organized meetings, seminars, and panels, as well as published articles in magazines, journals, and newspapers. At the same time, they strategically invoked treaties and the threat of litigation in formal and informal communications with state officials, through lobbying politicians, drafting official union documents, and making arguments in domestic court cases. The legal struggle thus unfolded simultaneously in the courtroom and in the public sphere.

8.1.1 Legal Discourse as a Tool of Education, Pressure, and Empowerment

The mobilization efforts of public sector workers took off with the establishment of *derneks* (associations) and journals where workers discussed how to advance their professional interests and establish unions. Education workers were at the forefront of the struggle. The first notable effort came in 1986 with the launch of *abece* (abc), a journal aimed at organizing education workers. It was initiated by eight labor activists who had been in the governing cadres of the leftist teachers' association, Tüm Öğretmenler Birleşme ve Dayanışma Derneği (TÖB-DER, Teachers' Unification and Solidarity Association), which had been shut down after the coup.[3]

The articles published in *abece* covered a wide range of topics, from the need for education reform to the current problems faced by education workers, but the right to unionize was a recurring theme and the journal played a central role in the unionization efforts. As subscriptions grew, reaching 5,000 by 1988, a group of activists, including the founders of *abece*, established the proto-union Eğitimciler Derneği (Eğit-Der, Educators' Association). At the time, education workers were prohibited from joining professional associations or participating in political activities, broadly construed. To circumvent this, retired teachers became regular members of Eğit-Der, while active teachers

---

[3] Tahsin Doğan, "Eğit-Der 35 Yaşında," *abece*, Winter 2023, issue 371.

registered as "honorary members." Their numbers soon reached 25,000, far outnumbering the regular members. The goal was to build enough momentum to transition from Eğit-Der to Eğit-Sen (Eğitimciler Sendikası, Educators' Union) – a professional association to a full-fledged union – which they managed to do in 1990. Other branches of public sector work followed suit and established their *derneks*, such as ÇAYAD (postal workers' association) and BEM-DER (municipal workers' association). To this day, the education workers' union is the largest subunion within KESK and has brought the majority of trade union rights cases to the ECtHR.

In order to examine how international human rights law figured into the early unionization movement, I conducted a systematic analysis of the first sixty-five issues of *abece* published between 1986 and 1991. The journal started as a monthly publication, though the schedule varied: nine issues appeared in 1986 and 1990, and eleven in 1991.[4] The journal provided a rich archive of news articles, opinion pieces, and coverage of unionization workshops and meetings, including written transcripts of keynote speeches delivered at these events, documenting this key period of union organizing carried out in the shadow of international human rights law. The discussions in *abece* offer an insider's view of how the labor activists who later founded the largest sub-union within KESK mobilized support, and the discursive and legal strategies they used to attract education workers to join the movement.

Since the early days of the workers' unionization efforts, human rights served as a prominent frame through which labor activists articulated their demands in legal terms and mobilized support for the nascent movement.[5] The opening article of the first issue of *abece* calls attention to the poverty teachers lived in, the hardships they endure at work, and the need to organize to collectively fight against these challenges.[6] The article then introduces the journal's broader

---

[4] Though the journal has continued to be published, with some disruptions, up until today, I was not able to access most of the issues published between 1992 and 1996. When I conducted my fieldwork in Turkey, KESK did not have any systematic archival material from this period either. See Appendix II for a discussion on the difficulties of accessing archival material on public sector unions in Turkey.

[5] I did not conduct a systematic analysis of how much class-based language was used in these issues, because themes such as capitalism, exploitation, working class, collective power/struggle of workers were pervasive throughout all the issues.

[6] *abece*, April 1986, issue 1.

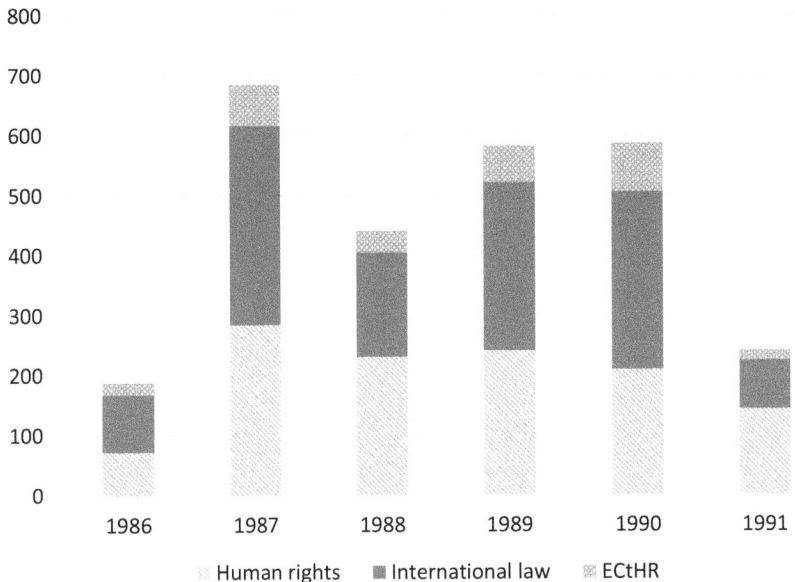

Figure 8.2 References to human rights law and discourse in *abece*
Source: *abece*, 1986–1991.

aims and the issues it intends to cover, including union struggles abroad and the protections offered by international human rights law. Figure 8.2 charts the annual number of references to concepts related to international human rights. Despite some fluctuation across the years, international law, human rights, and the ECtHR were consistent reference points in all issues of the *abece* from the beginning.[7] In 1990 – the year Eğit-Sen was established – each issue (around fifty pages) made an average of sixty-five references to these themes.[8] Headlines were direct and politically charged. The July 1987 cover asked, "Do human rights exist, or not?"[9] The December 1989 cover featured a photo of police beating a protester, with the caption "Human Rights Day, Turkey '89."[10]

During these early years, the labor lawyers were still surveying multiple institutions and had not yet identified the ECtHR as their target

---

[7] The references to the ECtHR include both references to the Court and to the Convention.
[8] There were nine issues in 1990 and a total of 585 references made.
[9] *abece*, July 1987, issue 17.   [10] *abece*, December 1989, issue 45.

institution or filed any cases (Chapter 5). Nonetheless, the possibility of ECtHR litigation, as well as the binding nature of the European Convention, already served as a mobilizing force for workers and a source of political leverage. As soon as Turkey accepted the right of individual petition to the ECtHR in 1987, *abece* issued an editorial analyzing the implications of this new development for trade union rights and the importance of Article 11.[11] The following year, Mesut Gülmez traveled to Strasbourg in order to study the ECtHR's case law on trade union rights.[12] He would later spearhead *Tüm Haber Sen and Çınar v. Turkey* (2006) and *Demir and Baykara v. Turkey* (2008), two precedent-setting cases.

Legal scholars and lawyers such as Işıklı and Gülmez actively used *abece* to inform and mobilize workers. Articles by or citing these two figures frequently appeared throughout the journal. An early example is a 1986 interview with Işıklı, where he laid out the legal basis for public sector workers' union rights under international law, including the ILO Conventions, United Declaration of Human Rights (UDHR), the European Convention, and the European Social Charter (Işıklı, December 1986). Işıklı and Gülmez contributed twelve articles in total and they were frequently mentioned (eighty-one times) in other pieces. The journal also featured a standing *"hukuk köşesi"* (legal corner) that reported on relevant domestic and international legal developments, including the decisions of international courts and organizations.

Labor leaders at union events similarly invoked international legal protections to help overcome workers' fears and inspire action. At an evening event organized for educators, Ali Bozkurt, then president of Eğit-Der, called on the audience:

> My fellow teachers, those who took away your right to unionize have done so by scaring and depoliticizing you. If you really want a democratic system based on human rights [...] lift your head up and say, "that's enough!" Demand your rights to unionize, bargain, and strike. It is possible to do this through legal means.[13]

Similarly, Şükran Ketenci, a prominent journalist and labor activist speaking at a panel organized by Eğit-Der, delivered a rallying message to the teachers, emphasizing their power: "you pose a serious threat to those who want the status quo to continue. How can they not be afraid

---

[11] *abece*, March 1987, issue 12.   [12] Interview with Mesut Gülmez, April 2015.
[13] *abece*, January 1989, issue 34, p. 7.

of you? It is not an easy task to bring together this many people who are not allowed to unionize." Then she went on to refence Işıklı and Gülmez to reiterate the public sector workers' right to unionize under international law and the ILO Conventions:

> They pacified, repressed, and depoliticized masses. The economic inequality has only become worse, they made it impossible for us to demand our rights, they keep exploiting us. Could they have done any of this before [the] September 12 [1980 coup]? [...] I wish the whole country could be as fearless as all of you [teachers] who fill in this room.[14]

One of the organizers of Eğit-Der, likewise, wrote the opening piece for the February 1990 issue to motivate education workers: "The unionization efforts must be supplemented with collective action. We must give a chance to our struggle because the international laws provide a legal basis for it."[15] Another activist referenced legal scholars such as Işıklı and Gülmez to remind his fellow teachers of their rights to unionize under international law, and told them that it was now up to them to act: "whether the legal human rights of teachers will actually be realized is up to the collective struggle of teachers in Turkey."[16]

Activists also referenced international laws in their pleas to politicians to legalize trade union rights for public sector workers. In October 1989, Eğit-Der organized the first major Trade Union Rights Assembly, attended by opposition party leaders, Erdal İnönü and Necmettin Erbakan, as well as the Minister of Education, Avni Akyol. In his opening speech, the president of Eğit-Der, Feyzullah Ertuğrul stated: "That public servants in Turkey have the rights to unionize, engage in collective bargaining, and strike based on the ILO Conventions and the European Convention on Human Rights is now well-known."[17] Both Işıklı and Gülmez gave speeches at the event, calling on politicians, including those in the audience, to make legislative changes explicitly protecting public sector workers' unionization rights in accordance with international laws.[18] Even teachers who were barred from regular membership at Eğit-Der directly appealed to the Minister of Education to legalize the right to unionize as it "is a basic human right in democracies."[19] Similarly, in an opening speech he

---

[14] *abece*, January 1989, issue 34, pp. 27–28.   [15] *abece*, February 1990, issue 47.
[16] *abece*, October 1989, issue 43, p. 36.   [17] *abece*, October 1989, issue 43, p. 8.
[18] *abece*, October 1989, issue 43.   [19] *abece*, October 1989, issue 43, p. 31.

gave at the celebration of Eğit-Der's second anniversary, which was attended by representatives from opposition parties, Ertuğrul gave a detailed talk on the protections provided by various international laws and defended the right to unionize as a human right.[20]

8.1.2 Culmination in Union Formation

Right before the first unions were established in 1990, Eğit-Der released a report, prepared by a committee that included Işıklı and Gülmez, citing the ILO and the European Convention to justify the right to unionize, bargain, and strike. The report concluded by calling for broader alliances with private sector unions and efforts to shift public opinion among teachers and the general population.[21] A related declaration issued by the presidents of Eğit-Der branches stressed that Turkey is one of the few countries where teachers lacked union rights and pledged that Eğit-Der would lead the struggle for "teachers to claim their unionization rights protected under international laws."[22]

The campaign activists led by relying on international law finally culminated in the formation of Turkey's first public sector unions in 1990. Teachers led the charge, forming Eğitim İşkolu Kamu Görevlileri Sendikası (Eğitim-İş) and Eğitimciler Sendikası (Eğit-Sen).[23] By the 1991 general elections, six additional unions had formed in other sectors. These early unions, established by leftist public sector workers, merged to form KESK in 1995.

Interviews with labor leaders similarly underscore the importance of legal reassurance in launching the union effort. Ayhan Erdoğan, a founding member of KESK, recalled: "Alpaslan Işıklı and Mesut Gülmez [...] supported us by providing very clear explanations with legal reasoning on the right to establish trade unions."[24] Erhan Karaçay, a veteran unionist who later filed a successful application on the right to take collective action at the ECtHR (*Karaçay v. Turkey* 2007), emphasized the supremacy conferred upon international laws by the Constitution and said: "we [the public sector workers] made our debut relying on Article 90 of the Constitution."[25] İsmail Çınar, founder and first president of Tüm Haber, emphasized the reliance on Article 11 of

---

[20] *abece*, March 1990, issue 48.   [21] *abece*, June 1990, issue 51, pp. 19–22.
[22] *abece*, September 1989, issue 42, p. 15.
[23] These unions merged under Eğitim-Sen in 1995.
[24] Interview with Ayhan Erdoğan, April 2015
[25] Interview with Erhan Karaçay, April 2015.

the European Convention and the broader legal framework provided by international law.[26]

These retrospective accounts highlight the formative role that international law – and the legal scholars who interpreted it – played in launching Turkey's public sector union movement. Even in the absence of enabling domestic legislation, activists based their claims on binding international commitments and translated legal discourse into mass mobilization.

8.1.3 Grassroots Mobilization in the Shadow of International Law

In response to the establishment of the first public sector unions, the government retaliated by sealing the union offices, preventing unionists from holding their meetings by police force, and initiating criminal and disciplinary action against union founders and members. To nip the nascent unionization efforts in the bud, the Ministry of Interior issued a circular in February 1991 banning all public sector workers from joining or establishing unions. But the workers remained undeterred; they were confident in the legitimacy and legality of their actions. Much like the BSG activists, they filed their grievances at international institutions and, without waiting for rulings, they pressured the government through mass mobilization. The safeguards provided by international human rights law emboldened public sector workers to engage in protest actions deemed illegal under domestic law.

In 1991, leaders of Eğitim-İş and Eğit-Sen filed separate complaints with the ILO CFA regarding violations of public sector workers' right to unionize, including the forced relocation of activists and the arrest of founding members, as well as interference with collective bargaining rights. Before the CFA issued its decision, members of Eğit-Sen staged a bold act of defiance: On September 14, 1991, they gathered in front of their union headquarters and broke the government-imposed seals on the doors without official permission. The ILO responded swiftly, issuing decisions in late 1991 and again in 1992, condemning the persecution of unionists and called on the Turkish government to pass legislation explicitly recognizing public sector workers' trade union rights. Yet, as discussed in Chapter 5, Turkish high courts continued to dismiss workers' legal claims, refusing to apply ILO conventions or CFA rulings. As a result, the public sector workers and their lawyers targeted the ECtHR.

---

[26] Email communication with İsmail Çınar, January 2018.

The applications to the ECtHR that produced the landmark judgments took more than a decade to be finalized. *Tüm Haber Sen v. Turkey* (2006), concerning the right to establish trade unions, was filed in 1995, and *Demir and Baykara v. Turkey* (2008), addressing collective bargaining rights, was filed in 1997. The ECtHR took eleven years to reach a final judgment in each case. Once again, the workers did not wait for Strasbourg. Throughout the 1990s, KESK unions built their strength in the streets.

As one interviewee put it, "KESK was built based on *sokak mücadelesi*" (struggle in the streets), and, as many others similarly emphasized, the movement prioritized "*fiili mücadele*" (rank-and-file mobilization) above all else.[27] KESK organized massive protests across the 1990s, many centered in Ankara, with tens of thousands pouring into the capital from around the country. These included the 1992 "*Hak Direnişi*" (Rights Struggle), a large protest event jointly organized with private sector unions in 1994, and a massive demonstration with hundreds of thousands of public sector workers in 1995. These notable demonstrations were accompanied by innovative protest activities, including work stoppages – since going on a strike was illegal for public servants – hunger strikes, and civil disobedience acts, such as violating the public sector dress code or collectively requesting sick leave.[28] These actions were met with police violence and harsh disciplinary and legal consequences. Between 1996 and 1998, 242 Eğitim-Sen members were forcibly relocated to different cities, 101 were sentenced to prison, and nearly 19,000 members faced disciplinary measures for union activity.[29] KESK's collective action and the police repression had become so routinized that the media coined the term *cop zammı* ("truncheon raise") to refer to wage increases won through street protests.[30]

---

[27] Interview with İrfan Kaygısız, April 2015. *Fiili mücadele* literally means "action-based-struggle," but in this context, it could be interpreted as rank-and-file mobilization.

[28] "İşçi Eylemlerine Memurlar da Katıldı", *Milliyet*, June 22, 1991, p. 10; "Memur Grevi Sıkıntısı," *Milliyet*, July 13, 1992.

[29] Prison sentences were not yet final at the time the report was published. Of the 242 exile decisions, 122 were revoked due to Eğitim-Sen's initiatives (Eğitim-Sen 1998: 89).

[30] See for instance, "Memura 'Cop Zammı' Geliyor," *Milliyet*, January 18, 1994. p. 18. For an earlier example on police repression against these protests, see "Memur-Polis Çatıştı," *Milliyet*, March 28, 1991.

While "*fiili mücadele*" remained central, legal advocacy continued in parallel. KESK unions continued to use international laws and pending cases at the ECtHR to justify their existence and basic trade union rights in legal forums and in their lobbying efforts. During the 1990s, KESK unions filed a total of three complaints with the ILO CFA regarding violations of freedom of association and fifteen applications to the ECtHR. Eğitim-Sen's founding constitution in 1995, as well as its current version, make multiple references to international human rights agreements, stating that the union "uses its rights based on international agreements, including the Universal Declaration of Human Rights, the ILO Conventions, the European Convention on Human Rights, and the European Social Charter. Based on the understanding that these agreements are binding in domestic law, it seeks to change the Constitution and domestic laws to reach contemporary standards" (3b). Similarly, KESK's current constitution states that one of its fundamental goals is "fighting for the full realization of all rights and freedoms based on universal human rights instruments and international law and agreements" (4c). KESK unions regularly issued reports and working papers urging the government to adopt legislation explicitly recognizing public sector workers' rights to unionize, bargain collectively, and strike.[31] In domestic courtrooms, KESK lawyers persistently cited Turkey's obligations under international law to push back against the legal repression of union activity.

Together, these efforts illustrate how international law functioned not simply as a source of legal protections, but as a political resource that public sector workers used to legitimize union activity, challenge state repression, and expand political space. The long delays of ECtHR judgments did not stall the movement; instead, workers mobilized in anticipation of legal recognition, treating international law as leverage rather than resolution. Thus, they reshaped the practice of legal struggle, not by waiting for judicial affirmation, but by asserting their rights through mass, organized action on the ground.

8.1.4 Framing the Fight: Class, Struggle, and the Absence of Rights Discourse

Despite the simultaneous use of international law and direct-action strategies, neither human rights nor the ECtHR cases shaped the

---

[31] See for example, Eğitim-Sen, *Fourth General Assembly Working Report, 1998–2000*. Ankara: Eğitim-Sen.

language of *on-stage* mobilization of public sector workers during the 1990s. In order to examine the discursive frames used by KESK in their public campaigns, I conducted a systematic review of all articles on public sector workers' mobilization in *Milliyet* from 1990 to 1995, which is the period that marks the height of their "*fiili mücadele.*" As one of Turkey's major mainstream newspapers with accessible online archives, *Milliyet* offers insight into the discursive strategies KESK employed in its public mobilization. A total of 251 articles covered public sector workers' mobilization, including twenty-two op-eds during this period. Of these, only five made any reference to human rights, and one of those was in the context of Kurdish minority rights, rather than trade union rights. One other article covered a demonstration in Ankara where protestors invoked international law. The intended audience of this protest was clearly international, rather than domestic, as the workers held up banners in English, such as "Not toys, real unions," "Keep up with ILO Acts 87, 98, 151," and "European Social Act §5."[32]

Instead, the dominant discursive frame was class-based. Common slogans included "Workers and civil servants hand in hand, on to general strike," "We want collective bargaining, not charity," "Strike is a right, we will fight hard," "Long live the solidarity of workers."[33] They also organized inventive protests, including burning their pay slips, staging mock markets to sell personal items in protest of poverty wages, and sending thousands of telegrams to the government.[34] In one striking example, protestors carried an empty coffin with a sign that said "lived in debt, died in debt."[35] Calls for democratization, which had been a salient theme in left-wing politics in the aftermath of the coup, also featured prominently in protest materials, along with slogans for peace and an end to state violence, owing to KESK's alliance with the Kurdish movement.[36]

Media statements by union leaders and rank-and-file workers similarly focused on material hardships and their right to organize without

---

[32] The latter was likely a reference to Article 5 of the ESC on the right to organize.
[33] "Yüzde 25'e isyan," *Milliyet*, July 1990; "Memurlar Hükümeti Son Kez Uyardı," *Milliyet*, February 23, 1994; "Memurların Eylem Günü," *Milliyet*, June 16, 1992; "Memurlar Yollara Düştü," *Milliyet*, June 16, 1993.
[34] "İşçi Eylemlerine Memurlar da Katıldı," *Milliyet*, June 22, 1991, p. 10; "Memur Grevi Sıkıntısı," *Milliyet*, July 13, 1992.
[35] "Sendika hakkını isteyen memurları polis copladı," *Milliyet*, January 14, 1994.
[36] See Chapter 5 for more on this alliance.

any references to human rights. For example, Vicdan Baykara, head of the Kamu Çalışanları Sendikaları Platformu (KÇSP) – a precursor to KESK – and later the applicant in *Demir and Baykara v. Turkey*, told *Milliyet* during a demonstration joined by 4,000 workers: "we reject the draft legislation which aims to turn our unions into associations by not recognizing our rights to engage in collective bargaining and strike."[37] Notably, there was no reference to human rights. Protesters commonly spoke of personal hardship in emotive, everyday terms: "We cannot afford to buy meat," or "My spouse cries every day."[38]

The absence of references to human rights discourse in KESK's public-facing campaigns stands in marked contrast to the BSG, whose on-stage mobilization explicitly invoked human rights language (Chapter 7). This difference can be explained in part by the differing resonance of human rights within the political climates in which the two movements emerged. By 2009, when the BSG was formed, human rights had become a widely accepted framework for advocacy, and the ECtHR had established its authority in shaping employment policy across Europe. Human rights discourse had by then entered the global vernacular, offering a common vocabulary for justice claims across movements (Moyn 2018). By contrast, when KESK was being established in the early 1990s, human rights had not yet achieved the same public resonance in Turkey. The country accepted the jurisdiction of the ECtHR in 1990, and its landmark rulings on the Kurdish cases, which brought national fame to the Court, started to be issued in 1996 and onwards. Although Turkey's human rights violations were regularly condemned in EU progress reports and covered in domestic media, human rights had not yet crystallized as a public framing tool in the labor movement. It was only towards the end of the 1990s that the human rights discourse began to gain broader traction among leftist activists, particularly in the Kurdish movement, who increasingly used it to frame grievances in public campaigns (Babül 2020).

8.2 BEYOND LITIGATION: THE MATERIAL IMPACT OF HUMAN RIGHTS MOBILIZATION

The analysis thus far shows that during the foundational years, KESK utilized international litigation and direct-action strategy

---

[37] "Memurlar hükümeti son kez uyardı," *Milliyet*, February 23, 1994.
[38] "Utanıyoruz," *Milliyet*, July 1990.

simultaneously. While public sector workers did not frame their demands in the language of human rights during protests or in movement slogans, references to international human rights law underpinned their claims in official communications, legal arguments, and lobbying efforts. Ratified treaties and pending cases before the ECtHR gave public sector workers a legal basis for justifying their existence, defying domestic restrictions, and attracting new members to the movement. Even though human rights discourse was absent from street protests, activists continued to remind Turkish judges and politicians of their international obligations through legal means and lobbying activities. This strategic use of international law was particularly effective because it unfolded during a period of intensified Europeanization, when Turkey's aspiration to join the EU heightened the political significance of compliance with international legal norms. The key question, once again, is whether this strategic use of human rights law produced any material gains for public sector workers. Much like the BSG, the Turkish labor activists achieved some of their goals well before any favorable rulings were delivered by the ECtHR.

In contrast to the institutional ties between the British labor movement and the Labour Party, Turkish workers faced a fragmented political landscape. In the aftermath of the 1980 coup, many leaders of organized labor were imprisoned, tortured, or killed. Türkiye İşçi Partisi (TİP, Workers Party of Turkey) was banned, and workers in Turkey no longer had direct ties with any of the remaining parties.[39] Nonetheless, their persistent lobbying, grounded in references to international law, began to shape party positions. Leading up to the 1991 elections, nearly all major parties promised to align domestic labor legislation with international standards.[40] The post-coup ruling party, ANAP, expressed general support for international law but remained silent on public sector union rights. The opposition parties, Sosyaldemokrat Halkçı Parti (SHP, Social Democratic People's Party) and Doğru Yol Partisi (DYP, True Path Party), formed a coalition after winning the

---

[39] TİP briefly merged with the Communist Party of Turkey in 1987 to form Türkiye Birleşik Komünist Partisi (United Communist Party of Turkey) but the Constitutional Court closed the party in 1991. The case was taken to the ECtHR and the Court delivered a violation judgment (*Case of United Communist Party of Turkey and Others v. Turkey*, 1998), but the party was never reestablished until 2010.

[40] See Gülmez (1992) for a detailed discussion on the campaign materials of competing parties in the 1991 elections.

elections and pledged to protect the rights of public sector workers. SHP explicitly promised that "all workers' and civil servants' trade union rights will be fully secured," and that "working conditions will be brought in line with standards recommended by the EEC and the ILO" (SHP Election Bulletin 1991). The new coalition government appointed a labor-friendly Labor Minister, Mehmet Moğultay, who in a letter to Eğit-Sen stated: "Making sure that all workers, including those in the public sector, are granted their trade union rights is our priority."[41] In 1993, the government ratified ILO Conventions 87 (freedom of association) and 151 (public sector union rights), signaling its commitment to labor reform.

The most important victory of the Turkish labor activists was the creation and operation of public sector unions on the legal basis provided by international human rights law, despite the absence of domestic legislation. As noted earlier, education workers formed the first unions in 1990, citing international treaties to justify their existence. Even the right-wing *derneks* that had initially denounced public sector workers' right to unionize followed suit. By 1992, forty-two new trade unions were formed. That same year, the left-wing unions came together to form KÇSP, which became KESK in 1995. In 1991, Eğit-Sen reported 10,000 members, and Eğitim-İş 20,000.[42] After the merger of these unions, Eğitim-Sen claimed its membership at 99,045 in 1995, composing 14 percent of the public education sector.[43] KESK reported a total membership of 391,500 in 1996, representing nearly 10 percent of all public sector workers (Koç 2013). These membership levels, despite state repression and legal ambiguity, indicate that public sector workers overcame fears of retaliation by relying on the legal grounding provided by international human rights law.

In July 1995, the Turkish parliament finally passed a new constitutional amendment recognizing public sector workers' right to join and establish trade unions (Article 53). Ironically, the amendment came just one month before Tüm Haber Sen filed its petition with the ECtHR. Since domestic legal remedies had been exhausted, the union had no choice but to pursue international litigation. Moreover, the labor activists criticized the amendment for failing to guarantee

---

[41] Eğit-Sen, Olağan Genel Kurul Sonuç Bildirgesi, 1992.
[42] ILO Complaint, Case No. 1577, April 13, 1991; ILO Complaint, Case No. 1583, May 15, 1991. Official statistics on union membership were released in 2002.
[43] Eğitim-Sen 1, Dönem Çalışma Raporu, July 1995.

public sector unions' rights to engage in collective bargaining and to strike, effectively diminishing unions to the status of *derneks*. In 2001, Article 51 of the Constitution was amended to guarantee all workers the right to organize and bargain collectively. This paved the way for the passage of Law No. 4688, the Public Servants' Trade Unions Act. While the new legislation did not grant a right to strike, it prohibited discrimination based on union membership and officially recognized public sector workers' right to engage in collective bargaining (Chapter 6).

As noted above, the Court took nearly a decade to issue its final rulings on these landmark cases. Yet during this long interim, public sector workers successfully advanced many of their demands by drawing on the broader context of Turkey's Europeanization, which boosted the ECtHR's judicial authority in the country. Even the pending cases at the ECtHR, along with the lawyers' repeated references to international instruments in domestic courts and other formal settings, generated sufficient pressure for public sector workers to secure some of their basic trade union rights in domestic law. Turkey's EU membership process began in 1987, when the state formally applied to become a member of the EEC, the predecessor to the EU. Its candidacy was formalized in 1999 and followed by the start of membership negotiations in 2005, creating additional external pressure for domestic legal reform. While the ECtHR is separate from the EU, the European Commission viewed compliance with ECtHR rulings as an important indicator of democratic reform and regularly referenced them in its candidacy evaluations. The Commission's 2005 Progress Report, for instance, cited the attempted closure of Eğitim-Sen to emphasize the importance of aligning judicial decisions with the European Convention (*Eğitim ve Bilim Emekçileri Sendikası v. Turkey* 2012). Many of the reforms and joint projects included in Turkey's action reports submitted to the Council of Europe's Committee of Ministers were undertaken as part of the EU accession process. Public sector workers effectively capitalized on this environment, using the leverage of EU monitoring to push for reforms in line with the European Convention and broader domestic legal change.

In sum, Turkish labor activists successfully mobilized international human rights law to initiate a trade union movement and influence legislative reform. Many of their key gains were achieved during the 1990s, well before any rulings were issued by the ECtHR. By invoking the authority of ratified treaties and the legal leverage of pending litigation, activists were able to establish the first public sector unions in Turkey and win partial legal recognition of their rights. This early success shows how international legal norms can shape domestic outcomes even in the absence of final judgments, particularly when mobilized strategically in a favorable political climate.

8.3 FROM MOBILIZATION TO MARGINALIZATION: COOPTATION AND CONTROL IN THE AKP ERA

By the end of the 1990s, KESK had already become a formidable force in the public sector. The protections provided by international human rights law made it clear that the government was not going to be able to contain KESK with brute force and outright bans. When the AKP came to power in 2002, the government swiftly adopted a new strategy: undermining the power of KESK through cooptation. The approach proved effective as KESK began to lose momentum and its ability to mobilize rank-and-file members weakened. Although KESK increased its applications to the ECtHR during this period, without the mobilization power, human rights litigation did little to improve the structural problems public sector unions faced.

The AKP's rise to power under Recep Tayyip Erdoğan's leadership marked a new chapter in Turkish politics. The government promoted a model of "moderate Islam" that promised to align democratic reforms, market liberalization, and EU integration with a conservative moral framework grounded in Islamic values. Erdoğan's rise was hailed in the West as a democratic model for the Muslim world.[44] In its early years, the AKP lifted the state of emergency in the Kurdish provinces, abolished the death penalty, and took steps to address torture and ill-treatment through police training programs and legal reforms. In recognition of these efforts, the EU formally started accession talks with Turkey in 2005.

Why, then, did KESK lose so much power under a regime that professed commitment to democratization and integration with Europe? The 2016 coup attempt brought the answer into sharp relief,

---

[44] For example, an article in *The Economist* explained the "importance of backing Erdoğan" by noting that, "[i]f democracy is to be successfully fostered across the Muslim world, especially in Arab countries, it is vital to encourage this Turkish exemplar." "The Importance of Backing Erdoğan," *The Economist*, January 29, 2004, www.economist.com/leaders/2004/01/29/the-importance-of-backing-erdogan.

exposing the depth of power abuse under the AKP and the steady erosion of union power through repression, blacklisting, and state-aligned unionism. In the wake of the coup attempt, the government declared a state of emergency that lasted for two years and carried out a sweeping purge under the pretext that hundreds of thousands of people had participated in the plot to overthrow the government and assassinate Erdoğan. More than 130,000 public sector workers – including teachers, university professors, top military officials, lawyers, and judges – were dismissed by emergency decrees issued without parliamentary approval or due process.[45] Hundreds of media outlets were shut down and more than 1,000 schools and universities were closed. Over 70,000 people were detained during this period. Those targeted not only lost their jobs or faced criminal investigations, but many were also banned from public employment and had their passports revoked, forcing many to seek refuge in Europe and North America.[46]

The extent of the purge in such a short amount of time lent retrospective credibility to KESK's long-standing claims about dissident blacklisting in the public sector. They also revealed how far-reaching the government's control mechanisms had become, exposing the infrastructure of exclusion and favoritism that had been quietly expanding throughout the 2000s. Even the EU Commissioner overseeing Turkey's accession noted that the rapid purges suggested that the lists had been prepared prior to the coup and that the government had been waiting for the right time to act on them.[47] While the majority of those purged were accused of ties to the Gülen movement, the AKP's former ally turned scapegoat, the purges were also used to suppress all dissent, including leftist public sector workers not affiliated with Gülen.[48]

---

[45] The data is from a report published by the main opposition party, CHP (the Republican People's Party) in July 2018. The report is based on executive orders, which included lists of purged individuals, published in the Official Gazette of the state.

[46] "Erdoğan's 'Enemies' Find Sanctuary Close to Home," *Politico*, April 3, 2018, www.politico.eu/article/turkey-erdogan-enemies-find-sanctuary-in-greece-asylum/.

[47] "Turkey Has Arrested 6,000 since the Failed Coup. The EU Said That's from a Pre-Prepared List," *The Independent*, July 18, 2016, www.independent.co.uk/news/world/europe/turkey-coup-attempt-erdogan-government-arrests-military-uprising-eu-commissioner-a7142426.html.

[48] Fethullah Gülen is a cleric residing in the US who was accused by the Turkish government of leading a terrorist organization responsible for the 2016 coup attempt. The AKP had previously maintained a close alliance with Gülen, particularly in its early rise to power and efforts to restructure the state bureaucracy, an

According to a 2021 report by the ITUC, more than 11,000 members of KESK were dismissed due to their trade union activities during the state of emergency.[49] With no due process and dismissals carried out through executive decrees, there has been no credible evidence linking thousands of individuals to the attempted coup.

What the purges brought to light instead was the scale of favoritism and corruption that had taken root in the public sector during the AKP's consolidation of power. In an effort to justify the purges to the military, the National Security Minister declared that they had just discovered that military school exams had been stolen between 2000 and 2014.[50] Such scandals have surfaced before in the AKP era, including leaked letters requesting political favoritism and allegations of stolen civil service entrance exams.[51] In a mirror image of the UK's blacklisting of construction workers, the AKP–Gülen alliance appeared to maintain a "whitelist" – a patronage system that favored allies from the lowest levels of public service to top state positions. But with checks and balances systematically dismantled as the AKP expanded its control over the military (Akça and Balta-Paker 2013), the judiciary (Özbudun 2014, 2015), and the police force (Özbudun 2014; Tuğal 2012), no formal inquiry was ever conducted into these allegations.

A key component of this patronage system was the corporatist–clientelist relationship between the AKP and Memur-Sen, a public sector union. Authoritarian regimes often coopt labor to consolidate

---

alliance widely acknowledged though difficult to document in detail (Taş 2015; Tuğal 2012). The relationship famously broke down after a massive corruption scandal erupted in 2013, implicating Erdoğan and other top AKP officials through leaked recordings. Erdoğan denied the allegations, claiming the recordings were fabricated, and later characterized his past cooperation with Gülen as a result of having been "deceived." This framing was widely adopted by AKP supporters after the failed coup attempt. "'We Were Deceived' Erdoğan Says, Accusing 'Parallel Structure' of Misinformation – Türkiye News," *Hürriyet Daily News*, March 20, 2015, www.hurriyetdailynews.com/we-were-deceived-erdogan-says-accusing-parallel-structure-of-misinformation-79936.

[49] ITUC, 2021, *Observations on Turkey in the 2021 Report on the Application of International Labor Standards*, Addendum to the 2020 Report of the ILO Committee of Experts on the Application of Conventions and Recommendations.

[50] "Milli Savunma Bakanı Fikri Işık canlı yayında açıkladı," *Hürriyet*, July 29, 2016, www.hurriyet.com.tr/gundem/bakan-isiktan-flas-aciklamalar-40175342.

[51] Part of the 2010 exam was canceled after allegations that the exam had been stolen. "2010 KPSS'nin 'Genel Yetenek ve Genel Kültür' Kısmı Iptal Edildi," *Cumhuriyet*, August 1, 2016, www.cumhuriyet.com.tr/haber/2010-kpssnin-genel-yetenek-ve-genel-kultur-kismi-iptal-edildi-577684.

their power (Caraway, Cook, and Crowley 2015; Kim and Gandhi 2010; Robertson 2007), and the AKP began cultivating ties with Memur-Sen almost immediately after taking office, well before it openly embraced authoritarian governance. Though the clientelist ties between Memur-Sen and the AKP have never been a subject of legal scrutiny, labor scholars and journalists have documented widespread favoritism toward Memur-Sen members, particularly in hiring and promotion decisions (Çelik 2014; Gürcan and Mete 2017).[52] Figure 8.3 illustrates the dramatic growth in Memur-Sen's membership – twenty-five-fold since 2002 – with a significant spike even during the AKP's initial "liberal" phase.[53] Although Kamu-Sen, another pro-government union, maintained some presence, both KESK and Kamu-Sen saw their membership decline relative to the tripling of the overall public sector workforce. Hence, Memur-Sen's expansion substantially eroded KESK's organizational power.

A key indicator of the direct government control in public sector unionism is that since 2005, workers' union dues are covered almost fully by the government, a practice condemned by the ILO.[54] That same year, a journalist exposed that the president of Kamu-Sen made a direct plea to the government for this financial support in order to strengthen pro-government unions, namely Kamu-Sen and Memur-Sen, against KESK.[55] In addition to the difficulties KESK faced in attracting members to a union on the losing side, the government's alliance with Memur-Sen preserves an institutional system where constitutionally protected trade union rights are, in effect, devoid of any meaning. As discussed in Chapter 6, the government structured the collective bargaining agreement process in such a way that Memur-Sen,

---

[52] The ties between the two institutions are no secret; for example, after serving as the president of Memur-Sen for seven years, Ahmet Gündoğdu was elected to parliament for the AKP in 2015.

[53] The government only started to release official membership numbers in 2002.

[54] Public sector workers who are union members receive a "premium" to offset the union fees they pay. The ILO prohibits schemes that make trade unions financially dependent on a public body and undermine the autonomy of trade unions. For related ILO decision, see ILO Freedom of Association, *Digest of Decisions and Principles of the Freedom of Association Committee of the Governing Body of the ILO*, Geneva, International Labour Office, Fifth (revised) edition, 2006, p. 96, paras. 466–467.

[55] "Memur Sendikalarını 5 YTL dize getirmiş," Memurlar.Net, September 3, 2005, www.memurlar.net/haber/28255/memur-sendikalarini-5-ytl-dize-getirmis.html.

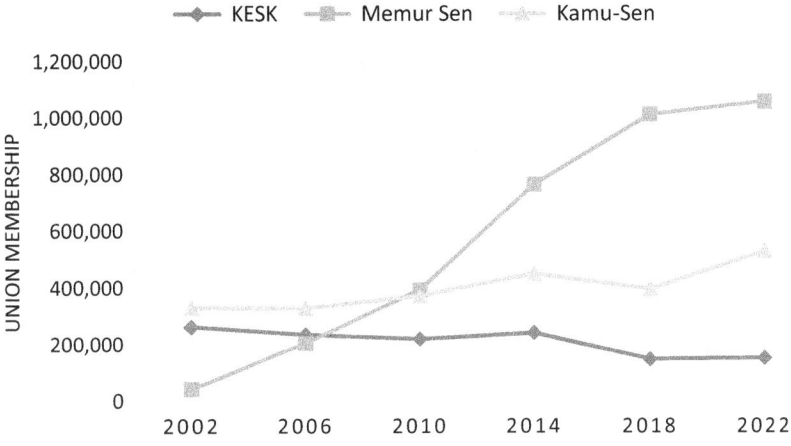

Figure 8.3 Membership levels in public sector unions
Source: Ministry of Labor and Social Security.

as the largest union in the public sector, seals the deal for all 3.5 million public sector workers, while KESK has virtually no say at the bargaining table. KESK has consistently accused Memur-Sen of failing to defend workers' interests, even settling for lower pay raises than the government's original offer in 2014.[56] The existing system can best be described as a consultation, as there is no real negotiation, and workers have no bargaining power to pressure the government. In case of disagreement, workers have to accept the decision of the arbitration board, since they are not legally allowed to strike. Memur-Sen not only denounces public sector workers' right to strike but has also sued KESK members over strike activity.[57] The ties between the AKP and Memur-Sen is based on the understanding that Memur-Sen members receive preferential access to jobs and promotion in return for political loyalty (Gürcan and Mete 2017).

The consolidation of state power under the AKP regime and its alliance with Memur-Sen ultimately marginalized KESK and curtailed its ability to organize public sector workers. As Eğitim-Sen's general secretary at the time, Sakine Esen Yılmaz put it, "The employer is the

---

[56] KESK. "Memur-Sen Yöneticileri Hakkında Suç Duyurusu," December 26, 2014, www.kesk.org.tr/2014/12/26/memur-sen-yoneticileri-hakkinda-suc-duyurusu/.
[57] "Sendikacıdan 'grev' yapan memura suç duyurusu," Memurlar.Net, April 17, 2011, www.memurlar.net/haber/193633/sendikacidan-grev-yapan-memura-suc-duyurusu.html.

state, the violator is the state as well as the judge [and] the legislator ... We are very weak in the face of such a structure."[58] The KESK unionists I interviewed uniformly pointed to structural disempowerment policies as their primary obstacle in organizing. Oya Aydın, a former KESK lawyer, bluntly put it:

> How many members did KESK have in 2000 and how many members does it have now? And, what about Memur-Sen? There is a serious barrier to the right to organize. You can't become a member of a dissident trade union. If you do, you are on the losing team.[59]

Although overt police violence against protestors declined relative to the 1990s, state repression of KESK's union activities has persisted, evidenced by the ECtHR cases. Eğitim-Sen has faced multiple closure attempts, KESK members continue to face disciplinary and criminal penalties for union activity, and many KESK leaders have been detained or imprisoned.[60] Compared to the 1990s, when KESK endured bans and police crackdowns yet maintained its mobilizing capacity, the AKP's cooptation strategy in the post-2000 period proved to be far more effective in containing public sector worker unionism. Through institutionalized favoritism, the government undercut grassroots organizing and rendered legal mobilization increasingly symbolic, devoid of the rank-and-file strength that had once amplified its power.

8.3.1 Human Rights Litigation with Weak Mobilization: A Strategy of Despair?

As KESK's ability to influence state policy through lobbying was nullified in the post-2000 period, its reliance on human rights litigation intensified. The number of applications KESK brought before the ECtHR more than tripled from the 1990s to the 2000s (Chapter 5). In all post-2000 judgments involving KESK, the Court found at least one violation.[61] The ECtHR remained responsive to KESK's cases on

---

[58] Interview with Esen Yılmaz, May 2015.
[59] Interview with Oya Aydın, May 2015.
[60] A mass arrest of KESK members and leaders occurred in 2012 under the KCK operations. The government declared the KCK to be the urban arm of the PKK. See Chapter 4 for a detailed discussion of human rights violations KESK faced in the post-2000 period and the relevant ECtHR case law.
[61] The ECtHR issued fifty-two judgments in response to KESK's claims from 2000 to 2021. Additionally, the Court issued sixteen decisions where applicants' claims were rendered inadmissible or were struck out.

trade union rights, even amid a broader period of judicial restraint in the post-2010 period, largely because almost all of these cases concerned repeat violations.[62] KESK unions regularly publicized these violation judgments, highlighting their broader implications for public sector workers through websites, membership pamphlets, and periodic reports addressing Turkey's violations of ECtHR, EU, and ILO norms. Eğitim-Sen, as the largest KESK union and the most active in Strasbourg litigation, played a leading role in these efforts. Overall, mobilizing human rights law became a central pillar of KESK's strategy against government repression.

Without the capacity to mobilize rank-and-file at the domestic level, however, increased reliance on international human rights law proved to be of little help in addressing the problems KESK faced in the post-2000 period. Although Turkey remained mostly receptive to pressure from Europe to democratize and improve its human rights record until about the mid-2010s, KESK lost its ability to leverage international law to influence state behavior.[63] In many ways, it had been easier for activists to name and shame Turkey for the blatant rights violations it committed in the 1990s. In contrast, post-2000 repression relied on more covert tactics. The government passed superficial legislative reforms that appeared to grant public sector workers rights to collective bargaining and action, while in practice they are able to exercise neither (Chapter 6). Most importantly, the AKP–Memur-Sen alliance was unlikely to be undone by litigating at an international court, and KESK lacked the means to fight against this system of cooptation through any other means.

KESK lawyers and activists are acutely aware of the limitations of ECtHR litigation. All interviewees consistently pointed to the government's evasion strategies in avoiding compliance with the rulings. Still, many emphasized the importance of documenting the repeated violations. At the end of one interview, after Öztürk Türkdoğan, who was a legal advisor to the healthcare union (SES) and KESK at the time,

---

[62] Only one of the twenty-eight cases KESK brought before the ECtHR between 2010 and 2021 is a high-importance case.

[63] In addition to the state of emergency measures taken after the coup attempt, the Syrian war marked a turning point in Turkey's relations with Europe. In 2015, Turkey signed an agreement with the EU to keep Syrian refugees from crossing into the EU in exchange for €6 billion. Erdoğan has since used the threat of letting refugees into the EU to resist any pressure from Europe.

complained at length about the shortcomings of the execution of judgments and Turkey's unwillingness to comply, I asked him why KESK unions continue to take cases to the ECtHR. He explained, "this is a rights struggle. We cannot simply stop bringing our cases to the ECtHR because Turkey refuses to comply."[64] For KESK lawyers, litigation serves as a record of the abuses public sector workers suffer under AKP rule.

Moreover, although the process is slow, ECtHR judgments can offer partial relief to individual applicants. Türkdoğan observed that in cases involving disciplinary and criminal penalties, the government often lifted sanctions after ECtHR judgments.[65] Mehmet Tiryaki, who was one of Eğitim-Sen's lead lawyers, similarly noted that compensation awards "may help ease their pain a bit," though he criticized the ECtHR for reducing damages in recent cases.[66] The analysis of the direct impact of ECtHR cases in Chapter 6 corroborates this pattern: While Turkey frequently evades structural reform, it generally complies with individual measures prescribed by the Committee of Ministers. Consequently, KESK lawyers started to take every eligible case they lost at the domestic level to the ECtHR, resulting in a flood of repetitive cases. This litigation strategy has also been adopted by the Kurdish lawyers (Chapter 5). In cases where states drag their feet on systemic changes, activists continue to litigate at human rights courts in order to document the truth and obtain some relief to individual applicants (Kurban 2020; Van der Vet 2012).

Despite this flood of cases, all interviewees emphasized that litigation was never their preferred strategy. During the formative years, there was no question that human rights litigation had a secondary role. As İrfan Kaygısız, a KESK activist, recalled: "*Fiili mücadele* was the priority [in the initial years]. The legal struggle fed, supported, and facilitated it."[67] Today, however, the ECtHR litigation is seen more as a symbolic gesture; the activists and the lawyers acknowledge their inability to force the government to undertake systemic changes. Nonetheless, some

---

[64] Interview with Öztürk Türkdoğan, May 2015.
[65] Interview with Öztürk Türkdoğan, May 2015.
[66] Interview with Mehmet Tiryaki, May 2015. In the 2018 general elections, Tiryaki was elected to the parliament as a member of the pro-Kurdish Peoples' Democratic Party (Halkların Demokratik Partisi, HDP). He currently serves under the YSP, which was established in response to the looming threat of an HDP ban ahead of the 2023 elections.
[67] Interview with İrfan Kaygısız, April 2015.

union leaders continue to frame litigation and *fiili mücadele* as complementary. Esen Yılmaz, for instance, noted that "the two [litigation and *fiili mücadele*] are moving in parallel. In some ways, we have to litigate so much because of the repression we face in our *fiili mücadele*."[68] Other union leaders and lawyers similarly confirmed this more favorable opinion that KESK prioritizes direct action today, despite difficulties.

Some of the lower-rank union officials at KESK, however, expressed greater skepticism. While they affirmed KESK's commitment to grassroots action, they were unsure of its ability to deliver: "In the first years, the law was secondary," one noted. "Putting direct pressure on the employer, bargaining, and taking direct action were essential. Now, the legal struggle has become the primary way to address problems. This is, undoubtably, troublesome."[69] Another remarked, "As KESK lost its militant edge, it wound up relying more on ECtHR litigation."[70] Compared to the organization's foundational period, several members now observe that litigation and direct action strategies are divorced from one another: "if a case is being taken to the ECtHR, that means it is already lost [in *fiili mücadele*]."[71]

This disillusionment with the ECtHR cases and its limited impact is also shared by KESK lawyers. As Tiryaki noted, "We are not that keen on applying to the ECtHR. We don't prefer to [litigate] because it takes so long. [By the time the judgment is delivered], the violation has already done its harm."[72] At the same time, once all domestic remedies are exhausted, they see no alternative. Even critical lower-rank officials were quick to defend the strategy as a reluctant necessity:

> We should recognize the following. It is not that we have given up everything and turned our face to Europe or that we delegated our work to international support. That is out of the question. The existing situation is already a weak one. The labor movement's effective use of the ECtHR and human rights is already limited [due to its weak position]. We should not attribute our own weakness to human rights itself.[73]

On the whole, KESK's shift toward ECtHR litigation indicates a strategic adjustment to political realities rather than a change in

---

[68] Interview with Esen Yılmaz, May 2015.
[69] Interview with KESK member #1, April 2015.
[70] Interview with KESK member #2, April 2015.
[71] Interview with KESK member #2, April 2015.
[72] Interview with Mehmet Tiryaki, May 2015.
[73] Interview with KESK member #3, April 2015.

normative orientation. Activists remain committed to direct action but are constrained by a hostile domestic environment. In the post-2000 period, human rights litigation has become less a catalyst for mobilization than a tool for documentation and symbolic accountability – a strategy not of hope, but of despair.

8.4 CONCLUSION

KESK's mobilization of human rights and its changing litigation strategy provide significant insights into the impact of ECtHR judgments across different contexts. As in the BSG case, the foundational years of KESK demonstrate the catalytic effects of human rights law on social movements and the ability of activists to achieve some of their goals without waiting for a final ruling. But unlike the BSG, Turkish public sector workers did not build their movement based on the favorable rulings of the ECtHR, nor did they frame the public face of their struggle in human rights language. Instead, Turkish labor activists used the power of ratified international treaties and the potential of international litigation to dynamize their movement and defend themselves against state restrictions during the initial years. By referencing the legality of public sector workers' trade union rights and the prospect of turning to international courts, they helped assuage fears among workers in a post-coup environment and drew new members into a fledgling movement. Concurrently, they invoked these legal norms in their dealings with state officials – through lobbying, official union documents, and domestic court cases – long before any judgment was issued in Strasbourg. The aims of the labor activists in these initial years were simple and pressing: to lift the ban on public sector unionization. With strong grassroots support, they established their unions and leveraged legal reforms ensuring the rights to unionize and to engage in collective bargaining without waiting for the final ruling of the ECtHR.

In the post-2000 period, however, KESK's mobilization power declined significantly as the AKP government shifted to more covert forms of repression. Rather than banning public sector workers from engaging in unions, the AKP government developed a corporatist–clientelist relationship with a rival union, Memur-Sen, to coopt and control the public sector workforce. As this strategy took hold, KESK's membership dwindled, and its capacity to exert pressure – either domestically or internationally – waned. Despite significantly increasing the number of cases it brought to the ECtHR, KESK could no longer leverage litigation to influence state behavior. KESK lawyers and activists recognize the limitations of this approach: ECtHR rulings may offer symbolic or individual relief, but they are unlikely to drive the systemic change needed to address current conditions. KESK's experience illustrates the limits of international legal mobilization when grassroots capacity is weakened. Within the current system of government cooptation of the public sector, KESK's international litigation efforts are unlikely to produce any changes beyond the lives of individual applicants before the ECtHR.

Nevertheless, the AKP's early efforts to neutralize KESK show how much power the union once held. The fact that it had to be coopted was a testament to the formidable force KESK had become. In the 1990s, labor activists built a powerful movement through legal ingenuity, mass organizing, and the strategic invocation of international norms. They succeeded in founding the first public sector unions in Turkey and, at least for a time, reshaped the landscape of labor rights without waiting for permission from the courts. KESK's trajectory highlights a broader theme of this book: The power of international human rights law is not found in courts alone, but in the political and organizational conditions that give legal norms traction.

CHAPTER 9

LITIGATING IN HARD TIMES
Fragile Gains, Enduring Struggles

The 1980s ushered in a new era for labor movements across the world. Organized labor entered a period of decline with the implementation of neoliberal policies that thwarted trade unions' organizing power. Much of this decline was spurred by the changing dynamics of industrial relations under globalization. Cracking down on the collective power of trade unions through direct state repression was a necessary part of facilitating this new economic model. In such a hostile environment, where workers faced legal restrictions or state violence against collective action, the rank-and-file mobilization that for decades had been labor's source of strength became harder to sustain. This book has analyzed the causes and consequences of one major strategy taken up by labor to combat neoliberal policies: claiming labor rights as human rights.

The concurrent rise of human rights institutions at the international level and neoliberal policies at the domestic level set the ground for labor to adopt this strategy. In Europe, the ECtHR emerged as one of the few institutional sites to which organized labor could turn in order to claim some basic trade union rights. A small group of committed lawyers stepped up to guide labor activists in this tumultuous time and drew their attention to the availability of international legal remedies. After probing multiple international venues, they identified the ECtHR as a court that was receptive enough to hear labor's claims and authoritative enough for its judgments to carry some weight with member states. In response to the cases brought by workers, the ECtHR issued landmark rulings that recognized core trade union rights as human rights. These judgments marked a significant departure from the Court's earlier case law and carried broad implications for labor rights. They ushered in the golden era for trade unions in the Court's jurisprudence, as the freedom of association was reinterpreted to include the right to form unions, bargain collectively, and strike. These key cases, brought primarily by labor activists in Turkey and the UK, helped establish new standards for trade union rights across Europe.

International courts, however, are not necessarily in the immediate orbit of politicians. Without pressure from below, governments tend to implement superficial measures to fulfill the requirements of distant supervisory bodies that have limited knowledge about actual labor conditions on the ground. Yet the Turkish and UK cases instruct us that the most transformative impact of ECtHR jurisprudence comes not from individual remedies, but from its potential to energize grassroots mobilization. Contrary to critics who argue that human rights regimes further undermine or depoliticize labor struggles, litigation at an international court can catalyze and amplify worker-led movements. Labor activists do not just take human rights to court – they take them to the streets, drawing strength from the moral force of human rights claims to gain legitimacy, deflect repression, and build broader public support. As a result, workers often achieve concrete gains not necessarily through legal victories, but through the political leverage that rights-based mobilization can generate.

When litigation at the ECtHR is coupled with grassroots organizing, workers are able to pressure governments to respond to their demands before a final ruling is even issued. In the aftermath of Turkey's 1980 military coup, human rights law provided public sector workers a legal foundation to challenge bans on unionization and mobilize despite the risks. These efforts culminated in the establishment of KESK, Turkey's first public sector union confederation, and secured labor activists the right to unionize years before the ECtHR handed down its decision. The blacklisted workers' case shows that even when workers ultimately lose the ECtHR case, they are able to achieve some of their core aims by mobilizing human rights law and language in their campaigns. The possibility of a favorable ruling gave activists leverage to pressure the government, demand legislative reforms, and cite international obligations in domestic legal forums. While KESK activists relied on human rights law to carve out organizing space in a repressive legal climate, the BSG strategically used rights discourse in its public campaigns to recast trade unionists as bearers of human rights and build alliances with other advocacy groups.

These findings contribute to a growing body of scholarship that emphasizes the role of domestic pro-compliance groups in facilitating the implementation of human rights law. Grassroots mobilization is not merely a potential byproduct of collective international litigation, but it is often a prerequisite for litigation to matter on the ground. Social movements – not just experts, professionals, or politicians – can facilitate compliance with human rights courts. Even in liberal democracies with strong rule-of-law traditions, grassroots mobilization is critical for pressuring state officials to secure labor protections. While much of the human rights literature highlights the catalytic potential of human rights law for social movements, this book has empirically shown how litigation at a human rights court can initiate, strengthen, and sustain mobilization from below.

This book also advances legal mobilization theory by demonstrating the mechanisms through which litigation at an international court can spur and sustain grassroots activism. Unlike in domestic litigation, obtaining a verdict from an international court requires years of lengthy litigation. Labor activists do not merely sit on their hands while their lawyers argue their case. Instead, the mobilizing effects of international litigation unfold during that waiting period, well before any final ruling is issued. Moreover, because these courts are distant, unfamiliar, and have limited impact, they do not necessarily possess the same symbolic power over activists as domestic courts often do. Contrary to the studies on vernacularization of human rights, where intermediaries try to persuade local groups or activists to view their grievances through a human rights lens (Chua 2020; Merry 2006), or research showing that activists develop a rights-consciousness as they participate and socialize in legal mobilization (McCann 1994; Tsutsui 2018), I showed that labor activists engage in *strategic mobilization of human rights*. In this model, lawyers still serve an important role as intermediaries to draw activists' attention to the legal remedies at the international level, but they do not attempt to instill a rights-based consciousness among movement participations. Workers view human rights law not as a moral cause around which to build a movement, but as one of several tools available in their broader tactical arsenal. Their commitment to their class identity and camaraderie is not easily displaced by litigation in an international court, nor by the adoption of human rights language in their campaigns.

In Turkey, the safeguards provided by international laws helped ease the fears of new members and provided legal justification for workers to demand basic trade union rights. In the UK, the blacklisted workers used human rights discourse to gain access to a public discourse in which human rights language had become the dominant language of social justice. But workers in both cases were reluctant to shed their class-based identities to embrace a human rights activist identity or to build in-group solidarity ties around human rights. This duality was most pronounced among BSG members who deliberately referenced human rights *on-stage*, but hardly ever talked about human rights in their *off-stage* internal meetings.

Workers' approach to human rights is characterized by caution and pragmatism. One could hardly blame them. Labor rights have historically held a secondary place in human rights law. The ECtHR – established as a civil and political rights court – only began to recognize basic labor rights as human rights in the post-2000 period after decades of rejecting workers' claims. Workers' perceptions of international law took ideological root during the pre-1980 period when unions were strong actors representing workers' interests. They did not need to appeal to an international human rights court in order to claim their basic trade union rights; they were able to resolve their disputes through the bargaining power of their unions. Particularly in the UK, workers still refer to a "glorious past" when unions were major political players.

Other activist groups – such as LGBTQ activists or women's organizations, whose claims fall within core issue areas of international human rights law, or those without a comparable "glorious past" – may approach human rights with less ambivalence. That said, skepticism toward legal remedies is a common feature of both domestic and international legal mobilization. States often evade rulings of international courts (Búzás 2021) or meet only the minimum standards set by international law (Von Staden 2018). The narrow scope of human rights frameworks can leave activists disillusioned, particularly when seeking more ambitious or revolutionary goals. But legal mobilization scholars have shown that nascent movements can develop a collective identity around rights-claiming, despite their doubts about courts' ability to deliver transformative outcomes (McCann 1994; Scheingold 1974). Thus, the prior existence of a strong collective identity and ideological grounding is essential for activists to adopt the kind of instrumental approach – one that treats human rights not as ends in themselves but as tools to pursue broader goals – documented in this book.

The strategic approach that lawyers and activists take toward human rights indicates that their connection to human rights laws and institutions is a tenuous one. Because human rights do not shape activists' legal consciousness or collective identity formation, activists may discard the framework if it no longer serves their purposes. Alternatively, it is possible for labor activists to shed their skepticism and embrace human rights off-stage over time. My observations on trade union activism suggest that two conditions would need to change for such a switch to occur in workers' attitudes. First, the ECtHR would need to show renewed responsiveness to trade union rights claims – not just continue issuing violation rulings on repetitive cases. Second, the alliances workers form with other human rights groups would need to deepen and endure. Sustained engagement and consistent cooperation on human rights activities could facilitate the formation of new subjectivities and gradually cultivate a shared rights-based identity. However, it does not seem likely that the ties between human rights and organized labor will endure if current trends continue.

9.1 RISE OF BACKLASH, REPRESSION, AND AUTHORITARIANISM

As the union between labor and human rights grew stronger states devised new strategies to undermine the power of labor movements and the authority of international human rights courts. Organized labor faced not only intensified but also newly adapted forms of repression at the same time as a wave of political backlash started to mount against international organizations tasked with protecting workers' rights.

Temporal analysis of KESK's mobilization from the late 1980s through the 2000s shows that the type and intensity of state repression shapes how labor movements strategically mobilize human rights. The Turkish state adapted to the rise of public sector workers' movement by using new forms of repression. In the early years, unionization efforts by public sector workers were not perceived as an existential threat to the regime. Nevertheless, the state met KESK's mobilization with overt repression: new legal restrictions against union activity and use of police violence to suppress protests. Human rights law became a tool for KESK to galvanize a movement and assert its right to exist. By the end of the 1990s, KESK had not only leveraged domestic legal protections on the right to unionize, but it also gained popularity, attracting workers from across the public sector to join its movement.

9.1 RISE OF BACKLASH, REPRESSION, AND AUTHORITARIANISM

When the AKP government came to power in 2002, it immediately identified KESK as a major threat against its authority and turned to a more insidious form of repression: cooptation. As the government formed clientelist ties with a state-backed union, KESK weakened from within and lost its capacity to grow and retain members. ECtHR litigation, once a strategic tool to mobilize workers, became a strategy of despair – providing relief to individual members seeking remedies against overt forms of government repression, but unable to rally masses against the systemic erosion of public sector unionism.

A more concerning development still – not only for organized labor, but for all human rights activists – is the growing backlash against the ECtHR. From concerted efforts to limit the Court's authority to open threats of withdrawal, member states have employed a wide range of tactics to weaken the influence of the ECtHR. The UK has been at the forefront of these efforts, as it used its previous Committee of Ministers chairmanship to promote reforms aimed at curbing the Court's ability to effectively scrutinize human rights violations occurring in member states (Voeten 2020). Parallel to these efforts, successive Conservative governments have attempted to repeal the Human Rights Act and sever the ECtHR's influence over the British legal system, though these threats did not materialize. Turkey, meanwhile, has openly disregarded ECtHR judgments in high-profile cases by refusing to release political prisoners, including in *Kavala v. Turkey* (2020) and *Selahattin Demirtas v. Turkey (No. 2)* (2020).[1] Other states, including liberal democracies and transitioning regimes, have joined the bandwagon by denouncing ECtHR rulings or backing efforts to diminish the Court's authority, as discussed in Chapter 5.

This mounting pressure contributed to a period of retrenchment at the ECtHR, not only on trade union rights, but across other issue areas as well. The Court has grown especially reluctant to issue violation judgments against liberal democracies (Stiansen and Voeten 2020). Notably, British labor lawyers have lost every trade union rights case they have submitted to the ECtHR within the past fifteen years – a trend consistent with the overall decline in violation judgments against

---

[1] New cases may soon be added, as one involving a current member of parliament is already pending before the ECtHR (*Atalay v. Turkey* 2024), and another – concerning the arrest and political ban of the main opposition leader, Ekrem İmamoğlu – is likely to be appealed unless the government yields to domestic protests and growing international pressure, including from the CoE.

the UK. The ILO has also come under fire. In 2012, the employers' group posed a challenge against the ILO CEACR's incorporation of the right to strike under the freedom of association provisions. Examples of political backlash against other international human rights institutions indicate that the ECtHR and the ILO are not alone in their struggle to maintain their authority and legitimacy (Hillebrecht 2021; Madsen, Cebulak, and Wiebusch 2018; Voeten 2022). This cumulative pressure on these institutions is constricting what was already a narrow space for organized labor to assert its rights through international legal channels.

9.2 BEYOND BACKLASH AND REPRESSION

In the face of new forms of state repression against labor activism and growing backlash against international courts, a critical reader may ask: So what? What is the use of KESK if a state-aligned union has come to dominate public sector unionization? What does the blacklisted workers' mobilization mean for organized labor in the UK, if trade union membership has been on a downward trajectory since the 1980s? Does it matter that the ECtHR once championed trade union rights if that period of judicial activism has since been curtailed by political backlash? Returning to a critical question posed at the beginning of this book: Can human rights courts really become counterforces against the declining power of organized labor?

To answer these questions, we must recall the historical moment in which labor activists turned to claiming labor rights as human rights – a moment when revolutionary change and a return to the golden years of organized labor were no longer possible. In order to counter the effects of neoliberalism, unions experimented with a variety of strategies, ranging from partnership with employers or governments to coalition building with other grassroots activists (Baccaro, Hamann, and Turner 2003; Frege and Kelly 2004; Ibsen and Tapia 2017). None of these strategies so far has succeeded in reversing the long-term decline in unionization or collective bargaining rates. But they offer glimpses of hope and, in certain cases, secured concrete gains. When the conditions are ripe, human rights litigation can be one such tool, mobilizing the rank-and-file. Still, the challenges confronting workers are systemic and multilayered. Reversing these trends will likely require wholesale changes not just in domestic employment relations but also in the global economy. When workers turned to the ECtHR, their expectations – which were already curbed by the realities of the post-1980

9.2 BEYOND BACKLASH AND REPRESSION

period – were targeted gains, rather than sweeping changes in the industrial balance of power.

Claiming labor rights as human rights is no panacea for the complex problems organized labor has been facing in the past four decades. But the movements it sustained – and those it sparked – helped workers achieve some concrete goals. Perhaps more importantly, these movements are likely to have enduring effects beyond the current moment of backlash and repression. The BSG is a case in point. These workers organized an independent movement against a powerful alliance of employers and the state while keeping the unions at arm's length. Using human rights law and language, they fought against decades of blacklisting in the construction industry and systematic surveillance by the police at the same time as they demanded accountability from unions regarding the representatives who had been complicit. Their campaign succeeded in gaining political and public traction, and may set an example for workers in other industries grappling with similar patterns of blacklisting. In addition to organizing blacklisted workers, the BSG formed alliances with other groups to reveal systemic surveillance – through collusion between multinational companies and the police – of a wide group of leftist activists.

In Turkey, human rights law provided the legal foundation for public sector workers to unionize for the first time in the aftermath of a coup that had violently dismantled the country's leftist infrastructure. While the cooptation of public sector unionism clipped KESK's wings in the post-2000 period, there is little reason to assume that the status quo in Turkey will remain unchallenged indefinitely. Even in more consolidated autocracies, like Egypt, workers have been able to fight against decades of cooptation to establish independent unions (Bishara 2018). Social movement scholars remind us that movements transpire in the form of cycles: They rise and fall, go underground when faced with repression, but they often resurface when the political climate softens (McCann 2020; Tarrow 2022). But even in moments of retreat, they often leave behind legacies – radical aspirations for future waves of mobilization, or organizational structures that later efforts can build upon (McCann 2020).[2]

---

[2] On the importance of historical legacies in the form of pre-existing institutions and alliances for unions, see also Anner (2015); Caraway, Cook, and Crowley (2015); Murillo and Schrank (2005).

The establishment of KESK matters not only for the material gains it acquired for public sector workers during the height of its mobilization, but also because it became a civic institution that created space for active resistance by backing opposition candidates in national elections, collaborating with the Kurdish movement in peace initiatives, and upholding democratic and inclusive governance structures even as Turkish democracy continued to slide into authoritarianism. Historically, unions have played critical roles in democratic transitions and in challenging authoritarian rule (Collier and Collier 2002; Rueschemeyer, Stephens, and Stephens 1992). KESK has similar potential to become a key actor in democratization when the tide turns against authoritarianism in Turkey.

The backlash against international human rights institutions poses a serious challenge against the judicial authority and public legitimacy of international courts. At the same time, insights from studies on judicial politics remind us that the mounting pressure against the ECtHR is not unexpected, particularly after a period in which it expanded the scope of human rights protections and delivered rulings on highly polarizing political matters. Just as movements often face state repression once they make advances for social justice, courts can provoke political backlash that leads them into periods of retrenchment following judicial activism (Carrubba, Gabel, and Hankla 2008; Larsson et al. 2017; McCann and Lovell 2005; Stiansen and Voeten 2020). Compared to their domestic counterparts, international courts operate on more precarious institutional footing because states can defy, denounce, or simply exit these institutions in ways that would be unthinkable for national legal systems.

Despite rhetorical attacks by politicians and negative media portrayal, however, current research shows that the general public does not necessarily reject the authority of international courts over national institutions. Most people do not view international courts' power as inherently illegitimate, nor do they uniformly accept the claim that such courts impose unacceptable "sovereignty costs" – the idea that international courts should not override national court decisions or constrain state autonomy (Madsen et al. 2022). Even ethnonationalists and Euroskeptics do not oppose international courts' violation rulings against their own country so long as the rulings align with their ideological position (Madsen et al. 2022). Nevertheless, the rise of the far right adds fuel to the backlash since these international courts are not designed to issue rulings that resonate with ethno-nationalist or authoritarian sentiments.

Yet there are also signs of a backlash against this backlash. In addition to pressure from pro-compliance groups urging states to uphold their obligations and maintain their ties to international human rights regimes, counter-movements opposing states' withdrawal efforts have gained traction among broad segments of society. The major wave of protests involving thousands of people against the Turkish government's unilateral decision to withdraw from the Istanbul Convention, a CoE treaty on violence against women, is a case in point.[3]

At a time when debates over the democratic deficit of international courts – namely, the power vested in the hands of unelected judges sitting at international courts – have intensified, *Labor in Hard Times* underscores the indirect ways in which international courts can invigorate social movements and amplify the voices of marginalized groups. The mobilization efforts of BSG and KESK workers show that the field of human rights laws, institutions, and discourses can provide important tools for workers to contest repression, secure tangible victories, and expand political space in hostile political environments. But labor's commitment to human rights is a marriage of convenience rather than one of passion. Organized labor will likely continue to reinvent new repertoires of contention to regain its collective power and unite workers.

---

[3] Ece Toksabay and Ali Kucukgocmen, "Women Protest as Turkey Quits Violence-on-Women Treaty," *Reuters*, July 1, 2021, www.reuters.com/world/middle-east/turkey-formally-quits-treaty-prevent-violence-against-women-2021-07-01/.

APPENDIX I

Strasbourg Labor Cases Database (StrasLab)

The Strasbourg Labor Cases Database (StrasLab) catalogs all labor-related cases brought before the ECtHR from its inception in 1960 through 2017, in sampled two-year intervals (odd-numbered years), as well as all precedent-setting labor cases ("case reports") from 1998 to 2017.[1] Complementing this dataset, I also compiled a separate list of all trade union rights cases at the ECtHR from 1960 to 2020, in order to provide a fuller picture of this issue area where the Court has issued some of its most influential rulings. This list includes all cases in which Article 11 (freedom of association) was invoked or found to have been violated in the context of trade union rights. Cases brought by individuals or employers challenging the rights and protections afforded to trade unions – such as those involving closed shop agreements – are excluded from this list, though they are included in the broader labor rights database. All judgments and decisions of the ECtHR are publicly available through the Court's official online repository, HUDOC.[2]

Unlike most existing studies of the ECtHR, which focus exclusively on judgments (rulings on the merits), I include both judgments and decisions on admissibility (Cichowski 2016; Helfer and Voeten 2014; Hillebrecht 2014). Failed cases on admissibility provide insights into the kinds of grievances individuals attempt to pursue through the Court and the boundaries drawn by the Court around what counts as a fundamental human right. They demonstrate the process through which the ECtHR folds new labor rights into the Convention

---

[1] StrasLab will be made publicly available, with accompanying documentation, via an academic open-data repository after publication.
[2] The HUDOC database, available at https://hudoc.echr.coe.int, provides access to all ECtHR judgments and decisions that meet the Court's basic eligibility criteria, such as the requirement that a petition is submitted within four months of the final domestic decision. The Court receives thousands of applications each year, the vast majority of which are dismissed at the outset for failing to meet these criteria. Unlike the US Supreme Court, however, the ECtHR does not exercise discretionary review; it issues a ruling on every case brought before it.

framework as well as the "novel rights claims" (Polletta 2000) the Court "kills" by declaring them inadmissible (Cover 1983; Lovell, McCann, and Taylor 2016).[3] Overall, the database includes general identifiers – such as the articles invoked, the date of application, and the ruling – along with basic information about the issue at stake and the outcome of the ruling.

StrasLab was developed with the help of a team of twenty trained undergraduate research assistants. The coding work was completed in two stages. First, I developed a screening scheme to identify potential labor-related cases, based on keyword searches and the invocation of Convention articles commonly associated with labor rights.[4] These include Articles 2, 3, 4, 8, 9, 10, 11, 12, 13, and 14, Article 1 of Protocol 1, Articles 2, 3, and 4 of Protocol 4, Article 1 of Protocol 7, and Article 1 of Protocol 12. Since the ECtHR was initially established as a civil and political rights court, there are not any articles that expressly protect labor rights, aside from freedom from slavery and servitude (Article 4) and a reference to trade union rights under freedom of association (Article 11). After this initial screening, the research assistants reviewed each case and identified the labor cases, which they coded into a shared spreadsheet based on a set of written guidelines.

Defining what counts as a labor rights case presented certain challenges, given that the Convention does not explicitly protect labor rights. The changing approach of the ECtHR toward labor rights over the past few decades is itself a testament to the indeterminate nature of human rights. To address this ambiguity, I drew on several sources to develop coding guidelines: the ECtHR's summary judgments on "work-related rights," "trade union rights," "forced labor," and "surveillance at workplace" – which are available as factsheets on the ECtHR's official website; international legal instruments that more clearly protect labor rights – especially those of the ILO and the ESC; and legal scholarship on labor case law at the ECtHR (Dorssemont, Lörcher, and Schömann 2013; Ewing and Hendy 2010; Mantouvalou 2013; Sychenko 2017). Additionally, discussions on the Workers' Health and Safety Watch

---

[3] In order to avoid duplication, I excluded any preliminary decisions once a final judgment on the merit was issued.
[4] I conducted a keyword search in the HUDOC database using the root "work*" to capture the word "work" and its derivatives, as well as the French equivalent "trava*," since some case documents are available only in French.

listserv in Turkey, where civil society activists debate which incidents constitute a work-related injury or death, broadened and informed my understanding of labor rights. This group regularly compiles monthly and annual data on worker fatalities, and their conversations offered a valuable perspective on how labor violations are defined and documented. While developing the guidelines, my purpose was to cast a wide net and include all rights violation claims that arose in the workplace or were experienced by workers due to their employment. In addition to the general guidelines I provided to the research team, I maintained a growing list of sample cases to include or exclude. In order to ensure consistency and reliability across the coding work, I reviewed all included and excluded cases – based on the brief summaries written by the students – before finalizing the database.

APPENDIX II

Qualitative Data

RESEARCH DESIGN AND METHODOLOGY

This book is grounded in qualitative methodology and draws on rich data collected over a period of eleven years beginning in 2013, including interviews, archival materials, participant observation, media coverage, social media, parliamentary records, and reports by NGOs and international organizations. Most of the fieldwork was conducted over a sixteen-month period between 2013 and 2018.[1] In the UK, I was primarily based in London, where most trade union activism was concentrated, and traveled to Newcastle and Bristol for interviews and meetings. In Turkey, I was primarily based in Istanbul, with additional trips to Ankara and Diyarbakır for interviews and archival research. My data sources included interviews; participant observation at events, meetings, demonstrations, and social gatherings organized by labor activists, as well as domestic court hearings; archival materials such as union magazines, meeting notes, reports, and pamphlets; parliamentary debates; social media; online news platforms; documentation related to the execution of ECtHR rulings (HUDOC-EXEC); legal reforms; domestic court rulings; reports on policy implementation; and ILO CFA complaints from both Turkey and the UK.

The primary purpose of the fieldwork was to explore the local dynamics of legal mobilization. Fieldwork data combined with case law analysis is commonly used by legal mobilization scholars, allowing researchers to examine both the drivers of legal mobilization and the radiating effects of litigation outside of the courtroom (Chua 2020; Cichowski 2007; Conant 2002; Mayo-Adam 2020; McCann 1994; Moustafa 2018; Pavone 2022; Stern 2013; Sundstrom 2012; Vanhala 2010). Specifically, I sought to: (1) investigate the process through

---

[1] I also conducted a few follow-up interviews in 2024 to update key developments discussed in earlier interviews.

which labor lawyers and activists come to mobilize human rights litigation and discourse, as well as document their hopes, doubts, and critiques about ECtHR litigation; (2) examine the roles played by different groups of activists in legal mobilization, with attention to their organizational structures and the power imbalances shaped by their access to legal, political, financial, and international resources; (3) track how labor activists mobilize around human rights litigation; (4) analyze the measures states take in compliance with ECtHR rulings and the real impact of these measures from the perspective of workers on the ground; (5) understand the cultural drivers of workers' movements – such as legal consciousness, solidarity, motivations, and collective identity formations – and the extent to which human rights inform these dynamics.

During my fieldwork, I analyzed the activities of five overlapping groups involved in organized labor's legal mobilization: (1) *legal professionals*, including labor lawyers working independently, in pro-union legal firms, or as in-house counsel for trade unions; (2) *social movement actors* – workers engaged in political mobilization, with or without union support, to advance workers' rights, such as members of the BSG or public sector workers that eventually established KESK; (3) *pro-labor organizations* – legal advocacy groups (e.g., Liberty in the UK) or think tanks (e.g., the Institute of Employment Rights) that support litigation or publish labor rights reports but do not mobilize grassroots support; (4) *trade unions*, primarily those involved in ECtHR litigation, though I also interviewed unionists who had not used the ECtHR, to capture their perspectives;[2] (5) *academics* who supported the ECtHR litigation efforts or labor activists. These categories are not mutually exclusive. For example, some academics served as legal counsel on ECtHR cases, and many social movement actors were also members of trade unions. In total, I conducted thirty-five semi-structured interviews in Turkey and thirty-four in the UK. The length of each interview lasted between half an hour and three hours. In addition to my formal interviews in the UK, I gathered substantial data through

---

[2] In the UK, I interviewed representatives and lawyers from RMT, Unite, GMB (which later merged into Unite), and Unison, as well as from two major trade union federations: the TUC and the ITUC. In Turkey, most of my interviews concentrated on KESK lawyers and activists, but I also conducted a few interviews with private sector union representatives and lawyers to investigate their limited experiences with the ECtHR. These unions were DİSK, Liman-İş, Birleşik Metal-İş, and Petrol-İş.

informal conversations with blacklisted workers at demonstrations, meetings, and pub gatherings.[3] In Turkey, I conducted all interviews in Turkish.

The interviews provided essential information on why and how organized labor turned to the ECtHR, and how lawyers and activists interpreted the Court's impact. Interviews with legal professionals and scholars were especially helpful in reconstructing litigation strategies (Chapter 5). I cross-checked information provided to me during interviews against a range of other sources, including participant observation, archival research, media reports, and official records. Through these documents, I conducted process tracing of landmark cases from Turkey and the UK to analyze the litigation strategies of the lawyers.[4] I also tracked major political developments that triggered a change in activists' strategies or institutional responses to unionists' claims.

In order to examine how labor lawyers identify the best venue to direct their litigation efforts at the international level, I supplemented StrasLab with a list of complaints brought by Turkish and British unions before the ILO's CFA from 1980 to 2021 ($n = 47$).[5] The CFA allows unions, employers, and states to bring forward complaints concerning violations of freedom of association. Because most ECJ labor cases originate through preliminary references from national courts, rather than as strategic filings by unions, I did not conduct a systematic review of ECJ cases. Instead, I relied on secondary literature to identify key cases and drew on British labor lawyers' accounts to understand their attitudes toward the ECJ.

In my analysis of the impact of ECtHR rulings, I first analyzed the direct impact of ECtHR rulings. Chapter 6 draws on the ECtHR's database on execution of judgments (HUDOC-EXEC) to trace the individual and general measures undertaken by Turkey and the UK in compliance with the violation rulings on trade union rights. The

---

[3] Throughout the book, I identify the names of activists and lawyers I interviewed, as this research does not pose any reasonable risk to the research subjects in addition to the risks they face in their daily lives by engaging in activism or representing clients. There are two exceptions to this. I do not identify the names of lower-rank KESK members who expressed some critical thoughts about the administration. I also do not identify the names of blacklisted workers with whom I engaged in informal conversations during demonstrations or events.

[4] McCann (1994) provides an empirical example of this process at the domestic level. I also followed Bennett and Checkel (2014) for process tracing.

[5] Pending cases are not included in the list.

database includes both governments' action reports on compliance as well as the CM's response to these reports. While the ECtHR has formally invited NGO participation in the supervision process since 2006, reports from NGOs are sporadic and they are extremely rare in trade union rights cases. Therefore, in order to assess the actual impact, I analyzed reports from trade unions, pro-labor organizations, legal scholars, as well as relevant progress reports published by international organizations, like the EU and the ILO, and government agencies.

The final two empirical chapters take a broader lens to analyze the indirect effects of litigation through an examination of trade union activism by KESK in Turkey and the BSG in the UK. Interviews gave voice to my respondents and provided insights into the motivations, strategies, and reflections of activists and lawyers. That said, I am mindful of the limitations of relying solely on interviews, which privilege discursive interpretation and may not fully capture the "unconscious cognitive processes" that shape action and behavior (Vaisey 2009; see also Jerolmack and Khan 2014).[6] Participant observation and archival research helped address some of these limitations by allowing me to trace practices and patterns that were not always articulated in the interviews and to situate actors' narratives within a broader context. In Turkey, the height of KESK's grassroots mobilization was from the late 1980s to the mid-1990s. Interviews with lawyers and activists active during this period provided retrospective accounts based on memory. Archival materials, including speeches given by activists or campaign materials, offered more direct evidence of their behavior, such as how they mobilized human rights law and language as a legal basis in establishing their unions.

CASE STUDY: BLACKLIST SUPPORT GROUP IN THE UK

For the BSG case in the UK, the participant observations at BSG events, including internal meetings, pub gatherings, dinners, and domestic court hearings with the workers provided valuable data. These settings allowed me to observe how activists articulating their grievances, interacting with one another, or strategizing for their next

---

[6] Ultimately, this book adopts "methodological pluralism" by using a wide range of qualitative data (Lamont and Swidler 2014), while keeping in mind that interviews provide information about how interview subjects characterize their own behavior when prompted by the interviewer to consider it.

event within their everyday environments. Because BSG members adapted their language depending on their audience, observing them in multiple arenas was critical. During internal meetings, I paid close attention to how they strategized, and whether and how they engaged with human rights discourse when they were not concerned about public-facing messaging.

I was often the only woman present at BSG events, which were predominantly attended by white male workers. Occasionally, wives of blacklisted workers, women journalists, and activists from allied campaigns were also present. Since I was a frequent participant in their events, after a while I became a familiar face. Yet, as blacklisted workers, many remained acutely aware of the possibility of being subjects of surveillance. On one occasion, during an informal gathering after a meeting, a blacklisted worker half-jokingly suggested I might be the spy among them, since there was always "at least one." Aside from that moment, I generally felt welcome, and I often participated in their demonstrations by holding signs or helping with set-up. While these minor contributions helped me immerse myself in the field, I did not participate in these events solely for the purposes of blending in as a researcher; I genuinely supported their cause.[7] That said, I was not part of the movement and did not participate in decision-making or planning.[8]

In addition to following BSG-specific events, I attended workshops, training sessions, and seminars related to other trade union rights activities, such as those organized by the pro-labor institutions or trade unions. These events brought together academics, politicians, and legal experts to discuss policy reforms on labor rights and implications of ECtHR litigation. I observed the actors involved in the ECtHR litigation process and how legal experts conveyed information about human rights law to workers and trade union activists.

My analysis of BSG activism also draws on three additional sources: social media analysis of the BSG Facebook page, media analysis of coverage of the blacklisting scandal, and an analysis of House of

---

[7] For immersive ethnography, see Schatz (2009); Simmons and Smith (2017).
[8] Since my purpose was to understand the impact of human rights litigation for workers, my sympathy and minor contributions to the activists' cause did not compromise my position as a researcher. Many activist-scholars conduct fieldwork on topics they are personally committed to (Chua 2020; Gallagher 2022; McCann and Lovell 2020; Milli Lake 2020).

Commons minutes on blacklisting (Chapter 7). The BSG Facebook page is a public platform which was established by the BSG leaders to share campaign updates, promote litigation efforts, and call out blacklisting companies. Other members of the group, including those not formally affiliated with the BSG, also post about blacklisting and trade union activities. A graduate student assisted me by systematically identifying and coding all posts referencing the ECtHR and human rights from 2010 to 2019, including metadata such as dates and authors. In order to assess the extent to which British politicians adopted BSG's human rights framing, I analyzed House of Commons debates that referenced both "blacklisting" and "human rights" between 2009 and 2020. All debates are publicly available online and searchable by keyword.

To explore how the BSG activists presented themselves to the media, I analyzed all articles on the BSG published in *The Guardian* from 2011 to 2019. The purpose of this analysis was not to track media framing of blacklisting in a nationally representative outlet, but rather to examine how BSG activists articulated their grievances in a platform that offered them visibility and support. *The Guardian* was well suited for this purpose because it is widely read on the left and it closely followed the blacklisting scandal. I examined opinion pieces written by BSG activists and news stories in which they were quoted, in order to understand how they sought to represent their claims and shape public narratives about blacklisting.

CASE STUDY: PUBLIC SECTOR UNION MOBILIZATION IN TURKEY

In Turkey, nearly all of the qualitative data I collected focused on the litigation and mobilization activities of KESK (and its predecessor organizations), as this union confederation brought the overwhelming majority of trade union rights cases before the ECtHR and combined grassroots mobilization with legal advocacy during its foundational years. Since the public sector workers' mobilization started in the late 1980s and peaked in the mid-1990s, an investigation of KESK's early organizing required extensive archival research on campaign materials, pamphlets, meeting reports, and annual reports of KESK. Accessing these materials, however, presented several challenges.

I visited KESK's headquarters in Ankara in 2018. Upon inquiring about the archives, I was led to the top floor of the building, where three rooms were filled with documents, pamphlets, and booklets related to KESK's activities, but none were organized. At the time, an archivist had only been recently hired to systematize and digitize these materials. In short, the archives were in the making when I visited KESK. I gathered bits and pieces of relevant material from KESK as well as from my interviewees – particularly trade union leaders from the 1990s – who had preserved key documents from that period for their personal records. One can hope that as KESK formalizes its archival infrastructure and provides a secure place for documents, more unionists will contribute their personal collections to ensure broader access. I had better luck with Eğitim-Sen, KESK's largest sub-union, which had digitized several key documents, including annual progress reports from the early 1990s.

One of the most valuable sources for conducting systematic research on KESK's activism in its foundational years (1986–1991) was the journal *abece*. As discussed in Chapter 8, the journal was launched by labor activists in the education sector and played an important role in organizing education sector workers and disseminating information about trade union rights. In addition to coverage of key union events, op-eds, and interviews, the journal also included transcripts of some of the keynote speeches delivered at public events and internal meetings. I worked with two research assistants to digitize all sixty-five issues published during this period and analyze their content.[9] The research assistants, both of whom were fluent in Turkish, completed the coding work on Nvivo, a qualitative data analysis software, based on a coding scheme I developed. While the journal continues to be published today, I was not able to access most of the issues published in the 1990s. Nonetheless, the available editions provide rich material to trace how public sector workers used international human rights law in their organizing efforts and as a legal basis in KESK's formative years.

I complemented the *abece* analysis with archival research on *Milliyet*, one of the two major mainstream newspapers in Turkey in the 1990s. My goal was to examine whether and how KESK used human rights language in its public campaigns in the 1990–1995 period, which marked the height of public sector mobilization. Compared to the BSG's campaigns, the public sector workers' mobilization efforts gained a lot more traction in the media as thousands of workers joined these

---

[9] Each issue was approximately fifty pages long.

protests. Given this broader media presence, I chose a mainstream newspaper to analyze how public sector unions framed their demands. Fortunately, the newspaper's archive from this period is accessible online. One graduate student, also fluent in Turkish, assisted me on this project by identifying all articles on public sector workers' mobilization and coding basic information such as the type of protest, location, estimated turnout, and organizing groups, as well as the frames and slogans used by demonstrators.[10]

---

[10] We searched for the words "memur" (public servant) combined with one of the following words "gösteri" (demonstration), "yürüyüş" (march), "eylem" (protest/action), and "grev" (strike).

REFERENCES

Acar, Elif Öznur, and Aysıt Tansel. 2016. "Defining and Measuring Informality: The Case of Turkish Labor Market." *Sosyoekonomi* 24 (28): 147–74. www.sosyoekonomijournal.org/Sosyoekonomi24(28).pdf.

Adaman, Fikret, Ayşe Buğra, and Ahmet İnsel. 2009. "Societal Context of Labor Union Strategy: The Case of Turkey." *Labor Studies Journal* 34 (2): 168–88. https://doi.org/10.1177/0160449X07309937.

Ahmad, Feroz. 1985. "The Transition to Democracy in Turkey." *Third World Quarterly* 7 (2): 211–26.

Akça, İsmet, and Evren Balta-Paker. 2013. "Beyond Military Tutelage? Turkish Military Politics and the AKP Government." In *Debating Security in Turkey: Challenges and Changes in the Twenty-First Century*, 77–92. New York: Routledge.

Albiston, Catherine R. 2005. "Bargaining in the Shadow of Social Institutions: Competing Discourses and Social Change in Workplace Mobilization of Civil Rights." *Law & Society Review* 39 (1): 11–49. https://doi.org/10.1111/j.0023-9216.2005.00076.x.

Albiston, Catherine Ruth, ed. 2011. "The Dark Side of Litigation as a Social Movement Strategy." *Iowa Law Review Bulletin* 96 (2011): 61–77.

Almeida, Paul, and Linda Brewster Stearns. 1998. "Political Opportunities and Local Grassroots Environmental Movements: The Case of Minamata." *Social Problems* 45 (1): 37–60. https://doi.org/10.2307/3097142.

Alston, Philip, and Ryan Goodman. 2013. *International Human Rights: The Successor to International Human Rights in Context: Law, Politics and Morals: Text and Materials*. Oxford: Oxford University Press.

Alter, Karen J. 1998. "Who Are the 'Masters of the Treaty'? European Governments and the European Court of Justice." *International Organization* 52 (1): 121–47. https://doi.org/10.1162/002081898550572.

——— 2014. *The New Terrain of International Law: Courts, Politics, Rights*. Princeton, NJ: Princeton University Press.

Alter, Karen J., Emilie M. Hafner-Burton, and Laurence R. Helfer. 2019. "Theorizing the Judicialization of International Relations." *International Studies Quarterly* 63 (3): 449–63. https://doi.org/10.1093/isq/sqz019.

Alter, Karen J., Laurence R. Helfer, and Mikael Rask Madsen. 2016. "How Context Shapes the Authority of International Courts." *Law and Contemporary Problems* 79 (1): 1–36.

Alter, Karen J., and Jeannette Vargas. 2000. "Explaining Variation in the Use of European Litigation Strategies: European Community Law and British Gender Equality Policy." *Comparative Political Studies* 33 (4): 452–82.

Anagnostou, Dia. 2013. *The European Court of Human Rights: Implementing Strasbourg's Judgements on Domestic Policy*. Edinburgh: Edinburgh University Press.

ed. 2014. *Rights and Courts in Pursuit of Social Change: Legal Mobilisation in the Multi-Level European System*. London: Bloomsbury.

Andersen, Ellen Ann. 2006. *Out of the Closets and into the Courts: Legal Opportunity Structure and Gay Rights Litigation*. Ann Arbor: University of Michigan Press.

Anderson, Carol. 2003. *Eyes off the Prize: The United Nations and the African American Struggle for Human Rights, 1944–1955*. Cambridge: Cambridge University Press.

Anner, Mark. 2009. "Two Logics of Labor Organizing in the Global Apparel Industry." *International Studies Quarterly* 53 (3): 545–70. https://doi.org/10.1111/j.1468-2478.2009.00546.x.

2015. "Labor Control Regimes and Worker Resistance in Global Supply Chains." *Labor History* 56 (3): 292–307. https://doi.org/10.1080/0023656X.2015.1042771.

Anner, Mark, and Teri Caraway. 2010. "International Institutions and Workers' Rights: Between Labor Standards and Market Flexibility." *Studies in Comparative International Development* 45 (2): 151–69. https://doi.org/10.1007/s12116-010-9064-x.

Armstrong, Elizabeth A., and Mary Bernstein. 2008. "Culture, Power, and Institutions: A Multi-Institutional Politics Approach to Social Movements." *Sociological Theory* 26 (1): 74–99. https://doi.org/10.1111/j.1467-9558.2008.00319.x.

Arrington, Celeste L. 2016. *Accidental Activists: Victim Movements and Government Accountability in Japan and South Korea*. Ithaca, NY: Cornell University Press. https://doi.org/10.7591/9781501703379.

2019. "The Mechanisms behind Litigation's 'Radiating Effects': Historical Grievances against Japan." *Law & Society Review* 53 (1): 6–40. https://doi.org/10.1111/lasr.12392.

Ayoub, Phillip. 2016. *When States Come Out: Europe's Sexual Minorities and the Politics of Visibility*. Cambridge Studies in Contentious Politics. New York: Cambridge University Press.

Babül, Elif M. 2020. "Radical Once More: The Contentious Politics of Human Rights in Turkey." *Social Anthropology/Anthropologie Sociale* 28 (1): 50–65. https://doi.org/10.1111/1469-8676.12740.

Baccaro, Lucio, Kerstin Hamann, and Lowell Turner. 2003. "The Politics of Labour Movement Revitalization: The Need for a Revitalized Perspective." *European Journal of Industrial Relations* 9 (1): 119–33. https://doi.org/10.1177/0959680103009001455.

Baccaro, Lucio, and Chris Howell. 2017. *Trajectories of Neoliberal Transformation: European Industrial Relations since the 1970s*. 1st ed. Cambridge: Cambridge University Press.

Bach, Stephen, and Lorenzo Bordogna. 2016. *Public Service Management and Employment Relations in Europe: Emerging from the Crisis*. Routledge Critical Studies in Public Management. New York: Routledge. https://doi.org/10.4324/9781315724096.

Bates, Ed. 2010. *The Evolution of the European Convention on Human Rights: From Its Inception to the Creation of a Permanent Court of Human Rights*. Oxford: Oxford University Press.

Batura, Justine. 2023. "A European Dialogue on Strike Action: The Strike Ban for German Civil Servants between Karlsruhe and Strasbourg." Verfassungs Blog: On Matters Constitutional, December 20, 2023. https://verfassungsblog.de/a-european-dialogue-on-strike-action/?utm_source=chatgpt.com.

Baxi, Upendra. 2008. *The Future of Human Rights*. Oxford: Oxford University Press. https://doi.org/10.1093/acprof:oso/9780195690439.001.0001.

Belge, Ceren. 2006. "Friends of the Court: The Republican Alliance and Selective Activism of the Constitutional Court of Turkey." *Law Society Review* 40 (3): 653–92. https://doi.org/10.1111/j.1540-5893.2006.00276.x.

Benford, Robert D., and David A. Snow. 2000. "Framing Processes and Social Movements: An Overview and Assessment." *Annual Review of Sociology* 26: 611–39.

Bennett, Andrew, and Jeffrey T. Checkel, eds. 2014. *Process Tracing: From Metaphor to Analytic Tool*. Cambridge: Cambridge University Press.

Bishara, Dina. 2018. *Contesting Authoritarianism: Labor Challenges to the State in Egypt*. Cambridge Middle East Studies. Cambridge: Cambridge University Press. https://doi.org/10.1017/9781108147873.

Blaydes, Lisa. 2020. *State of Repression: Iraq under Saddam Hussein*. Princeton, NJ: Princeton University Press.

Bob, Clifford. 2002. "Merchants of Morality." *Foreign Policy* 129 (March): 36–45. https://doi.org/10.2307/3183388.

Bogg, A., and K. D. Ewing. 2014. "The Implications of the RMT Case." *Industrial Law Journal* 43 (3): 221–52.

Bogg, A. L. 2005. "Employment Relations Act 2004: Another False Dawn for Collectivism?" *Industrial Law Journal (London)* 34 (1): 72–82. https://doi.org/10.1093/ilj/34.1.72.

Bogg, Alan. 2022. "Wilson and Palmer: A Biographical Portrait of a Landmark Case." In *Landmark Cases in Labour Law*, edited by Alan

Bogg, A. C. L. Davies, and Jeremias Adams-Prassl, 209–43. Gordonsville, VA: Hart Publishing.

Bogg, Alan, and Keith Ewing. 2014. "The Implications of the RMT Case." *Industrial Law Journal* 43 (3): 221–52. https://doi.org/10.1093/indlaw/dwu015.

———. 2021. "Kostal UK Ltd v Dunkley: A Reply to John Bowers QC." *Industrial Law Journal* 50 (1): 125–29.

Boratav, Korkut, and Erinç Yeldan. 2006. "Turkey, 1980–2000: Financial Liberalization, Macroeconomic (In-)Stability, and Patterns of Distribution." In *External Liberalization in Asia, Post-Socialist Europe, and Brazil*, edited by Lance Taylor, 417–55. New York: Oxford University Press.

Brems, Eva. 2011. "Transitional Justice in the Case Law of the European Court of Human Rights." *International Journal of Transitional Justice* 5 (2): 282–303.

Brown, Wendy. 2004. "'The Most We Can Hope For...': Human Rights and the Politics of Fatalism." *South Atlantic Quarterly* 103 (2): 451–63.

———. 2006. "American Nightmare: Neoliberalism, Neoconservatism, and De-Democratization." *Political Theory* 34 (6): 690–714.

Brown, William, Simon Deakin, David Nash, and Sarah Oxenbridge. 2000. "The Employment Contract: From Collective Procedures to Individual Rights." *British Journal of Industrial Relations* 38 (4): 611–29. https://doi.org/10.1111/1467-8543.00182.

Bruun, Niklas. 2014. "Prohibition of Discrimination under Article 14 European Convention on Human Rights." In *The European Convention on Human Rights and the Employment Relation*, edited by Filip Dorssemont, Klaus Lörcher, and Isabelle Schömann, 367–80. Oxford: Hart.

Brysk, Alison. 2000. *From Tribal Village to Global Village: Indian Rights and International Relations in Latin America*. Stanford, CA: Stanford University Press.

———. 2009. *Global Good Samaritans: Human Rights as Foreign Policy*. Oxford: Oxford University Press.

Buğra, Ayse. 2007. "Poverty and Citizenship: An Overview of the Social-Policy Environment in Republican Turkey." *International Journal of Middle East Studies* 39 (1): 33–52. https://doi.org/10.1017/S0020743807212528.

Burgess, S., Carol Propper, and D. Wilson. 2001. *Explaining the Growth in the Number of Applications to Industrial Tribunals, 1972–1997*. Employment Relations Research Series No. 10. London: Department of Trade and Industry.

Burke-White, William. 2004. "International Legal Pluralism." *Michigan Journal of International Law* 25 (4): 963–79.

REFERENCES

Busch, Marc L. 2007. "Overlapping Institutions, Forum Shopping, and Dispute Settlement in International Trade." *International Organization* 61 (04). https://doi.org/10.1017/S0020818307070257.

Búzás, Zoltán I. 2021. *Evading International Norms: Race and Rights in the Shadow of Legality*. 1st ed. Pennsylvania Studies in Human Rights. Philadelphia: University of Pennsylvania Press.

Çalı, Başak. 2010. "The Logics of Supranational Human Rights Litigation, Official Acknowledgment, and Human Rights Reform: The Southeast Turkey Cases before the European Court of Human Rights, 1996–2006." *Law & Social Inquiry* 35 (02): 311–37. https://doi.org/10.1111/j.1747-4469.2010.01187.x.

Çali, Başak, and Anne Koch. 2014. "Foxes Guarding the Foxes? The Peer Review of Human Rights Judgments by the Committee of Ministers of the Council of Europe." *Human Rights Law Review* 14 (2): 301–25. https://doi.org/10.1093/hrlr/ngu007.

Caraway, Teri L, Maria Lorena Cook, and Stephen Crowley. 2015. *Working through the Past: Labor and Authoritarian Legacies in Comparative Perspective*. Ithaca: Cornell University Press.

Carrubba, Clifford J., Matthew Gabel, and Charles Hankla. 2008. "Judicial Behavior under Political Constraints: Evidence from the European Court of Justice." *American Political Science Review* 102 (4): 435–52. https://doi.org/10.1017/S0003055408080350.

Caserta, Salvatore, and Mikael Rask Madsen. 2024. "When the Sun, the Moon and the Stars Align: Litigating LGBTQIA+ Rights and the Death Penalty in East Africa and the Caribbean." *European Journal of International Law* 35 (3): 727–50. https://doi.org/10.1093/ejil/chae040.

Cebulak, Pola, Marta Morvillo, and Stefan Salomon. 2024. "Strategic Litigation in EU Law: Who Does It Empower?" *German Law Journal* 25 (6): 800–821. https://doi.org/10.1017/glj.2024.56.

Çelik, Aziz. 1996. "Bahar Eylemleri 1989." In *Türkiye sendikacılık ansiklopedisi*, edited by Turkey Kültür Bakanlığı and Türkiye Ekonomik ve Toplumsal Tarih Vakfı, vol. 1, 103–4. Istanbul: Kültür Bakanlığı ve Tarih Vakfı'nın ortak yayınıdır.

———. 2010. *Vesayetten siyasete Türkiye'de sendikacılık (1946-1967)*. 1. baskı. Araştırma-inceleme dizisi 254. Cağaloğlu, İstanbul: İletişim.

———. 2014. "Mücadeleden Vesayete Türkiye'de Kamu Görevlileri Sendikacılığı." *Eleştirel Pedagoji* 34 (Temmuz-Ağustos): 1–8.

Chayes, Abram, and Antonia Handler Chayes. 1998. *The New Sovereignty: Compliance with International Regulatory Agreements*. Cambridge: Harvard University Press. https://doi.org/10.4159/9780674262638.

Checkel, Jeffrey T. 2005. "International Institutions and Socialization in Europe: Introduction and Framework." *International Organization* 59 (4): 801–26. https://doi.org/10.1017/S0020818305050289.

REFERENCES

Chouliaraki, Lilie. 2013. *The Ironic Spectator: Solidarity in the Age of Post-Humanitarianism*. 1st ed. Cambridge, MA: Polity.

Chua, Lynette J. 2012. "Pragmatic Resistance, Law, and Social Movements in Authoritarian States: The Case of Gay Collective Action in Singapore: Pragmatic Resistance." *Law & Society Review* 46 (4): 713–48. https://doi.org/10.1111/j.1540-5893.2012.00515.x.

2019. "Legal Mobilization and Authoritarianism." *Annual Review of Law and Social Science* 15 (1): 355–76.

2020. *The Politics of Love in Myanmar: LGBT Mobilization and Human Rights as a Way of Life*. Stanford University Press. https://doi.org/10.1515/9781503607453.

CIA (Central Intelligence Agency). 2012. *The World Factbook 2012*. Washington, DC: Central Intelligence Agency. www.cia.gov/the-world-factbook/.

Cichowski, Rachel A. 2006. "Courts, Rights, and Democratic Participation." *Comparative Political Studies* 39 (1): 50–75. https://doi.org/10.1177/0010414005283217.

2007. *The European Court and Civil Society: Litigation, Mobilization and Governance*. Themes in European Governance. Cambridge: Cambridge University Press.

2016. "The European Court of Human Rights, Amicus Curiae, and Violence against Women." *Law & Society Review* 50 (4): 890–919. https://doi.org/10.1111/lasr.12236.

Cichowski, Rachel, and Elizabeth Chrun. 2017. "European Court of Human Rights Database (ECHRdb)." 1.0. http://depts.washington.edu/echrdb/.

Cizre-Sakallıoğlu, Ümit. 1992. "Labour and State in Turkey: 1960–80." *Middle Eastern Studies* 28 (4): 712–28. https://doi.org/10.1080/00263209208700926.

Clark, Jon, and Mark Hall. 1992. "The Cinderella Directive? Employee Rights to Information about Conditions Applicable to Their Contract or Employment Relationship." *Industrial Law Journal (London)* 21 (2): 106–18. https://doi.org/10.1093/ilj/21.2.106.

Clark, Jon, Roy Lewis, and Lord Wedderburn, eds. 1983. *Labour Law and Industrial Relations: Building on Kahn-Freund*. Oxford: Oxford University Press.

Clark, Jon, and Lord Wedderburn. 2012. "Juridification – a Universal Trend? The British Experience in Labor Law." In *Juridification – a Universal Trend? The British Experience in Labor Law*, 163–90. De Gruyter. https://doi.org/10.1515/9783110921472.163.

Coleman, Christopher, Laurence D. Nee, and Leonard S. Rubinowitz. 2007. "Social Movements and Social-Change Litigation: Synergy in the Montgomery Bus Protest." *Law & Social Inquiry* 30 (4): 663–737. https://doi.org/10.1111/j.1747-4469.2005.tb01143.x.

Collier, Ruth Berins, and David Collier. 2002. *Shaping the Political Arena: Critical Junctures, the Labor Movement, and Regime Dynamics in Latin America*. Notre Dame, IN: University of Notre Dame Press.

Colling, Trevor. 2006. "What Space for Unions on the Floor of Rights? Trade Unions and the Enforcement of Statutory Individual Employment Rights." *Industrial Law Journal* 35 (2): 140–60. https://doi.org/10.1093/indlaw/dwl011.

Collins, Hugh, Keith Ewing, and Aileen McColgan. 2012. *Labour Law. Law in Context*. Cambridge: Cambridge University Press.

Conant, Lisa. 2002. *Justice Contained: Law and Politics in the European Union*. Ithaca, NY: Cornell University Press.

— 2006. "Individuals, Courts, and the Development of European Social Rights." *Comparative Political Studies* 39 (1): 76–100. https://doi.org/10.1177/0010414005283218.

Conant, Lisa, Andreas Hofmann, Dagmar Soennecken, and Lisa Vanhala. 2017. "Mobilizing European Law." *Journal of European Public Policy* 25 (9): 1376–89. https://doi.org/10.1080/13501763.2017.1329846.

Cook, Linda J. 2010. "More Rights, Less Power: Labor Standards and Labor Markets in East European Post-Communist States." *Studies in Comparative International Development* 45 (2): 170–97. https://doi.org/10.1007/s12116-010-9065-9.

Corntassel, Jeff. 2007. "Towards a New Partnership? Indigenous Political Mobilization and Co-Optation During the First UN Indigenous Decade (1995-2004)." *Human Rights Quarterly* 29 (1): 137–66. https://doi.org/10.1353/hrq.2007.0005.

Cover, Robert. 1983. "The Supreme Court, 1982 Term – Foreword: Nomos and Narrative." *Harvard Law Review* 97 (1): 4–68.

Crouch, Colin. 1997. "The Terms of the Neo-Liberal Consensus." *The Political Quarterly (London. 1930)* 68 (4): 352–60. https://doi.org/10.1111/1467-923X.00103.

Dai, Xinyuan. 2007. *International Institutions and National Policies*. Cambridge: Cambridge University Press.

Danchin, Peter G. 2011. "Islam in the Secular Nomos of the European Court of Human Rights." *Michigan Journal of International Law* 32 (4): 663–720.

Dancy, Geoff. 2017. "Searching for Deterrence at the International Criminal Court." *International Criminal Law Review* 17 (4): 625–55. https://doi.org/10.1163/15718123-01704007.

Dancy, Geoff, and Verónica Michel. 2016. "Human Rights Enforcement From Below: Private Actors and Prosecutorial Momentum in Latin America and Europe." *International Studies Quarterly* 60 (1): 173–88. https://doi.org/10.1111/isqu.12209.

Dancy, Geoff, and Florencia Montal. 2017. "Unintended Positive Complementarity: Why International Criminal Court Investigations

May Increase Domestic Human Rights Prosecutions." *American Journal of International Law* 111 (3): 689–723. https://doi.org/10.1017/ajil.2017.70.

Dancy, Geoffrey, and Christopher Fariss. 2018. "The Heavens Are Always Fallen: A Neo-Conservative Approach to Human Rights in Global Society: The Future of Human Rights Scholarship." *Law and Contemporary Problems* 81 (4): 73–100.

Daniels, Gary, and John McIlroy. 2009. *Trade Unions in a Neoliberal World British Trade Unions under New Labour.* Routledge Research in Employment Relations. New York: Routledge.

Davenport, Christian. 2007. *State Repression and the Domestic Democratic Peace.* Cambridge Studies in Comparative Politics. Cambridge: Cambridge University Press.

2014. *How Social Movements Die: Repression and Demobilization of the Republic of New Africa.* Cambridge Studies in Contentious Politics. Cambridge: Cambridge University Press. https://doi.org/10.1017/CBO9781139649728.

Davies, A. C. L. 2008. "One Step Forward, Two Steps Back? The Viking and Laval Cases in the ECJ." *Industrial Law Journal (London)* 37 (2): 126–48. https://doi.org/10.1093/indlaw/dwn001.

Davies, Paul, and Mark Freedland. 2007. *Towards a Flexible Labour Market: Labour Legislation and Regulation since the 1990s.* Oxford Monographs on Labour Law. Oxford: Oxford University Press.

Deakin, Simon, Sarah Fraser Butlin, Colm McLaughlin, and Aleksandra Polanska. 2015. "Are Litigation and Collective Bargaining Complements or Substitutes for Achieving Gender Equality? A Study of the British Equal Pay Act." *Cambridge Journal of Economics* 39 (2): 381–403. https://doi.org/10.1093/cje/bev006.

Department for Business, Innovation and Skills. 2009. *The Blacklisting of Trade Unionists: Revised. Draft Regulations.* London: Department for Business, Innovation and Skills.

Diani, Mario. 2013. "Brokerage." In *The Wiley-Blackwell Encyclopedia of Social and Political Movements*, edited by Donatella Della Porta, Bert Klandermans, Doug McAdam, and David A. Snow, 1st ed. Hoboken, NJ: Wiley. https://doi.org/10.1002/9780470674871.wbespm017.

Dickens, Linda, and Mark Hall. 2010. "The Changing Framework of Employment Relations." In *Industrial Relations: Theory and Practice*, edited by Trevor Colling and Mike Terry, 69–96, 3rd ed. Chichester: John Wiley.

Dinas, Elias, and Ezequiel Gonzalez-Ocantos. 2021. "Defending the European Court of Human Rights: Experimental Evidence from Britain." *European Journal of Political Research* 60 (2): 397–417. https://doi.org/10.1111/1475-6765.12404.

DİSK-AR (Türkiye Devrimci İşçi Sendikaları Konfederasyonu Araştırma Dairesi). 2017. *Sendikalaşma ve Toplu İş Sözleşmesi Raporu (Ağustos 2017)*. Istanbul: DİSK-AR.

Disney, Richard, Amanda Gosling, and Stephen Machin. 1995. "British Unions in Decline: Determinants of the 1980s Fall in Union Recognition." *Industrial & Labor Relations Review* 48 (3): 403–19. https://doi.org/10.1177/001979399504800302.

Djupe, P. A., A. R. Lewis, T. G. Jelen, and C. D. Dahan. 2014. "Rights Talk: The Opinion Dynamics of Rights Framing." *Social Science Quarterly* 95 (3): 652–68.

Doğan, Mustafa G. 2010. "When Neoliberalism Confronts the Moral Economy of Workers: The Final Spring of Turkish Labor Unions." *European Journal of Turkish Studies* 11 (October). https://doi.org/10.4000/ejts.4321.

Donald, Alice, Debra Long, and Anne-Katrin Speck. 2020. "Identifying and Assessing the Implementation of Human Rights Decisions." *Journal of Human Rights Practice* 12 (1): 125–48. https://doi.org/10.1093/jhuman/huaa003.

Dorssemont, Filip, Klaus Lörcher, and Isabelle Schömann. 2013. *The European Convention on Human Rights and the Employment Relation*. 1st ed. Oxford: Hart. https://doi.org/10.5040/9781474200301.

Drooghenbroeck, Sébastien van. 2014. "Labour Law Litigation and Fair Trial Under Article 6 ECHR." In *The European Convention on Human Rights and the Employment Relation*, edited by Filip Dorssemont, Klaus Lörcher, and Isabelle Schömann, 159–82. Oxford: Hart.

Duffy, Helen. 2018. *Strategic Human Rights Litigation: Understanding and Maximising Impact*, 1st ed. Oxford: Hart. https://doi.org/10.5040/9781509922000.

Dukes, Ruth. 2011. "The Right to Strike under UK Law: Something More Than a Slogan?: NURMT v SERCO, ASLEF v London & Birmingham Railway Ltd." *Industrial Law Journal (London)* 40 (3): 302–11. https://doi.org/10.1093/indlaw/dwr012.

Dukes, Ruth, and Eleanor Kirk. 2024. "Legal Change and Legal Mobilisation: What Does Strategic Litigation Mean for Workers and Trade Unions?" *Social & Legal Studies* 33 (4): 479–500. https://doi.org/10.1177/09646639231204942.

Duranti, Marco. 2017. *The Conservative Human Rights Revolution: European Identity, Transnational Politics, and the Origins of the European Convention*. New York: Oxford University Press.

Dzehtsiarou, Kanstantsin. 2015. *European Consensus and the Legitimacy of the European Court of Human Rights*. Cambridge: Cambridge University Press.

Earl, Jennifer, and Jessica Maves Braithwaite. 2022. "Layers of Political Repression: Integrating Research on Social Movement Repression." *Annual Review of Law and Social Science* 18: 227–48.

Earl, Jennifer, and Sarah A. Soule. 2010. "The Impacts of Repression: The Effect of Police Presence and Action on Subsequent Protest Rates." In *Research in Social Movements, Conflicts and Change*, edited by Patrick G. Coy, 30:75–113. Leeds: Emerald Group. https://doi.org/10.1108/S0163-786X(2010)0000030006.

ECtHR. 2003. "Factsheet – Work-Related Rights." Council of Europe. Published June 12,; last updated March 2024. www.echr.coe.int/documents/d/echr/fs_work_eng?utm_source=chatgpt.com.

⸻ 2012. "Factsheet – Slavery, Servitude and Forced Labour." Council of Europe.. www.echr.coe.int/documents/d/echr/fs_forced_labour_eng?utm_source=chatgpt.com.

⸻ 2014. "Factsheet – Trade Union Rights." Council of Europe. www.echr.coe.int/documents/d/echr/fs_trade_union_eng?utm_source=chatgpt.com.

⸻ 2017. "Factsheet – Surveillance at Workplace." Council of Europe. www.echr.coe.int/documents/d/echr/FS_Workplace_surveillance_ENG?utm_source=chatgpt.com.

⸻ 2018. "Overview 1959–2017." www.echr.coe.int/documents/d/echr/Annual_report_2018_ENG. [no longer available]

⸻ 2021. "Annual Report 2020." Annual Reports. www.echr.coe.int/annual-reports.

⸻ 2022. "Overview 1959–2021." www.echr.coe.int/documents/d/echr/Overview_19592021_ENG.

⸻ 2023. "Annual Report 2022." Annual Reports. www.echr.coe.int/annual-reports.

⸻ 2025. Pending Applications 2025. *Statistics Monthly 2025*. www.echr.coe.int/documents/d/echr/stats-pending-month-2025-bil.

Eder, Mine. 2010. "Retreating State? Political Economy of Welfare Regime Change in Turkey." *Middle East Law and Governance* 2 (2): 152–84. https://doi.org/10.1163/187633710X500739.

Elver, Hilal. 2014. *The Headscarf Controversy: Secularism and Freedom of Religion*. Religion and Global Politics. Oxford: Oxford University Press.

Engel, David M., and Frank W. Munger. 2003. *Rights of Inclusion: Law and Identity in the Life Stories of Americans with Disabilities*. Chicago Series in Law and Society. Chicago: University of Chicago Press.

Engstrom, Par, ed. 2019. *The Inter-American Human Rights System: Impact Beyond Compliance*. Cham: Springer International Publishing. https://doi.org/10.1007/978-3-319-89459-1.

Engstrom, Par, and Peter Low. 2019. "Mobilising the Inter-American Human Rights System: Regional Litigation and Domestic Human Rights Impact in Latin America." In *The Inter-American Human Rights System: Impact

Beyond Compliance, edited by Par Engstrom, 23–58. Studies of the Americas. London: Palgrave Macmillan. https://doi.org/10.1007/978-3-319-89459-1_2.

Epp, Charles R. 1998. *The Rights Revolution: Lawyers, Activists, and Supreme Courts in Comparative Perspective*. Chicago: University of Chicago Press.

——— 2009. *Making Rights Real: Activists, Bureaucrats, and the Creation of the Legalistic State*. Chicago: University of Chicago Press.

Erken, Elif. 2021. "Non-Governmental Organisations and National Human Rights Institutions Monitoring the Execution of Strasbourg Judgments: An Empirical Perspective on Rule 9 Communications." *Human Rights Law Review* 21 (3): 724–51. https://doi.org/10.1093/hrlr/ngab007.

Eskridge, William N. 1991. "Reneging on History? Playing the Court/Congress/President Civil Rights Game." *California Law Review* 79 (3): 613. https://doi.org/10.2307/3480831.

Evans, Stephen, John Goodman, and Leslie Hargreaves. 1985. "Unfair Dismissal Law and Changes in the Role of Trade Unions and Employers' Associations." *Industrial Law Journal (London)* 14 (2): 91–108.

Ewing, K D. 1993. "Trade Union Derecognition and Personal Contracts: A Note on Recent Developments." *Industrial Law Journal* 22 (4): 297–303. https://doi.org/10.1093/ilj/22.4.297.

——— 2003. "The Implications of Wilson and Palmer." *Industrial Law Journal* 32 (1): 1–22.

——— 2009a. "Ruined Lives: Blacklisting in the Construction Industry. Union of Construction, Allied Trades and Technicians." Union of Construction, Allied Trades and Technicians. www.ier.org.uk/product/ruined-lives-blacklisting-construction-industry/.

——— 2009b. "Employment Act 2008: Implementing the ASLEF Decision–A Victory for the BNP?" *Industrial Law Journal (London)* 38 (1): 50–57. https://doi.org/10.1093/indlaw/dwn027.

——— 2011. "United Kingdom." In *The Right to Strike in the EU The Complexity of the Norms and Safeguarding Efficacy*, edited by Carmen La Macchia, 95–129. Rome: Ediesse.

——— 2021. "Contesting Austerity: The Role of Trade Unions in the UK." In *Contesting Austerity: A Socio-Legal Inquiry*, edited by Anusceh Farahat and Xabier Arzoz, 193–211. Oxford: Hart.

Ewing, K. D., and John Hendy. 2010. "The Dramatic Implications of Demir and Baykara." *Industrial Law Journal (London)* 39 (1): 2–51. https://doi.org/10.1093/indlaw/dwp031.

——— 2014. "International Litigation Possibilities in European Collective Labour Law: ECHR." In *The Economic and Financial Crisis and Collective Labour Law in Europe*, edited by Niklas Bruun, Isabelle Schömann, and Klaus Lörcher, 295–322. London: Bloomsbury. https://doi.org/10.5040/9781474201735.ch-011.

2016. "The Trade Union Act 2016 and the Failure of Human Rights." *Industrial Law Journal (London)* 45 (3): 391–422. https://doi.org/10.1093/indlaw/dww027.

Ewing, Keith D., John Hendy, and Carolyn Jones, eds. 2016. *A Manifesto for Labour Law: Towards a Comprehensive Revision of Workers' Rights*. London: Institute of Employment Rights.

Felstead, Alan, and Nick Jewson, eds. 1999. *Global Trends in Flexible Labour*. London: Macmillan Education UK. https://doi.org/10.1007/978-1-349-27396-6.

Finnemore, Martha. 1996. "Norms, Culture, and World Politics: Insights from Sociology's Institutionalism." *International Organization* 50 (2): 325–47. https://doi.org/10.1017/S0020818300028587.

Finnemore, Martha, and Kathryn Sikkink. 1998. "International Norm Dynamics and Political Change." *International Organization* 52 (4): 887–917. www.jstor.org/stable/2601361.

Flanagan, Robert J. 2006. *Globalization and Labor Conditions: Working Conditions and Worker Rights in a Global Economy*. New York: Oxford University Press.

Flanders, Allan D. 1974. "The Tradition of Voluntarism." *British Journal of Industrial Relations* 12 (3): 352–70. https://doi.org/10.1111/j.1467-8543.1974.tb00012.x.

Ford, Michael, and John Hendy. 2007 *ASLEF v. UK*. Liverpool: Institute of Employment Rights.

Fourcade-Gourinchas, Marion, and Sarah L. Babb. 2002. "The Rebirth of the Liberal Creed: Paths to Neoliberalism in Four Countries." *American Journal of Sociology* 108 (3): 533–79. https://doi.org/10.1086/367922.

Frege, Carola, and John Kelly. 2004. *Varieties of Unionism*. Oxford: Oxford University Press. https://doi.org/10.1093/acprof:oso/9780199270149.001.0001.

Fudge, Judy. 2015. "Constitutionalizing Labour Rights in Canada and Europe: Freedom of Association, Collective Bargaining, and Strikes." *Current Legal Problems* 68 (1): 267–305. https://doi.org/10.1093/clp/cuv003.

Galanter, Marc. 1974. "Why the 'Haves' Come Out Ahead: Speculations on the Limits of Legal Change." *Law & Society Review* 9 (1): 95–160.

——— 1983. "The Radiating Effects of Courts." In *Empirical Theories About Courts*, edited by Keith O. Boyum and Lynn Mather, 117–42. New York: Longman.

Gallagher, Janice K. 2022. *Bootstrap Justice: The Search for Mexico's Disappeared*. Oxford: Oxford University Press.

Gallagher, Janice K., Gabrielle Kruks-Wisner, and Whitney K. Taylor. 2024. *Claim-Making in Comparative Perspective: Everyday Citizenship Practice and Its Consequences*. 1st ed. Cambridge: Cambridge University Press. https://doi.org/10.1017/9781009028820.

Gearty, Conor. 2010. "Against Judicial Enforcement." In *Debating Social Rights*, edited by Virginia Mantouvalou and Conor Gearty, 1–82. London: Bloomsbury.

Gentile, Antonina, and Sidney Tarrow. 2009. "Charles Tilly, Globalization, and Labor's Citizen Rights." *European Political Science Review* 1 (3): 465–93. https://doi.org/10.1017/S175577390999018X.

Gill, Stephen. 1995. "Globalisation, Market Civilisation, and Disciplinary Neoliberalism." *Millennium: Journal of International Studies* 24 (3): 399–423. https://doi.org/10.1177/03058298950240030801.

Ginsburg, Tom. 2006. *Judicial Review in New Democracies: Constitutional Courts in Asian Cases*. Digital printing [der Ausg.] 2003. Cambridge: Cambridge University Press.

Glas, Lize R. 2020. "From Interlaken to Copenhagen: What Has Become of the Proposals Aiming to Reform the Functioning of the European Court of Human Rights?" *Human Rights Law Review* 20 (1): 121–51. https://doi.org/10.1093/hrlr/ngaa001.

Glasius, Marlies. 2018. "What Authoritarianism Is . . . and Is Not: A Practice Perspective." *International Affairs* 94 (3): 515–33. https://doi.org/10.1093/ia/iiy060.

Glendon, Mary Ann. 1991. *Rights Talk: The Impoverishment of Political Discourse*. New York: Free Press.

Goffman, Erving. 2007. *The Presentation of Self in Everyday Life*. Repr. London: Penguin Books.

Gomez-Mera, Laura, and Andrea Molinari. 2014. "Overlapping Institutions, Learning, and Dispute Initiation in Regional Trade Agreements: Evidence from South America." *International Studies Quarterly* 58 (2): 269–81. https://doi.org/10.1111/isqu.12135.

González-Ocantos, Ezequiel A. 2016. *Shifting Legal Visions: Judicial Change and Human Rights Trials in Latin America*. 1st ed. Cambridge: Cambridge University Press. https://doi.org/10.1017/CBO9781316535509.

Goodman, Ryan, and Derek Jinks. 2008. "Incomplete Internalization and Compliance with Human Rights Law." *European Journal of International Law* 19 (4): 725–48. https://doi.org/10.1093/ejil/chn039.

⸺. 2013. *Socializing States: Promoting Human Rights through International Law*. Oxford: Oxford University Press.

Graber, Mark A. 1993. "The Nonmajoritarian Difficulty: Legislative Deference to the Judiciary." *Studies in American Political Development* 7 (1): 35–73. https://doi.org/10.1017/S0898588X00000687.

Greenhill, Brian, Layna Mosley, and Aseem Prakash. 2009. "Trade-Based Diffusion of Labor Rights: A Panel Study, 1986–2002." *American Political Science Review* 103 (4): 669–90. https://doi.org/10.1017/S0003055409990116.

Grewal, Sharanbir, and Erik Voeten. 2015. "Are New Democracies Better Human Rights Compliers?" *International Organization* 69 (2): 497–518. https://doi.org/10.1017/S0020818314000435.

Guillaume, C. 2015. "Understanding the Variations of Unions' Litigation Strategies to Promote Equal Pay: Reflection on the British Case." *Cambridge Journal of Economics* 39 (2): 363–79. https://doi.org/10.1093/cje/bev004.

Gülmez, Mesut. 1988. *Sendikal hakların uluslararası kuralları ve Türkiye: (UÇÖ/ILO sözleşme ve ilkeleri)*. Ankara: Türkiye ve Orta Doğu Amme İdaresi Enstitüsü yayınları.

———. 1992. "Hükümet Programında Sendikal Haklar ve Memur Sendikacılığı." *Amme İdaresi Dergisi* 25 (1): 3–26.

———. 2002. *Kamu Görevlileri Sendika ve Toplu Görüşme Hukuku: 788'den 4688'e: 1926-2001*. Türkiye ve Orta Doğu Amme İdaresi Enstitüsü, yayın no. 309. Ankara: Türkiye ve Orta Doğu Amme İdaresi Enstitüsü.

———. 2013. "1924'ten 1982'ye Anayasal Sendikal Haklar ve Ulusalüstü Kurallarla Uyumlu 'Yeni' Anayasa İçin Öneriler." *Sosyal Haklar Uluslararası Sempozyumu* V: 67–98.

———. 2014. "Toplu eylem hakkına dahil protesto eylemi yasa dışı grev değildir yargıtay 7. hukuk dairesi karar eleştirisi." *Çalışma ve Toplum* 43 (4): 244–62.

Gürcan, Efe Can, and Berk Mete. 2017. *Neoliberalism and the Changing Face of Unionism: The Combined and Uneven Development of Class Capacities in Turkey*. Cham: Springer.

Haddad, Heidi Nichols. 2018. *The Hidden Hands of Justice: NGOs, Human Rights, and International Courts*. Cambridge: Cambridge University Press.

Hafner-Burton, Emilie. 2009. *Forced to Be Good: Why Trade Agreements Boost Human Rights*. Ithaca, NY: Cornell University Press. https://doi.org/10.7591/9780801458705.

———. 2013. *Making Human Rights a Reality*. Princeton, NJ: Princeton University Press.

Hafner-Burton, Emilie M., and Kiyoteru Tsutsui. 2005. "Human Rights in a Globalizing World: The Paradox of Empty Promises." *American Journal of Sociology* 110 (5): 1373–1411. https://doi.org/10.1086/428442.

———. 2007. "Justice Lost! The Failure of International Human Rights Law to Matter Where Needed Most." *Journal of Peace Research* 44 (4): 407–25. https://doi.org/10.1177/0022343307078942.

Hafner-Burton, Emilie M., David G. Victor, and Yonatan Lupu. 2012. "Political Science Research on International Law: The State of the Field." *American Journal of International Law* 106 (1): 47–97.

Haglund, Jillienne. 2020. *Regional Courts, Domestic Politics, and the Struggle for Human Rights*. 1st ed. Cambridge: Cambridge University Press. https://doi.org/10.1017/9781108776561.

Hall, Peter, and David Soskice. 2001. *Varieties of Capitalism: The Institutional Foundations of Comparative Advantage*. Oxford: Oxford University Press. https://doi.org/10.1093/0199247757.001.0001.

Hall, Stuart. 2005. "New Labour's Double-Shuffle." *Review of Education, Pedagogy, and Cultural Studies* 27 (4): 319–35. https://doi.org/10.1080/10714410500338907.

Hamann, Kerstin, and John Kelly. 2004. "Unions as Political Actors: A Recipe for Revitalization?" In *Varieties of Unionism: Strategies for Union Revitalization in a Globalizing Economy*, edited by Carola Frege and John Kelly, 31–44. Oxford: Oxford University Press.

Hansen, Randall. 2023. *War, Work, and Want: How the OPEC Oil Crisis Caused Mass Migration and Revolution*. New York: Oxford University Press.

Hardy, Jane, Line Eldring, and Thorsten Schulten. 2012. "Trade Union Responses to Migrant Workers from the 'New Europe': A Three Sector Comparison in the UK, Norway and Germany." *European Journal of Industrial Relations* 18 (4): 347–63. https://doi.org/10.1177/0959680112461464.

Harlow, Carol, and Richard Rawlings. 1992. *Pressure Through Law*. Abingdon: Routledge.

Harvey, David. 2005. *A Brief History of Neoliberalism*. Oxford: Oxford University Press.

Hassel, Anke. 1999. "The Erosion of the German System of Industrial Relations." *British Journal of Industrial Relations* 37 (3): 483–505. https://doi.org/10.1111/1467-8543.00138.

Hathaway, Oona A. 2002. "Do Human Rights Treaties Make a Difference?" *The Yale Law Journal* 111 (8): 1935–2042. https://doi.org/10.2307/797642.

Hawkins, Darren, and Wade Jacoby. 2010. "Partial Compliance: A Comparison of the European and Inter-American Courts of Human Rights Engagement and Escape: International Legal Institutions and Public Political Contestation." *Journal of International Law and International Relations* 6 (1): 35–86.

Health and Safety Watch/Turkey. 2024. *İş Cinayetleri Raporları (Workplace Homicide Reports*. Istanbul: İşçi Sağlığı ve İş Güvenliği Meclisi. https://www.isigmeclisi.org/is-cinayetleri-raporlari

Helfer, Laurence R. 1999. "Forum Shopping for Human Rights." *University of Pennsylvania Law Review* 148 (2): 285–400.

2008. "Redesigning the European Court of Human Rights: Embeddedness as a Deep Structural Principle of the European Human Rights Regime." *European Journal of International Law* 19 (1): 125–59. https://doi.org/10.1093/ejil/chn004.

Helfer, Laurence R., and Anne-Marie Slaughter. 1997. "Toward a Theory of Effective Supranational Adjudication." *The Yale Law Journal* 107 (2): 273–391. https://doi.org/10.2307/797259.

Helfer, Laurence R., and Erik Voeten. 2014. "International Courts as Agents of Legal Change: Evidence from LGBT Rights in Europe." *International Organization* 68 (1): 77–110. https://doi.org/10.1017/S0020818313000398.

———. 2020. "Walking Back Human Rights in Europe?" *European Journal of International Law* 31 (3): 797–827. https://doi.org/10.1093/ejil/chaa071.

Hendickx, Frank, and Aline van Bever. 2014. "Article 8 ECHR: Judicial Patterns of Employment Privacy Protection." In *The European Convention on Human Rights and the Employment Relation*, edited by Filip Dorssemont, Klaus Lörcher, and Isabelle Schömann, 183–208. Oxford: Hart.

Hendrix, Cullen S., and Wendy H. Wong. 2013. "When Is the Pen Truly Mighty? Regime Type and the Efficacy of Naming and Shaming in Curbing Human Rights Abuses." *British Journal of Political Science* 43 (3): 651–72. https://doi.org/10.1017/S0007123412000488.

Hendy, John, and K. D. Ewing. 2005. "Trade Unions, Human Rights and the BNP." *Industrial Law Journal (London)* 34 (3): 197–216. https://doi.org/10.1093/indlaw/dwi015.

Herzfeld Olsson, Petra. 2013. "Every Natural or Legal Person Is Entitled to the Peaceful Enjoyment of His or Her Possessions: Article 1, Protocol 1 to the European Convention on Human Rights." In *The European Convention on Human Rights and the Employment Relation*, edited by Klaus Lörcher, Isabelle Schömann, and F. Dorssemont, 381–414. Oxford: Hart.

Hilbink, Lisa. 2009. "The Constituted Nature of Constituents' Interests: Historical and Ideational Factors in Judicial Empowerment." *Political Research Quarterly* 62 (4): 781–97. https://doi.org/10.1177/1065912909349628.

Hilbink, Thomas. 2006. "The Profession, the Grassroots and the Elite: Cause Lawyering for Civil Rights and Freedom in the Direct Action Era." In *Cause Lawyers and Social Movements*, edited by Austin Sarat and Stuart A. Scheingold, 60–83. Stanford, CA: Stanford University Press.

Hill, Daniel W. 2010. "Estimating the Effects of Human Rights Treaties on State Behavior." *Journal of Politics* 72 (4): 1161–74. https://doi.org/10.1017/S0022381610000599.

Hillebrecht, Courtney. 2014. *Domestic Politics and International Human Rights Tribunals: The Problem of Compliance*. Cambridge Studies in International and Comparative Law. New York: Cambridge University Press.

———. 2016. "The Deterrent Effects of the International Criminal Court: Evidence from Libya." *International Interactions* 42 (4): 616–43. https://doi.org/10.1080/03050629.2016.1185713.

———. 2021. *Saving the International Justice Regime: Beyond Backlash against International Courts*. Cambridge: Cambridge University Press. https://doi.org/10.1017/9781009052610.

Hilson, Chris. 2002. "New Social Movements: The Role of Legal Opportunity." *Journal of European Public Policy* 9 (2): 238–55. https://doi.org/10.1080/13501760110120246.

Hirschl, Ran. 2004. "The Political Origins of the New Constitutionalism." *Indiana Journal of Global Legal Studies* 11 (1): 71–108. https://doi.org/10.2979/gls.2004.11.1.71.

———. 2008. "The Judicialization of Mega-Politics and the Rise of Political Courts." *Annual Review of Political Science* 11 (1): 93–118. https://doi.org/10.1146/annurev.polisci.11.053006.183906.

Hodson, Loveday C. 2014. "Activists and Lawyers in the ECtHR: The Struggle for Gay Rights." In *Rights and Courts in Pursuit of Social Change: Legal Mobilisation in the Multi-Level European System*, edited by Dia Anagnostou, 181–204. Oxford: Hart.

Hofmann, Andreas, and Daniel Naurin. 2021. "Explaining Interest Group Litigation in Europe: Evidence from the Comparative Interest Group Survey." *Governance* 34 (4): 1235–53. https://doi.org/10.1111/gove.12556.

Holzhacker, Ronald. 2013. "State-Sponsored Homophobia and the Denial of the Right of Assembly in Central and Eastern Europe: The 'Boomerang' and the 'Ricochet' between European Organizations and Civil Society to Uphold Human Rights." *Law & Policy* 35 (1-2): 1–28. https://doi.org/10.1111/j.1467-9930.2012.00371.x.

Hopgood, Stephen. 2015. *The Endtimes of Human Rights*. Ithaca, NY: Cornell University Press.

House of Commons Scottish Affairs Committee. 2014. *Blacklisting in Employment: Interim Report. Ninth Report of Session 2012-13*, HC 1071. London: The Stationery Office.

Howell, Chris. 1996. "Women as the Paradigmatic Trade Unionists? New Work, New Workers and New Trade Union Strategies in Conservative Britain." *Economic and Industrial Democracy* 17 (4): 511–43. https://doi.org/10.1177/0143831X96174002.

———. 2009. "The Transformation of French Industrial Relations: Labor Representation and the State in a Post-Dirigiste Era." *Politics & Society* 37 (2): 229–56.

Human Rights Watch. 2004. *Last Chance for Turkey's Displaced?* Human Rights Watch Briefing Paper. www.hrw.org/legacy/backgrounder/eca/turkey/2004/10/index.htm.

Hunt, Alan. 1990. "Rights and Social Movements: Counter-Hegemonic Strategies." *Journal of Law and Society* 17 (3): 309–28. https://doi.org/10.2307/1410156.

Hyman, Richard. 1988. *The Political Economy of Industrial Relations: Theory and Practice in a Cold Climate*. Basingstoke: Macmillan.

Ibsen, Christian Lyhne, and Maite Tapia. 2017. "Trade Union Revitalisation: Where Are We Now? Where to Next?" *Journal of Industrial Relations* 59 (2): 170–91. https://doi.org/10.1177/0022185616677558.

ILO. 2020. *International Labour Standards on Occupational Safety and Health.* Washington, DC: International Labor Organization. www.ilo.org/global/standards/subjects-covered-by-international-labour-standards/occupational-safety-and-health/lang–en/index.htm.

IMF. 2024. *World Economic Outlook Database.* Washington, DC: International Monetary Fund. www.imf.org/en/Publications/WEO/weo-database/2024/October.

Işıklı, Alpaslan. 1986. *2821 Sayılı Sendikalar Kanunu İle 2822 Sayılı Toplu İş Sözleşmesi Grev ve Lokavt Kanununun Uluslararası Normlara Aykırılığı.* Publication No. 1986/11. Ankara: Yol-İş Sendikası.

ITUC. 2014. *Global Rights Index.* Brussels, Belgium: International Trade Union Confederation. www.ituc-csi.org/ituc-global-rights-index-2014.

——— 2022. *Global Rights Index.* Brussels, Belgium: International Trade Union Confederation. www.ituc-csi.org/ituc-global-rights-index-2022.

Jacquot, Sophie, and Tommaso Vitale. 2014. "Law as Weapon of the Weak? A Comparative Analysis of Legal Mobilization by Roma and Women's Groups at the European Level." *Journal of European Public Policy* 21 (4): 587–604. https://doi.org/10.1080/13501763.2014.887138.

Jay, Zoë. 2022. "A Tale of Two Europes: How Conflating the European Court of Human Rights with the European Union Exacerbates Euroscepticism." *British Journal of Politics and International Relations* 24 (4): 563–81.

Jeffries, Judson L. 2002. "Black Radicalism and Political Repression in Baltimore: The Case of the Black Panther Party." *Ethnic and Racial Studies* 25 (1): 64–98.

Jerolmack, Colin, and Shamus Khan. 2014. "Talk Is Cheap: Ethnography and the Attitudinal Fallacy." *Sociological Methods & Research* 43 (2): 178–209. https://doi.org/10.1177/0049124114523396.

Jo, Hyeran, and Beth A. Simmons. 2016. "Can the International Criminal Court Deter Atrocity?" *International Organization* 70 (3): 443–75. https://doi.org/10.1017/S0020818316000114.

Johnson, Krista. 2006. "Framing AIDS Mobilization and Human Rights in Post-Apartheid South Africa." *Perspectives on Politics* 4 (04). https://doi.org/10.1017/S1537592706060415.

Joint Committee on Human Rights. 2004. *Scrutiny of Bills: Sixth Progress Report. Thirteenth Report of Session 2003–04.* London: The Stationery Office. https://publications.parliament.uk/pa/jt200304/jtselect/jtrights/102/102.pdf?utm_source=chatgpt.com.

Joppke, Christian. 2013. "Double Standards? Veils and Crucifixes in the European Legal Order." *European Journal of Sociology* 54 (1): 97–123. https://doi.org/10.1017/S0003975613000040.

Kadivar, Mohammad Ali. 2018. "Mass Mobilization and the Durability of New Democracies." *American Sociological Review* 83 (2): 390–417. https://doi.org/10.1177/0003122418759546.

Kahn-Freund, Otto. 1972. *Labour and the Law*. 24th Hamlyn Lectures. London: Stevens for the Hamlyn Trust.

Kahraman, Filiz. 2018. "A New Era for Labor Activism? Strategic Mobilization of Human Rights Against Blacklisting." *Law & Social Inquiry* 43 (4): 1279–1307. https://doi.org/10.1111/lsi.12299.

——— 2023. "What Makes an International Institution Work for Labor Activists? Shaping International Law through Strategic Litigation." *Law & Society Review* 57 (1): 61–82. https://doi.org/10.1111/lasr.12643.

——— 2025. Strasbourg Labor Rights Database (StrasLab), Version 1.0.

——— 2026. "Instrumentalizing Human Rights: The On-Stage and Off-Stage of the Blacklisted Workers' Movement." *Perspectives on Politics*. Forthcoming.

Kang, Susan L. 2012. *Human Rights and Labor Solidarity: Trade Unions in the Global Economy*. Pennsylvania Studies in Human Rights. 1st ed. Philadelphia: University of Pennsylvania Press.

Keck, Margaret E., and Kathryn Sikkink. 1998. *Activists beyond Borders: Advocacy Networks in International Politics*. Ithaca, NY: Cornell University Press.

Keil, Roger. 2009. "The Urban Politics of Roll-with-It Neoliberalization." *City: Analysis of Urban Change, Theory, Action* 13 (2-3): 230–45. https://doi.org/10.1080/13604810902986848.

Keith, Linda Camp. 2002. "Constitutional Provisions for Individual Human Rights (1977-1996): Are They More Than Mere 'Window Dressing?'" *Political Research Quarterly* 55 (1): 111–43. https://doi.org/10.2307/3088068.

Kelemen, R. Daniel. 2011. *Eurolegalism: The Transformation of Law and Regulation in the European Union*. Cambridge, MA: Harvard University Press. https://doi.org/10.4159/harvard.9780674061057.

——— 2016. "The Court of Justice of the European Union in the Twenty-First Century." *Law and Contemporary Problems* 79 (1): 117–40.

Kelly, John E. 1998. *Rethinking Industrial Relations: Mobilization, Collectivism and Long Waves*. Routledge Studies in Employment Relations. London: Routledge. https://doi.org/10.4324/9780203213940.

Kent, Avidan, Nikos Skoutaris, and Jamie Trinidad, eds. 2019. *The Future of International Courts: Regional, Institutional and Procedural Challenges*. Routledge Research in International Law. 1st ed. Abingdon: Routledge. https://doi.org/10.4324/9780429463280.

Keohane, Robert O., Andrew Moravcsik, and Anne-Marie Slaughter. 2000. "Legalized Dispute Resolution: Interstate and Transnational." *International Organization* 54 (3): 457–88. https://doi.org/10.1162/002081800551299.

Keyder, Çağlar. 2005. "Globalization and Social Exclusion in Istanbul." *International Journal of Urban and Regional Research* 29 (1): 124–34. https://doi.org/10.1111/j.1468-2427.2005.00574.x.

Kim, Wonik, and Jennifer Gandhi. 2010. "Coopting Workers under Dictatorship." *The Journal of Politics* 72 (3): 646–58. https://doi.org/10.1017/S0022381610000071.

Kinderman, Daniel. 2005. "Pressure from Without, Subversion from Within: The Two-Pronged German Employer Offensive." *Comparative European Politics* 3 (4): 432–63. https://doi.org/10.1057/palgrave.cep.6110064.

King, Desmond, and Stewart Wood. 1999. "The Political Economy of Neoliberalism: Britain and the United States in the 1980s." In *Continuity and Change in Contemporary Capitalism*, edited by Herbert Kitschelt, Peter Lange, Gary Marks, and John D. Stephens, 371–97. Cambridge: Cambridge University Press.

Koç, Canan, and Yıldırım Koç. 2009. *Kesk tarihi*. Epos yayınları 53, 61. Maltepe-Ankara: Epos.

Koç, Yıldırım. 2013. "KESK: Nereden Nereye?" *Teori* 286: 3–16.

Kochenov, Dimitry. 2008. *EU Enlargement and the Failure of Conditionality: Pre-Accession Conditionality in the Fields of Democracy and the Rule of Law*. European Monographs 59. Alphen aan den Rijn: Kluwer Law International.

Koenig, Matthias. 2015. "Governance of Religious Diversity at the European Court of Human Rights." In *International Approaches to Governing Ethnic Diversity*, edited by Jane Boulden, Will Kymlicka, Jane Boulden, and Will Kymlicka, 51–78. Oxford: Oxford University Press.

Koh, Harold Hongju. 2005. "Internalization through Socialization." *Duke Law Journal* 54 (4): 975–82.

Koopmans, Ruud. 1993. "The Dynamics of Protest Waves: West Germany, 1965 to 1989." *American Sociological Review* 58 (5): 637–58. https://doi.org/10.2307/2096279.

Krieger, Joel. 1983. *Undermining Capitalism: State Ownership and the Dialectic of Control in the British Coal Industry*. Princeton, NJ: Princeton University Press.

Kriesi, Hanspeter, Ruud Koopmans, Jan Willem Duyvendak, and Marco G. Giugni. 1995. *New Social Movements in Western Europe: A Comparative Analysis*. New ed. Vol. 5. Minneapolis: University of Minnesota Press.

Küçüksu, Aysel. 2022. "Enforcing Rights Beyond Litigation: Mapping NGO Strategies in Monitoring ECtHR Judgement Implementation." *Human Rights Law Review* 22 (2). https://doi.org/10.1093/hrlr/ngac013.

Kurban, Dilek. 2020. *Limits of Supranational Justice: The European Court of Human Rights and Turkey's Kurdish Conflict*. Cambridge: Cambridge University Press.

Kurban, Dilek, Deniz Yükseker, and Ayşe Betül Çelik. 2006. "Overcoming a Legacy of Mistrust: Towards Reconciliation between the State and the Displaced." https://doi.org/10.13140/rg.2.1.1774.6002.

REFERENCES

Kutal, Metin. 2015. "'Sendikalar ve Toplu İş Sözleşmesi' Yasasının Kimi Hükümlerinin İptali İstemi ile Anayasa Mahkemesine Açılan Davaya İlişkin Notlar." *Çalışma ve Toplum* 1 (44): 13–28.

Lake, Milli. 2018. *Strong NGOs and Weak States: Pursuing Gender Justice in the Democratic Republic of Congo and South Africa*. Cambridge: Cambridge University Press. https://doi.org/10.1017/9781108297745.

Lamont, Michèle, and Ann Swidler. 2014. "Methodological Pluralism and the Possibilities and Limits of Interviewing." *Qualitative Sociology* 37 (2): 153–71. https://doi.org/10.1007/s11133-014-9274-z.

Larsson, Olof, Daniel Naurin, Mattias Derlén, and Johan Lindholm. 2017. "Speaking Law to Power: The Strategic Use of Precedent of the Court of Justice of the European Union." *Comparative Political Studies* 50 (7): 879–907. https://doi.org/10.1177/0010414016639709.

Levitt, Peggy, and Sally Merry. 2009. "Vernacularization on the Ground: Local Uses of Global Women's Rights in Peru, China, India and the United States." *Global Networks* 9 (4): 441–61. https://doi.org/10.1111/j.1471-0374.2009.00263.x.

Louis, Julien. 2022. "The Judicialisation of European Trade Union Confederation Action: From the Viking and Laval Cases to Defending Fundamental Social Right." *European Trade Union Institute*. https://doi.org/10.2139/ssrn.4243469.

Lovell, George I. 2012. *This Is Not Civil Rights: Discovering Rights Talk in 1939 America*. Chicago: University of Chicago Press.

Lovell, George I., M. McCann, and K. Taylor. 2016. "Covering Legal Mobilization: A Bottom-Up Analysis of Wards Cove v. Atonio." *Law & Society Inquiry* 41 (1): 61–99. https://doi.org/10.1111/lsi.12143.

Lubow, Alexis, and Susanne K. Schmidt. 2021. "A Hidden Champion? The European Court of Justice as an Agenda-setter in the Case of Posted Workers." *Public Administration (London)* 99 (2): 321–34. https://doi.org/10.1111/padm.12643.

Madlingozi, Tshepo. 2013. "Post-Apartheid Social Movementsand Legal Mobilisation." In *Socio-Economic Rights in South Africa: Symbols or Substance?*, edited by Ben Cousins, Jackie Dugard, Malcolm Langford, and Tshepo Madlingozi, 92–130. Cambridge: Cambridge University Press. https://doi.org/10.1017/CBO9781139108591.006.

Madsen, Mikael Rask. 2004. "France, the United Kingdom and the 'Boomerang' of the Internationalization of Human Rights." In *Human Rights Brought Home: Socio-Legal Perspectives of Human Rights in the National Context*, edited by Simon Halliday and Patrick Schmidt, 57–86. London: Bloomsbury.

    2007. "From Cold War Instrument to Supreme European Court: The European Court of Human Rights at the Crossroads of International and National Law and Politics: The European Court of Human

REFERENCES

Rights." *Law & Social Inquiry* 32 (1): 137–59. https://doi.org/10.1111/j.1747-4469.2007.00053.x.

———. 2016. "The Challenging Authority of the European Court of Human Rights: From Cold War Legal Diplomacy to the Brighton Declaration and Backlash." *Law and Contemporary Problems* 79 (1): 141–78.

———. 2018. "Rebalancing European Human Rights: Has the Brighton Declaration Engendered a New Deal on Human Rights in Europe?" *Journal of International Dispute Settlement* 9 (2): 199–222. https://doi.org/10.1093/jnlids/idx016.

———. 2021. "The Narrowing of the European Court of Human Rights? Legal Diplomacy, Situational Self-Restraint, and the New Vision for the Court." *European Convention on Human Rights Law Review* 2 (2): 180–208.

Madsen, Mikael Rask, Pola Cebulak, and Micha Wiebusch. 2018. "Backlash against International Courts: Explaining the Forms and Patterns of Resistance to International Courts." *International Journal of Law in Context* 14 (2): 197–220. https://doi.org/10.1017/S1744552318000034.

Madsen, Mikael Rask, Juan A.Mayoral, AntonStrezhnev, and Erik Voeten. 2022. "Sovereignty, Substance, and Public Support for European Courts' Human Rights Rulings." *American Political Science Review* 116 (2): 419–38. https://doi.org/10.1017/S0003055421001143.

Mantouvalou, Virginia. 2006. "Servitude and Forced Labour in the 21st Century: The Human Rights of Domestic Workers." *Industrial Law Journal (London)* 35 (4): 395–414. https://doi.org/10.1093/indlaw/dwl029.

———. 2013. "Labour Rights in the European Convention on Human Rights: An Intellectual Justification for an Integrated Approach to Interpretation." *Human Rights Law Review* 13 (3): 529–55. https://doi.org/10.1093/hrlr/ngt001.

Marks, Susan. 2011. "Human Rights and Root Causes." *Modern Law Review* 74 (1): 57–78. https://doi.org/10.1111/j.1468-2230.2010.00836.x.

Matsuda, Mari J. 1987. "Looking to the Bottom: Critical Legal Studies and Reparations Minority Critiques of the Critical Legal Studies Movement." *Harvard Civil Rights-Civil Liberties Law Review* 22 (2): 323–400.

Mayo-Adam, Erin. 2020. *Queer Alliances: How Power Shapes Political Movement Formation*. Stanford, CA: Stanford University Press.

McAdam, Doug. 1983. "Tactical Innovation and the Pace of Insurgency." *American Sociological Review* 48 (6): 735. https://doi.org/10.2307/2095322.

———. 1996. "Conceptual Origins, Current Problems, Future Direction." In *Comparative Perspectives on Social Movements*, edited by Doug McAdam, John D. McCarthy, and Mayer N. Zald, 1st ed., 23–40. Cambridge: Cambridge University Press.

———. 1999. *Political Process and the Development of Black Insurgency, 1930-1970.* 2nd ed. Chicago: University of Chicago Press.
McAdam, Doug, Sidney Tarrow, and Charles Tilly. 2001. *Dynamics of Contention.* New York: Cambridge University Press.
McCammon, Holly J. 2012. *The U.S. Women's Jury Movements and Strategic Adaptation: A More Just Verdict.* New York: Cambridge University Press.
McCann, Michael W. 1994. *Rights at Work: Pay Equity Reform and the Politics of Legal Mobilization.* Chicago: University of Chicago Press.
———. 2006. "Law and Social Movements: Contemporary Perspectives." *Annual Review of Law and Social Science* 2 (1): 17–38. https://doi.org/10.1146/annurev.lawsocsci.2.081805.105917.
———. 2014. "The Unbearable Lightness of Rights: On Sociolegal Inquiry in the Global Era." *Law & Society Review* 48 (2): 245–73.
McCann, Michael W., and Filiz Kahraman. 2021. "On the Interdependence of Liberal and Illiberal/Authoritarian Legal Forms in Racial Capitalist Regimes... The Case of the United States." *Annual Review of Law and Social Science* 17 (1): 483–503. https://doi.org/10.1146/annurev-lawsocsci-111720-012237.
McCann, Michael W., and George Lovell. 2020. *Union by Law: Filipino American Labor Activists, Rights Radicalism, and Racial Capitalism.* Chicago Series in Law and Society. Chicago: University of Chicago Press.
McCann, Michael W., and Terry Lovell. 2005. "Conversations with Critical Legal Studies." In *The Politics of Method in the Human Sciences: Positivism and Its Epistemological Others*, edited by George Steinmetz, 253–72. Durham, NC: Duke University Press.
McCann, Michael W., and Helena Silverstein. 1998. "Rethinking Law's 'Allurements': A Relational Analysis of Social Movement Lawyers in the United States." In *Cause Lawyering: Political Commitments and Professional Responsibilities*, edited by Austin Sarat and Stuart Scheingold, 261–92. Oxford: Oxford University Press. https://doi.org/10.1093/oso/9780195113198.003.0009.
McCarthy, William Edward John. 1992. *Legal Intervention in Industrial Relations: Gains and Losses.* Oxford: Blackwell.
McCartin, Joseph A. 2005. "Democratizing the Demand for Workers' Rights: Toward a Re-Framing of Labor's Argument." *Dissent* 52 (1): 61–71. https://doi.org/10.1353/dss.2005.0010.
Mehta, Kalika. 2024. *Strategic Litigation and Corporate Complicity in Crimes under International Criminal Law: A TWAIL Analysis.* Abingdon: Routledge.
Meierhenrich, Jens. 2008. *The Legacies of Law: Long-Run Consequences of Legal Development in South Africa, 1652–2000.* Cambridge: Cambridge University Press.

REFERENCES

Merry, Sally Engle. 2006. "Transnational Human Rights and Local Activism: Mapping the Middle." *American Anthropologist* 108 (1): 38–51. https://doi.org/10.1525/aa.2006.108.1.38.

———. 2016. *The Seductions of Quantification: Measuring Human Rights, Gender Violence, and Sex Trafficking*. Chicago Series in Law and Society. Chicago: University of Chicago Press.

Merry, Sally Engle, and Rachel E. Stern. 2005. "The Female Inheritance Movement in Hong Kong: Theorizing the Local/Global Interface." *Current Anthropology* 46 (3): 387–409. https://doi.org/10.1086/428800.

Merry, Sally Engle, Peggy Levitt, Mihaela Şerban Rosen, and Diana H. Yoon. 2010. "Law from Below: Women's Human Rights and Social Movements in New York City: Women's Human Rights and Social Movements." *Law & Society Review* 44 (1): 101–28. https://doi.org/10.1111/j.1540-5893.2010.00397.x.

Meyer, John W., John Boli, George M. Thomas, and Francisco O. Ramirez. 1997. "World Society and the Nation-State." *American Journal of Sociology* 103 (1): 144–81. https://doi.org/10.1086/231174.

Mitchell, Timothy. 1991. "The Limits of the State: Beyond Statist Approaches and Their Critics." *American Political Science Review* 85 (1): 77–96. https://doi.org/10.2307/1962879.

Moravcsik, Andrew. 2000. "The Origins of Human Rights Regimes: Democratic Delegation in Postwar Europe." *International Organization* 54 (2): 217–52. https://doi.org/10.1162/002081800551163.

Moustafa, Tamir. 2018. *Constituting Religion: Islam, Liberal Rights, and the Malaysian State*. 1st ed. Cambridge: Cambridge University Press. https://doi.org/10.1017/9781108539296.

Moyn, Samuel. 2012. *The Last Utopia: Human Rights in History*. Cambridge, MA: Belknap Press of Harvard University Press.

———. 2018. *Not Enough: Human Rights in an Unequal World*. Cambridge, MA: Harvard University Press. https://doi.org/10.4159/9780674984806.

Muller, Edward N., and Erich Weede. 1990. "Cross-National Variation in Political Violence: A Rational Action Approach." *Journal of Conflict Resolution* 34 (4): 624–51. https://doi.org/10.1177/0022002790034004003.

Murillo, M. Victoria, and Andrew Schrank. 2005. "With a Little Help from My Friends: Partisan Politics, Transnational Alliances, and Labor Rights in Latin America." *Comparative Political Studies* 38 (8): 971–99. https://doi.org/10.1177/0010414004274402.

NeJaime, Douglas. 2010. "Winning through Losing." *Iowa Law Review* 96 (3): 941–1012.

Neumayer, Eric. 2005. "Do International Human Rights Treaties Improve Respect for Human Rights?" *Journal of Conflict Resolution* 49 (6): 925–53. https://doi.org/10.1177/0022002705281667.

Novitz, Tonia. 2003. *International and European Protection of the Right to Strike: A Comparative Study of Standards Set by the International Labour Organization, the Council of Europe and the European Union*. Oxford Monographs on Labour Law International and European Protection of the Right to Strike. Oxford: Oxford University Press.
———. 2007. "Labour Rights as Human Rights: Implications for Employers' Free Movement in an Enlarged European Union." *Cambridge Yearbook of European Legal Studies* 9: 357–86. https://doi.org/10.5235/152888712802746911.
O'Brien, Kevin J. 1996. "Rightful Resistance." *World Politics* 49 (1): 31–55. https://doi.org/10.1353/wp.1996.0022.
O'Brien, Kevin J., and Yanhua Deng. 2015. "The Reach of the State: Work Units, Family Ties and 'Harmonious Demolition.'" *The China Journal* 74 (July): 1–17. https://doi.org/10.1086/681660.
O'Donnell, Guillermo A. 1973. *Modernization and Bureaucratic-Authoritarianism; Studies in South American Politics*. Politics of Modernization Series, No. 9. Berkeley: Institute of International Studies, University of California.
OECD (Organisation for Economic Co-operation and Development). 2023. Average Usual Weekly Hours Worked on the Main Job. OECD Employment and Labour Market Statistics (database). www.oecd.org/en/data/indicators/hours-worked.html.
OECD and AIAS. 2021. Institutional Characteristics of Trade Unions, Wage Setting, State Intervention and Social Pacts (ICTWSS) Database. www.oecd.org/en/data/datasets/oecdaias-ictwss-database.html.
Okafor, Obiora Chinedu. 2007. *The African Human Rights System, Activist Forces and International Institutions*. Cambridge: Cambridge University Press. https://doi.org/10.1017/CBO9780511494048.
Ong, Aihwa. 2006. *Neoliberalism as Exception: Mutations in Citizenship and Sovereignty*. Durham, NC: Duke University Press.
Öniş, Ziya. 2006. "Varieties and Crises of Neoliberal Globalisation: Argentina, Turkey and the IMF." *Third World Quarterly* 27 (2): 239–63.
O'Sullivan, M., T. Turner, M. Kennedy, and J. Wallace. 2015. "Is Individual Employment Law Displacing the Role of Trade Unions?" *Industrial Law Journal* 44 (2): 222–45. https://doi.org/10.1093/indlaw/dwv010.
Özbudun, Ergun. 1996. "Democratization in the Middle East: Turkey – How Far from Consolidation?" *Journal of Democracy* 7 (3): 123–38.
———. 2014. "The Post-1980 Legal Framework for Interest Group Associations." In *Strong State and Economic Interest Groups: The Post-1980 Turkish Experience*, 41–54. Berlin: De Gruyter. https://doi.org/10.1515/9783110859966.41.
———. 2015. "Turkey's Judiciary and the Drift toward Competitive Authoritarianism." *The International Spectator* 50 (2): 42–55. https://doi.org/10.1080/03932729.2015.1020651.

Özdoğan, Kiraz. 2015. "Kamu Sendikalarında Etnisite ve Sınıf İlişkisinin Kuruluşu: Yurtsever Emekçiler." *Toplum ve Kuram* 10 (1): 99–110.

Özerdem, Alpaslan, and Tim Jacoby. 2007. "Conflict Induced Internal Displacement." In *Human Rights in Turkey*, edited by Zehra F. Kabasakal Arat, 159–69. Philadelphia: University of Pennsylvania Press.

Passalacqua, Virginia. 2021. "Legal Mobilization via Preliminary Reference: Insights from the Case of Migrant Rights." *Common Market Law Review* 58 (3): 751–76. https://doi.org/10.54648/cola2021049.

Pavone, Tommaso. 2022. *The Ghostwriters: Lawyers and the Politics behind the Judicial Construction of Europe*. Cambridge Studies in Law and Society. Cambridge: Cambridge University Press.

Pavone, Tommaso, and Øyvind Stiansen. 2022. "The Shadow Effect of Courts: Judicial Review and the Politics of Preemptive Reform." *American Political Science Review* 116 (1): 322–36. https://doi.org/10.1017/S0003055421000873.

Pedriana, Nicholas. 2006. "From Protective to Equal Treatment: Legal Framing Processes and Transformation of the Women's Movement in the 1960s." *American Journal of Sociology* 111 (6): 1718–61. https://doi.org/10.1086/499911.

Peters, Birgit, and Johan Karlsson Schaffer. 2013. "The Turn to Authority beyond States." *Transnational Legal Theory* 4 (3): 315–35. https://doi.org/10.5235/20414005.4.3.315.

Pevehouse, Jon C. 2005. *Democracy from Above: Regional Organizations and Democratization*. Cambridge: Cambridge University Press.

Pollert, Anna. 2007. "Britain and Individual Employment Rights: 'Paper Tigers, Fierce in Appearance but Missing in Tooth and Claw.'" *Economic and Industrial Democracy* 28 (1): 110–39. https://doi.org/10.1177/0143831X07073031.

Polletta, Francesca. 1999. "'Free Spaces' in Collective Action." *Theory and Society* 28 (1): 1–38.

———. 2000. "The Structural Context of Novel Rights Claims: Southern Civil Rights Organizing, 1961–1966." *Law & Society Review* 34 (2): 367–406. https://doi.org/10.2307/3115087.

Polletta, Francesca, and James M. Jasper. 2001. "Collective Identity and Social Movements." *Annual Review of Sociology* 27 (1): 283–305. https://doi.org/10.1146/annurev.soc.27.1.283.

Posner, Eric A. 2014. *The Twilight of Human Rights Law*. Inalienable Rights Series. Oxford: Oxford University Press.

Postnikov, Evgeny, and Ida Bastiaens. 2014. "Does Dialogue Work? The Effectiveness of Labor Standards in EU Preferential Trade Agreements." *Journal of European Public Policy* 21 (6): 923–40. https://doi.org/10.1080/13501763.2014.910869.

Przeworski, Adam, and John Sprague. 1986. *Paper Stones: A History of Electoral Socialism.* Chicago: University of Chicago Press.

Rajagopal, Balakrishnan. 2003. *International Law from Below: Development, Social Movements, and Third World Resistance.* Cambridge: Cambridge University Press.

Risse, Thomas, Steve C. Ropp, and Kathryn Sikkink. 1999. *The Power of Human Rights: International Norms and Domestic Change.* Cambridge Studies in International Relations 66. Cambridge: Cambridge University Press.

Risse, Thomas, and Kathryn Sikkink. 1999. "The Socialization of International Human Rights Norms into Domestic Practices: Introduction." In *The Power of Human Rights*, edited by Thomas Risse, Stephen C. Ropp, and Kathryn Sikkink, 1st ed., 1–38. Cambridge: Cambridge University Press. https://doi.org/10.1017/CBO9780511598777.002.

Ritter, Emily Hencken, and Courtenay R. Conrad. 2016. "Human Rights Treaties and Mobilized Dissent against the State." *Review of International Organizations* 11 (4): 449–75. https://doi.org/10.1007/s11558-015-9238-4.

Robertson, Graeme B. 2007. "Strikes and Labor Organization in Hybrid Regimes." *American Political Science Review* 101 (4): 781–98. https://doi.org/10.1017/S0003055407070475.

Rodríguez-Garavito, A. César. 2005. "Nike's Law: The Anti-Sweatshop Movement, Transnational Corporations, and the Struggle over International Labor Rights in the Americas." In *Law and Globalization from Below*, edited by Boaventura De Sousa Santos and César A. Rodríguez-Garavito, 1st ed., 64–91. Cambridge: Cambridge University Press. https://doi.org/10.1017/CBO9780511494093.003.

Rodríguez-Garavito, César, and Diana Rodríguez-Franco. 2015. *Radical Deprivation on Trial: The Impact of Judicial Activism on Socioeconomic Rights in the Global South.* 1st ed. Cambridge: Cambridge University Press. https://doi.org/10.1017/CBO9781139940849.

Rosenberg, Gerald N. 2008. *The Hollow Hope: Can Courts Bring about Social Change?* Chicago: University of Chicago Press. https://press.uchicago.edu/ucp/books/book/chicago/H/bo193463251.html.

Rosenfeld, Jake. 2014. *What Unions No Longer Do.* 1st ed.. Cambridge, MA: Harvard University Press.

Rueschemeyer, Dietrich, Evelyne Huber Stephens, and John D. Stephens. 1992. *Capitalist Development and Democracy.* Chicago: University of Chicago Press.

Ryan, Bernard. 1997. "Pay, Trade Union Rights and European Community Law." *International Journal of Comparative Labour Law and Industrial Relations* 13: 305–25.

REFERENCES

Sarat, Austin, and Stuart A. Scheingold. 2006. *Cause Lawyers and Social Movements*. Stanford, CA: Stanford University Press.

Savage, Larry. 2009. "Workers' Rights as Human Rights: Organized Labor and Rights Discourse in Canada." *Labor Studies Journal* 34 (1): 8–20. https://doi.org/10.1177/0160449X08328889.

Savage, Larry, and Charles W. Smith. 2017. *Unions in Court: Organized Labour and the Charter of Rights and Freedoms*. Vancouver: UBC Press.

Schatz, Edward, ed. 2009. *Political Ethnography: What Immersion Contributes to the Study of Power*. Chicago: University of Chicago Press.

Scheingold, Stuart A. 1974. *The Politics of Rights: Lawyers, Public Policy, and Political Change*. New Haven, CT: Yale University Press.

Schimmelfennig, Frank, and Ulrich Sedelmeier. 2005. *The Europeanization of Central and Eastern Europe*. Cornell Studies in Political Economy. Ithaca, NY: Cornell University Press.

Schmidt, Christopher W. 2018. *The Sit-Ins: Protest and Legal Change in the Civil Rights Era*. Chicago Series in Law and Society. Chicago: University of Chicago Press.

Schuck, Peter H. 1993. "Public Law Litigation and Social Reform." *Yale Law Journal* 102 (7): 1763–86. https://doi.org/10.2307/796831.

Schulman, Jason. 2019. "Next Labour? Changes in British Union-Labour Party Relations since the Election of Tony Blair." *Employee Responsibilities and Rights Journal* 31 (2): 115–30. https://doi.org/10.1007/s10672-019-09331-0.

Scott, James C. 2000. *Weapons of the Weak: Everyday Forms of Peasant Resistance*. New Haven, CT: Yale University Press.

Seidman, Gay. 2007. *Beyond the Boycott: Labor Rights, Human Rights, and Transnational Activism*. New York: Russell Sage Foundation.

⸻. 2008. "Transnational Labour Campaigns: Can the Logic of the Market Be Turned Against Itself?" *Development and Change* 39 (6): 991–1003. https://doi.org/10.1111/j.1467-7660.2008.00525.x.

Shapiro, Martin. 1986. *Courts: A Comparative and Political Analysis*. Chicago, IL: University of Chicago Press.

Sikkink, Kathryn. 2011. *The Justice Cascade: How Human Rights Prosecutions Are Changing World Politics*. 1st ed. New York: W. W. Norton.

Simmons, Beth A. 2009. *Mobilizing for Human Rights: International Law in Domestic Politics*. New York: Cambridge University Press.

Simmons, Erica S., and Nicholas Rush Smith. 2017. "Comparison with an Ethnographic Sensibility." *PS: Political Science & Politics* 50 (1): 126–30.

Slaughter, Anne-Marie. 2003. "A Global Community of Courts." *Harvard International Law Journal* 44: 191–211.

Smith, Dave. 2014. "Focus: The UK Blacklisting Scandal." *International Union Rights* 21 (1): 3–4.

———. 2017. "No Blacklist Justice for Britain's Agency Staff." *Morning Star*, May 2. https://morningstaronline.co.uk/a-dc1a-no-blacklist-justice-for-britains-agency-staff-1.

Smith, Dave, and Phil Chamberlain. 2016. *Blacklisted: The Secret War between Big Business and Union Activists : The Full Story*. 2nd ed. Oxford: New Internationalist.

Smith, Jackie, Charles Chatfield, and Ron Pagnucco, eds. 1997. *Transnational Social Movements and Global Politics: Solidarity beyond the State*. 1st ed. Syracuse Studies on Peace and Conflict Resolution. Syracuse, NY: Syracuse University Press.

Smith, Jackie, Ron Pagnucco, and George A. Lopez. 1998. "Globalizing Human Rights: The Work of Transnational Human Rights NGOs in the 1990s." *Human Rights Quarterly* 20 (2): 379–412.

Smith, Paul. 2009. "New Labour and the Commonsense of Neoliberalism: Trade Unionism, Collective Bargaining and Workers' Rights." *Industrial Relations Journal* 40 (4): 337–55. https://doi.org/10.1111/j.1468-2338.2009.00531.x.

Smith, Paul, and Gary Morton. 1993. "Union Exclusion and the Decollectivization of Industrial Relations in Contemporary Britain." *British Journal of Industrial Relations* 31 (1): 97–114. https://doi.org/10.1111/j.1467-8543.1993.tb00382.x.

———. 2009. "Employment Legislation: New Labour's Neoliberal Legal Project to Subordinate Trade Unions." In *Trade Unions in a Neoliberal World*, edited by Gary Daniels and John McIlroy, 225–49. Abingdon: Routledge. https://doi.org/10.4324/9780203887738-14.

Snow, David A., and Robert Benford. 1992. "Master Frames and Cycles of Protest." In *Frontiers in Social Movement Theory*, edited by Aldon D. Morris and Carol McClurg Mueller, 133–55. New Haven, CT: Yale University Press.

Snow, David A., Sarah A. Soule, and Hanspeter Kriesi. 2008. "Mapping the Terrain." In *The Blackwell Companion to Social Movements*, edited by David Snow, Sarah A. Soule, and Hanspeter Kriesi, 3–16. Oxford: Wiley-Blackwell.

Somers, Margaret R., and Christopher N. J. Roberts. 2008. "Toward a New Sociology of Rights: A Genealogy of 'Buried Bodies' of Citizenship and Human Rights." *Annual Review of Law and Social Science* 4 (1): 385–425.

Staggenborg, Suzanne. 1988. "The Consequences of Professionalization and Formalization in the Pro-Choice Movement." *American Sociological Review* 53 (4): 585–605. https://doi.org/10.2307/2095851.

Staton, Jeffrey K., and Will H. Moore. 2011. "Judicial Power in Domestic and International Politics." *International Organization* 65 (3): 553–87. https://doi.org/10.1017/S0020818311000130.

Steinberg, Marc W. 1999. "The Talk and Back Talk of Collective Action: A Dialogic Analysis of Repertoires of Discourse among Nineteenth-Century English Cotton Spinners." *American Journal of Sociology* 105 (3): 736–80. https://doi.org/10.1086/210359.
Stern, Rachel E. 2013. *Environmental Litigation in China: A Study in Political Ambivalence*. Cambridge Studies in Law and Society. Cambridge: Cambridge University Press. https://doi.org/10.1017/CBO9781139096614.
Stiansen, Øyvind. 2019. "Delayed but Not Derailed: Legislative Compliance with European Court of Human Rights Judgments." *International Journal of Human Rights* 23 (8): 1221–47. https://doi.org/10.1080/13642987.2019.1593153.
Stiansen, Øyvind, and Erik Voeten. 2020. "Backlash and Judicial Restraint: Evidence from the European Court of Human Rights." *International Studies Quarterly* 64 (4): 770–84. https://doi.org/10.1093/isq/sqaa047.
Stone Sweet, Alec. 2000. *Governing with Judges: Constitutional Politics in Europe*. Oxford: Oxford University Press. https://doi.org/10.1093/0198297718.001.0001.
Stone Sweet, Alec, and Helen Keller. 2008. "Assessing the Impact of the ECHR on National Legal Systems." In *A Europe of Rights: The Impact of the ECHR on National Legal Systems*, edited by Helen Keller and Alec Stone Sweet, 677–711. Oxford: Oxford University Press.
Stone Sweet, Alec, and Martin Shapiro. 2002. *On Law, Politics, and Judicialization*. Oxford: Oxford University Press.
Sundstrom, Lisa McIntosh. 2012. "Advocacy beyond Litigation: Examining Russian NGO Efforts on Implementation of European Court of Human Rights Judgments." *Communist and Post-Communist Studies* 45 (3-4): 255–68. https://doi.org/10.1016/j.postcomstud.2012.06.003.
——— 2014. "Russian NGOs and the European Court of Human Rights: A Spectrum of Approaches to Litigation." *Human Rights Quarterly* 36 (4): 844–68.
Sundstrom, Lisa McIntosh, Valerie Sperling, and Melike Sayoglu. 2019. *Courting Gender Justice: Russia, Turkey, and the European Court of Human Rights*. Oxford Scholarship Online. New York: Oxford University Press.
Sweeney, James A. 2013. *The European Court of Human Rights in the Post-Cold War Era: Universality in Transition*. Abingdon: Routledge.
Swidler, Ann. 1986. "Culture in Action: Symbols and Strategies." *American Sociological Review* 51 (2): 273–86. https://doi.org/10.2307/2095521.
Sychenko, Elena. 2017. *Individual Labour Rights as Human Rights: The Contributions of the European Court of Human Rights to Worker's Rights Protection*. Alphen aan den Rijn: Kluwer Law International B.V.

Tachau, Frank, and Metin Heper. 1983. "The State, Politics, and the Military in Turkey." *Comparative Politics* 16 (1): 17–33. https://doi.org/10.2307/421593.

Tam, Waikeung. 2012. *Legal Mobilization under Authoritarianism: The Case of Post-Colonial Hong Kong*. 1st ed. Cambridge: Cambridge University Press. https://doi.org/10.1017/CBO9781139424394.

Tarrow, Sidney. 1996. "Social Movements in Contentious Politics: A Review Article." *American Political Science Review* 90 (4): 874–83. https://doi.org/10.2307/2945851.

2001. "Transnational Politics: Contention and Institutions in International Politics." *Annual Review of Political Science* 4 (1): 1–20. https://doi.org/10.1146/annurev.polisci.4.1.1.

2010. "The Strategy of Paired Comparison: Toward a Theory of Practice." *Comparative Political Studies* 43 (2): 230–59. https://doi.org/10.1177/0010414009350044.

2022. *Power in Movement: Social Movements and Contentious Politics*. 4th ed. Cambridge: Cambridge University Press. https://doi.org/10.1017/9781009219839.

Taş, Hakkı. 2015. "Turkey – from Tutelary to Delegative Democracy." *Third World Quarterly* 36 (4): 776–91.

Tate, C. Neal, and Torbjörn Vallinder. 1995. *The Global Expansion of Judicial Power*. New York: New York University Press.

Taylor, Lance. 2006. "External Liberalization in Asia, Post-Socialist Europe, and Brazil." In *External Liberalization in Asia, Post-Socialist Europe, and Brazil*, edited by Lance Taylor, 3–60. Oxford: Oxford University Press. https://doi.org/10.1093/acprof:oso/9780195189322.003.0001.

Taylor, Whitney K. 2023. *The Social Constitution: Embedding Social Rights Through Legal Mobilization*. 1st ed. Cambridge: Cambridge University Press. https://doi.org/10.1017/9781009367738.

Taylor, Whitney K., and Sidney Tarrow. 2024. *Law, Mobilization, and Social Movements: How Many Masters?* 1st ed. Cambridge: Cambridge University Press. https://doi.org/10.1017/9781009493024.

Thörn, Håkan. 2006. *Anti-Apartheid and the Emergence of a Global Civil Society*. London: Palgrave Macmillan UK. https://doi.org/10.1057/9780230505698.

Tilly, Charles. 1995. "Globalization Threatens Labor's Rights." *International Labor and Working-Class History* 47: 1–23.

Towers, Brian. 1989. "Running the Gauntlet: British Trade Unions under Thatcher, 1979–1988." *Industrial and Labor Relations Review* 42 (2): 163–88. https://doi.org/10.2307/2523352.

Trif, Aurora. 2013. "Romania: Collective Bargaining Institutions under Attack." *Transfer* 19 (2): 227–37. https://doi.org/10.1177/1024258913480600.

Tsutsui, Kiyoteru. 2018. *Rights Make Might: Global Human Rights and Minority Social Movements in Japan*. Oxford: Oxford University Press.

Tsutsui, Kiyoteru, and Jackie Smith. 2018. "Human Rights and Social Movements: From the Boomerang Pattern to a Sandwich Effect." In *The Wiley Blackwell Companion to Social Movements*, edited by David A. Snow, Sarah A. Soule, Hanspeter Kriesi, and Holly J. McCammon, 1st ed., 586–601. Oxford: Wiley. https://doi.org/10.1002/9781119168577.ch33.

Tsutsui, Kiyoteru, Claire Whitlinger, and Alwyn Lim. 2012. "International Human Rights Law and Social Movements: States' Resistance and Civil Society's Insistence." *Annual Review of Law and Social Science* 8 (1): 367–96. https://doi.org/10.1146/annurev-lawsocsci-102811-173849.

Tuğal, Cihan. 2012. "Fight or Acquiesce? Religion and Political Process in Turkey's and Egypt's Neoliberalizations." *Development and Change* 43 (1): 23–51.

Tushnet, Mark. 2000. *Taking the Constitution Away from the Courts*. Princeton, NJ: Princeton University Press. https://doi.org/10.1515/9781400822973.

Uçkan, Banu. 2013. *4688 Sayılı Kamu Görevlileri Sendikaları ve Toplu Sözleşme Kanunu Çerçevesinde Türkiye'de Kamu Görevlileri Sendikacılığı*. Birinci baskı. Hukuk Kitapları Serisi 236. Kadıköy, İstanbul: Legal.

Vaisey, Stephen. 2009. "Motivation and Justification: A Dual-Process Model of Culture in Action." *American Journal of Sociology* 114 (6): 1675–1715. https://doi.org/10.1086/597179.

Van den Eynde, Laura. 2013. "An Empirical Look at the Amicus Curiae Practice of Human Rights NGOs before the European Court of Human Rights." *Netherlands Quarterly of Human Rights* 31 (3): 271–313. https://doi.org/10.1177/016934411303100304.

Van Der Vet, Freek. 2012. "Seeking Life, Finding Justice: Russian NGO Litigation and Chechen Disappearances before the European Court of Human Rights." *Human Rights Review* 13 (3): 303–25. https://doi.org/10.1007/s12142-012-0226-2.

———. 2018. "'When They Come for You': Legal Mobilization in New Authoritarian Russia." *Law & Society Review* 52 (2): 301–36. https://doi.org/10.1111/lasr.12339.

Vanhala, Lisa. 2010. *Making Rights a Reality? Disability Rights Activists and Legal Mobilization*. Cambridge Disability Law and Policy Series. New York: Cambridge University Press.

———. 2018. "Is Legal Mobilization for the Birds? Legal Opportunity Structures and Environmental Nongovernmental Organizations in the United Kingdom, France, Finland, and Italy." *Comparative Political Studies* 51 (3): 380–412. https://doi.org/10.1177/0010414017710257.

Vickers, Lucy. 2014. "Freedom of Religion and Belief, Article 9 ECHR and the EU Equality Directive." In *The European Convention on Human Rights and the Employment Relation,* edited by Filip Dorssemont, Klaus Lörcher, and Isabelle Schömann, 209–36. Oxford: Hart.

Voeten, Erik. 2013. "Public Opinion and the Legitimacy of International Courts." *Theoretical Inquiries in Law* 14: 209–36.

———. 2020. "Populism and Backlashes against International Courts." *Perspectives on Politics* 18 (2): 407–22.

———. 2022. "Is the Public Backlash against Globalization a Backlash against Legalization and Judicialization?" *International Studies Review* 24 (2): viac015. https://doi.org/10.1093/isr/viac015.

Von Staden, Andreas. 2018. *Strategies of Compliance with the European Court of Human Rights: Rational Choice Within Normative Constraints.* Pennsylvania Studies in Human Rights. Philadelphia: University of Pennsylvania Press,. https://doi.org/10.9783/9780812295153.

Vreeland, James Raymond. 2008. "Political Institutions and Human Rights: Why Dictatorships Enter into the United Nations Convention Against Torture." *International Organization* 62 (1): 65–101. https://doi.org/10.1017/S002081830808003X.

Waites, Matthew. 2019. "Decolonizing the Boomerang Effect in Global Queer Politics: A New Critical Framework for Sociological Analysis of Human Rights Contestation." *International Sociology* 34 (4): 382–401. https://doi.org/10.1177/0268580919851425.

Wallerstein, Michael, Miriam Golden, and Peter Lange. 1997. "Unions, Employers' Associations, and Wage-Setting Institutions in Northern and Central Europe, 1950–1992." *Industrial & Labor Relations Review* 50 (3): 379–401.

Waltz, Susan. 2001. "Universalizing Human Rights: The Role of Small States in the Construction of the Universal Declaration of Human Rights." *Human Rights Quarterly* 23 (1): 44–72.

Wang, Dan J., and Sarah A. Soule. 2016. "Tactical Innovation in Social Movements: The Effects of Peripheral and Multi-Issue Protest." *American Sociological Review* 81 (3): 517–48. https://doi.org/10.1177/0003122416644414.

Wedderburn of Charlton, Kenneth William. 1965. *The Worker and the Law.* Harmondsworth: Penguin Books.

———. 1991. *Employment Rights in Britain and Europe: Selected Papers in Labour Law.* London: Lawrence and Wishart.

Weiler, J. H. H. 1994. "A Quiet Revolution: The European Court of Justice and Its Interlocutors." *Comparative Political Studies* 26 (4): 510–34. https://doi.org/10.1177/0010414094026004006.

Weisband, Edward. 2006. "Verdictive Discourses, Shame and Judicialization in Pursuit of Freedom of Association Rights." In *The Legalization of Human Rights : Multidisciplinary Perspectives on Human Rights and Human Rights Law,* edited by Saladin Meckled-García and Basak

Çali, 135–61. Abingdon: Routledge. https://doi.org/10.4324/9780203008683-19.

Whyte, Jessica. 2019. *The Morals of the Market: Human Rights and the Rise of Neoliberalism*. London: Verso.

Wiener, Antje. 2007. "Contested Meanings of Norms: A Research Framework." *Comparative European Politics* 5 (1): 1–17.

Williams, Daniel K. 2019. *Defenders of the Unborn: The Pro-Life Movement before Roe v. Wade*. Oxford: Oxford University Press.

Wilson, Bruce M. 2009. "Institutional Reform and Rights Revolutions in Latin America: The Cases of Costa Rica and Colombia." *Journal of Politics in Latin America* 1 (2): 59–85. https://doi.org/10.1177/1866802X0900100203.

Winterton, Jonathan, and Ruth Winterton. 1989. *Coal, Crisis, and Conflict: The 1984–85 Miners' Strike in Yorkshire*. Manchester: Manchester University Press.

Wong, Wendy H. 2012. *Internal Affairs: How the Structure of NGOs Transforms Human Rights*. Ithaca, NY: Cornell University Press.

Wood, Elisabeth Jean. 2003. *Insurgent Collective Action and Civil War in El Salvador*. Cambridge Studies in Comparative Politics. Cambridge: Cambridge University Press. https://doi.org/10.1017/CBO9780511808685.

Wotipka, Christine Min, and Kiyoteru Tsutsui. 2008. "Global Human Rights and State Sovereignty: State Ratification of International Human Rights Treaties, 1965–20011." *Sociological Forum* 23 (4): 724–54. https://doi.org/10.1111/j.1573-7861.2008.00092.x.

Zemans, Frances Kahn. 1983. "Legal Mobilization: The Neglected Role of the Law in the Political System." *American Political Science Review* 77 (3): 690–703. https://doi.org/10.2307/1957268.

REFERENCES

EUROPEAN COURT OF HUMAN RIGHTS CASES CITED

AB Kurt Kellerman v. Sweden, Application No. 41579/98. Judgment, 26 October 2004.

Airey v. Ireland, Application No. 6289/73, Judgment (Merits), 9 October 1979.

Aizpurua Ortiz and Others v. Spain, Application No. 42430/05, Judgment (Merits and Just Satisfaction), 2 February 2010.

Almaz and Others v. Turkey, Application No. 55789/19 55896/19 55931/19, 56981/19, Decision, 19 November 2024.

Akarsubaşı v. Turkey, Application No. 70396/11, Judgment (Merits and Just Satisfaction), 21 July 2015.

Akdivar and Others v. Turkey, GC, Application No. 21893/93, Judgment (Merits and Just Satisfaction), 16 September 1996.

Akkoç v. Turkey, Application No. 22947/93 et al., Judgment (Merits and Just Satisfaction), 10 October 2000.

Antović and Mirković v. Montenegro, Application No. Judgment (Merits and Just Satisfaction), 28 November 2017.

Associated Society of Locomotive Engineers and Firemen (ASLEF) v. The United Kingdom, Application No. 11002/05, Judgment (Merits and Just Satisfaction), 27 February 2007.

Atalay v. Turkey, Application No. 11503/24, lodged 16 April 2024; communicated 16 September 2024.

Barış and Others v. Turkey, Application No. 66828/16, Decision, 14 December 2021.

Beck, Copp and Bazeley v. the United Kingdom, Application No. 48535/99 et al., Judgment (Merits and Just Satisfaction), 22 October 2002.

Brincat and Others v. Malta, Application No. 60908/11, Judgment (Merits and Just Satisfaction), 24 July 2014.

Brough v. the United Kingdom, Application No. 52962/11, Decision, 30 August 2016.

Bucur and Toma v. Romania, Application No. 40238/02, Judgment (Merits and Just Satisfaction), 8 January 2013.

C. N. v. the United Kingdom, Application No. 4239/08, Judgment (Merits and Just Satisfaction), 13 November 2012.

C. N. and V. v. France, Application No. 67724/09, Judgment (Merits and Just Satisfaction), 11 October 2012.

Chowdury and Others v. Greece, Application No. 21884/15, Judgment (Merits and Just Satisfaction), 30 March 2017.

Copland v. the United Kingdom, Application No. 62617/00, Judgment (Merits and Just Satisfaction), 3 April 2007.

Council of Civil Service Unions et al. v. The United Kingdom, Application No. 11603/85, Decision (Commission, Plenary), 20 January 1987.

REFERENCES

Dahlab v. Switzerland, Application No. 42393/98, Decision, 15 February 2001.

Danilenkov and Others v. Russia, Application No. 67336/01, Judgment (Merits and Just Satisfaction, 30 July 2009.

Dedecan and Ok v. Turkey, Application No. 22685/09, Judgment (Merits and Just Satisfaction), 22 September 2015.

Demir and Baykara v. Turkey, GC, Judgment (Merits and Just Satisfaction), 12 November 2008.

Dev Maden-Sen v. Turkey, Application No. 32980/96, Judgment, 12 September 1999.*Dikici v. Turkey*, Application No. 18308/02, Judgment (Merits and Just Satisfaction), 20 October 2009.

Dilek and Others v. Turkey, Application No. 74611/01 et al., Judgment (Merits and Just Satisfaction), 17 July 2007.

Dudgeon v. the United Kingdom, Application No. 7525/76, Judgment, 22 October 1981.

Ebrahimian v. France, Application No. 64846/11, Judgment (Merits and Just Satisfaction), 26 November 2015.

Eğitim ve Bilim Emekçileri Sendikası v. Turkey, Application No. 20641/05, Judgment (Merits and Just Satisfaction), 25 September 2012.

Eker v. Turkey, Application No. 26970/95, Decision, 20 May 1998.

Emel Boyraz v. Turkey, Application No. 61960/08, Judgment (Merits and Just Satisfaction), 2 December 2014.

Enerji Yapı-Yol-Sen v. Turkey, Application No. 68959/01, Judgment (Merits and Just Satisfaction), 21 April 2009.

Erenler and Others v. Turkey, Application No. 53310/10, Judgment (Merits and Just Satisfaction), 17 January 2023.

Ertaş Aydın and Others v. Turkey, Application No. 43672/98, Judgment (Merits and Just Satisfaction), 20 September 2005.

Eweida and others v. the United Kingdom, Application No. 48420/10, Judgment (Merits and Just Satisfaction), 15 January 2013.

Ezelin v. France, Application No. 11800/85, Judgment, 26 April 1991.

Fábián v. Hungary, GC, Application No. 78117/13, Judgment (Merits), 5 September 2017.

Fatma Akaltun Fırat v. Turkey, Application No. 34010/06, Judgment (Merits and Just Satisfaction), 10 September 2013.

Garcia Mateos v. Spain, Application No. 38285/09, Judgment (Merits and Just Satisfaction), 19 February 2013.

Guja v. Moldova, GC, Application No. 14277/04, Judgment (Merits and Just Satisfaction), 12 February 2008.

Gül and Others v. Turkey, Application No. 4870/02, Judgment (Merits and Just Satisfaction), 8 June 2010.

Güneri and Others v. Turkey, Application No. 42853/98 et al., Judgment (Merits and Just Satisfaction), 12 July 2005.

Gustafsson v. Sweden, GC, Application No. 15573/89, Judgment (Merits and Just Satisfaction), 25 April 1996.

H. M. v. Turkey, Application No. 34494/97, Judgment (Merits and Just Satisfaction), 8 August 2006.

Halford v. the United Kingdom, Application No. 20605/92, Judgment (Merits and Just Satisfaction), 25 June 1997.

Harman and Hewitt v. the United Kingdom, Application No. 20317/92, Judgment, 1 September 1993.

Heinisch v. Germany, Application No. 28274/08, Judgment (Merits and Just Satisfaction), 21 July 2011.

Hirst v. the United Kingdom (No. 2), GC, Application No. 74025/01, Judgment (Merits and Just Satisfaction), 6 October 2005.

Hulea v. Romania, Application No. 33411/05, Judgment of 2 October 2012.

Humpert and Others v. Germany, Application No. 59433/18 59477/18 59481/18, Judgment (Merits and Just Satisfaction), 14 December 2023.

I. B. v. Greece, Application No. 552/10, Judgment (Merits and Just Satisfaction), 3 October 2013.

İşçi and Others v. Turkey, Application No. 67483/12, Judgment (Merits and Just Satisfaction), 20 October 2020.

Junta Rectora Del Ertzainen Nazional Elkartasuna (ER.N.E.) v. Spain, Application No. 45892/09, Judgment, 21 April 2015.

Karaçay v. Turkey, Application No. 6615/03, Judgment (Merits and Just Satisfaction), 27 March 2007.

Karademirci and Others v. Turkey, Application No. 37096/97 et al., Judgment (Merits and Just Satisfaction), 25 January 2005.

Kavala v. Turkey, GC, Application No. 28749/18, Judgment (Merits and Just Satisfaction), 11 July 2022.

Kawogo v. the United Kingdom, Application No. 56921/09, Decision, 3 September 2013.

Kaya v. Turkey, Application No. 51194/19, Decision, 19 November 2024.

Kaya and Seyhan v. Turkey, Application No. 30946/04, Judgment (Merits and Just Satisfaction), 15 September 2009.

Kaymak and Others v. Türkiye, Application No. 62239/12, Judgment (Merits and Just Satisfaction), 20 June 2023.

Kjartan Ásmundsson v. Iceland, Application No. 60669/00, Judgment (Merits and Just Satisfaction), 12 October 2004.

Konstantin Markin v. Russia, Application No. 30078/06, Judgment (Merits and Just Satisfaction), 22 March 2012.

Köpke v. Germany, Application No. 420/07, Decision, 5 October 2010.

Koufaki and ADEDY v. Greece, Application No. 57665/12 et al., Decision, 7 May 2013.

L. C. B. v. the United Kingdom, Application No. 23413/94, Judgment, 9 June 1998.

L. E. v. Greece, Application No. 71545/12, Judgment (Merits and Just Satisfaction), 21 January 2016.

LO and NTF v. Norway, Application No. 45487/17, Judgment, 10 June 2021.

L. R. v. the United Kingdom, Application No. 49113/09, Decision, 14 June 2011.

Lautsi and Others v. Italy, GC, Application No. 30814/06, Judgments (Merits and Just Satisfaction), 18 March 2011.

Leyla Şahin v. Turkey, GC, Application No. 44774/98, Judgment (Merits and Just Satisfaction), 10 November 2005.

López Ribalda and Others v. Spain, GC, Application No. 1874/13 et al., Judgment (Merits and Just Satisfaction), 17 October 2019.

Lustig-Prean and Beckett v. the United Kingdom, Application No. 31417/96 et al., Judgment (Merits), 27 September 1999.

M. v. the United Kingdom, Application No. 16081/08, Decision, 1 December 2009.

M. A. and 39 Others v. the United Kingdom, Application No. 12519/86, Decision, 13 July 1987.

Massa v. Italy, Application No. 14399/88, Judgment (Merits and Just Satisfaction), 24 August 1993.

Matelly v. France, Application No. 10609/10, Judgment, 2 October 2014.

Meier v. Switzerland, Application No. 10109/14, Judgment (Merits and Just Satisfaction), 9 February 2016.

Melike v. Turkey, Application No. 35786/19, Judgment (Merits and Just Satisfaction), 15 June 2021.

Metin Turan v. Turkey, Application No. 20868/02, Judgment (Merits and Just Satisfaction), 14 November 2006.

Metrobus Ltd v. Unite the Union, UKHL 41, [2009] 1 WLR 1987.

Müslüm Çiftçi v. Turkey, Application No. 30307/03, Judgment (Merits and Just Satisfaction), 2 February 2010.

Mustafa Avcı v. Turkey, Application No. 39322/12, Judgment (Merits and Just Satisfaction), 23 May 2017.

N. K. M. v. Hungary, Application No. 66529/11, Judgment (Merits and Just Satisfaction, Section), 14 May 2013.

National Union of Belgian Police v. Belgium, Application No. 4464/70, Judgment (Merits), 27 October 1975.

National Union of Rail, Maritime and Transport Workers [RMT] v. The United Kingdom, Application No. 31045/10, Judgment (Merits and Just Satisfaction), 8 April 2014.

Nerva and Others v. the United Kingdom, Application No. 42295/98, Judgment (Merits and Just Satisfaction), 24 September 2002.

Norman v. the United Kingdom, Application No. 41387/17, Judgment (Merits and Just Satisfaction), 6 July 2021.

Obst v. Germany, Application No. 425/03, Judgment (Merits and Just Satisfaction), 23 September 2010.

Öneryıldız v. Turkey, Application No. 48939/99, Judgment, 30 November 2004.

Oya Ataman v. Turkey, Application No. 74552/01, Judgment (Merits and Just Satisfaction), 5 December 2006.

Palomo Sánchez and Others v. Spain, GC, Application No. 28955/06, Judgment (Merits and Just Satisfaction), 12 September 2011.

Paulet v. the United Kingdom, Application No. 6219/08, Judgment (Merits and Just Satisfaction), 13 May 2014.

Pay v. the United Kingdom, Application No. 32792/05, Decision, 16 September 2008.

Pellegrin v. France, GC, Application No. 28541/95, Judgment (Merits), 8 December 1999.

Perkins and R. v. the United Kingdom, Application No. 43208/98 et al., Judgment (Merits and Just Satisfaction), 22 October 2002.

Petrovic v. Austria, Application No. 20458/92, Judgment (Merits and Just Satisfaction), 27 March 1998.

POA and Others v. the United Kingdom, Application No. 59253/11, Communicated Case, 14 September 2011.

R (on the application of UNISON) v. Lord Chancellor, UKSC 51, [2017] 3 WLR 409.

R. A. and W. M. v. the United Kingdom, Application No. 12105/86, Decision on Admissibility, 13 October 1987.

Rantsev v. Cyprus and Russia, Application No. 25965/04, Judgment (Merits and Just Satisfaction), 7 January 2010.

Redfearn v. the United Kingdom, Application No. 47335/06, Judgment (Merits and Just Satisfaction), 6 November 2012.

RMT v. Serco Ltd; ASLEF v. London & Birmingham Railway Ltd, EWCA Civ 226, [2011] IRLR 399.

Rommelfanger v. Germany, Application No. 12242/86, Decision, 6 September 1989.

S. M. v. Croatia, Application No. 60561/14, Judgment (Merits and Just Satisfaction), 19 July 2018.

Sabeh El Leil v. France, GC, Application No. 34869/05, Judgment (Merits and Just Satisfaction), 29 June 2011.

Saime Özcan v. Turkey, Application No. 22943/04, Judgment (Merit and Just Satisfaction), 15 September 2009.

Schmidt and Dahlström v. Sweden, Application No. 5589/72, Judgment (Merits), 6 February 1976.

Schüth v. Germany, Application No. 1620/03, Judgment (Merits), 23 September 2010.

Secretary of State for Business and Trade v. Mercer, UKSC 12, Judgment of 17 April 2024.

Selahattin Demirtaş v. Turkey No. 2, GC, Application No. 14305/17, Judgment (Merits and Just Satisfaction), 22 December 2020.

Serco Ltd v. RMT, EWCA Civ 226, [2011] IRLR 399.

Sidabras and Džiautas v. Lithuania, Application No. 55480/00 et al., Judgment (Merits and Just Satisfaction), 27 July 2004.

Siebenhaar v. Germany, Application No. 18136/02, Judgment (Merits and Just Satisfaction), 3 February 2011.

Sigurður A. Sigurjónsso v. Iceland, Application No. 16130/90, Judgment (Merits and Just Satisfaction), 30 June 1993.

Siliadin v. France, Application No. 73316/01, Judgment (Merits and Just Satisfaction), 26 July 2005.

S. L. v. Sweden, Application No. 4475/70, Decision, 24 May 1971.

Smith and Grady v. the United Kingdom, Application No. 33985/96 et al., Judgment (Merits), 27 September 1999.

Smith v. the United Kingdom, Application No. 54357/15, Decision, 28 March 2017.

Sørensen and Rasmussen v. Denmark, GC, Application No. 52562/99 et al., Judgment (Merits and Just Satisfaction), 11 January 2006.

Sosyal-İş Union and Kodaş v. Turkey, Application No. 22726/93. Decision on Admissibility, 4 July 1995.

Stummer v. Austria, GC, Application No. 37452/02, Judgment (Merits and Just Satisfaction), 7 July 2011.

Süheyla Aydın v. Turkey, Application No. 25660/94, Judgment (Merits and Just Satisfaction), 24 May 2005.

Süleyman Çelebi and Others v. Turkey, Application No. 37273/10 et al., Judgment (Merits and Just Satisfaction), 24 May 2016.

Svenska Transportarbetareförbundet and Seko v. Sweden, Application No. 53507/99, Judgment, 2 July 2016.

Swedish Engine Drivers' Union v. Sweden, Application No. 5614/72, Judgment (Merits), 6 February 1976.

Syndicat Sosyal-Is Et Kodas v. Turkey, Application No. 22726/9, Decision, 4 July 1995.

Tek Gıda İş Sendikasi v. Turkey, Application No. 35009/05, Judgment (Merits and Just Satisfaction, 4 April 2017.

The National Association of Teachers in Further and Higher Education v. the United Kingdom, Application No. 28910/95, Decision, 16 April 1998.

Tüm Bel Sen v. Turkey, Application No. 38927/10 et al., Judgment (Merits and Just Satisfaction), 18 February 2014.

Tüm Emekliler Sendikası v. Turkey, Application No. 40903/06, Judgment. 19 December 2017.

Tüm Haber Sen and Çınar v. Turkey, Application No. 28602/95, Judgment (Merits), 21 February 2006.

Tyrer v. the United Kingdom, Application No. 5856/72, Judgment (Merits), 25 April 1978.

Ülger v. Turkey, Application No. 25321/02, Judgment (Merits and Just Satisfaction), 26 June 2007.

United Communist Party of Turkey and Others v. Turkey, Application No. 19392/92. Judgment. 30 January 1998.

Urcan and Others v. Turkey, Application No. 23018/04 et al., Judgment (Merits and Just Satisfaction), 17 July 2008.

V. C. L. and A. N. v. the United Kingdom, Application No. 77587/12, Judgment (Merits and Just Satisfaction), 16 February 2021.

Van Der Mussele v. Belgium, Application No. 8919/80, Judgment (Merits), 23 November 1983.

Vilho Eskelinen and Others v. Finland, GC, Application No. 63235/00, Judgment (Merits and Just Satisfaction), 19 April 2007.

Vilnes and Others v. Norway, Application No. 52806/09 et al., Judgment (Merits and Just Satisfaction), 5 December 2013.

Wilson, National Union of Journalists and Others v. The United Kingdom, Application No. 30668/96 et al., Judgment (Merits and Just Satisfaction), 2 July 2002.

X v. Federal Republic of Germany, Application No. 6049/73, Decision, 14 December 1974.

Yilmaz v. Turkey, Application No. 793/18, Communicated Case, 8 January 2019.

Young, James and Webster v. The United Kingdom, Application No. 7601/76 et al., Judgment (Merits), 31 August 1981.

Zengin v. Turkey, Application No. 23143/93, Decision, 8 September 1997.

Zengin v. Turkey, Application No. 43178/18, Communicated Case, 8 January 2019.

INDEX

Note: Page references in italic indicate tables or figures.

A Manifesto for Labour Law, 121
abece, 206–10, *207*
Acheson, Steve, 176, 178–79, 190
African Court on Human and Peoples' Rights, 77
Alter, Karen J., 28, 42
Aydın, Oya, 224

backlash
   ECtHR, 99, 104, 186, 235–36, 238–39
   ILO, 236
   legal mobilization, 46–47, 235–36
Baykara, Vicdan, 215
Blacklist Support Group (BSG)
   alliance formation, 188–89
   class-based discourse, 193–96, 199, 233
   domestic litigation, 179–80, 187–88, 197–98
   ECtHR litigation, 180
   ECtHR litigation strategy, 180–82, 185
   formation of, 177
   goals of, 179
   human rights framework, 176–78, 183–87, 194, 197–200, 233, 237
   human rights framework, effects of, 186–87, 196–99
   human rights framework, influence of lawyers, 182–83, 185, 195–96
   media relations, 190–91
   mobilization, external, 5, 17, 182, 193, 231–32
   mobilization, internal, 192–93
   mobilization, tactical innovations, 188
   parliamentary advocacy, 191–92
Blacklisted (Smith and Chamberlain, 2016), 184
blacklisted workers
   Acheson, Steve, 176, 178–79, 190
   Brough, Terence, 181
   ECtHR litigation, 177
   employment tribunals, 176, 178–79, 181, 185
   government inaction, 66, 178
   police involvement in, 177, 189, 198
   scope of blacklisting, 1–2, 176–77
   Smith, Dave, 1–2, 4–5, 181–82, 184–86, 189–90, 194–95
   union involvement, 183–85
   See also Blacklist Support Group (BSG); Consulting Association; ICO
Blair, Tony, 65–67, 149, 152, 178, 191
Bogg, Alan, 150–51
Bozkurt, Ali, 208
Brough, Terence, 181

Cameron, David, 186–87
Campaign Opposing Police Surveillance (COPS), 188–89
Candoğan, Gökhan, 129–30
Chamberlain, Phil, 184
Çınar, İsmail, 201, 210–11
CoE. *See* Council of Europe (CoE)
Colombia, 40, 43, 70
Committee of Ministers (CM)
   cases, closing, 150
   compliance negotiations, 141, 159, 161, 166–67
   compliance with ECtHR rulings, analysis of, 142–43, 167–68, 170–72, 218
   ECtHR proceedings, length of, 144
   as enforcement mechanism, 140
   evaluation process, 166–68, 170–72
   evaluations, problems with, 169
   minimal state compliance, 139–40, 144, 157, 172–73
Consulting Association
   blacklist, 1–2, 177
   Crossrail use of, 185
   police collaboration with, 189, 198
   prosecutions, 2
   raid on, 1, 179, 189
COPS, 188–89
Corbyn, Jeremy, 191, 197
Council of Europe (CoE)
   collective complaint mechanism, 80

INDEX

Committee of Independent Experts, 116
  and ECtHR, 10, 14, 77, 79–80
  expansion of, 56, 81
  human rights, 6–7
  Istanbul Convention, 239
  Parliamentary Assembly of the Council of Europe (PACE), 77, 90
  Russia, 57
  Turkey, 82, 142
  United Kingdom, 65
  See also Committee of Ministers (CM); ECtHR
Czech Republic, 143

Denmark, 99–100, 104
Digest of Decisions and Principles of the Freedom of Association Committee of the Governing Body of the ILO (ILO, 2006), 222
Duffy, Helen, 40

ECJ
  and national law, 107
  pay equity, 112
  trade union rights, 107, 112, 116–17, 119–20
ECSR, 7, 80, 155–56
ECtHR
  backlash against, 99, 104, 186, 235–36, 238–39
  Brighton Declaration (2012), 99
  compliance with, 10, 13–14, 34, 140–44
  conservative origins of, 79–80
  Copenhagen Declaration (2018), 99–100
  direct access, 76
  evasion of rulings, 14, 34, 144, 157, 162, 226, 233
  fair trial, 86
  formation of, 77
  ILO, reference of, 118, 127
  institutional structure, 76–77, 82
  judges, 27, 77–78, 81, 100–1, 103
  litigation costs, 109, 121
  proceedings, length of, 144
  process, 77–78, 84
  rise to prominence, 7–8, 80–82
  rulings, execution of, 140–42
  Turkey, 144
  See also ECtHR compliance, Turkey; ECtHR compliance, United Kingdom; labor cases, ECtHR; labor rights
ECtHR compliance, Turkey, *146*
  Article 10 compliance, 158–59
  Article 11 compliance, 158–61
  Article 13 compliance, 160
  Article 14 compliance, 161–62
  collective action, 165–69
  collective action, limitations and violations, 169
  collective bargaining, 163–64
  collective bargaining, limitations and violations, 164–66
  evasion of, 162
  right to unionize, 157–59
  right to unionize, limitations and violations, 159–62
  violations, core areas, 157
  See also KESK
ECtHR compliance, United Kingdom, *147*
  Article 11 compliance, 149, 154–56
  control of union membership, 151–52
  control of union membership, limitations and violations, 152–53
  right to strike, 154–55
  right to unionize, 149–50
  right to unionize, limitations and violations, 150–51
Eğitim-Sen
  constitution, 213
  cooptation, 223–24
  Eğit-Der, 205–6, 208–10
  Eğitim-İş, 204, 210–11
  Eğit-Sen, 131–33, 206, 210–11
  government support, 217
  membership, 217
  mobilization, 225
  repression of, 134, 158–59
  sanctions against individuals, 167
Egypt, 237
Erdoğan, Ayhan, 127, 210
Ertuğrul, Feyzullah, 209–10
ESC, 65, 80, 116
ETUC, 123
European Committee on Social Rights (ECSR), 7, 80, 155–56
European Convention on Human Rights
  Article 1 of Protocol 86, 87
  Article 2, 92–93
  Article 3, 92–93
  Article 4, 82, 90–91
  Article 6, 58, 86
  Article 8, 87–88, 93
  Article 9, 91–92
  Article 10, 88, 132
  Article 11, 6, 56, 58, 75, 80, 83, 94, 97, 99–100, 102, 124, 127, 129, 132, 149
  Article 14, 87–88
  Article 25, 71
  drafting of, 188
  ECtHR use of, 83
  labor standards, 107
  as living instrument, 81
  Turkey, 71, 209–10
  United Kingdom, 3–4, 55, 65, 181
  See also ECtHR compliance, Turkey; ECtHR compliance, United Kingdom

293

INDEX

European Court of Human Rights (ECtHR).
    See ECtHR
European Court of Justice (ECJ). See ECJ
European Social Charter (ESC), 65, 80, 116
European Trade Union Confederation
    (ETUC), 123
Ewing, Keith, 4, 120–21, 150, 153, 180–81

Ford, Michael, 118, 122, 192
France, 57, 62–63, 90, 143

Germany, 62, 102–3
Gülen, Fethullah, 220–21
Gülmez, Mesut, 125, 129, 167, 204, 208

Harman, Harriet, 123
Helfer, Laurence R., 27–28, 141
Hendy, Lord John, 106, 113–16, 120–22, 150,
    180–81, 195
Hewitt, Patricia, 123
human rights
    human rights regimes, 32–34
    illiberal practices, 24–25
    International Criminal Court (ICC), 45
    narrative framing, 43–44, 47
    and neoliberalism, 11
    regime type, 24
    strategic mobilization, 5–6, 12, 39, 41,
        43–51, 197–99, 232, 234
    See also human rights courts; NGOs
human rights courts
    compliance with, 13–14, 22, 28, 34–35, 142,
        226
    extensive authority, 28, 115, 118, 127
    external enforcement, 42, 51
    grassroots mobilization, 5–6, 231–32
    institutional capacity, 108–9
    judicial process, 41
    labor litigation, 18, 230–31
    repression, 42, 47, 59, 234–35
    state inaction, 12–13
    See also ECtHR

ICC, 45
ICO
    construction industry investigation, 179
    Consulting Association investigation, 1,
        177, 179, 189
    Kerr prosecution, 2, 179
IER, 121
ILO
    backlash, 236
    Committee of Experts on the Application of
        Conventions and Recommendations
        (CEACR), 101, 119–20
    Committee on Freedom of Association
        (CFA), 115–16, 118–19, 204, 211, 213

Convention 87, 71, 101, 126
Convention 98, 71
Convention 151, 126
ECJ rulings, 119–20
extensive authority, 28, 115, 118, 127
political pressure upon, 101–2
trade union rights, 9, 80, 107, 119
United Kingdom, 65–66, 178
İmamoğlu, Ekrem, 235
Information Commissioner's Office. See ICO
Institute of Employment Rights (IER),
    121
Inter-American Court of Human Rights, 77,
    108
International Criminal Court (ICC), 45
International Labor Organization (ILO). See
    ILO
International Trade Union Confederation
    (ITUC), 61, 70, 221
Işıklı, Alpaslan, 125, 129, 204, 208
Italy, 58
ITUC, 61, 70, 221

judicial authority
    effects of, 28
    extensive authority, 28, 115, 118, 127
    mobilization, 46
judicial responsiveness, 27–28, 47

Kamu Emekçileri Sendikaları Konfederasyonu
    (KESK). See KESK
Karaçay, Erhan, 130, 210
Kaygısız, İrfan, 129–30, 226
Kerr, Ian, 2
KESK, 146–48
    2016 state of emergency, 221
    as civic institution, 238
    class-based discourse, 214, 233
    collective action, 146–48, 166, 169, 227
    collective bargaining, 165
    constitution, 213
    cooptation of labor, 219, 223–25, 228–29
    education unions, 206
    formation of, 124, 201, 210, 231
    government reaction to, 202
    human rights discourse, 176, 215, 225
    Kurdish movement, 128–34, 158–59
    litigation, cost of, 109
    litigation, domestic, 213
    litigation, ECtHR, 124, 128, 133, 212–13,
        218, 224–29
    litigation, effects of, 215–19
    litigation, ILO, 213
    litigation strategies, 128–30
    media relations, 214–15
    membership, 217
    Milliyet, 214

294

mobilization, 212, 228
police violence, 171
public sector unions, 74, 106, 169, 229
public sector unions, government control, 165, 222–23
state repression, 161–62, 224, 234–35
sürgün davaları, 134, 146–48, 159–61
Yurtsever Emekçiler, 131
See also Eğit-Sen
Khan, Imran, 189

labor
   activism, 9, 22
   collective bargaining, 61–63, *61–62*
   human rights, 4–6, 11–12, 230–31
   litigation, international courts, 3–4, 18, 233
   neoliberalism, countering, 236–39
   organizational failures, 60
   political opportunities, 25–26, 30, 32
   See also human rights; legal mobilization; repression
labor, Turkey
   abece, 206–10, *207*
   AKP favoritism and corruption, 221–22
   Bahar Eylemleri, 203
   Birleşik Metal İş, 102
   collective action, 129–30
   collective bargaining, 126–28
   Devrimci İşçi Sendikaları Konfederasyonu (DİSK), 68–69, 102, 124, 171
   Enerji Yapı-Yol-Sen, 129–30
   hukuk mücadelesi, 202–3
   human rights framework, 201, 206–7, *207*, 237
   Kamu-Sen, 222
   Kurdish Human Rights Project (KHRP), 131
   litigation, ECtHR, 126, 210–11
   litigation, ILO, 125–26, 211
   litigation, private sector unions, 124
   Memur-Sen, 165, 169, 221–23, *223*
   public sector unions, 3, 17, 71–72, 124–25, 128, 203–4, *204*, 210, 222
   public sector unions, influence of lawyers, 204–5
   public sector unions, state repression, 211
   rights violations, 157
   Tüm Bel Sen, 127, 163–64, 201
   Tüm Haber Sen, 126, 158, 210, 217
   Türkiye İşçi Sendikaları Konfederasyonu, 68
   TürkMetal, 102
   Yurtsever Emekçiler, 131
   See also ECtHR compliance, Turkey; Eğit-Sen; KESK
labor, United Kingdom
   collective bargaining, 111–12
   employment tribunals, 109, 111–13, 176, 178–79, 181, 184–85
   Institute of Employment Rights (IER), 121
   international courts, 116–17
   judicial conservatism, domestic, 111
   legislative reform, 111–12
   litigation, ECJ, 114–17, 119–20
   litigation, ECtHR, 112–14, 117–18
   litigation, ILO, 115–16, 118–19
   Union of Construction, Allied Trades and Technicians (UCATT), 180–81, 183
   Unite, 183, 190–91, 197
   See also blacklisted workers; ECtHR compliance, United Kingdom
labor cases, ECtHR
   diversity of, 84–85, *84–85*
   fair trial, 86
   forced labor, 90–91
   freedom of expression, 88
   freedom of religion, 91–92
   job access and security, 89
   pay and benefits, 87
   political context, 78–79, *79*
   privacy and surveillance, 93
   workplace discrimination, 87–88
   workplace health and safety, 92–93
labor rights
   blacklisting, 2–3, 182
   collective bargaining, 99, 120
   public sector unions, 75–76
   right to strike, 101–3
   rollback of, 100–1, 234
   See also trade union rights
Lawrance, Stephen, 189
lawyers
   cause lawyers, 109–10, 120–23, 135
   international litigation, 29–30, 114
   international litigation, cost of, 108–9
   and labor, 23
   legal mobilization, 9, 14–15, 134
   litigation strategies, 45, 106–8, 120–23, 134–35
   tensions, 110
legal mobilization
   case law, favorable, 27
   grassroots mobilization, 5–6, 12, 15, 40–42, 232
   international legal pluralism, 22–23
   international vs. domestic, 39
   judicial legitimacy, 28–29
   judicial responsiveness, 27–28, 47
   legal opportunities, 26, 30–32
   litigation, indirect effects, 5, 34–35, 38, 40–42, 46
   political backlash, 46–47, 235–36
   repression, covert, 47
   rights-based identity, 15–16, 233

legal mobilization (cont.)
  standing, 27
  state inaction, 12–13
  theoretical insights, 38–39
  See also ECtHR; judicial authority; lawyers
Lester, Anthony, 123
Liberty, 114, 122–23

Madsen, Mikael R., 28
McCann, Michael W., 38, 40, 44, 195
McCluskey, Len, 190–91
McDonnell, John, 191
Merry, Sally Engle, 14–15, 48
Milliyet, 214
Mobilizing for Human Rights (Simmons, 2009), 36
Moğultay, Mehmet, 217
Moyn, Samuel P., 44

National Council for Civil Liberties (NCCL). *See* Liberty
neoliberalism
  features of, 59–60
  labor mobilization, inhibition of, 4, 7, 16, 18, 55, 59, 69, 72–73
  rise of, 60–61
The Netherlands, 99
NGOs
  CM, reports to, 143, 171–72
  goals, misalignment of, 110
  human rights, 36, 48
  and institutional capacity, 108–9
  state accountability, 13, 36
  third-party intervention, 115
  United Kingdom, 94
  United States, 108

Owens, Declan, 195

Phillips, Victoria, 113–14, 195
Posner, Eric A., 10

repression
  covert, 47
  Eğitim-Sen, 134, 158–59
  human rights courts, 42, 47, 234–35
  KESK, 161–62, 224, 234–35
  public sector unions, Turkey, 211
research design, 16–18
Romania, 57–58, 62–63, 62
Russia, 57, 141

Savage, Larry, 38
Scottish National Party (SNP), 191, 193
Simmons, Beth A., 36
Smith, Dave, 1–2, 4–5, 181–82, 184–86, 189–90, 194–95

SNP, 191, 193
social movements
  alliances, fostering of, 45–46, 234
  cyclical nature, 237
  definition, 35
  discursive frames, 43–44
  domestic advocacy, 44–45
  grassroots mobilization, 34–37, 43, 46
  group identity, 47–49
  human rights, 11, 37–38
  issues addressed, 37
  legal consciousness, 48
  litigation, 13, 15–16, 32
  NGOs, importance of, 36
  tactical innovation, 44
  See also labor
Spain, 62, 99
StrasLab
  content of, 16, 83
  freedom of expression, 88
  trade union rights, 17, 75–76, 100

Tarrow, Sidney, 46
Tiryaki, Mehmet, 226–27
Tomlinson, Ricky, 190
trade union rights, 155–56
  blacklisted workers, 2–3
  collective bargaining, 163–66
  ECJ, 107, 117, 119–20
  ECtHR, conservative phase, 6–8, 56, 83, 94–96
  ECtHR, expansion phase, 56–58, 96–99, 106, 117–18
  ECtHR, litigation strategy (KESK), 128–30, 133–34
  ECtHR, litigation strategy (UK), 120–23
  ECtHR, retrenchment phase, 99–103
  ECtHR litigation, 8, 56–58, *57*, 75–76, 83, 95, 106–8, 113–15, 126, 134, *146–48*, 224–25, 230–31
  ECtHR rulings, compliance with, 139–44, 156–57, 172–73
  as human rights, 16–17
  ILO, 9, 118–19
  litigation, cost of, 109
  membership selection, 151–53
  public sector workers, Turkey, 6–7
  restrictions on, Turkey, 69–72
  right to strike, 154–56, 166–69
  right to unionize, 149–51, 157–62
  Thatcher government (UK), 64, 123
Trades Union Congress (TUC), 115, 123, 178
TUC, 115, 123, 178
Türkdoğan, Öztürk, 128, 225–26
Turkey
  1961 constitution, 68
  1982 constitution, 69, 72, 125, 156

2004 constitutional amendment, 157
2016 state of emergency, 219–20
Adalet ve Kalkınma Partisi (AKP), 69, 219
anti-union policies, *61–62*, 69–71, 125, 211
Doğru Yol Partisi, 216–17
economy, 69–70
ECtHR, 55
European Convention on Human Rights, 71, 210
European Union, integration with, 71
Gülen movement, 220–21
International Labor Organization, 71
labor reform, 71, 217
Law No. 657, 167, 170
Law No. 4688, 158, 161, 163–65, 170, 218
Law No. 6009, 164
Law No. 6289, 158, 164–65
Law No. 6356, 167, 169
Sosyaldemokrat Halkçı Parti, 216–17
Türkiye İşçi Partisi, 68, 216
See also labor, Turkey

United Kingdom (UK)
anti-union policies, 64–66, 105–6, 116
Employment Act (1988), 116
Employment Appeal Tribunal, 151
Employment Relations Act, 2004 (ERA 2004), 149, 152
Employment Relations Act, 2008 (ERA 2008), 152
Employment Relations Act, 2010, 180
European Convention on Human Rights, 3–4, 55, 65, 181

European Social Charter (ESC), 65
Human Rights Act (HRA), 67, 114, 118, 154–55, 186–87, 235
Joint Committee on Human Rights (JCHR), 150, 153
litigation, cost of, 109
National Union of Journalists (NUJ), 105–6
Strikes (Minimum Service Requirements) Act (2023), 156
Trade Union Act (2016), 156
Trade Union and Labour Relations (Consolidation) Act (TULRCA, 1992), 149–52, 155
See also blacklisted workers; ICO; labor, United Kingdom
United Nations (UN), 7, 80, 116, 118, 185
United States (US)
cause lawyers, 109
individual rights, 43
marriage equality, 43
mobilization, 14
NGOs, 108
pay equity, 38, 40
public interest litigation, 111

Wedderburn of Charlton, Kenneth William, 115, 123
Wilson, David, 105–6

Yılmaz, Sakine Esen, 223–24, 227

CAMBRIDGE STUDIES IN LAW AND SOCIETY

Books in the Series

Diseases of the Will: Alcohol and the Dilemmas of Freedom
Mariana Valverde

The Politics of Truth and Reconciliation in South Africa: Legitimizing the Post-Apartheid State
Richard A. Wilson

Modernism and the Grounds of Law
Peter Fitzpatrick

Unemployment and Government: Genealogies of the Social
William Walters

Autonomy and Ethnicity: Negotiating Competing Claims in Multi-Ethnic States
Yash Ghai

Constituting Democracy: Law, Globalism and South Africa's Political Reconstruction
Heinz Klug

The Ritual of Rights in Japan: Law, Society, and Health Policy
Eric A. Feldman

Governing Morals: A Social History of Moral Regulation
Alan Hunt

The Colonies of Law: Colonialism, Zionism and Law in Early Mandate Palestine
Ronen Shamir

Law and Nature
David Delaney

Social Citizenship and Workfare in the United States and Western Europe: The Paradox of Inclusion
Joel F. Handler

Law, Anthropology, and the Constitution of the Social: Making Persons and Things
Edited by Alain Pottage and Martha Mundy

Judicial Review and Bureaucratic Impact: International and Interdisciplinary Perspectives
Edited by Marc Hertogh and Simon Halliday

Immigrants at the Margins: Law, Race, and Exclusion in Southern Europe
Kitty Calavita

Lawyers and Regulation: The Politics of the Administrative Process
Patrick Schmidt

Law and Globalization from Below: Towards a Cosmopolitan Legality
Edited by Boaventura de Sousa Santos and César A. Rodríguez-Garavito

Public Accountability: Designs, Dilemmas and Experiences
Edited by Michael W. Dowdle

Law, Violence and Sovereignty among West Bank Palestinians
Tobias Kelly

Legal Reform and Administrative Detention Powers in China
Sarah Biddulph

The Practice of Human Rights: Tracking Law between the Global and the Local
Edited by Mark Goodale and Sally Engle Merry

Judges beyond Politics in Democracy and Dictatorship: Lessons from Chile
Lisa Hilbink

Paths to International Justice: Social and Legal Perspectives
Edited by Marie-Bénédicte Dembour and Tobias Kelly

Law and Society in Vietnam: The Transition from Socialism in Comparative Perspective
Mark Sidel

Constitutionalizing Economic Globalization: Investment Rules and Democracy's Promise
David Schneiderman

The New World Trade Organization Knowledge Agreements: Second Edition
Christopher Arup

Justice and Reconciliation in Post-Apartheid South Africa
Edited by François du Bois and Antje du Bois-Pedain

Militarization and Violence against Women in Conflict Zones in the Middle East: A Palestinian Case-Study
Nadera Shalhoub-Kevorkian

Child Pornography and Sexual Grooming: Legal and Societal Responses
Suzanne Ost

Darfur and the Crime of Genocide
John Hagan and Wenona Rymond-Richmond

Fictions of Justice: The International Criminal Court and the Challenge of Legal Pluralism in Sub-Saharan Africa
Kamari Maxine Clarke

Conducting Law and Society Research: Reflections on Methods and Practices
Simon Halliday and Patrick Schmidt

Planted Flags: Trees, Land, and Law in Israel/Palestine
Irus Braverman

Culture under Cross-Examination: International Justice and the Special Court for Sierra Leone
Tim Kelsall

Cultures of Legality: Judicialization and Political Activism in Latin America
Javier Couso, Alexandra Huneeus, and Rachel Sieder

Courting Democracy in Bosnia and Herzegovina: The Hague Tribunal's Impact in a Postwar State
Lara J. Nettelfield

The Gacaca Courts, Post-Genocide Justice and Reconciliation in Rwanda: Justice without Lawyers
Phil Clark

Law, Society, and History: Themes in the Legal Sociology and Legal History of Lawrence M. Friedman
Edited by Robert W. Gordon and Morton J. Horwitz

After Abu Ghraib: Exploring Human Rights in America and the Middle East
Shadi Mokhtari

Adjudication in Religious Family Laws: Cultural Accommodation, Legal Pluralism, and Gender Equality in India
Gopika Solanki

Water on Tap: Rights and Regulation in the Transnational Governance of Urban Water Services
Bronwen Morgan

Elements of Moral Cognition: Rawls' Linguistic Analogy and the Cognitive Science of Moral and Legal Judgment
John Mikhail

Mitigation and Aggravation at Sentencing
Edited by Julian V. Roberts

Institutional Inequality and the Mobilization of the Family and Medical Leave Act: Rights on Leave
Catherine R. Albiston

Authoritarian Rule of Law: Legislation, Discourse and Legitimacy in Singapore
Jothie Rajah

Law and Development and the Global Discourses of Legal Transfers
Edited by John Gillespie and Pip Nicholson

Law against the State: Ethnographic Forays into Law's Transformations
Edited by Julia Eckert, Brian Donahoe, Christian Strümpell and Zerrin Özlem Biner

Transnational Legal Ordering and State Change
Edited by Gregory C. Shaffer

Legal Mobilization under Authoritarianism: The Case of Post-Colonial Hong Kong
Waikeung Tam

Complementarity in the Line of Fire: The Catalysing Effect of the International Criminal Court in Uganda and Sudan
Sarah M. H. Nouwen

Political and Legal Transformations of an Indonesian Polity: The Nagari from Colonisation to Decentralisation
Franz von Benda-Beckmann and Keebet von Benda-Beckmann

Pakistan's Experience with Formal Law: An Alien Justice
Osama Siddique

Human Rights under State-Enforced Religious Family Laws in Israel, Egypt, and India
Yüksel Sezgin

Why Prison?
Edited by David Scott

Law's Fragile State: Colonial, Authoritarian, and Humanitarian Legacies in Sudan
Mark Fathi Massoud

Rights for Others: The Slow Home-Coming of Human Rights in the Netherlands
Barbara Oomen

European States and Their Muslim Citizens: The Impact of Institutions on Perceptions and Boundaries
Edited by John R. Bowen, Christophe Bertossi, Jan Willem Duyvendak, and Mona Lena Krook

Environmental Litigation in China: A Study in Political Ambivalence
Rachel E. Stern

Indigeneity and Legal Pluralism in India: Claims, Histories, Meanings
Pooja Parmar

Paper Tiger: Law, Bureaucracy and the Developmental State in Himalayan India
Nayanika Mathur

Religion, Law and Society
Russell Sandberg

The Experiences of Face Veil Wearers in Europe and the Law
Edited by Eva Brems

The Contentious History of the International Bill of Human Rights
Christopher N. J. Roberts

Transnational Legal Orders
Edited by Terence C. Halliday and Gregory Shaffer

Lost in China? Law, Culture and Society in Post-1997 Hong Kong
Carol A. G. Jones

Security Theology, Surveillance and the Politics of Fear
Nadera Shalhoub-Kevorkian

Opposing the Rule of Law: How Myanmar's Courts Make Law and Order
Nick Cheesman

Ironies of Colonial Governance: Law, Custom and Justice in Colonial India
James Jaffe

The Clinic and the Court: Law, Medicine and Anthropology
Edited by Ian Harper, Tobias Kelly, and Akshay Khanna

The World of Indicators: The Making of Government Knowledge through Quantification
Edited by Richard Rottenburg, Sally E. Merry, Sung-Joon Park, and Johanna Mugler

Contesting Immigration Policy in Court: Legal Activism and Its Radiating Effects in the United States and France
Leila Kawar

The Quiet Power of Indicators: Measuring Governance, Corruption, and Rule of Law
Edited by Sally Engle Merry, Kevin E. Davis, and Benedict Kingsbury

Investing in Authoritarian Rule: Punishment and Patronage in Rwanda's Gacaca Courts for Genocide Crimes
Anuradha Chakravarty

Contractual Knowledge: One Hundred Years of Legal Experimentation in Global Markets
Edited by Grégoire Mallard and Jérôme Sgard

Iraq and the Crimes of Aggressive War: The Legal Cynicism of Criminal Militarism
John Hagan, Joshua Kaiser, and Anna Hanson

Culture in the Domains of Law
Edited by René Provost

China and Islam: The Prophet, the Party, and Law
Matthew S. Erie

Diversity in Practice: Race, Gender, and Class in Legal and Professional Careers
Edited by Spencer Headworth, Robert L. Nelson, Ronit Dinovitzer, and David B. Wilkins

A Sociology of Constitutions: Constitutions and State Legitimacy in Historical-Sociological Perspective
Chris Thornhill

A Sociology of Transnational Constitutions: Social Foundations of the Post-National Legal Structure
Chris Thornhill

Genocide Never Sleeps: Living Law at the International Criminal Tribunal for Rwanda
Nigel Eltringham

Shifting Legal Visions: Judicial Change and Human Rights Trials in Latin America
Ezequiel A. González-Ocantos

The Demographic Transformations of Citizenship
Heli Askola

Criminal Defense in China: The Politics of Lawyers at Work
Sida Liu and Terence C. Halliday

Contesting Economic and Social Rights in Ireland: Constitution, State and Society, 1848–2016
Thomas Murray

Buried in the Heart: Women, Complex Victimhood and the War in Northern Uganda
Erin Baines

Palaces of Hope: The Anthropology of Global Organizations
Edited by Ronald Niezen and Maria Sapignoli

The Politics of Bureaucratic Corruption in Post-Transitional Eastern Europe
Marina Zaloznaya

Revisiting the Law and Governance of Trafficking, Forced Labor and Modern Slavery
Edited by Prabha Kotiswaran

Incitement on Trial: Prosecuting International Speech Crimes
Richard Ashby Wilson

Criminalizing Children: Welfare and the State in Australia
David McCallum

Global Lawmakers: International Organizations in the Crafting of World Markets
Susan Block-Lieb and Terence C. Halliday

Duties to Care: Dementia, Relationality and Law
Rosie Harding

Insiders, Outsiders, Injuries, and Law: Revisiting "The Oven Bird's Song"
Edited by Mary Nell Trautner

Hunting Justice: Displacement, Law, and Activism in the Kalahari
Maria Sapignoli

Injury and Injustice: The Cultural Politics of Harm and Redress
Edited by Anne Bloom, David M. Engel, and Michael McCann

Ruling Before the Law: The Politics of Legal Regimes in China and Indonesia
William Hurst

The Powers of Law: A Comparative Analysis of Sociopolitical Legal Studies
Mauricio García-Villegas

A Sociology of Justice in Russia
Edited by Marina Kurkchiyan and Agnieszka Kubal

Constituting Religion: Islam, Liberal Rights, and the Malaysian State
Tamir Moustafa

The Invention of the Passport: Surveillance, Citizenship and the State, Second Edition
John C. Torpey

Law's Trials: The Performance of Legal Institutions in the US "War on Terror"
Richard L. Abel

Law's Wars: The Fate of the Rule of Law in the US "War on Terror"
Richard L. Abel

Transforming Gender Citizenship: The Irresistible Rise of Gender Quotas in Europe
Edited by Eléonore Lépinard and Ruth Rubio-Marín

Muslim Women's Quest for Justice: Gender, Law and Activism in India
Mengia Hong Tschalaer

Children as 'Risk': Sexual Exploitation and Abuse by Children and Young People
Anne-Marie McAlinden

The Legal Process and the Promise of Justice: Studies Inspired by the Work of Malcolm Feeley
Jonathan Simon, Rosann Greenspan, Hadar Aviram

Gift Exchanges: The Transnational History of a Political Idea
Grégoire Mallard

Measuring Justice: Quantitative Accountability and the National Prosecuting Authority in South Africa
Johanna Mugler

Negotiating the Power of NGOs: Women's Legal Rights in South Africa
Reem Wael

Indigenous Water Rights in Law and Regulation: Lessons from Comparative Experience
Elizabeth Jane Macpherson

The Edge of Law: Legal Geographies of a War Crimes Court
Alex Jeffrey

Everyday Justice: Law, Ethnography, and Injustice
Sandra Brunnegger

The Uncounted: Politics of Data in Global Health
Sara L. M. Davis

Transnational Legal Ordering of Criminal Justice
Gregory Shaffer and Ely Aaronson

Five Republics and One Tradition
Pablo Ruiz-Tagle

The Law Multiple: Judgment and Knowledge in Practice
Irene van Oorschot

Health as a Human Right: The Politics and Judicialisation of Health in Brazil
Octávio Luiz Motta Ferraz

Shari'a, Inshallah: Finding God in Somali Legal Politics
Mark Fathi Massoud

Policing for Peace: Institutions, Expectations, and Security in Divided Societies
Matthew Nanes

Rule of Law Intermediaries: Brokering Influence in Myanmar
Kristina Simion

Lactation at Work: Expressed Milk, Expressing Beliefs, and the Expressive Value of Law
Elizabeth A. Hoffmann

The Archival Politics of International Courts
Henry Redwood

Global Pro Bono: Causes, Context, and Contestation
Edited by Scott L. Cummings, Fabio de Sa e Silva
and Louise G. Trubek

The Practice and Problems of Transnational Counter-Terrorism
Fiona de Londras

Decoupling: Gender Injustice in China's Divorce Courts
Ethan Michelson

Anti-Constitutional Populism
Martin Krygier, Adam Czarnota and Wojciech Sadurski

Lawyers in Conflict and Transition
Kieran McEvoy, Louse Mallinder and Anna Bryson

The Ghostwriters: Lawyers and the Politics behind the Judicial Construction of Europe
Tommaso Pavone

The Sentimental Court: The Affective Life of International Criminal Justice
Jonas Bens

Practices of Reparations in International Criminal Justice
Christoph Sperfeldt

Seeking Supremacy: The Pursuit of Judicial Power in Pakistan
Yasser Kureshi

The Power of the Jury: Transforming Citizens into Jurors
Nancy S. Marder

Undue Process: Persecution and Punishment in Autocratic Courts
Fiona Feiang Shen-Bayh

Discounting Life: Necropolitical Law, Culture, and the Long War on Terror
Jothie Rajah

Clean Air at What Cost? The Rise of Blunt Force Regulation in China
Denise Sienli van der Kamp

Law and Precarity: Legal Consciousness and Daily Survival in Vietnam
Tu Phuong Nguyen

Prosecutors, Voters and The Criminalization of Corruption in Latin America: The Case of Lava Jato
Ezequiel A. Gonzalez-Ocantos and Paula Muñoz Chirinos

Entangled Domains: Empire, Law and Religion in Northern Nigeria
Rabiat Akande

The Social Constitution: Embedding Social Rights Through Legal Mobilization
Whitney K. Taylor

Out of Place: Fieldwork and Positionality in Law and Society
Edited by Lynette J. Chua and Mark Fathi Massoud

Negotiating Legality: Chinese Companies in the U.S. Legal System
Ji Li

Law and Jewish Difference: Ambivalent Encounters
Mareike Riedel

A Sociology of Post-Imperial Constitutions: Suppressed Civil War and Colonized Citizens
Chris Thornhill

The Regulation of Prostitution in China: Law in the Everyday Lives of Sex Workers, Police Officers, and Public Health Officials
Margaret L. Boittin

Immoral Traffic: An Ethnography of Law, NGOs, and the Governance of Prostitution in India
Vibhuti Ramachandran

From Manners to Rules: Advocating for Legalism in South Korea and Japan
Celeste L. Arrington

Risk and Resistance: How Feminists Transformed the Law and Science of AIDS
Aziza Ahmed

Moral Autopsy: Truths, Secrets, and the Judicial Afterlives of Communist Secret Service Archives
Saygun Gökarıksel

Courts, Constitutions and Karma: Buddhism, Monasticism and Connection in Sri Lanka's Legal Multiverse
Ben Schonthal

Terror on Trial: An Ethnography of French Courts
Sharon Weill, Dénis Salas, Antoine Mégie and Christiane Bésnier

Labor in Hard Times: Workers' Legal Mobilization at the European Court of Human Rights
Filiz Kahraman

For EU product safety concerns, contact us at Calle de José Abascal, 56–1°,
28003 Madrid, Spain or eugpsr@cambridge.org

www.ingramcontent.com/pod-product-compliance
Ingram Content Group UK Ltd.
Pitfield, Milton Keynes, MK11 3LW, UK
UKHW020328280226
468510UK00020B/394